Frommer's®

Buenos Aires

3rd Edition

by Michael Luongo

Here's what the critics say about Frommer's:

"Amazingly easy to use. Very portable, very complete."
—**BOOKLIST**

"Detailed, accurate, and easy-to-read information
for all price ranges."
—**GLAMOUR MAGAZINE**

"I   "

"From   al feel

WILEY

Wiley Publishing, Inc.

918, 211
Buenos Aires

ABOUT THE AUTHOR

Michael Luongo has written on Argentina for the *New York Times, National Geographic Traveler, Bloomberg News, Out Traveler,* and many other publications. He is also the co-author of *Frommer's Argentina*. His debut novel, *The Voyeur,* was published by Alyson Books in 2007, and he has several other travel books. He has visited more than 80 countries and all seven continents, but few places have stolen his heart like Argentina. Highlights of his travels there include riding Juan Perón's coffin through the streets of Buenos Aires during his 2006 reburial, and wearing Evita's perfume to a dinner party. Visit him at www.michaelluongo.com and www.misterbuenosaires.com.

Published by:

WILEY PUBLISHING, INC.

111 River St.
Hoboken, NJ 07030-5774

ISBN 978-0-470-44972-1

Editor: Shelley W. Bance with Jamie Ehrlich
Production Editor: Michael Brumitt
Cartographer: Roberta Stockwell
Photo Editor: Richard Fox
Production by Wiley Indianapolis Compositio

Front cover photo: Painted facade near Museo
Back cover photo: Patrons at the Limbo Club

For information on our other products and ser
contact our Customer Care Department withir
U.S. at 317/572-3993 or fax 317/572-4002.

Wiley also publishes its books in a variety of el
appears in print may not be available in electro

Manufactured in the United States of America

**ORLAND PARK
PUBLIC LIBRARY**
A Natural Connection

**14921 Ravinia Avenue
Orland Park, IL 60462**

**708-428-5100
orlandparklibrary.org**

9 SHOPPING 188

10 BUENOS AIRES AFTER DARK 213

11 SIDE TRIPS FROM BUENOS AIRES 235

APPENDIX A: FAST FACTS & WEBSITES 262

APPENDIX B: SURVIVAL SPANISH 267

INDEX 270

LIST OF MAPS

For Patti Lupone, whose Broadway Evita inspired a starry-eyed 10-year-old boy to develop a lifelong obsession with a woman and a city.

ACKNOWLEDGMENTS

Big thanks to my editors, Jamie Ehrlich and Shelley Bance, and to Kathleen Warnock for introducing me to the Frommer's bunch, to Maureen Clarke, Ensley Eikenberg, Kelly Regan, P.J. Campbell, and to everyone in the Hoboken office for their support during the work on this book. Thanks to Inés Segarra of the Argentine Tourism Office in New York for her endless help and to her assistant Lucia Mallea. To Alejandro Bertolo, the Consul General, and to Verónica Garcia, and everyone in the Argentine Consular Office in New York, and to Eduardo Piva in Miami, and to Ambassador Héctor Marcos Timerman in Washington and his wife Anabelle Sielecki of Mendel Wines. To Carlos Enrique Mayer and everyone at the National Tourism Office, and to everyone at the Buenos Aires City Tourism office. Thanks to Gabriel Miremont, Pablo Vazquez, Liliana and everyone at Museo Evita, and to Marta Granja, Carlos Francavilla, and Alberto and the "cat ladies" for help in Recoleta Cemetery. To Cristina Alvarez, Miguel Cuberos, and Juan Gandublia and Raul Zaffaroni for their support of my work, and to President Cristina Fernandez de Kirchner for her mix of Argentine glamour and politics whenever I run into her here in Argentina. To Luis Formaiano and Lawrence Wheeler, who are like big brothers and without whom I could achieve nothing in Argentina. For Juanita and the Madres, and to Tulio and the Islas Malvinas veterans for helping me better understand Argentina's deepest wounds, and to Cristian Bonaventura for helping me understand today's military. For Marcos Wolff for advice over the years. To Mario, for his friendship, though who will always be my tristeza porteña. For my landlord Martin and Katrin, Anna, Lucia and the Best Rentals staff, and to Ruben and his family. To Sandra Borello of Borello Travel, and Javier and Diego and the rest of her staff. For Rafael Meyer and Mauro and the Say Hueque staff. For Sorrel Moseley-Williams and Bonnie Tucker of the Buenos Aires Herald, Kristie Robinson and Carla Peluffo of the Argentimes, and Soledad Vallejos of Pagina 12 and Eduardo Carrera of Critica and Lorena Lemos of Perfil, Alicia Quazzolo and Fernando of Radio Nacional, the glamorous Teté Coustarot of Radio 10, and all the other local journalists for their interviews and advice. For Ileda Bustos and everyone at the Bloomberg Buenos Aires office. To Gabriel of the Four Seasons, Cecilia of the Alvear, and Laura of the Sheraton for advice, and sometimes gossip. A big thanks to Ricardo and everyone at Aerolíneas. Thanks to Caryn Carbonaro for introducing me to tango, and Eduardo, Nora, Suzanna, Michele, Marithe, and Laura Chummers for continuing, and for Marina Palmer too. To Luciana Arias and Jorge Arias, and Ines and Mariella of TangoModa's special world. For Helen Halldórsdóttir and friends at Mano a Mano. For Augustin, Miguel, Mariana, Roxanna, and Edgardo of La Marshall, and Marcelo and Cesar of CHA. To Carlos Melia and Alfredo Ferreyra, and to Marta Pasquali, Monika Varela, and Tamara Levinson, Carla and Julian of Dedios for advice, and to Steve Blackman, Ignacio Kliche, and David Goldfein for making Punta amazing. To Leva Levitt, Mara Tekach Ball, Holly Murten, and Ambassador Earl Anthony Wayne, and the staff of the U.S. Embassy for all their help and advice. To Clarisa Poblete for helping me remember Argentina in New York. Pedro Bevilacqua of the National Archives, and to Felix and Jorge Biondo of El General and Dr. Hipolito Barreriro for more on Juan and Evita. To George Carrancho of American for putting up with my flight changes, and to Ingrid Breyer for being my eternal sounding board and to my roommates Harry and Khoa in New York for taking care of things while I am gone. Thanks also to Richard Burnett in Canada for forwarding that e-mail that told me about the first Buenos Aires book, and to all my editors over the years for whom I have written on this wonderful city. Certainly I am missing many who made living in Argentina special, but please know that you're loved and appreciated!

—Michael Luongo

AN INVITATION TO THE READER

In researching this book, we discovered many wonderful places—hotels, restaurants, shops, and more. We're sure you'll find others. Please tell us about them, so we can share the information with your fellow travelers in upcoming editions. If you were disappointed with a recommendation, we'd love to know that, too. Please write to:

Frommer's Buenos Aires, 3rd Edition
Wiley Publishing, Inc. • 111 River St. • Hoboken, NJ 07030-5774

AN ADDITIONAL NOTE

Please be advised that travel information is subject to change at any time—and this is especially true of prices. We therefore suggest that you write or call ahead for confirmation when making your travel plans. The authors, editors, and publisher cannot be held responsible for the experiences of readers while traveling. Your safety is important to us, however, so we encourage you to stay alert and be aware of your surroundings. Keep a close eye on cameras, purses, and wallets, all favorite targets of thieves and pickpockets.

Other Great Guides for Your Trip:

Frommer's Spanish PhraseFinder & Dictionary
Frommer's Argentina
Frommer's Chile & Easter Island
Frommer's Peru
Frommer's Equador & the Galápagos Islands
Frommer's South America

FROMMER'S STAR RATINGS, ICONS & ABBREVIATIONS

Every hotel, restaurant, and attraction listing in this guide has been ranked for quality, value, service, amenities, and special features using a **star-rating system**. In country, state, and regional guides, we also rate towns and regions to help you narrow down your choices and budget your time accordingly. Hotels and restaurants are rated on a scale of zero (recommended) to three stars (exceptional). Attractions, shopping, nightlife, towns, and regions are rated according to the following scale: zero stars (recommended), one star (highly recommended), two stars (very highly recommended), and three stars (must-see).

In addition to the star-rating system, we also use **six feature icons** that point you to the great deals, in-the-know advice, and unique experiences that separate travelers from tourists. Throughout the book, look for:

(Finds)   Special finds—those places only insiders know about

(Fun Facts)   Fun facts—details that make travelers more informed and their trips more fun

(Moments)   Special moments—those experiences that memories are made of

(Overrated)   Places or experiences not worth your time or money

(Tips)   Insider tips—great ways to save time and money

(Value)   Great values—where to get the best deals

The following abbreviations are used for credit cards:

AE	American Express	**DISC**	Discover	**V**	Visa
DC	Diners Club	**MC**	MasterCard		

FROMMERS.COM

Now that you have this guidebook to help you plan a great trip, visit our website at **www.frommers.com** for additional travel information on more than 4,000 destinations. We update features regularly to give you instant access to the most current trip-planning information available. At Frommers.com, you'll find scoops on the best airfares, lodging rates, and car rental bargains. You can even book your travel online through our reliable travel booking partners. Other popular features include:

- Online updates of our most popular guidebooks
- Vacation sweepstakes and contest giveaways
- Newsletters highlighting the hottest travel trends
- Podcasts, interactive maps, and up-to-the-minute events listings
- Opinionated blog entries by Arthur Frommer himself
- Online travel message boards with featured travel discussions

What's New in Buenos Aires

What's New, Buenos Aires? It's the title of one of the most famous songs about this exciting city and it's never more true than today. Many new tourists are pouring into the Argentine capital and there are plenty of things to enjoy, most of which are highlighted in this guide.

PLANNING YOUR TRIP You have more choices these days for flying from North America to Buenos Aires. Since our last edition, **American Airlines** has nearly doubled its capacity at JFK airport. In addition, it began direct flights from Miami to Montevideo. Contact the airline at $\textcircled{C}$ **800/433-7300** in the U.S. or 11/4318-1111 in Buenos Aires.

ACCOMMODATIONS The "Where to Stay" chapter has been completely revamped in this edition. You'll find many of your favorite hotels, but many new boutique hotels are noted, particularly in the Palermo Viejo area. One of the best of these is the **Bo-Bo** hotel (Guatemala 4882, btw. Borges and Thames; $\textcircled{C}$ **11/4774-0505**; www.bobohotel.com). It's a mix of old and new, with each room individually styled, and a staff that gives excellent personal service. See p. 77. Or try the family-run **La Otra Orilla** (Julian Alvarez 1779, btw. El Salvador and Costa Rica; $\textcircled{C}$ **11/4867-4070** or 11/4863-7426; www.otraorilla.com.ar). In this tranquil oasis from the city, the rooms are quiet and charming and there's a relaxing garden

patio. See p. 78. Also new is a boutique hotel, **The Glu** (Godoy Cruz, 1733 btw. Gorriti and Honduras; $\textcircled{C}$ **800/405-3072** in the U.S., or 11/4831-4646 in Buenos Aires; www.thegluhotel.com). It's family-run, with simple decor, and it sets you in the heart of Palermo's action. Specially made windows and walls allow you to still get sleep at the end of the day. See p. 77.

One more sign that Buenos Aires continues to be the gay capital of Latin America is the opening of **The Axel Hotel** (Venezuela 649, btw. Peru and Chacabuco; $\textcircled{C}$ **11/4136-9393;** www.axelhotels.com). Located in San Telmo, it's open to anyone, regardless of orientation, and the spectacular atrium lobby has social and dining areas. A glass-bottom pool hung from the third level allows you to watch people swim far above your head. See p. 70.

Following requests from readers, the apartment listings have been expanded in the "Where to Stay" chapter. After renting an apartment or even staying a few days in a hotel in Buenos Aires, you might want to move here permanently, so check out the tips for expat living in the city. See p. 80.

DINING The "Where to Dine" chapter also has been significantly revamped since the last edition, with an even greater variety of ethnic restaurants listed, as well as some new, trendy spots. If you're looking for a romantic night out with your partner, be sure to check out the new San

Telmo restaurant **647 Club** (647 Tacuari, at Chile; ✆ 11/4331-3026; www.club 647.com). It's high on ambience, with delicious, creative cuisine under the direction of Executive Chef Guillermo Testón, and you may find yourself dining here more than once. See p. 99. Also noted are more places serving Asian cuisine. **Tandoor** (Laprida 1293, at Charcas; ✆ 11/4821-3676; www.tandoor.com.ar) is an upscale, elegant Indian restaurant, concentrating on cuisine from different regions of India, with an emphasis on family recipes. It was opened by two former engineers from India, one of whom came to Argentina because of his obsession with tango. See p. 105. Though it's been open for a few years, a Palermo standby has been added: **Sudestada.** (Guatemala 5602, at Fitzroy; ✆ 11/4776-3777) serves a mix of Asian, Vietnamese, and Thai food, with a variety of menu items to make anyone happy. See p. 112.

SIGHTSEEING Face-lifts are popular in Buenos Aires, even for historical buildings. With the city's 2010 Bicentennial coming up, the city is being renovated like crazy. Yet, in typical Argentine fashion, much is behind schedule. Look at newly renovated **Casa Rosada, Tribunales, Plaza Congreso,** and repaved and replanted areas along **Avenida 9 de Julio** and **Avenida de Mayo.** Sadly, one of the city's most glorious buildings, the **Teatro Colón,** should have had renovations completed by mid-2008. A new timeline is for mid-2010, but considering how much work needs to be done, and how badly the renovation has been botched, that's optimistic. Still, it's worth a trip to see the exterior; visit the website, www.teatrocolon.org.ar, for updates and information about when partial visits might resume.

SHOPPING Numerous stores of all kinds are listed for adults and kids alike,

including several more clothing shops for women. If you have a shoe fetish and a lot of cash to burn through, head to **Mishka Shoes,** in Palermo (El Salvador 4673, at Armenia; ✆ 11/4833-6566; www.mishka shoes.com). It has exquisite handmade shoes as well as custom-made ones. See p. 203. **Raffaello by Cesar Franco** (Florida 165, btw. Bartolomo Mitre and Peron, in the Güemes shopping center; ✆ 11/4343-1935 or 11/4331-1771; www.raffaello buenosaires.com) has clothes with a theatrical flair, a reflection of Franco's start designing clothes for the stage. See p. 204. Men can look to such shops as **Prototype** (Arguibel 2867, at Arce; ✆ 11/4773-8812; www.prototypeweb.com) for a clean, metrosexual look. See p. 204. Men looking for nightlife attire to meet the beautiful women of Buenos Aires should check out **Bokura,** in Palermo (El Salvador 4677, btw. Armenia and Malabia; ✆ 11/4833-3975; www.bokura.com.ar). See p. 202. If you're visiting with your little girl, head to **Casa Barbie** (Scalabrini Ortiz 3170, btw. Cerviño and Cabello; ✆ 0810/4444-BARBIE [227243]; www.barbie-stores.com), also in Palermo. You can shop, get a beauty makeover, or even sit for tea and coffee. Pink is the new black, after all. See p. 211.

AFTER DARK One of the new bars is the very popular **Sugar** (Costa Rica 4619, at Armenia; ✆ 11/15-6894-2002; www.sugarbuenosaires.com). Owned by two Brits and an American, this Palermo Soho spot is trendy with English-speaking expats who've made Buenos Aires their home. See p. 221. Also, check out **Mano a Mano** at Plaza Bohemia (Maipu 444, at Corrientes; ✆ 11/15-5865-8279). This Thursday-only *milonga* (tango salon) is run by Helen Halldórsdóttir, an Iceland native who everyone calls La Vikinga. See p. 230.

The Best of Buenos Aires

A country's tragedy has become a tourist's opportunity, and in between the two is a vastly improved economy for Buenos Aires, the glamorous capital of Argentina. Until the peso crisis of December 2001, Buenos Aires was regarded as Latin America's most expensive city. Many on the South American tourist crawl avoided this sophisticated and beautiful city altogether, staying in the cheaper capitals of the countries that surrounded it. However, because the peso, once on par with the U.S. dollar, has fallen to less than a third of its former value, tourists from all over the world are flocking to this city, often called the Paris of South America. Since the 2007 edition of this guide, however, prices have gone up, most significantly at hotels. Still, the city is a relative bargain, roughly 30% cheaper for a vacation than North America or Europe. Tourism has become the third most important component of Argentina's economy, with Buenos Aires the main recipient of visitors.

In spite of the 2001 peso crisis, the beauty of Buenos Aires is still here and always will be. The city is undergoing renovations to renew its wealth of architecture, much of which dates from nearly a century ago, in time for the pending 2010 Bicentennial. (As with all things Argentine, however, many projects are behind schedule.) Stroll through the neighborhoods of Recoleta or Palermo, full of buildings with marble neoclassical facades on broad tree-lined boulevards, or tour the historic Avenida de Mayo, designed to rival Paris's Champs-Elysées. European immigrants to Buenos Aires, mostly from Spain and Italy, have brought with them the warm ways of Mediterranean culture, with friends, family, and conversation as the most important things in life.

The crisis also has had a remarkable effect on the country's soul. Argentines as a whole are becoming more self-reflective, looking at themselves and the reasons why their country fell into so much trouble and trying to find answers. This has led, ironically, to an incredible flourishing of all things Porteño, the word Buenos Aires locals use to describe both themselves and the culture of their city. Unable to import expensive foods from overseas, Buenos Aires's restaurants are concentrating instead on cooking with Argentine staples, such as Pampas grass–fed beef, and using locally produced, organic ingredients as seasonings. What has developed is a spectacular array of Argentine–nouvelle cuisine of incredible quality and originality. Chefs can't seem to produce it fast enough in the ever-expanding array of Buenos Aires restaurants, particularly in the trendy Palermo Viejo district on the city's north side.

This new Argentine self-reliance and pride are not just limited to its restaurants. The same thing has happened with the country's fashion. In the go-go 1990s, when the peso was pegged to the U.S. dollar, Argentines loaded up on European labels and made shopping trips to the malls of Miami for their clothing. Now, however, even the middle class cannot afford to do this anymore. Instead, with necessity as the mother of invention, young Argentine designers have opened up their own shops and boutiques in the Palermo Soho neighborhood, putting other Argentines to work sewing, selling, and modeling their designs. Women, especially, will find fantastic and utterly unique fashions in Buenos Aires that you won't find anywhere else in the world. And, if you're looking for leather goods, say no more. The greatest variety and quality of leather goods in the world are found all over town.

Importantly, the most Porteño thing of all, the tango, has also witnessed an explosive growth. Up until the peso crisis, Argentines worried that the dance would die out as young people bopped instead to American hip-hop and European techno. But the peso crisis and the self-reflection it created helped bolster the art form's popularity: Tourists can now see a different form of tango every night of their stay. More importantly to residents, the traditional, 1930s-style *milongas* (tango salons) have opened in spaces all over town. These are drawing not only the typical tango dancers, but also young Argentines who have rediscovered their grandparents' favorite dance and expats who've made Buenos Aires the world's new hot city, just like Prague at the end of the Cold War.

The city is also home to an incomparable array of theaters and other traditional performance spaces. Buenos Aires's numerous museums, many in beautiful neoclassical structures along broad, tree-lined Avenida Libertador, are as exquisite as the treasures they hold. There's no time like the present to visit Buenos Aires, a city rich in cultural excitement, at reasonable prices that are welcome during a worldwide recessionary period.

1 FROMMER'S FAVORITE BUENOS AIRES EXPERIENCES

- **Best Tango Shows for Tourists:** Tango, a beautiful dance that tells the pained history of the city's immigrant poor from the beginning of the 20th century, is the ultimate Buenos Aires–defining experience. For an authentic historical look, see the tango show **El Querandí,** Perú 302 (© **11/4345-0331**), which traces the dance's roots from brothel slums, when only men danced it, to its current leggy sexiness. See p. 225. **Señor Tango,** Vieytes 1653 (© **11/4303-0212**), adds Hollywood glamour and Fosse-esque dance moves, as well as horses trampling the stage, in the city's most popular show. See p. 226. You'll find a more gracious experience at **Esquina Carlos Gardel,** Carlos Gardel 3200 (© **11/4876-6363**), in the Abasto neighborhood, where Carlos Gardel, the city's most famous tango crooner, actually lived and worked. A classical

symphony accompanies the more traditional instruments in this show. See p. 226.

- **Best Tango Hall for the Experienced or Those Who Want to Watch the Experienced:** If you're an expert tango dancer, or want to at least watch the people who are, head to a *milonga* (tango salon). **El Niño Bien,** Humberto I, no. 1462 (© **11/4483-2588**), is like taking a step back in time as you watch patrons dance in an enormous Belle Epoque–era hall under ceiling fans. The best dancers come here to show off, though you'll also find instructors looking to mingle with shy potential students who watch from the sidelines. See p. 227. **Salón Canning,** Scalabrini Ortiz 1331 (© **11/4832-6753**), in Palermo Hollywood, has what many local dancers call the best tango floor in all of Buenos Aires—a hard, smooth, parquet surface perfect for this dance. The tight space, however, is not big enough for the tango-challenged. See p. 230. For a mix between a *milonga* and a show, head to the Thursday-only **Mano a Mano at Plaza Bohemia** (Maipu 444, at Corrientes © **11/15-5865-8279**), run by Helen Halldórsdóttir, a native of Iceland whom tango lovers all over Buenos Aires simply call La Vikinga. See p. 230.

- **Best Architecture Walks:** Buenos Aires abounds in beautiful architecture, especially after its very self-conscious and ambitious rebuilding project for Argentina's 1910 Centennial celebration of its independence from Spain. The plan was put into action in the 1880s, and by the turn of the 20th century, entire neighborhoods had been rebuilt. The French Beaux Arts movement was at its worldwide height at that point, meaning much of the city looks more like Paris than any other Latin American city. **Avenida de Mayo,** the city's official processional route linking the Presidential Palace (Casa Rosada) to the National Congress Building, is the longest and best-preserved example of this. (See p. 179 for a walking tour of this area.) The corner buildings along the wide **Diagonal Norte,** also known as **Avenida Sáenz Peña,** are all topped with fantastic neoclassical domes, from the street's beginning at the Plaza de Mayo until it hits the **Obelisco,** Buenos Aires's defining monument, at Avenida 9 de Julio, the world's widest boulevard. Don't miss the neighborhoods of San Telmo and Monserrat either, with their balconied late-19th and early-20th-century structures, most of which are gracefully decaying as they await gentrification once the economy improves.

- **Best Park Walks:** The Palermo Park system runs along Avenida Libertador and is one of the world's most beautiful

parks. You could spend more than a day here, wandering this tree- and monument-lined part of the city, and still not see it all. Within the system are numerous small parks such as the Rose Garden and the Japanese Gardens, as well as museums such as the **Museo de Arte Latinoamericano de Buenos Aires (MALBA),** Av. Figueroa Alcorta 3415 (© **11/4808-6500;** p. 149), and the **Museo Nacional de Bellas Artes,** Av. del Libertador 1473 (© **11/4803-0802;** p. 148). In the Argentine spring—late September and early October—the weather is at its best, and the jacaranda trees here are in their purple-bloomed glory, making this the best time to stroll. In summer months, locals who can't escape the city come to jog, sunbathe, and while away the day in this area. See chapter 7.

- **Best Bird-Watching:** Proof that nature is stronger than whatever humankind throws at it is just a brisk walk away from Buenos Aires's tallest office structures at the **Ecological Reserve** (along the Costanera, near Puerto Madero; © **11/4893-1588**). In the 1960s and 1970s, demolished buildings and construction debris were dumped into the Río de La Plata. Nature responded by wrapping it with sediment and then grass and small plants, creating a home for a myriad of birds. Wander on your own with caution, as there are still rough areas, or ask a tour company about bird-watching tours. See p. 143.

- **Best (& Most Heartbreaking) Political Experience:** Argentina's political history is a long series of ups and downs, some more tragic than others. Perhaps the worst occurred between 1976 and 1982, when a military government, bent on destroying what it considered political enemies, ruled the country. During that time, up to 30,000 people, mostly college-age, were secretly murdered, their bodies never found, giving them the name *los desaparecidos,* meaning "the disappeared ones." The **Asociación Madres de Plaza de Mayo** is an organization that aims for justice for their murdered children and marches on the Plaza de Mayo every Thursday at 3:30pm, giving speeches and handing out fliers. They also run a university with a store and library full of books on this painful period of history that has yet to come to an end. See p. 133.

- **Best Evita Experiences:** Visit the Plaza de Mayo, the political heart of Argentina, and look to the facade of the **Casa Rosada (Presidential Palace;** p. 126). The northern balcony, with its three French doors, is where Evita addressed her adoring fans. Just as many people come to pay their respects now at the **Recoleta Cemetery** (p. 136), where she was laid to rest in a tomb belonging to the family of her wealthy father. To understand why it has taken Argentina more than 50 years to come to terms with this controversial woman, visit the **Museo Evita,** Calle Lafinur 2988 (© 11/4807-9433), in Palermo, where the story of her life is told through personal objects. See p. 147.
- **Best Museums:** The **MALBA** (Museo de Arte Latinoamericano de Buenos Aires), Av. Figueroa Alcorta 3415 (© 11/4808-6500), houses an extensive and interesting modern art collection. The building itself is as unique as the art, and nothing is more impressive than the giant sculpture of a man doing pushups suspended over the escalator bay in the central atrium. See p. 149. The **Museo Nacional de Bellas Artes,** Av. del Libertador 1473 (© 11/4803-0802), was built into a former water-pump station and houses an impressive art collection, including many Picasso drawings. See p. 148.
- **Best Ethnic Neighborhoods:** With a population that is nearly all white and either of Spanish or Italian descent,

Buenos Aires, on the surface, does not seem to be a very ethnically diverse city, despite its cosmopolitan nature. However, head to the neighborhood of **Once,** around Calle Tucumán in particular, for a still-thriving Jewish community. You'll find numerous kosher restaurants, stores, and other businesses owned by or catering to this community. See p. 42. Then head to **Belgrano,** to the city's north, for its Chinatown. Most people in Buenos Aires know nothing of this community, a flourishing, busy area of restaurants, shops, and other businesses. If you're in town for the Chinese New Year, the Dragon Parade is a fun affair to check out. See p. 28.

- **Best Outdoor Markets:** There's no market like the **San Telmo Antiques Fair,** held every Sunday in Plaza Dorrego, the old colonial heart of the San Telmo district. You'll find lots of small antiques and collectibles dealers here along with some kitschy souvenirs, local crafts, and lots of free live tango dancing as good as anything that you might pay 355 pesos to see onstage. The **Feria de Plaza Francia,** in front of the Recoleta Cemetery, is another market you shouldn't miss, with great crafts, live music, and a beautiful setting on a grassy hill. See p. 192 and 193, respectively.
- **Best Shopping Experiences:** There's no shortage of **top designer shops** along Calle Alvear, with the same high quality and high style you find throughout North America and Europe, at slightly lower prices befitting the Argentine economy. **Leather** shops abound on Calle Florida, near Galerías Pacífico, and you can even have items custom-made while you're here. For the best quality high-design items for fashion and home, my favorite shop is **Tienda Puro Diseño Argentino,** (Gorriti 5953, btw. Arevalo and Ravignani;

© **11/4776-8037;** www.purodiseno.com.ar; p. 205). For little **boutiques** specializing in the sexy styles Argentine women favor wearing, wander the cobblestone streets of **Palermo Soho** and **Palermo Hollywood.** See chapter 9.

- **Best High-Building Vista Points:** Odd-looking as it might be, the **Palacio Barolo,** Av. de Mayo 1370 (© **11/4383-1065**), designed by an architect who took Dante's *Inferno* a little too literally, is finally open to the public for tours. Previously only open to office workers, now anyone can see the building's interesting interior. Its tower, which once made it the tallest building in all of South America, provides a sweeping view up and down Avenida de Mayo, as well as across the entire city. See p. 134. The **Torre Monumental,** Av. Libertador 49 (© **11/4311-0186**), better known by its old name, the British Clock Tower, has a fantastic view to the Río de la Plata and up and down Avenida Libertador. So what if the tower represents a country with which Argentina has had some arguments over the years? It's the view that counts now. See p. 139.

- **Best Oddball Museums:** Two modern-day necessities—taxes and toilets—are honored in two different small museums in Buenos Aires. The **Tax Museum,** Hipólito Yrigoyen 370, at Defensa (© **11/4347-2396**), contains historical items relating to money, coins, and taxes throughout Argentine history. It is one of only three museums of this type in the world. See p. 145. The **Museo del Patrimonio,** Av. Córdoba 1750, museum entrance at Riobamba 750 (© **11/6319-1882**), in the Aguas Argentinas building, better known as the Water Palace, is really about waterworks, but it contains what surely must be the largest

toilet collection in the world. Kids will have a blast here. See p. 148.
- **Best Museums for Kids:** Its name is **Museo de los Niños (Children's Museum),** Av. Corrientes 3247 (© **11/4861-2325**), and this is certainly a great place to bring the young ones. Full of displays on various careers, presented in a fun way, you'll wish you'd had such a place when you were young. See p. 145. In the **Museo Participativo de Ciencias,** it's forbidden *not* to touch the displays. This place (inside the Centro Cultural de Recoleta; © **11/4807-3260**) is full of science displays and other exhibits that are so much fun, kids won't know they're educational too! See p. 146.

- **Best People-Watching:** Pedestrianized **Calle Florida** is not the elegant shopping street it might have been a generation ago, but all kinds of Porteños find their way here, especially at lunchtime. Day and night, musicians, tango dancers, broken-glass walkers, comedians, and the like entertain the crowds along this street. At night, **Avenida Santa Fe** also has an interesting array of people who pop into stores, gossip at sidewalk cafes, and just check each other out. See p. 155 and 189, respectively.

- **Best Nightlife Street:** Whether you want to eat at a *parrilla* (an Argentine steakhouse), try some nouvelle cuisine, have some drinks, or do some dancing, **Calle Báez** in Las Cañitas is the place to go. This busy street in Palermo has such great restaurants as **Novecento,** Báez 199 (© **11/4778-1900**), **El Estanciero,** Báez 202 (© **11/4899-0951**), and numerous other choices. Savor the night afterwards over drinks at trendy **Soul Café,** Báez 352 (© **11/4776-3905**). This street has some of the most intensely packed nightlife on any 3 blocks of Buenos Aires.

2 THE BEST HOTEL BETS

- **Most Luxurious Hotel Choices:** The two hotels cited here top my list of hotel choices, and they top the lists of travel magazines as well. The **Alvear Palace Hotel,** Av. Alvear 1891 (© 11/4808-2100), is a gilded confection of carved marble and French furniture. It's the ultimate grand hotel experience in Buenos Aires, complete with butler service. See p. 72. The **Four Seasons Hotel,** Posadas 1086–88 (© 800/819-5053 in the U.S. and Canada), offers a more subdued form of luxury (elegant without flash), with quiet pampering and a chance to hide away in the hotel's walled garden. See p. 73.

- **Best Historic Hotels:** The **Marriott Plaza Hotel,** Calle Florida 1005 (© 888/236-2427 in the U.S.), is the oldest of the grand hotels still operating in Buenos Aires, and its location on Plaza San Martín can't be beat. See p. 65. The **Hotel Castelar** (© 11/4383-5000) sits on Avenida de Mayo, once the city's most glamorous street. This hotel, adorned with Italian marble and bronze, was once the favorite choice of Lorca and other Spanish writers in the 1930s, when Buenos Aires was the intellectual and literary capital of the Spanish-speaking world. See p. 70.

- **Best See-and-Be-Seen Hotels:** The **Faena Hotel and Universe,** Martha Salotti 445 (© 11/4010-9000), located in the Puerto Madero district, is the fashionista's see-and-be-seen choice. The hotel was designed with lots of bars in the lobby and a pool in the front of the hotel, so that anyone coming in would know exactly who else was around. See p. 64. Within Recoleta, the new **Park Hyatt Buenos Aires,** Av. Alvear 1661 (© 11/5171-1234), built into the old Palacio Duhau, has the best garden in the city. It's here that ladies who lunch come to be seen,

and businesspeople make decisions over coffee or drinks alfresco.

- **Best Boutique Hotels:** With the tourism boom, boutique hotels have become all the rage in Buenos Aires. These are some of the best, and the newest. **Home** in Palermo Viejo, Honduras 5860 (© 11/4778-1008), creates a home away from home that's both trendy and welcoming. This is also where the Bush twins stayed during their infamous time in the Argentine capital. See p. 77. Nearby, **Soho All Suites** is sleek and stylish, and the site of some fashionable local parties (Honduras 4762; © 11/4832-3000). See p. 78. **Bo-Bo,** in Palermo (Guatemala 4882, btw. Borges and Thames; © 11/4774-0505; www.bobohotel.com), is housed in a European-style mansion from 1920, and each of the seven rooms follows a different design aesthetic. See p. 77.

- **Best Budget Hotel:** French miracle chain **Hotel Ibis,** Hipólito Yrigoyen 1592 (© 11/5300-5555), wins in this category hands down. Though these places are alike the world over, the efficient service and location overlooking Congreso make for an excellent hotel choice. All the rooms look the same, but with the low prices, you can easily ignore that. See p. 76.

- **Best Hotel Gyms:** The **Marriott Plaza Hotel,** Calle Florida 1005 (© 888/236-2427 in the U.S.), has an enormous gym, with more than enough equipment so there's no waiting. See p. 65. The gym in the **Pan Americano,** Carlos Pellegrini 551 (© 800/227-6963 in the U.S.), must be seen to be believed. It sits in a three-story glass box on the building's roof, so you feel like you're floating over Avenida 9 de Julio while at the pool or especially on the treadmills. See p. 67.

- **Best Hotel Pools:** In the hot Southern Hemisphere summer months (Dec–Mar), any pool will be a welcome treat in Buenos Aires, but two of them really stand out. The **Pan Americano,** Carlos Pellegrini 551 (℃ **800/227-6963** in the U.S.), has a combination indoor/outdoor pool on the roof of the hotel, so you feel like you're swimming on top of the city and Avenida 9 de Julio. See p. 67. The **Four Seasons,** Posadas 1086–1088 (℃ **800/819-5053** in the U.S. and Canada), has the only garden swimming pool in Recoleta. When lounging poolside at the walled garden complex, you feel like you're in a resort, though still in the heart of the city. See p. 73.

- **Best Business Hotel:** With its location away from the noise of the city in Puerto Madero, and with one of the largest convention centers in all of Buenos Aires, the **Hilton Buenos Aires,** Av. Macacha Güemes 351 (℃ **800/445-8667** in the U.S.), is a logical choice for travelers on business. Its business center, complete with translation services, is also one of the largest in the city. See p. 64.

3 THE BEST DINING & CAFE BETS

- **Best *Parrilla*:** You probably heard of this place long before coming to Buenos Aires, and **Cabaña las Lilas,** Alicia Moreau de Justo 516 (℃ **11/4313-1336**), deserves every bit of its reputation. It's expensive for sure, running about 142 pesos ($38/£27) for a complete meal, but it's worth it: The cuts of beef are so soft, they almost melt in your mouth. In spite of the price, it's casual too, so you can come in sneakers and shorts. See p. 89.

- **Best Cafe Experiences: Café Tortoni,** Av. de Mayo 825 (℃ **11/4342-4328**), might not have the best service in town, but its incredible history and beauty more than make up for it. This was and still remains Argentina's intellectual coffee spot of choice; and even the culture-seeking tourists don't overwhelm the space. See p. 97. Sit outside at **La Biela,** Av. Quintana 596 (℃ **11/4804-0449**), in glamorous Recoleta, overlooking the world-famous Recoleta Cemetery. From the view to Iglesia Pilar to the wonderful shade of the gum trees on its sidewalk, this is Buenos Aires at its best. See p. 104.

- **Best Authentic Old Buenos Aires Dining:** Buenos Aires is full of trendy places, but the surefire bets are where Porteños have eaten for decades. Ham hangs from the rafters and steaks are as thick as the crowds at the Spanish eatery **Plaza Asturias,** Av. de Mayo 1199 (℃ **11/4382-7334**). The staff is so busy that you might get hurt while trying to find the restroom, with all the running around they do. See p. 106. For more than 40 years, fish lovers have flocked to **Dora,** Reconquista 1076, at Paraguay (℃ **11/4311-2891**), an unpretentious, but high-quality and high-priced spot that has moved from its last location, yet still has the same level of service and quality. See p. 93.

- **Best Seafood:** Argentina has a long coastline, but the turf, not the surf, has always provided chefs with culinary inspiration. Two places have defied this trend: **Dora,** Reconquista 1076, at Paraguay (℃ **11/4311-2891**), the unpretentious seafood spot where businesspeople and those in the know have eaten for 40 years (p. 93); and **Olsen,** in Palermo Viejo, at Gorriti 5870 (℃ **11/4776-7677**), which prepares seafood with an interesting twist—Scandinavian-style, with flavors different from those in other city restaurants. See p. 112.

- **Best Italian Restaurant:** With more than half the residents of Buenos Aires from Italian immigrant stock, it's hard to go wrong in finding good Italian food: Most *parrillas* serve an excellent array of pastas, usually homemade on the premises. The best formal Italian dining experience in the city, however, is **Piegari,** Posadas 1042 (✆ 11/4328-4104), in the Recoleta la Recova area, near the Four Seasons hotel. The selection of food concentrating on northern Italian cuisine is superb, with a stunning array of risottos. See p. 102.

- **Best French Restaurant: La Bourgogne,** Av. Alvear 1891 (✆ 11/4805-3857), in the Alvear Palace, is hands down the best French restaurant in Buenos Aires and the recipient of numerous awards. Yes, it's very formal and very expensive, but what else do you expect from such a place? See p. 101.

- **Best Restaurant for Kids: Garbis,** Scalabrini Ortiz 3190, at Cerviño (✆ 11/4511-6600), is an Armenian restaurant chain, with what one British expat loves to call a "jumpee castle" where she can bring her kids. The best one is in Palermo Soho, and adults can eat in peace while the kids entertain themselves on the indoor playground. See p. 114.

- **Best Value Restaurants:** Little-known family-run **Juana M,** Carlos Pellegrini 1535 (✆ 11/4326-0462), a small *parrilla* on the very end of Avenida 9 de Julio, in the Recoleta district, wins this distinction. There are great cuts of meat and an unlimited salad bar; and most meals with drinks are priced under the 18 pesos ($4.85/£3.40) mark. See p. 103. If you're in Puerto Madero, head straight to **La Bisteca,** Av. Alicia Moreau de Justo 1890 (✆ 11/4514-4999), a chain restaurant with an all-you-can-eat menu offering high-quality cuts of meat and a generous salad bar. It's a huge space, but the seating arrangements create a sense of intimacy; at these prices, it can't be beat. See p. 92.

Buenos Aires in Depth

What the traveler sees in Buenos Aires today is a result of a confluence of factors. The beautiful, glorious, at times decrepit city is the greatest artifact of Argentina's hopes to rise as a world power on the global stage. The city is the capital of what was once among the world's wealthiest countries, and South America's most powerful, drawing its strength from the bounty of its agricultural hinterland, the labor of its immigrants, and the way its political and intellectual elite dealt with the masters of Europe. The architecture, culture, atmosphere, and sense of nostalgia now present in the city are all vestiges of its physical and spiritual transformation at the turn of the 20th century. From boulevards lined with Parisian buildings, to government headquarters of marble from European quarries, to the conversation-filled cafes, the fashion boutiques and art galleries, what one sees now in Buenos Aires is what was, what could have been, and what Buenos Aires still longs to be in the eyes of the world.

1 BUENOS AIRES TODAY

The recent years in Buenos Aires have seen it evolve from its worst economic tumble, the 2001–02 pesos crisis, to a buoyant era, floating on apparent prosperity due to a tourism boom, a new political era, and high prices for its commodities on the global market. In December 2001, the Argentine peso, once on a par with the U.S. dollar, collapsed to less than a third of its former value. Unemployment rose to more than 20%, businesses shut down, and many people who trusted the banking system lost their entire life savings overnight. Television images across the world showed momentary social cohesion, such as members of the middle class banging pots in the streets and shouting at police officers, followed by social breakdown, when those same police officers shot rioters on the pedestrianized shopping streets in the city's downtown.

While no one watching the news at the beginning of 2002 could have guessed that Buenos Aires would experience a tourism boom, that was exactly the result. With hotels, restaurants, and shopping at nearly a third of their former prices, the most expensive capital in South America suddenly became a bargain destination. Tourism now is the third most important sector of the economy. The peso crisis also forced locals to make do with their own resources by cooking with Argentine ingredients, designing clothes for a local market with local materials, and turning inward to their own culture, particularly the tango, for entertainment. Argentine culture was regenerated, which created a more dynamic city for tourists.

Politics also changed in recent years, with the election of the Peronist Néstor Kirchner into office in 2003. At the same time, commodities Argentina is famous for—grain and beef—rose in value throughout the world, particularly with the growth of China and other Asian nations. The same was true for petroleum prices, which rose substantially in the first decade of the millennium. The turnaround of the economy of Buenos Aires, and the nation as a whole, has been spectacular.

This new economic situation led to inflation, however, with tourism a major driver. Much of the recent residential high-rise construction in Buenos Aires, particularly in Palermo and Puerto Madero, was speculated on the premise that foreigners would buy apartments to rent to foreigners, hardly sustainable.

Following on her husband's success in steering the country around, former First Lady and Buenos Aires province Senator Cristina Fernandez de Kirchner was elected as the president in 2007. The election was taken with delight both around the world and within the country, but soon her immense popularity crashed. Her government began to put out false inflation figures, claiming it was held at various points between 1% to 7%, when it was as high as 30%. The government enacted price controls and tariffs on grain and beef exports, causing international trade on these commodities to plummet at a time of high demand from China and Asia. Argentina's chance to grow wealthy from its natural bounty, as it had 100 years before, was lost.

As Argentina prepares for its 2010 Bicentennial, Buenos Aires is being spiffed up. The city has renovated historical buildings, repaved and replanted boulevards, and expanded its subway system. Yet even this is not without its controversies. The restoration of the Teatro Colón, the most important symbol of Buenos Aires's golden period, is years behind schedule with corruption at every level. If, at the 1910 Centennial, Teatro Colón represented the city in its most glorious period, the process of the restoration shows what it has become 100 years later—a city of opportunity lost, but one that still longs, no matter how difficult it is now, to return to glory. How the city weathers the global recession remains to be seen.

2 LOOKING BACK AT BUENOS AIRES

In 1880, 300 years after the permanent founding of Buenos Aires, the city was officially made the capital of Argentina. From then on, Buenos Aires experienced a period of explosive growth and wealth, laying the foundation for the glory days that Argentines recall. Trade with Europe expanded, with cattle and grain from the newly conquered hinterlands as the main exports. Millions of immigrants came from Italy, Spain, and other countries, filling the city's slums, primarily in the southern sections of La Boca and San Telmo. To this day, there are almost as many Italian last names as Spanish in Argentina. Even the language spoken in Argentina seems almost like Italian-accented Spanish, with its rhythm and pitch. *Lunfardo,* the street dialect associated with tango, owes many of its words to immigrant Italian.

The exponential growth of this time means that Buenos Aires—unlike Salta, Córdoba, and other old Argentine cities—retains few colonial buildings besides its churches.

Today, as a visitor mindful of Argentina's past several decades of political and economic chaos, it is difficult for me to make sense of the ostentatiously built infrastructure remaining from this earlier time. In essence, between 1880 and 1910, Argentina assumed the height of its wealth and power. Built at great expense of labor, money, and determination, Buenos Aires was the imperial capital of a country hungry to assert its importance on the world stage. Indeed, at the turn of the 20th century, Argentina was one of the 10 wealthiest countries in the world.

THE CULTURAL GROWTH OF THE 1920S & 1930S

Argentina's economic expansion, its wealth and sense of power during the turn of the 20th century laid the groundwork for strong cultural growth by the 1920s and

1930s. During this period, traditions that had always existed among the lower classes came into international recognition. Tango had always been associated with the lower classes, but one man changed all of that. In 1917, Carlos Gardel, who began his career singing as a child in Buenos Aires's Abasto Market, recorded what is considered the first important tango song—"Mi Noche Triste," which launched him to stardom. Throughout the 1920s, Gardel toured in France. Seeing that Parisians accepted tango, Argentina's upper classes embraced it as well. By the middle of the 1920s, tango became the country's most important musical form; its history is akin to the rise of jazz in the United States. Gardel died at the age of 44, on June 24, 1935, in a plane crash in Colombia, solidifying his status as one of Argentina's most important cultural icons.

The same period saw a flowering of literature and theater. Jorge Luis Borges published short stories on the gangsters and lower classes in Buenos Aires. By the 1930s, with Civil War and repression in Spain, Buenos Aires became the preeminent center of Spanish-language culture. Federico García Lorca lived in Buenos Aires briefly between 1933 and 1934, staying at the Castelar Hotel on Avenida de Mayo.

The 1930s were also a golden age for radio and cinema. Many stars came of age at this time, including Tita Morello and Libertad Lamarque. The Argentine film industry's only South American rival was Rio de Janeiro. Even there, however, stars such as Carmen Miranda, long before Hollywood discovered her, emulated the style of Buenos Aires. With the widening of Avenida Corrientes in the 1930s, many theaters opened here, making it the Broadway of Buenos Aires.

Buenos Aires glittered as the cultural capital of Argentina, pulling fame-seeking young men and women from the provinces. In 1934, one teenage girl from the city of Junín in the Province of Buenos Aires would come to do just that, changing Argentine history forever. Though accounts differ as to exactly how Maria Eva Duarte came to Buenos Aires—whether she was escorted by members of her family or with Augustin Magaldi, one of the country's top tango singers—she was in Buenos Aires for her very first time at the tender age of 15. With little but looks, charm, and persistence, Ms. Duarte moved through a succession of jobs and men, in theater, radio, and film. Eventually, with success as an actress, she would meet her most powerful boyfriend of all.

THE PERÓN YEARS

Juan Perón's popularity was anchored by an earthquake that occurred on January 15, 1944, in San Juan, a city near Mendoza, while he served as the head of the country's labor division. About 10,000 people died and nearly half the city was left homeless. The event was Perón's ultimate public relations opportunity. He arranged a fundraiser for the victims of the earthquake with a star-studded concert in Luna Park, a stadium in Buenos Aires. Though they actually met earlier, legend places the gala as where Perón and Evita met.

Fearing his rise to power, the military government arrested Perón and imprisoned him on Juan García Island in the Tigre Delta. A near revolt occurred in Buenos Aires, and the government quickly released him. On October 17, 1945 (the most important date in the Peronist calendar), Perón spoke to a crowd from a balcony at the Casa Rosada and announced that elections would be forthcoming. Feeling the need to legitimize their relationship, Eva and Perón married secretly in Los Toldos, the town of her birth, using the civil registry, and later married in a Catholic ceremony in La Plata, the provincial capital of Buenos Aires Province, overseen by a priest relative of Perón's.

Perón became president in 1946 in an election marked by fraud and brutality on both sides. Though Juan technically had the power, he could not have retained his popularity without Eva. With their power based in workers' unions, the couple launched numerous economic and work initiatives, many along the lines of Communist-style 5-year plans. Employment and wages spiked. Argentina's middle class owes its existence to this period.

After Evita's long insistence, women received the right to vote in 1947, and the presidential elections of 1951 were the first in which women participated. Wanting to legitimize her power within the government, Evita sought to be vice president on the 1951 election ballots, but Perón forced her to decline. Stricken with cervical cancer, Evita was dying, and forfeiting this final fight worsened her health. She voted in the elections from her hospital bed. She was so weak for the inaugural parade through Buenos Aires that they doped her up with painkillers and strapped her body to a wood frame, hidden by an oversized fur coat, so she could wave to crowds.

On July 26, 1952, Evita finally died. A 2-week mourning period ensued, and millions poured into Buenos Aires to pay their final respects. Knowing that without Evita his days might soon be over, Perón commissioned a monument to her, which was never completed, and had her body embalmed to be preserved forever.

A period of economic instability ensued, exacerbated by Perón's own policies. In 1955, the military deposed him and stole Evita's body, sending it on a journey lasting 17 years. Images of the Peróns were banned; even uttering their names was an offense.

Perón bounced through various countries—Paraguay, Panama, Venezuela, the Dominican Republic—before settling in Spain, ruled by longtime ally Francisco Franco. In Panama, he met his future third wife and vice president, nightclub dancer Isabel Martínez.

While Perón was exiled, Evita's body was returned to him, and his power base in Argentina strengthened, allowing his return to the presidency in 1973. Still, his arrival was wrought with chaos. Gun battles broke out at Ezeiza Airport when his plane landed. When he died in 1974, Isabel replaced him. Neither as strong as her husband nor his previous wife, Isabel could not hold onto the country for very long. She took on the nickname Isabelita, to bring back the memory of her predecessor and she supposedly held séances over the coffin of Evita in order to absorb her power. Despite her efforts, on March 24, 1976, she was deposed in a military coup headed by Jorge Rafael Videla.

THE DIRTY WAR & ITS AFTERMATH

The regime of Jorge Rafael Videla, established as a military junta, carried out a campaign to weed out anybody suspected of having Communist or Peronist sympathies. (Ironically, it was in this period that Evita was finally laid to rest in her current tomb in Recoleta Cemetery.) Congress was closed, censorship imposed, and unions banned. Over the next 7 years, during this "Process of National Reorganization"—a period now known as the Guerra Sucia (Dirty War) or El Proceso—between at least 10,000 and 30,000 intellectuals, artists, activists, and others were tortured or executed by the Argentine government. The mothers of these *desaparecidos* (the disappeared ones) began holding Thursday afternoon vigils in front of the presidential palace in Buenos Aires's Plaza de Mayo as a way to call international attention to the plight of the missing, an action which continues to this day. President Videla finally relinquished power to Roberto Violo in 1981. Violo would only serve as an interim president before being ousted by yet another military dictator, Leopoldo Galtieri, at the end of 1981.

With the Argentine population growing increasingly vocal about human rights abuses and the worsening economy, President Galtieri sought a patriotic distraction—invading the Falkland Islands, which the British had taken from Argentina in 1833.

The disastrous war, in which more than 900 died, ended the military regime. An election in 1983 restored constitutional rule and brought Raúl Alfonsín, of the Radical Civic Union, to power. In 1989, political power shifted from the Radical Party to the Peronist Party (established by Juan Perón), the first democratic transition in 60 years. Carlos Saúl Ménem, a former governor from the province of La Rioja, won the presidency by a surprising margin.

A strong leader, Ménem pursued an ambitious but controversial agenda, with the privatization of state-run institutions as its centerpiece. With the peso pegged to the dollar, Argentina enjoyed unprecedented price stability, allowing Ménem to deregulate and liberalize the economy. For many Argentines, it meant a kind of prosperity they had not seen in years. The policies, however, devastated manufacturing, and the export market virtually ended. The chasm between rich and poor widened, squeezing out much of the middle class and eroding social support systems. This destroyed investor confidence, and the national deficit soared.

After 10 years as president, Ménem left office. By that time, an alternative to the traditional Peronist and Radical parties, the center-left FREPASO political alliance, had emerged on the scene. The Radicals and FREPASO formed an alliance for the October 1999 election, and the alliance's candidate, running on an anti-corruption campaign, defeated his Peronist competitor.

Less charismatic than his predecessor, President Fernando de la Rúa was forced to reckon with the recession. In an effort to eliminate Argentina's ballooning deficit, de la Rúa followed a strict regimen of government spending cuts and tax increases recommended by the International Monetary Fund (IMF). However, crippled economic growth and political infighting prevented de la Rúa from implementing other reforms to stimulate the economy. An economic crisis loomed.

The meltdown arrived with a run on the peso in December 2001. Government efforts to restrict the run by limiting depositor bank withdrawals fueled anger through society, and Argentines took to the streets in sometimes violent demonstrations. De la Rúa resigned on December 20, as Argentina faced the worst economic crisis of its history. A series of interim governments did little to improve the situation. Peronist President Eduardo Duhalde unlocked the Argentine peso from the dollar on January 1, 2002, and the currency's value quickly tumbled. Within a few months, several presidents came and went, and people died in street protests. The country's default to the IMF was the largest in history.

Argentina's economic crisis severely eroded the population's trust. Increased poverty, unemployment surpassing 20%, and inflation hitting 30% resulted in massive emigration. *Piqueteros* and *cartoneros,* the protestors and the homeless, became a visible presence throughout Buenos Aires and other large cities, as the unemployed in rural areas picked garbage for a living.

Ironically, those who could not flee built a stronger nation. While under Ménem, Argentina idolized Europe and the United States, but now citizens had to look to their own historical and cultural models, things authentically Argentine. The tango—long expected to die out as a dance for the older generation—found new enthusiasts among the young.

The country further stabilized by 2003, with the election of Néstor Kirchner, the governor of the Province of Santa Cruz in

Patagonia, a province made wealthy by oil exploration. Kirchner had proven his economic savvy by sending the province's investments overseas just before the collapse of the peso. A left-wing Peronist, he saw many of his friends disappear under the military regime. He reopened investigations into this dark period in Argentina's history and also went after the most corrupt members of Ménem's regime. A consolidator of power, he and his senator wife—Cristina Fernandez de Kirchner, became the country's most important political couple. Under Kirchner, economic stability returned, with exports of soy, oil, and meat pumping the economy, and a cheap peso. An overall global boom meant there was a hungry market for the raw material Argentina produces, especially with China and other Asian economies. Tourism became the third most important economic sector under his administration, with many well-off foreigners deciding to stay and invest in property and business.

Yet Kirchner could hardly be called a reformist and Argentine politics remained mired in a myriad of bitter rivalries, exacerbated by a weak bureaucratic civil service and compromised judiciary. Corruption scandals, such as public works backhanders and a Venezuelan cash-in-suitcase election donation, failed to dent the president's popularity, buoyed by a consumer boom and relative prosperity. Sure to win a second term, Kirchner surprised everybody when he put his wife forward instead, and she won the presidency in October 2007 with 45% of the vote, making her the country's first elected female leader.

3 ARCHITECTURE

The vast majority of what visitors see in Buenos Aires today was built in the explosive period between 1880 and 1910, just after the city became the capital of Argentina, and in preparation for the country's Centennial. As a result, very little of Buenos Aires's colonial heritage exists today, save for Cabildo and Catedral Metropolitano surrounding Plaza de Mayo, both of which have been altered dramatically over time, and several churches within Monserrat and San Telmo.

REDESIGNING STREETS

Instead of Spain, it was France to which Buenos Aires looked when re-envisioning the city. The idea was to take the principles that Baron Georges-Eugène Haussmann used in Paris as a new foundation for the capital. The concept of diagonals, grand structures, parks, and vista points were put in place all over the city.

Developers laid new boulevards over the original Spanish colonial grid. The most important was Avenida de Mayo, which opened in 1893 and would serve as the government procession route, linking the Casa Rosada or Presidential Palace on its eastern end with the new Congreso on its western terminus. Lined with Beaux Arts and Art Nouveau buildings, according to the styles of the time, it became the cultural and nightlife center of the city. Diagonal Norte and Diagonal Sur were also laid out. Diagonal Norte was completed through the 1930s and, as such, its buildings seem a mix of neoclassical and Art Deco elements. Each building is capped with a corner dome, creating a sweeping vista meant to connect the Plaza de Mayo and the Casa Rosada to the Tribunales Building in Plaza Libertad. The sweeping designs of Diagonal Norte and Avenida de Mayo were meant to provide philosophical and physical connections between the Executive, Judicial, and Legislative branches of government. This point becomes lost to a degree with the addition of the Obelisco in 1936, marking the 400th anniversary of the (unsuccessful) founding of the city, blocking the view to Tribunales. The Obelisco sits in the oval Plaza de República, all of which was once the site of Iglesia de San Nicolás where the Argentine flag was first displayed on August 23, 1812. Like the Eiffel Tower in Paris, many hated the Obelisco when it was first built, but it has become the most important symbol of the city. The grand architectural plans for Diagonal Sur never came to fruition. Though it began grandly, with the City Legislature Building, over time it became lined with buildings lacking distinction, and it has no vista point. The widest boulevard in the world, Avenida 9 de Julio, was planned in 1888 as well, but its construction didn't begin until 1937. It was worked on in various stages, beginning with the center portion that exists today, and then widened by a street block once again on each side. Today, what appears to be the front of Teatro Colón is actually the back of the structure facing what was once an obscure street.

Technically, Avenida 9 de Julio is incomplete. The same grand expansion of the street that created the underground portions of the Teatro Colón was meant to extend all the way to Avenida Libertador. Ironically, the plan to redesign Buenos Aires to look like Paris would have meant the destruction of the Belle Epoque French Embassy. France refused to sell the structure and the boulevard's northern terminus here forms a beautiful vista point and gives an idea of what was destroyed here. At the southern end of the boulevard, the Health Department building was too large a structure to demolish, so the boulevard simply goes around it. It was from this building, looking out onto Avenida 9 de Julio, that Evita gave her speech giving up her candidacy for the vice presidency. From one end to the other, with the Obelisco as its fulcrum, the grand boulevard that is Avenida 9 de Julio seems out of kilter, the low-rise buildings that line it out of balance with its expanse. This is itself a function of grand plans that could never be fulfilled, and an obsession with a city's desire to have world acclaim for its streets.

GRAND ARCHITECTURE

As the streets were rebuilt, grand plans were announced to build what were to become the city's most iconic structures. One of the earliest of these was the Water Palace, originally designed in 1877. At first, it was meant as a reaction to the yellow fever epidemic raging through San Telmo and the city's need for a clean water supply. But as the wealthy residents constructed nearby mansions and the city was poised to become the capital of the country, what was simply a structure for water pumps transformed into an exquisite, high-Victorian style, built with more than 300,000 glazed Royal Doulton bricks shipped from Britain, and interior workings from Belgium. It opened in 1887 and is the earliest example of how, for the next several decades, Buenos Aires would continually outdo itself, creating over-the-top public buildings, each competing with other government projects and the nearby homes of the wealthiest oligarchs.

Perhaps the grandest of all was the Congreso building. Opened in 1906, after nearly 9 years of work, and built in a Greco-Roman style with strong Parisian Beaux Arts influences, Congreso is the city's most imposing building. One of the main architects was Victor Meano, who was also involved in designing the Teatro Colón, but he was murdered before completion of either building. Certain elements within the structure call to mind the Argentine desire to emulate other countries. The overall scheme of the building, with its wings and central dome, mimics the U.S. Capitol in Washington, D.C. The bronze ornamentation at the roofline simulates that of the Paris Opera

House, and the grand entrance, capped by bronze horses, is almost a direct copy of the Brandenburg Gate in Berlin. Though the exterior walls are made of Argentine granite, the building's interior is lavishly decorated with woods, tiles, marbles, bronzes, and other material imported from Europe. The Teatro Colón opened in 1908 and was perhaps the grandest example of Buenos Aires's desire to compete with the capitals of Europe. It, too, is filled with exquisite imported materials. After its opening, Italy's greatest opera stars, such as Enrico Caruso, graced its stage. Finally, by the 1910 Centennial, after nearly 3 decades as a construction site, the former simple trading post on the Pampas—once considered worthless by the powers in Madrid—was transformed by the best of Europe.

Yet for all its desire to transform itself architecturally to rival Europe, Buenos Aires was more likely the Dubai or Beijing of its time. While the city had the wealth and resources to pay for the massive rebuilding, it lacked the know-how and imported talent, labor, and materials from Europe. Buenos Aires needed the countries it competed with in order to transform itself in their image, something that to this day remains a sticking point.

4 ARGENTINA IN POPULAR CULTURE

RECOMMENDED BOOKS

Fiction lovers have a rich seam to mine regarding Argentine writing. Jorge Luis Borges is the country's grandfather of literature with his elegant short stories combining symbolism, fantasy, and reality to create metaphysical narratives that have been translated all over the world. *Labyrinths* and *A Universal History of Iniquity* are just two of his collections from a prolific career. Julio Cortázar is another giant of letters who, like Borges, was very much influenced by European ideas and lived abroad for many years in Paris. His novel *Hopscotch* has an unconventional narrative that requires reading twice to give two different versions. His story *The Droolings of the Devil* was adapted into the famous arthouse movie *Blow Up,* by Michelangelo Antonioni. Another Borges-influenced writer is Ernesto Sábato, whose *On Heroes and Tombs* is one of the most thorough artistic expressions of Buenos Aires ever written. *The Tunnel,* by the same author, is a compelling read about an obsessed painter. Less lauded abroad but more indicative of Argentine rural life is the work of Horacio Quiroga. A tragic figure (he committed suicide in 1937), Quiroga's stories are mostly set in the jungle frontier of Misiones and combine the supernatural and bizarre to create stories that are enjoyed by both young and old and can be seen as a predecessor to magical realism. *The Decapitated Chicken* and *The Exiles* are both short-story collections that are available in English. A seminal book in Argentine literature is the 19th-century gaucho poem *Martin Fierro,* by José Hernández, a compulsory read for all Argentine students.

Popular modern writers include Manuel Puig, whose *Kiss of the Spider Woman* was adapted into a movie of the same name. It deals with sex and repression, using popular movies and cultural references to keep the narrative flowing. Puig's background as a screenwriter can also be seen in other books such as *Betrayed by Rita Hayworth* and *Heartbreak Tango.* An excellent book discussing Puig's life is the biography *Manuel Puig and the Spider Woman,* by academic Suzanne Jill Levine. Osvaldo Soriano's *Shadows* and *A Funny Dirty Little War* are popular critiques of Argentine society, while Federico Andahazi's *The Anatomist* is an entertaining and somewhat bawdy work of historical fiction.

For an outsider's take on Argentine culture, read *In Patagonia,* by Bruce Chatwin, one of the most famous travelogues ever written. *Chasing Che,* by Patrick Symmes, is an eloquent description of the writer's attempt to retrace the road trip of the famous revolutionary. Miranda France's *Bad Times in Buenos Aires* is an excellent impression of an expat's frustrating attempt to live in Argentina. For something more light and fun, read *Kiss and Tango,* by Marina Palmer, the warts-and-all confessions of a tango-dancing *gringa.* Women should take note that, as exciting and romantic as the men of the *milongas* might seem to be, when Palmer finally settled down, she married a man who couldn't dance.

RECOMMENDED FILMS

Despite limited funding and very little exposure, the Argentine movie industry has a prodigious output, from slick mainstream features to grim independent films, with the occasional award-winning gem in between. Themes such as the breakdown of society, the Dirty War, the Malvinas war, and the sex wars provide rich pickings for young creative directors with little money, but lots of talent. Once in Buenos Aires, taking note of TV shows and theater productions in the small market that is Argentina, many local film stars move back and forth among various kinds of media.

Maria Luisa Bemberg is probably the most famous of late-20th-century Argentine filmmakers, and she specialized in period dramas. Her *Camila* (1984), which was Argentina's selection for the Oscars, and *Miss Mary* (1986) both deal with the feminine experience in Argentina, with Julie Christie starring in the latter. *The Official Story* (1985), by Luis Puenzo, and *The Night of the Pencils* (1986), by Hector Olivera, are two powerful dramas about the military dictatorship and how the repression even reached the nation's children. *Man Facing Southeast* (1986) and *The Dark Side of the Heart* (1992) are two compelling movies by Eliseo Subiela, the former having a sci-fi theme and the latter

an intriguing love story. The Italian neorealist style of filmmaking is a strong influence in Argentine cinema, and nowhere is it more evident than in the movies of Pablo Trapero. *Crane World* (1999) and *El Bonaerense* (2002) are two gritty working-class features, with the former a stark portrait of police corruption. Another master of everyday themes and deadpan comedy is Carlos Sorin. *Historias Minimas* (2003) and *Bombon the Dog* (2004) deal with love, life, and dogs. For something more mainstream but just as hilarious, *Tiempo de Valientes* (2008), by Damian Szifron, concerns two favorite Argentine subject matters—crime and psychoanalysis. *Blessed by Fire* (2004), by Tristan Bauer, is possibly one of the best movies made about the Falklands War, while grifter movie *Nine Queens* (2001), by Fabian Bielinsky, is so good that it was remade in Hollywood.

One of the first Hollywood movies on Buenos Aires is a lighthearted musical called *Down Argentine Way* (1940), by Irving Cummings, and stars the Brazilian Carmen Miranda. Robert Duvall's *Assassination Tango* (2002) is almost a personal project, and he stars along with his Argentine wife Luciana Pedraza. It is a slow movie, but highlights his obsession with Argentina and the tango, letting the city serve as a backdrop. Christopher Hampton's *Imagining Argentina* (2003), based on the book by Lawrence Thornton, details the Dirty War, and stars Emma Thompson and Antonio Banderas. More than likely, you've seen Alan Parker's *Evita* (1996), starring Madonna. While the film is often criticized, and not completely accurate, its cinematography is fantastic. So is its use of real Buenos Aires sites, such as the balcony of the Casa Rosada, where Evita once stood and entranced millions, as well as the use of Budapest as a stand-in for other scenes. For more authenticity, however, see the Argentine film *Eva Perón,* starring Esther Goris, which was produced almost as a response to the Madonna film.

Buenos Aires is one of the world's most important food cities. Its cuisine is a mix of influences, using homegrown staples such as the beef from cows fed off the grassland of the Pampas, to Italian staples such as pastas and rich sauces, and even underlying native Indian ingredients like *choclo,* a form of corn. With the Argentines' ensuing wealth and a desire to emulate what they saw as they traveled the rest of the world, French and other European influences came into the cuisine. The pretension of the go-go Ménem years of the 1990s, in particular, saw the rise of sushi and other Japanese items coming into vogue throughout Buenos Aires.

The most important Argentine staple is beef, and the world-famous Argentine steak is on top of every visitor's list to try as soon as possible. Sidewalk restaurants and cafes throughout Buenos Aires have a multitude of meat-based snacks such as *milanesas* (filet in bread crumbs) and *lomitos* (steak sandwiches). The ultimate cow experience is the epic Argentine *asado,* something to which the translation "barbecue" does no justice, as there is not a hotdog or hamburger in sight. Instead, you get a mouth-watering parade of every meat cut imaginable, such as *costillas* (ribs) and *bife de chorizo* (tenderloin). Offal is popular in the form of *mollejas* (sweetbread) and *chimchullinis* (intestine). A weekend invitation to a family *asado* should not be missed and, as you travel around, you will see such gatherings in the most unlikely places such as freeway curbs, street steps, and high-rise balconies. When Argentines want to celebrate, it is always with an *asado.* If such an invite is not forthcoming, settle for an *asado de tira* in any *parrilla* (grillhouse restaurant), with the ubiquitous empanadas for starters. You'll find these wonderful choices all over the city, whether in humble, family-run restaurants, such as **El Obrero** in La Boca,

to the most expensive *parrillas* in town, such as Recoleta's **La Cabaña.**

While beef is available throughout Buenos Aires, the neighborhood of Palermo Viejo reigns supreme in food experimentation. It is here that some of the most interesting examples of Argentine nouvelle cuisine were born, largely as a response to the peso crisis. With imported ingredients too expensive, many chefs began to take Argentine staples, such as beef and Italian food, and mix them with homegrown ingredients. Look to such restaurants as **Meridiano 58, Te Mataré Ramírez, Casa Cruz,** and **Bar Uriarte,** among many others, for this kind of cuisine. In addition, some chefs looked to ancient, indigenous staples, better known in Peru, for influence. These include restaurants such as **Bio,** a vegetarian restaurant that uses *quinoa,* the grain of the Incas, in some of its dishes, and **De Olivas i Lustres,** which uses the Incan grain *quinoa, yacare,* or river alligator, and *llama* in some of its dishes, many cooked in a Mediterranean fashion, a fantastic fusion of continents. Still, beyond the gourmet re-creations of star chefs, the Indian heritage of Buenos Aires remains in other staples, such as *locro,* the heavy winter stew with a mix of meats, and *chocla,* a large kernel corn.

With descendants of Italians making up more than half the population of Buenos Aires, Italian food cannot in any way be considered an ethnic specialty here. However, Middle Eastern influences exist in the city—a remnant of the immigrants who moved here after the breakup of the Ottoman Empire—in such restaurants as **Viejo Agump** and **Garbis.** Similarly, kosher restaurants, particularly with Sephardic influences, exist in Abasto. If you're craving peanut butter, considered a Middle Eastern food as the abundant peanuts were used as a substitute for sesame seeds, kosher shops will stave the craving.

Asian food is all over the city, with sushi in particular. Sushi's popularity during the Ménem years continued during the presidency of Fernando de la Rúa, whose economic advisors ate the dish during meetings and were nicknamed "the Sushi Club." In Buenos Aires, head to such places as **Kandi, Asia de Cuba,** the **Sushi Club,** and other restaurants to enjoy the raw fish. Recently, the raw fish trend has created another cultural fusion, born of immigration from Peru during the economic boom and the rise of Japanese-Argentine star chefs—Peruvian cuisine, itself, based on raw fish and best enjoyed in Palermo's **Ceviche.**

Regarding drinks, *mate* tea is a national obsession with groups of people consuming this bitter, green infusion on street corners, park benches, and at soccer games. Scan the city's parks on a hot day and you'll see it's carried by everyone enjoying the sun. Coffee is popular and served strong. For something different, try a *submarino*—a tall glass of hot milk dunked with a lump of dark chocolate (often in the shape of a submarine). Ice cream is indulged in at all hours and in the many parlors open until early morning, with a bewildering range of flavors topped by the national pride, *dulce de leche* (caramelized milk).

The Italian *digestif* Fernet has taken on a new life as the alcoholic drink of the young and is popular in late-night bars and discos. Argentine wine is some of the best in the world, with the powerful red Malbec from Mendoza the perfect companion for beef and the aromatic white Torrontes from Salta and La Rioja excellent with fish or pasta.

Planning Your Trip to Buenos Aires

A little advance planning can make the difference between a good trip and a great trip. What do you need to know before you go? When should you go? What's the best way to get there? How much should you plan on spending? What safety or health precautions are advised? All the basics are outlined in this chapter. For additional help in planning your trip and for more on-the-ground resources in Buenos Aires, see appendix A, "Fast Facts & Websites."

1 VISITOR INFORMATION

IN THE U.S. The Argentina Government Tourist Office has offices at 12 W. 56th St., New York, NY 10019 (© **212/603-0443;** fax 212/315-5545), and 2655 Le Jeune Rd., Penthouse Ste. F, Coral Gables, FL 33134 (© **305/442-1366;** fax 305/441-7029). For more details, consult Argentina's Ministry of Tourism website (see "Websites of Note," below).

IN CANADA Basic tourist information can be obtained at the Consulate General of Argentina, 2000 Peel St., Ste. 600, Montreal, Quebec H3A 2W5 (© **514/842-6582;** fax 514/842-5797; www.consargenmtl.com); for more details, consult Argentina's Ministry of Tourism website (see "Websites of Note," below).

IN THE U.K. For visitor information, contact the Embassy of Argentina in London (see "Entry Requirements," below) or consult Argentina's Ministry of Tourism website (see "Websites of Note," below).

IN BUENOS AIRES The central office of the **City Tourism Secretariat,** Calle Balcarce 360, in Monserrat (© **11/4313-0187**), is responsible for all visitor information on Buenos Aires, but is not open to the general public. Instead, the city uses several kiosks spread throughout various neighborhoods, which have maps and hotel, restaurant, and attraction information. For addresses and hours of these kiosks, see "Buenos Aires City Tourism Kiosks," below. In addition, individual associations often have their own tourist centers providing a wealth of information, such as that for the Calle Florida Business Association in a kiosk close to the end of Calle Florida as it hits Plaza San Martín.

The **Buenos Aires City Tourism Office** runs a hot line for information (© **11/4313-0187**) from 7:30am to 6pm Monday to Saturday, and Sunday 11am to 6pm.

Free tours are also provided by the city (find out more by calling © **11/4114-5791;** Mon–Fri 10am–4pm). The majority of the tours are in Spanish, but a few are also in English.

WEBSITES OF NOTE
- **www.argentina.travel** This Ministry of Tourism site has travel information for all of Argentina, including a virtual tour of the country's tourist regions, shopping tips, links to city tourist sites, and general travel facts. Similar information is on **www.turismo.gov.ar.**

- **www.buenosaires.gov.ar** A comprehensive government website set up by the city of Buenos Aires with some tourist links and news about the city.
- **www.bue.gov.ar** A comprehensive tourism website set up by the city of Buenos Aires with details on neighborhoods and a calendar of events in English and other languages. The website has lots of extremely detailed and useful information, but it can be cumbersome to work through its windows and pop-ups. Be patient with it.
- **www.palermoviejo.com** Find out what is going on in the city's trendiest neighborhood, full of the newest restaurants and shops. Palermo Viejo is further divided into Palermo Hollywood and Palermo Soho.
- **www.gopalermo.com.ar** This is another great website devoted to this rapidly changing part of the city, full of restaurants and shopping ideas.
- **www.welcomeargentina.com** This has great information on Argentina, and extensive details on things to do in Buenos Aires. Includes self-guided tour ideas, lists of hotels, and up-to-date information on restaurants and other trends.
- **www.guiaoleo.com.ar** This is only in Spanish, but it's a fantastic website for looking at different restaurants in Buenos Aires. Search by neighborhood or food type, and some entries include maps and photos to help you with your decision.
- **www.whatsupbuenosaires.com** This bilingual arts and culture website offers a glimpse at contemporary Buenos Aires, from news to music to photography to interviews.
- **www.subte.com.ar** This website explains in detail the workings of the Buenos Aires subway system and allows you to locate hotels and other sites of interest in relation to subway stops. It also includes downloadable maps and an interactive feature that allows you to figure out travel times between destinations.
- **www.embassyofargentina.us** This site contains up-to-date travel information from the Argentine embassy in Washington, D.C.

You can also send questions or requests for information to secturusa@turismo.gov.ar.

(Tips) Buenos Aires City Tourism Kiosks

The city of Buenos Aires has decided to bring information to the people. It closed its old central tourism information office and opened numerous tourism kiosks all over the city. In addition to those at the airport, here is a list of those located in the city center, including addresses and opening times.

- **Microcentro—Calle Florida:** Calle Florida 100, at Diagonal Norte. Open Monday to Friday from 9am to 6pm, Saturday, Sunday, and holidays 10am to 3pm.
- **San Telmo:** Defensa 1250, at San Juan. Open Monday to Friday from 11am to 5pm, Saturday and Sunday from 11am to 7pm.
- **Puerto Madero:** Alicia Moreau de Justo 200, at Dique 4 (Dock 4). Open Monday to Friday from 11am to 6pm, Saturday and Sunday from 11am to 7pm.
- **Retiro:** Retiro Bus Station, Window 83. Open Monday to Saturday from 7:30am to 1pm.
- **Recoleta:** Av. Quintana 596, at Ortiz. Open Monday to Friday from 10:30am to 6:30pm, Saturday and Sunday from 10am to 7pm.
- **Abasto:** Abasto Shopping Center, main level. Open daily 11am to 9pm.

MAPS

Ask at the front desk of your hotel for a copy of *The Golden Map* and *QuickGuide Buenos Aires* to help you navigate the city. Before leaving home, you can also get great maps ahead of time from the Buenos Aires–based company **De Dios**, which has laminated street maps (www.dediosonline.com).

Some of its maps are also themed, such as tango, shopping, or dining. Many neighborhoods in Buenos Aires now also have their own individual maps that you can often obtain at tourism kiosks. Free metro maps are available at ticket sales counters at every subway station, or visit www.subte.com.ar, the government's website for the subway system.

2 ENTRY REQUIREMENTS

PASSPORTS

Citizens of the United States, Canada, the United Kingdom, Australia, New Zealand, and South Africa require a passport to enter the country. No visa is required for citizens of these countries for tourist stays of up to 90 days. For more information concerning longer stays, employment, or other types of visas, contact the embassies or consulates in your home country. Usually, a hop by boat into neighboring Uruguay or crossing into Brazil (which might also require its own visa) during an Iguazú Falls excursion will allow a new 90-day tourist period. Take note that in January 2009, the Argentine government passed a reciprocity law, meaning that while not technically a visa, a one-time entry fee voucher, good for 10 years, must be paid by citizens of countries that charge Argentines to enter. For instance, Americans would have to pay $135, the same cost an Argentine bears to apply for a U.S. visa. As of this writing, the law has not been enforced and debate continues in Argentina whether to ignore or rescind the law, because of fears of reduction in tourism.

VISAS

To obtain a visa to Buenos Aires, contact the appropriate embassy or consulate in your home country.

IN THE U.S. Contact the Consular Section of the Argentine Embassy, 1811 Q St.

NW, Washington, DC 20009 (© **202/238-6401** or 202/238-6460). Consulates are also located in Los Angeles, California (© **323/954-9155/6**); Miami, Florida (© **305/577-9418**); Atlanta, Georgia (© **404/880-0805**); Chicago, Illinois (© **312/819-2610**); New York City (© **212/603-0400**); and Houston, Texas (© **713/871-8935**). For more information, visit www.embassyofargentina.us, with links to the various consulates in the U.S.

IN CANADA Contact the Embassy of the Argentine Republic, 81 Metcalfe Street, Ste. 700, Ottawa, Ontario K1P 5B4 (© **613/236-2351**; fax 613/235-2659; www.argentina-canada.net).

IN THE U.K. Contact the Embassy of the Argentine Republic, 65 Brooke St., London W1Y 4AH (© **020/7318-1300**; fax 020/7318-1301; seruni@mrecic.gov.ar; www.argentine-embassy-uk.org).

IN NEW ZEALAND Contact the Embassy of the Argentine Republic, Prime Finance Tower, Level 14, 142 Lambton Quay, P.O. Box 5430, Wellington (© **04/472-8330**; fax 04/472-8331; enzel@arg.org.nz; www.arg.org.nz).

IN AUSTRALIA Contact the Embassy of the Argentine Republic, John McEwen House, Level 2, 7 National Circuit, Barton, ACT 2600 (© **02/6273-9111**; fax 02/6273-0500; info@argentina.org.au; www.argentina.org.au).

MEDICAL REQUIREMENTS

Vaccinations are not required to enter Argentina, except for passengers arriving from countries where cholera and yellow fever are endemic.

CUSTOMS
What You Can Bring into Argentina

Travelers entering Argentina can bring personal effects—including clothes, jewelry, and professional equipment such as cameras and computers—without paying duty. In addition, they can bring in 21 liters (5½ gallons) of alcohol, 400 cigarettes, and 50 cigars duty-free.

What You Can Take Home From Argentina

U.S. Citizens: Returning U.S. citizens who have been away for at least 48 hours are allowed to bring back, once every 30 days, $800 worth of merchandise duty-free. You'll be charged a flat rate of duty on the next $1,000 worth of purchases. Any dollar amount beyond that is dutiable at whatever rates apply. On mailed gifts, the duty-free limit is $200. Be sure to have your receipts or purchases handy to expedite the declaration process. *Note:* If you owe duty, you are required to pay on your arrival in the United States, by cash, personal check, government or traveler's check, or money order, and in some locations, a Visa or MasterCard.

To avoid having to pay duty on foreign-made personal items you owned before leaving on your trip, bring along a bill of sale, insurance policy, jeweler's appraisal, or receipts of purchase. Or you can register items that can be readily identified by a permanently affixed serial number or marking—think laptop computers, cameras, and CD players—with Customs before you leave. Take the items to the nearest Customs office or register them with Customs at the airport from which you're departing. You'll receive, at no cost, a Certificate of Registration, which allows duty-free entry for the life of the item.

With some exceptions, you cannot bring fresh fruits and vegetables into the United States. For specifics on what you can bring back, download the invaluable free pamphlet *Know Before You Go* online at **www.cbp.gov**. (Click on "Travel," and then click on "Know Before You Go! Online Brochure.") Or contact the **U.S. Customs & Border Protection (CBP)**, 1300 Pennsylvania Ave., NW, Washington, DC 20229 (© **877/287-8667**) and request the pamphlet.

Canadian Citizens: Canada allows its citizens a C$750 exemption, and you're allowed to bring back duty-free one carton of cigarettes, one can of tobacco, 40 imperial ounces of liquor, and 50 cigars. In addition, you're allowed to mail gifts to Canada valued at less than C$60 a day, provided they're unsolicited and don't contain alcohol or tobacco (write on the package "Unsolicited gift, less than $60 value"). All valuables should be declared on the Y-38 form before departure from Canada, including serial numbers of valuables you already own, such as expensive foreign cameras. *Note:* The C$750 exemption can be used only once a year and only after an absence of 7 days. For a clear summary of Canadian rules, write for the booklet *I Declare,* issued by the **Canada Border Services Agency** (© **800/461-9999** in Canada or 204/983-3500; www.cbsa-asfc.gc.ca).

U.K. Citizens: Citizens returning from a non-E.U. country have a Customs allowance of 200 cigarettes; 50 cigars; 250 grams of smoking tobacco; 2 liters of still table wine; 1 liter of spirits or strong liqueurs (over 22% volume); 2 liters of fortified wine, sparkling wine, or other liqueurs; 60 cubic centimeters (mL) of perfume; 250 cubic centimeters (mL) of toilet water; and £145 worth of all other goods, including gifts and souvenirs. People younger than 17 cannot have the tobacco or alcohol allowance. For more information, contact **HM Customs & Excise** at © 0845/010-9000 (from outside the U.K., © 2920/501-261), or consult its website at www.hmrc.gov.uk.

Australian Citizens: The duty-free allowance in Australia is A$400 or, for those younger than 18, A$200. Citizens can bring in 250 cigarettes or 250 grams of loose tobacco, and 1.125 liters of alcohol. If you're returning with valuables you already own, such as foreign-made cameras, you should file form B263. A helpful brochure available from Australian consulates or Customs offices is *Know Before You Go*. For more information, call the **Australian Customs Service** at © 1300/363-263, or log on to www.customs.gov.au.

New Zealand Citizens: The duty-free allowance for **New Zealand** is NZ$700.

Citizens older than 17 can bring in 200 cigarettes, 50 cigars, or 250 grams of tobacco (or a mixture of all three if their combined weight doesn't exceed 250g); plus 4.5 liters of wine and beer, or 1.125 liters of liquor. New Zealand currency does not carry import or export restrictions. Fill out a certificate of export, listing the valuables you are taking out of the country; that way, you can bring them back without paying duty. Most questions are answered in a free pamphlet available at New Zealand consulates and Customs offices: *New Zealand Customs Guide for Travellers, Notice no. 4*. For more information, contact **New Zealand Customs,** The Customhouse, 17–21 Whitmore St., Box 2218, Wellington (© 04/473-6099 or 0800/428-786; www.customs.govt.nz).

3 WHEN TO GO

The seasons in Argentina are the reverse of those in the Northern Hemisphere. Buenos Aires is ideal in fall (Mar–May) and spring (Sept–Nov). The best travel deals are during April to June. The most beautiful time to visit, however, is October and November when the jacaranda trees are in bloom. "High season" is the period from December through February, with "low season" from June to August. In July and August, there's a slight rise in tourists because of North American summer and the South American ski season (tourists stop in Buenos Aires before heading to ski resorts). In December, you'll find pleasant weather for the most part. However, you won't find over-the-top Christmas decorations and rituals, in spite of the city's residents being overwhelmingly Catholic. In January and February, much of the city is abandoned by locals who flock to beach resorts in Mar del Plata or Uruguay. January is a time when many tourists do visit, resulting in overbooked hotels, yet many restaurants and sites have limited hours during this time period, often closing entirely from January 1 to January 15. You should call ahead to make sure a place is open.

WEATHER Except for a small tropical area in northern Argentina, the country lies in the temperate zone, characterized by cool, dry weather in the south, and warmer, humid air in the center. Accordingly, January and February can be terribly hot and humid—often in the high 90s to more than 100°F (38°C)—while winter (approximately June–Aug) can be overcast, chilly and wet (though you won't find snow). As in the rest of the world, global warming is shifting these trends, and sometimes odd heat waves or cold spells happen.

HOLIDAYS Public holidays are January 1 (New Year's Day), Good Friday, May 1 (Labor Day), May 25 (First Argentine Government), June 10 (National Sovereignty Day), June 20 (Flag Day), July 9

(Independence Day), August 17 (Anniversary of the Death of General San Martín), October 12 (Día de la Raza), December 8 (Immaculate Conception Day), and December 25 (Christmas). Most tourist businesses and restaurants, however, will remain open during all but Christmas and New Year's. Christmas itself is also celebrated on December 24, and many places will be closed that day as well.

Average Daytime Temperature (°F & °C) in Buenos Aires

	Jan	Feb	Mar	Apr	May	June	July	Aug	Sept	Oct	Nov	Dec
Temp (°F)	75	73	69	62	56	51	50	53	56	61	66	72
Temp (°C)	24	23	21	17	13	11	10	12	13	16	19	22

CALENDAR OF EVENTS

A few holidays and festivals are worth planning a trip around. The best place to get information for these events is through your local Argentina tourism office (see "Visitor Information," earlier in this chapter). The Buenos Aires Tourism Office also provides information on all these events through its website, www.bue.gov.ar, or by calling ℂ **11/4313-0187.** For an exhaustive list of events beyond those listed here, check http://events.frommers.com, where you'll find a searchable, up-to-the-minute roster of what's happening in cities all over the world.

FEBRUARY

Fiesta de las Murgas. The Buenos Aires version of Carnaval or Mardi Gras is not quite as colorful as that in Rio de Janeiro. Various neighborhoods have costumed street band competitions full of loud music and dancing. Every weekend in February.

Chinese Lunar New Year. Belgrano's Chinatown is small, but the dragon-blessing parade is a fun, intimate event that kids and adults are certain to enjoy. Beware of irresponsible firecracker users. The actual date of this holiday follows a lunar calendar. First Sunday of February.

Buenos Aires Fashion Week. Fashionistas will enjoy this event. Design is important to the city, the first ever designated by UNESCO as a world design capital. Visit www.bafweek.com for more information. Last week of February.

APRIL

Feria del Libro (Book Festival). This is one of the world's largest book festivals. Visit www.el-libro.org.ar for exact dates and the event schedule or call ℂ **11/4370-0600.** Late April to early May.

JULY

Buenos Aires Querible. Literally "lovable Buenos Aires," this event celebrates history and neighborhoods of the city, with events spread throughout town. Visit www.buenosairesquerible.gov.ar for more information. Mid-July.

Exposicion Rural. Gaucho and *estancia* culture invades the urban center, with this event held in La Rural, near Plaza Italia. Visit www.exposicionrural.com.ar for more information. Late July.

AUGUST

Buenos Aires Fashion Week. In August, you'll find the fashionistas gathering once again, this time for the spring and summer collections. Visit www.bafweek.com for more information. Late August.

SEPTEMBER

Festival Internacional de Buenos Aires. Theater lovers should try to visit during this 2-week event of international

theater programs. Visit www.festival
deteatroba.gov.ar, or call ℂ 11/4374-
2829 for more information. September
or October.

OCTOBER

World Tango Festival. This is celebrated with various events, many concentrated in the tango neighborhood of
San Telmo. See www.worldtangof
estival.com.ar for more information
and exact dates. Early to mid-October.

NOVEMBER

National Gay Pride Parade. The
parade goes down Avenida de Mayo.
Visit the Comunidad Homosexual de
Argentina website at www.cha.org.ar
for updated information. **Diversa,** the
national gay and lesbian film festival,
usually occurs near that period. Check
www.diversa.com.ar for the schedule.
First Saturday in November.

Argentine Open Polo Champion-
ships. The world's biggest polo event,
the **Argentine Open Polo Champion-**
ships, is held at the polo grounds in
Palermo, near the Las Cañitas neighborhood. It attracts moneyed crowds
from around the world, who get to
mingle with visiting British royalty. Call
the Argentine Polo Association (ℂ 11/
4343-0972) for more details. Late
November to early December.

DECEMBER

Midnight Mass on Christmas Eve
(Noche Buena). Though Argentina has
little in the way of Christmas ritual, the
mass at the Metropolitan Cathedral is a
beautiful spectacle. It is usually held at
10pm on Christmas Eve. In Argentina,
December 24 is a more important day
than December 25, and family dinners
are held on Christmas Eve rather than
Christmas Day.

4 GETTING THERE & GETTING AROUND

GETTING TO BUENOS AIRES
By Plane

Argentina's main international airport is
Ezeiza Ministro Pistarini (EZE; ℂ **11/**
4480-9538), located 42km (26 miles) to
the west of Buenos Aires. Allow at least 45
minutes to an hour for travel between the
airport and the city, more in rush hour.
You will be assessed a departure tax of
approximately $18 (£13) upon leaving the
country, payable in pesos, dollars, euros,
or by Visa credit card. For flights from
Buenos Aires to Montevideo (in Uruguay),
the departure tax is $8 (£5.70). Passengers
in transit and children younger than 2 are
exempt from this tax.

Below are the major airlines that fly
into Argentina from North America,
Europe, and Australia. Argentina's national

airline is **Aerolíneas Argentinas** (ℂ **800/**
333-0276 in the U.S. and Canada,
0810/222-86527 in Buenos Aires, or
1800/22-22-15 in Australia; www.aerolineas.
com.ar). The airline uses Miami as its U.S.
hub. While not having the most frequent
international connections to Buenos Aires,
Aerolíneas Argentinas provides an interesting
introduction to the excitement of Argentina
and its culture. The airline was also national-
ized at the beginning of 2009, so expect
changes in scheduling and frequency.

Other operators include **American Air-**
lines (ℂ **800/433-7300** in the U.S. or
11/4318-1111 in Buenos Aires; www.
americanair.com); **United Airlines** (ℂ **800/**
241-6522 in the U.S. or 0810/777-8648
in Buenos Aires; www.ual.com); **Air Can-**
ada (ℂ **888/247-2262** in Canada or

11/4327-3640 in Buenos Aires; www.air-canada.ca); **British Airways** (© 0845/773-3377 in the U.K. or 11/4320-6600 in Buenos Aires; www.britishairways.com); and **Iberia** (© 0870/609-0500 in the U.K. or 11/4131-1000 in Buenos Aires; www.iberia.com). **LAN Airlines,** formerly known as LanChile (© 866/435-9526 in the U.S. and Canada or 11/4378-2222 in Buenos Aires; www.lan.com), also provides connections from New York and Los Angeles to Buenos Aires via Santiago, and directly between Miami and Buenos Aires. **Continental Airlines** has flights from its hubs in Newark and Houston (© 800/525-0280; www.continental.com). **Qantas Airlines** of Australia (© 13-13-13 in Australia or 11/4514-4730 in Buenos Aires; www.qantas.com/au) has service from Sydney and Auckland, New Zealand, to Buenos Aires. For a complete list of airlines flying to Buenos Aires, see appendix A.

From New York, it's usually an overnight flight, about 11 hours. The small time difference of 1 to 3 hours, depending on the season, means there's little or no jet lag involved, depending on how you sleep on the plane.

Domestic airlines and flights to Uruguay use **Jorge Newbery Airport** (© 11/4514-1515), located only 15 minutes to the north, along the river from downtown.

The easiest way to travel Argentina's vast distances is by air. **Aerolíneas Argentinas** (© 800/333-0276 in the U.S. and Canada, 0810/222-86527 in Buenos Aires, or 1800/22-22-15 in Australia; www.aerolineas.com.ar) connects most cities and tourist destinations in Argentina, including Córdoba, Jujuy, Iguazú, Salta, and the beach resorts. Its competitor, **Southern Winds** (© 0810/777-7979; www.sw.com.ar), serves roughly the same routes. By American standards, domestic flights within Argentina are expensive. Technically, citizens and tourists get different airfares within Argentina. However, when booking through airline websites or even with travel agencies, tourists can sometimes get the Argentine rate.

If you plan to travel extensively in Argentina from Buenos Aires, consider buying the **Visit Argentina Pass,** issued by Aerolíneas Argentinas. You must purchase the pass in your home country—it cannot be purchased once you are in Argentina. This pass offers discounts for domestic travel in conjunction with your international Aerolíneas Argentinas ticket. Passes are purchasable as one-way coupons for flights within Argentina. Each segment ranges in price from $27 to $294 (£19–£209), depending on the destination, not including additional possible fees and taxes. Slightly higher, but still reduced rates, ranging from $38 to $382 (£27–£271), are available if you fly into Argentina via other airlines as well. Tickets are exchangeable by date but not by destination and are nonrefundable. For more information, contact the Aerolíneas office in your home country or visit **www.aerolineas.com**.

(Tips) U.S. Flight Connections

Be aware that while Argentina might not require a visa from your country of origin, continuing U.S. visa–requirement restrictions on connecting passengers from overseas have made connections via Canada or other countries easier for many non-American travelers. Foreign travelers using U.S. connections should contact the U.S. embassy in their country to find out restrictions, which are constantly changing, and incorporate the visa application time into the planning of their trip. This may also require an entirely new passport.

By Bus

The **Estación Terminal de Omnibus,** Av. Ramos Mejía 1680 (© **11/4310-0700**), located near Retiro Station, serves all long-distance buses. You would use this station when connecting to other parts of Argentina, or by long-distance coach from other countries. Due to the high cost of air transport for most South Americans, the continent is served by numerous companies offering comfortable, and at times luxurious, bus services to other capitals, often overnight. This is ideal for student and budget travelers.

Among the major bus companies that operate out of Buenos Aires are **La Veloz del Norte** (© **11/4315-2482**), serving destinations in the northwest, including Salta and Jujuy; **Singer** (© **11/4315-2653**), serving Puerto Iguazú as well as Brazilian destinations; and **T.A. Chevallier** (© **11/4313-3297**), serving points throughout the country.

The **Estación Terminal de Omnibus,** sometimes referred to as the Retiro Bus Station, is sprawling, enormous, and confusing. Just walking from one end to another takes about 15 minutes, given the ramps, crowds, and stairs through which you have to maneuver. Routes and platform locations rarely make it to the overhead boards, so they should never be relied on as the main source of information when trying to find your bus. In spite of the chaos readily observable here, there is an overarching order to the confusion. A color-coded system used at the ticket-counters explains, in general, which destinations of the country are served by which bus lines. Red, for instance, indicates the center of the country, including the province of Buenos Aires, dark blue the south, orange the north, green the northeast, light blue the central Atlantic coast, and gray the international destinations. However, at their sales counters, many bus companies indicate names of cities on their destination lists though they're no

longer served, so you may have to stand in a line to ask. Many companies also have more than one name, adding to the visual clutter at the ticket counters. To help you make sense of it all, use **www.tebasa.com.ar**, the terminal's website, while planning your trip. Click on the province where you are traveling and a list of bus companies and phone numbers will come up. Bus tickets can also be purchased at most travel agencies. This can cost slightly more, but can save a lot of confusion. You can also buy and download tickets ahead of time for select bus companies using the website **www.plataforma10.com**.

Getting into Town from the Airport

Taxis from the airport to the center of town cost about $30 to $40 (£21–£28). Take officially sanctioned transportation only available at the taxi kiosks, and do not accept transportation services from any private individuals. **Manuel Tienda León** (© **11/4314-3636**) is the most reliable transportation company, with buses and remises to and from the airport. Its buses cost about $18 (£13) and use a two-part hub system at its downtown terminal in Plaza San Martín to connect you in smaller buses to your final destination. This can take 1½ hours for connections.

GETTING AROUND

The best way (by far) to get around Buenos Aires is the metro—called the *subte*—the fastest, cheapest way to travel from neighborhood to neighborhood. Buses are also convenient in Buenos Aires, though less commonly used by tourists. The advantage of getting lost on a bus is that you'll be able to see parts of the city obviously not visible from the underground, and you'll stay oriented to your surroundings.

In addition to the maps in this book, you can usually get maps of metro and bus lines from tourist offices and most hotels. (Ask for the *QuickGuide Buenos Aires*.) All metro stations should have maps too, though they're rarely in good supply.

You will also find that Buenos Aires is a great walking city. The beauty of the Buenos Aires streets will pull you farther and farther along, until you realize just how many hours have passed since you began your stroll.

By Metro

Six *subte* lines connect commercial, tourist, and residential areas in the city Monday through Saturday from 5am to 11pm and Sunday and holidays from 8am to 10pm. The actual last train at any given station might be earlier, however, as the schedules are more of a guideline than a commitment. The flat fare is 1.10 pesos (30¢/20p). You can also buy a *subte pass* for 11 pesos ($3.15/£2.10), valid for 10 *subte* trips. Because the passes are relatively cheap, demagnetize easily, and do not work well in intense humidity, which is most of the summer, you might want to consider buying extra cards as backup. See the inside front cover of this guide for a *subte* map. Although the *subte* is the fastest and cheapest way to travel in Buenos Aires, the system can be crowded during rush hour and unbearably hot in summer as even the newest trains were designed without air-conditioning. After the subway has closed in the evening, it's best to take a taxi back to your hotel.

You should make sure to ride the A line, itself a tourist site, at least once during your stay in Buenos Aires. The A-line was the first line built, running along Avenida de Mayo, and it still uses the rickety but safe old wooden trains. Perú station, in particular, retains most of its turn-of-the-20th-century ornamentation, including advertising that mocks the old style from that time period and specially designed kiosks.

Neither the Recoleta nor Puerto Madero neighborhood has *subte* access, but most of Puerto Madero can be reached via the

L. N. Alem *subte* stop on the B line. (It's then a 5- to 20-min. walk, depending on which dock you're going to.) The D runs through Barrio Norte, which borders Recoleta, and depending on where exactly you're going, the area is a 5- to 10-minute walk away. Visit www.subte.com.ar for more information. The interactive site also gives estimated times and transfer information between stations.

Since the peso crisis, wildcat strikes on the subway have been common. However, the workers are usually very polite, often informing passengers ahead of time either by signs posted at the ticket windows of the designated strike time or by telling them before passing the turnstiles. And they never leave trains stuck midroute in the tunnels during these stoppages.

By Bus

There are 140 bus lines operating in Buenos Aires 24 hours a day. The fare is 1.10 pesos (30¢/20p). Pay your fare inside the bus at an electronic ticket machine, which accepts coins only, but will give change. Many bus drivers, provided you can communicate with them, will tell you the fare for your destination and help you with where to get off. The *Guia T* is a comprehensive guide to the buses, dividing the city up into various grids. This in itself presents a problem, however; rather than a flat map of the city, each neighborhood has its own page, making it nearly impossible for most foreigners to figure out. You can buy the guide at bookstores, newspaper kiosks, or on the *subte* from peddlers. Bus lines generally run on the main boulevards. Look for the numbered routes on the poles, which list the main points and neighborhoods the bus will pass through. It's a good idea to take note of main plazas, intersections, and other landmarks that are near your hotel to help with finding your way back. Even hotels on quiet side streets are usually close to a bus route. However, since it can be easy to get lost on the city's buses, I don't recommend them as your main mode of transportation while in Buenos Aires.

On Foot

You'll probably find yourself walking more than you had planned in this pedestrian-friendly city. Most of the center is small enough to navigate by foot, and you can connect to adjacent neighborhoods by catching a bus or taxi or using the *subte*. Additionally, plazas and parks all over the city supply wonderful places to rest, catch your breath, and watch the locals. Based on the Spanish colonial plan, Buenos Aires is a wobbly grid fanning out from the Plaza de Mayo, which makes it unlikely that you'll get too lost.

By Taxi

The streets of Buenos Aires are crawling with taxis. Fares are generally low, with an initial meter reading of 3.8 pesos ($1.10/72p) increasing 38 centavos every 200m (656 ft.) or each minute. *Remises* and radio-taxis are much safer than ordinary street taxis; *remises* are radio-taxis called in advance. Most of what the average tourist needs to see in the city involves a ride costing $3 to $7 (£2.15–£4.95). Radio-taxis, when hailed on the street, can be recognized by the plastic light boxes on their rooftops. If a cab is available, the word *libre* will flash in red on the windshield. Ordinary street taxis, more likely to be run by members of Buenos Aires's infamous taxi mafia, do not have these special lights. I personally have had few problems, but it's always best to err on the side of caution. If you speak English loudly with fellow passengers and are an obvious tourist, expect that your ride might last longer than it should, with strange route diversions ensuring a higher fare than normal. Being vigilant and having a general idea of where you are going, keeping in mind the one-way street system, can help to prevent this. Whenever I've been preoccupied with showing North American friends Buenos

Aires and lapsing into an intense conversation, this has happened often, with the driver using traffic problems as his excuse for the runaround.

A common taxi rip-off scam occurs when passengers don't know (in Spanish) the value of the bill(s) they present for payment, and the driver returns change for a smaller denomination than what he's actually been handed. Be sure to know in Spanish the value of your bill and announce it to the driver when requesting change. (Or make sure to have exact change and lots of coins and small bills.)

A rarely enforced law means taxi drivers can stop only if their passenger side is facing the curb. If you're being ignored by cabs with the red word *libre* (available) flashing on their windshield, cross the other side of the street and hail again.

Unlike European cities where taxi drivers go through extensive training to know their way around, Buenos Aires has no such training. Many taxi drivers here are from the provinces and simply do not know their way around Buenos Aires as well as they should. When heading to an off-the-beaten-path destination, or one along the miles-long *avenidas,* take note of the cross street when telling the driver where to go. Of course, it might be a fun learning venture for the both of you if you get lost. To request a taxi by phone (these drivers tend to be more experienced and safe), consider **Taxi Premium** (© 11/4374-6666), which is used by the Four Seasons Hotel, or **Radio Taxi Blue** (© 11/4777-8888), contracted by the Alvear Palace Hotel.

By Car

In Buenos Aires, travel by *subte* (subway), *remise*, or radio-taxi (radio-dispatched taxis, as opposed to street taxis) is easier and safer than driving yourself. Rush-hour traffic is chaotic, and parking is difficult. If you have rented a car, park it at your hotel or a nearby garage, and leave it there. Most daily parking charges do not exceed $8 or

$12 (£5.70–£8.50). Many recently built hotels have parking on the premises; others use nearby garages.

Many international car-rental companies operate in Argentina with offices at airports and in city centers. Here are the main offices in Buenos Aires for the major agencies: **Hertz,** Paraguay 1122 (© **800/645-3131** in the U.S., or 11/4816-8001 in Buenos Aires); **Avis,** Cerrito 1527 (© **800/331-1212** in the U.S., or 11/4300-8201 in Buenos Aires); **Dollar,** Marcelo T. de Alvear 523 (© **800/800-4000** in the U.S., or 11/4315-8800 in Buenos Aires); and **Thrifty,** Av. Leandro N. Alem 699 (© **800/367-2277** in the U.S., or 11/4315-0777 in Buenos Aires). Car rentals are expensive in Argentina, with standard rates beginning at about $50 to $60 (£36–£43) per day for a manual subcompact with unlimited mileage (ask for any special promotions, especially on weekly rates). Automatic cars will run about $100 (£71) per day. Check if your existing automobile insurance policy (or a credit card) covers insurance for car rentals.

5 MONEY & COSTS

The official Argentine currency is the **peso,** made up of 100 **centavos.** Money is denominated in notes of 2, 5, 10, 20, 50, and 100 pesos; and coins of 1, 2, and 5 pesos, and 1, 5, 10, 25, and 50 centavos. At the time this book went to press, the exchange rate was about 3.5 pesos to the U.S. dollar, and about 5 pesos to the British pound.

While prices in Argentina famously fell with the peso's devaluation in 2001, inflation has driven many prices up in recent years. Still, compared to North America and Europe, Argentina remains a relative bargain. Hotels however, are a general exception to that rule. Many four- and five-star- hotels have returned to their pre-devaluation rates, as the number of quality hotels has not kept up with the demand by visitors to one of the world's hottest travel destinations. As more and more Europeans (mostly from Western Europe) flock to Argentina, hotels are jacking up their prices because they know the euro is so strong. The average cost of a hotel room is from $50 to $400 (£36–£284) or more, with midrange hotels running about $150 (£107) a night in high season and $100 to $125 (£71–£89) in low season. Prices tend to be cheaper outside of Buenos Aires.

EXCHANGING MONEY

It's a good idea to exchange at least some money—just enough to cover airport incidentals and transportation to your hotel—before you leave home (though don't expect the exchange rate to be ideal), so you can avoid lines at airport ATMs. You can exchange money at your local American Express or Thomas Cook office or your bank. If you're far away from a bank with currency-exchange services, American Express offers traveler's checks and foreign currency, though with a $15 (£11) order fee and additional shipping costs, at www.americanexpress.com or © **800/807-6233.**

U.S. dollars are no longer as widely accepted in Buenos Aires as they were before and immediately after the December 2001 peso crisis. However, you can still use them to pay in some business-class hotels, and at restaurants and businesses catering to tourists. Such places will often post their own daily exchange rate at the counter. For the vast majority of your purchases, however, you will need pesos. You can convert your currency in hotels, *casas de cambio* (money-exchange houses), some banks, and at the airport. Exchange American Express traveler's checks for pesos in Buenos Aires at **American**

Express, Arenales 707 (© **11/4130-3135**). It is sometimes difficult to exchange traveler's checks outside the center of Buenos Aires, so plan ahead to have a sufficient amount of pesos on day trips.

ATMS

The easiest and best way to get cash away from home is from an ATM (automated teller machine). The **Cirrus** (© **800/424-7787;** www.mastercard.com) and **PLUS** (© **800/843-7587;** www.visa.com) networks span the globe; look at the back of your bank card to see which network you're on, and then call or check online for ATM locations at your destination. Be sure you know your personal identification number (PIN) before you leave home, and be sure to find out your daily withdrawal limit before you depart. Also keep in mind that many banks impose a fee every time a card is used at a different bank's ATM, and that fee can be higher for international transactions (up to $5/£3.55 or more) than domestic ones. On top of this, the bank from which you withdraw cash may charge its own fee. Ask your bank about international withdrawal fees.

ATMs are easy to access in Buenos Aires, but don't depend on finding them off the beaten path. Also, even if your bank allows a certain maximum daily amount to be withdrawn, usually in the range of $500 (£355), local ATM limits may be significantly lower (as little as $100/£71), so plan ahead if you know you need large amounts of cash, or test various cash machines before an emergency. While it's a bit of a pain, and sometimes results in higher fees, you can sometimes make multiple small withdrawals from the same bank machine, up to your own bank's limit. It is a good idea to let your bank know ahead of time that you will be using your ATM card overseas so it does not block transactions in an effort to prevent fraudulent ones.

CREDIT CARDS

Credit cards are another safe way to carry money. They also provide a convenient record of all your expenses, and they generally offer relatively good exchange rates. Visa, American Express, and MasterCard are accepted at most establishments in Buenos Aires. You can withdraw cash advances from your credit cards at banks or ATMs, but high fees make credit card cash advances a pricey way to get cash. Keep in mind that you'll pay interest from the moment of your withdrawal, even if you pay your monthly bills on time. Also, note that many banks now assess a 1% to 3% "transaction fee" on **all** charges you incur abroad (whether you're using the local currency or your native currency).

TRAVELER'S CHECKS

Traveler's checks are something of an anachronism from the days before the ATM made cash accessible at any time. Traveler's checks used to be the only sound alternative to traveling with dangerously large amounts of cash. They were as reliable as currency, but could be replaced if lost or stolen. Within the Pampas and rural areas of Buenos Aires Province, traveler's checks are especially welcomed by many establishments.

You can buy traveler's checks at most banks. They are offered in U.S. denominations of $20, $50, $100, $500, and sometimes $1,000. Generally, you'll pay a service charge ranging from 1% to 4%.

The most popular traveler's checks are offered by **American Express** (© **800/807-6233,** or 800/221-7282 for cardholders—the latter number accepts collect calls, offers service in several foreign languages, and exempts AmEx gold and platinum cardholders from the 1% fee); **Visa** (© **800/732-1322**)—AAA members can obtain Visa checks for a $9.95 fee (for checks up to $1,500) at most AAA offices or by calling © **866/339-3378;** and **MasterCard** (© **800/223-9920**).

What Things Cost in Buenos Aires	US$	UK£
Cup of regular coffee	2.00	1.40
Taxi from airport into Buenos Aires	30.00	21.30
Bus or subway fare	.29	.21
Moderate three-course meal for two, without alcohol	60.00	42.60
Room for two in moderately priced hotel	150.00	106.50

Be sure to keep a record of the traveler's checks serial numbers separate from your checks, in the event that they are stolen or lost. You'll get a refund faster if you know the numbers.

American Express, Thomas Cook, Visa, and **MasterCard** offer **foreign currency traveler's checks,** and they're accepted at locations where dollar checks may not be.

Another option is the new prepaid traveler's check cards, reloadable cards that work much like debit cards, but aren't linked to your checking account. The **American Express Travelers Cheque Card,** for example, requires a minimum deposit, sets a maximum balance, and has a one-time issuance fee of $14.95. You can withdraw money from an ATM (for a fee of $2.50 per transaction, not including bank fees), and the funds can be purchased in dollars, euros, or pounds. If you lose the card, your available funds will be refunded within 24 hours.

6 HEALTH

STAYING HEALTHY

Argentina requires no vaccinations to enter the country, except for passengers coming from countries where cholera and yellow fever are endemic.

Some people who have allergies can be affected by the pollution in Buenos Aires's crowded Microcentro, where cars and buses remain mired in traffic jams, belching out pollution. The beautiful spring blossoms also bring with them pollen, and even people not usually affected by plants might be thrown off seasonally and by species of plants different from those in North America and Europe. It's a good idea to pack a decongestant with you, or asthma medicine if you require it.

Because motor vehicle crashes are a leading cause of injury among travelers, walk and drive defensively. Do not expect buses and taxis to stop for you when crossing the street. Always use a seat belt, which has now become the law in Buenos Aires, even in taxis.

Most visitors find that Argentine food and water are generally easy on the stomach. Water and ice are considered safe to drink in Buenos Aires, though many people will prefer bottled water. However, you should be careful with Argentine steak. Because it is generally served very rare, if not almost raw inside, people with delicate digestive systems or immune deficiency should request it well done (*bien cocido*). You should also avoid street food and drinks served out of canisters at the ubiquitous festivals all over the city. Vegetarians should be aware that with so much leftover cow fat as a byproduct of the cattle industry, lard winds up being commonly used as a cooking ingredient and finds its way into many baked goods. Read labels and ask.

Buenos Aires's streets and sidewalks can be disgustingly unsanitary. While there is a pooper-scooper law on the books, dog owners seem to take delight in letting their pets relieve themselves in the middle of the sidewalk. Even the best neighborhoods are an obstacle course to walk through, and it's a good idea to continually watch where you're stepping. Wash your hands thoroughly after handling your shoes, even if you do not think you have stepped in anything. Roaches also love the city's streets as much as you do. If you don't want unwelcome visitors in shopping bags or pocketbooks, don't leave them sitting on the ground while you dine outdoors.

General Availability of Health Care

The medical facilities and personnel in Buenos Aires and the other urban areas in Argentina are very professional. Argentina has a system of socialized medicine, where basic services are free. Private clinics are inexpensive by Western standards.

Be aware that most drugs requiring a prescription in North America or Western Europe do not necessarily need one in Argentina. Hence, if you lose or run out of a medicine, it might not be necessary to schedule a doctor's appointment to get your prescription. The same goes if you become ill and are sure you know what you need. Many of the pharmacies in the Microcentro have English-speaking staff. Not all medicines, however, are a bargain in Argentina.

Pack **prescription medications** in your carry-on luggage, and carry them in their original containers, with pharmacy labels—otherwise they won't make it through airport security. Also bring copies of your prescriptions in case you lose your pills or run out. Don't forget an extra pair of contact lenses or prescription glasses. Carry the generic name of prescription medicines, in case a local pharmacist is unfamiliar with the brand name.

Though not strictly a health issue, plastic surgery has become an obsession for many Argentines. Depending on your view, Susana Gimenez, one of Argentina's most famous stars, is an example of either the dangers or delights of that obsession. Whether looking at the supposedly Botox-enhanced face of President Cristina Fernandez de Kirchner, or the everyday top-heavy stick-figure women on the sidewalks, you get a sense that facial and breast augmentation are the fashion here. In fact, it is so common that it is often covered in private health insurance. Because of the exchange rate, Argentina is also becoming a place for plastic-surgery tourism. If you are planning to be here for a long time and have been considering cosmetic procedures, Buenos Aires might be a place to have it done.

Common Ailments

AUSTRAL SUN The summer sun is hot and strong in Buenos Aires. It's best to bring sun block, though it is available in stores and pharmacies throughout the city. There are no beaches within the city proper, but many people go tanning in the Palermo and Recoleta parks or in the Ecological Reserve.

TROPICAL ILLNESSES Malaria is not an issue in Buenos Aires. However, the humid summer months of January and February mean you will sometimes find swarms of mosquitoes, particularly along the Río de la Plata and in parks. Bring repellent to avoid bites. To get advice about shots for various illnesses if you are traveling from Buenos Aires to the jungle for long periods of time, contact **Vacunar,** a chain of clinics specializing in vaccinations and preventative illness, with locations all over Buenos Aires (www.vacunar. com.ar). Keep in mind that many shots require a period of time before they become effective. They will also explain what is required in other countries if you are traveling to other parts of South America.

WHAT TO DO IF YOU GET SICK AWAY FROM HOME

For an English-speaking hospital, call **Clínica Suisso Argentino** (ⓒ 11/4304-1081). The **Hospital Británico** (ⓒ 11/4309-6600) also has English-speaking doctors. If you worry about getting sick away from home, you may want to consider **medical travel insurance** (see "Fast Facts" in appendix A). In most cases, your existing health plan will provide all the coverage you need, but call to make sure. Be sure to carry your identification card in your wallet. You should also ask for receipts or notes from the doctors, which you might need for your claim.

Any foreign consulate can provide a list of area doctors who speak English. If you get sick, consider asking your hotel concierge to recommend a local doctor—even his or her own. You can also try the emergency room at a local hospital. Many hospitals also have walk-in clinics for emergency cases that are not life-threatening; you may not get immediate attention, but you won't pay the high price of an emergency room visit.

If you suffer from a chronic illness, consult your doctor before your departure. For such conditions as epilepsy, diabetes, or heart problems, wear a **MedicAlert identification tag** (ⓒ 888/633-4298; www.medicalert.org), which will immediately alert doctors to your condition and give them access to your records through MedicAlert's 24-hour hot line.

For **additional emergency numbers,** see appendix A.

7 SAFETY

Petty crime has increased significantly in Buenos Aires as a result of Argentina's economic crisis. Travelers should watch out for pickpockets and purse-snatchers on the streets and on subways, buses, and trains. Tourists should take care not to be overly conspicuous, walking in pairs or groups when possible. Avoid demonstrations, strikes, and other political gatherings if they appear to be violent, though the vast majority of these are safe and peaceful.

In Buenos Aires, it's not recommended that you hail taxis off the street. You should call for a radio-taxi instead. Particular areas of the city considered to be unsafe are parts of Monserrat, especially at night, and La Boca. Parts of San Telmo have historically been considered dangerous, but in general that is no longer true. However, you should still take precautions. Particular caution should be taken when using the Constitución train station or while in that neighborhood, though I do not discuss it from a tourist standpoint, except in terms of a side trip to La Plata. In an emergency, call ⓒ 100 for police assistance. This is a free call.

See the "Women Travelers" section below for safety advice for women traveling in Argentina. With the increase in tourism, Buenos Aires has also engaged in a massive police-hiring program to ensure tourist safety, so you are generally never more than a block or two away from a police officer. In the event of an incident where you cannot find an officer, go to a hotel, restaurant, or shop and ask them to call the police for you. If you take a tour and feel you've been the victim of fraud or misrepresentation of any kind by businesses that serve tourists, or you have been the victim of a taxi scam, the tourism office has a special number for reporting this, and it can be called toll-free at ⓒ 0800/999-5000.

TRAVELERS WITH DISABILITIES

Buenos Aires is not a very accessible destination for travelers with disabilities. Four- and five-star hotels in Buenos Aires often have a few rooms designed for travelers with disabilities—check with the hotel in advance, and ask specific questions. Some hotels claim to be equipped for those with disabilities, but still have one or two stairs leading to their elevator bays, making wheelchair access impossible. American, Canadian and European-owned chains tend to be better at accessibility. Hotels with recent renovations sometimes will also have a room for those with limited capabilities and pull bars in the bathrooms. The tiny crowded streets of the Microcentro can often barely accommodate two people walking together, let alone a wheelchair, and sidewalk cutouts do not exist in all areas.

The city government's special task force COPINE, or the Comisión para la Plena Participación e Integración de las Personas con Necesidades Especiales, has recently put out a tourism guide called *Guía Turismo Accesible,* which lists a variety of resources and establishments for travelers with disabilities. Ask for it at tourism kiosks or at the airport upon arrival. They can also be reached at ✆ **11/4010-0300** ext. 13407 or by e-mail at copine@buenos aires.gov.ar.

Many travel agencies offer customized tours and itineraries for travelers with disabilities. **Flying Wheels Travel** (✆ **507/451-5005;** www.flyingwheelstravel.com) offers escorted tours and cruises that emphasize sports and private tours in minivans with lifts. **Access-Able Travel Source** (✆ **303/232-2979;** www.access-able.com) offers extensive access information and advice for traveling around the world with disabilities. **Accessible Journeys** (✆ **800/846-4537** or 610/521-0339; www.disabilitytravel.com) caters specifically to slow walkers and wheelchair travelers.

Within Buenos Aires, **Turismo Nuevo Mundo,** while not specializing in travel for those with limited disability, has put together many of such itineraries (Alicia Moreau de Justo 872, 10th floor; ✆ **11/4331-4573;** www.turismonuevomundo.com).

Organizations that offer assistance to travelers with disabilities include **Moss Rehab** (www.mossresourcenet.org), which provides a library of accessible-travel resources online; **SATH** (Society for Accessible Travel & Hospitality; ✆ **212/447-7284;** www.sath.org; annual membership fees: $45/£32 adults, $30/£21 seniors and students), which offers a wealth of travel resources for all types of disabilities and informed recommendations on destinations, access guides, travel agents, tour operators, vehicle rentals, and companion services; and the **American Foundation for the Blind** (AFB; ✆ **800/232-5463;** www.afb.org), a referral resource for the blind or visually impaired that includes information on traveling with Seeing Eye dogs.

Also check out the quarterly magazine *Emerging Horizons* ($14.95 per year, $19.95/£14 outside the U.S.; www.emerginghorizons.com), and *Open World* magazine, published by SATH (see above; subscription: $13 per year, $21/£15 outside the U.S.).

SENIOR TRAVEL

Argentines treat seniors with great respect, making travel for them easy. The Argentine term for a senior or retired person is *jubilado.* Discounts are usually available; ask when booking a hotel room or before ordering a meal in a restaurant. There are often discounts at theaters and museums too, or even free admission. **Aerolíneas Argentinas** (© 800/333-0276 in the U.S.; www.aerolineas.com.ar) offers a 10% discount on fares to Buenos Aires from Miami and New York for passengers 62 and older; companion fares are also discounted.

Members of **AARP** (formerly known as the American Association of Retired Persons), 601 E St. NW, Washington, DC 20049 (© 888/687-2277; www.aarp. org), get discounts on hotels, airfares, and car rentals. AARP offers members a wide range of benefits, including *AARP: The Magazine* and a monthly newsletter. Anyone over 50 can join.

The Alliance for Retired Americans, 8403 Colesville Rd., Ste. 1200, Silver Spring, MD 20910 (© 301/578-8422; www.retiredamericans.org), offers a newsletter six times a year and discounts on hotel and auto rentals; annual dues are $13 per person or couple. *Note:* Members of the former National Council of Senior Citizens receive automatic membership in the Alliance.

Many reliable agencies and organizations target the 50-plus market. **Elderhostel** (© 877/426-8056; www.elderhostel. org) arranges study programs for those ages 55 and over (and a spouse or companion of any age) in the U.S. and in more than 80 countries around the world. Most courses last 5 to 7 days in the U.S. (2–4 weeks abroad), and many include airfare, accommodations in university dormitories or modest inns, meals, and tuition. **Elder-Treks** (© 800/741-7956; www.eldertreks. com) offers small-group tours to off-the-beaten-path or adventure-travel locations, restricted to travelers 50 and older.

Recommended publications offering travel resources and discounts for seniors include: the quarterly magazine *Travel 50 & Beyond* (www.travel50andbeyond. com); *Travel Unlimited: Uncommon Adventures for the Mature Traveler*

(Avalon); *101 Tips for Mature Travelers,* available from Grand Circle Travel (© 800/221-2610 or 617/350-7500; www.gct.com); and *Unbelievably Good Deals and Great Adventures that You Absolutely Can't Get Unless You're Over 50* (McGraw-Hill), by Joann Rattner Heilman.

GAY & LESBIAN TRAVELERS

Argentina remains a very traditional, Catholic society that is fairly close-minded about homosexuality. Buenos Aires, however, is a more liberal exception to this rule. In particular, the Barrio Norte and San Telmo neighborhoods are gay- and lesbian-friendly, and gays and lesbians are part of the fabric of city life. Gay and lesbian travelers will find numerous clubs, restaurants, and even tango salons catering to them. Buenos Aires has become a major Latin American gay-tourism mecca since the peso crisis, outshining Rio de Janeiro in popularity for this market. Gay maps are now produced by the Buenos Aires Tourism Office for distribution with standard travel information, along with *The Ronda* which lists the gay scene (www. theronda.com.ar), and *G-Maps,* with an interior booklet and map (www.gmaps360. com). Most hotel concierges also easily provide this information, recognizing the importance of the emerging market. The locally produced website www.gayin buenosaires.com.ar also provides more details on sites of interest.

In 2003, Buenos Aires enacted a Civil Unions law for gay and lesbian couples—the first major Latin American city to do so. While there are visible venues and efforts, for the most part many gays and lesbians remain fairly closeted. Violence is sometimes aimed at the transgendered, even by police.

Be aware of a few rules of thumb in a city where close contact is normal. Women walk hand in hand on the street. Men kiss each other hello. However, when two men hold hands, it means they are gay. It's very rare to see men holding hands, but Buenos Aires is beginning to see surprisingly open expressions of male homosexuality, especially in Barrio Norte along Santa Fe at night.

The **International Gay and Lesbian Travel Association (IGLTA;** © **800/448-8550** or 954/776-2626; www.iglta.org) is the trade association for the gay and lesbian travel industry, and offers an online directory of gay- and lesbian-friendly travel businesses; go to their website and click on "Members." In February 2005, IGLTA hosted an international gay travel conference in Buenos Aires, with official Argentine government recognition of the event.

The **Comunidad Homosexual de Argentina (CHA;** © **11/4361-6382;** www.cha.org.ar) is the main gay- and lesbian-rights group in Argentina. They were the main proponents of the Civil Unions law, which they are attempting to expand to the entire country. They also run the annual Gay Pride March, known as Marcha del Orgullo Gay, in November.

Many agencies offer tours and travel itineraries specifically for gay and lesbian travelers. **Above and Beyond Tours** (© **800/397-2681;** www.abovebeyond tours.com) is the exclusive gay and lesbian tour operator for United Airlines. **Now, Voyager** (© **800/255-6951;** www.now voyager.com) is a well-known San Francisco–based gay-owned and -operated travel service. Chicago-based **Zoom Vacations** (© **866/966-6822;** www.zoom vacations.com) and New York–based **Steele Travel** (© **646/688-2274;** www. steeletravel.com) both offer specialized group itineraries and cruise vacations for Buenos Aires.

Pride Travel (© **11/5218-6556;** www. pride-travel.com) is an Argentina-based company specializing in inbound Buenos Aires travel and other trips throughout South America. **BueGay Travel** (© **11/4184-8290;** www.buegay.com.ar) handles gay tourism within Buenos Aires and other parts of Argentina. **Viajeras Travel** (© **11/4328-1857;** www.viajeras.net) is a woman-run travel company, specializing in travel for lesbian visitors to Buenos Aires. The women's scene is harder to tap than the men's scene, so this is a useful resource.

Daniel Porce Producciones, a gay-owned promotion company, also provides discounts to Howard Johnson and other hotels in Buenos Aires and other cities when booked through its website, www.dp producciones.com.ar (© **15/5817-3041**).

Owned by a Dutch expat, the **Royal Family** offers gay travel services and gay dinner get-togethers (© **11/4383-1026;** www.theroyalfamily.com.ar).

The affiliated gay websites of **PlanetOut. com, Gay.com Travel,** and **Outtraveler. com;** (www.planetout.com; www.gay. com; www.outtraveler.com) have provided gay and lesbian travelers with objective, timely, and trustworthy coverage of gay-owned and gay-friendly lodging, dining, sightseeing, nightlife, and shopping establishments in every important destination worldwide. These websites maintain an archive of past articles on gay spots around the globe, including many on Buenos Aires and Argentina. *Spartacus International Gay Guide* (Bruno Gmünder Verlag; www.spartacusworld.com/gayguide) and *Odysseus* (Odysseus Enterprises Ltd.) are good, annual English-language guidebooks focused on gay men, with some information for lesbians. You can get them from most gay and lesbian bookstores, or order them from **Giovanni's Room** bookstore, 1145 Pine St., Philadelphia, PA 19107 (© **215/923-2960;** www.giovannis room.com). Within Buenos Aires, the gay monthly magazine *Imperio* is available at virtually all central newspaper kiosks, or look for *Otra Guia,* sometimes sold at kiosks and available free in select venues. Both include maps and gay guides for Buenos Aires and other Argentine cities. The Buenos Aires–based gay news website www.sentidog.com.ar also has extensive local travel advertising.

WOMEN TRAVELERS

A woman achieved the highest position in Argentine society when Cristina Fernandez de Kirchner, the former First Lady and Senator, who is often nicknamed CFK, was elected president in 2007. She's not, however, the first female president—that distinction went to Juan Perón's third wife, Isabel, upon his death in 1974. What is remarkable beyond Cristina's winning is that her most challenging candidate was another woman, Elisa Carrió, head of the political party ARI, which stands for the Spanish translation for Alternative for a Republic of Equals. Combined, the two women received nearly 77% of all votes in the 2007 presidential elections. Still, in spite of political power and the very visible women-owned and -run businesses in the restaurant and tourism industries, Argentina remains, at heart, a sexist country. Media often use the term "businessmen" rather than inclusive terms, demonstrating the glass ceiling for women in many corporations, and female beauty is highly idealized above all other traits.

Women travelers will find that Argentine men are extremely flirtatious, and leering looks are common and rarely discreet, owing perhaps to the strong Italian influence in the country. While disconcerting, any looks and calls you might get are rarely more than that. Drunken men in clubs can sometimes be physically harassing and, according to many young pretty foreign visitors, will try to kiss you to show off to their friends. Women should be cautious when walking alone at night and should take a *remise* or radio-taxi after dark.

In the rare and unlikely event of an assault or sexual attack, contact the police immediately. More help can also be received from the **Centro de Estudios Cultura y Mujer (CECYM),** Guatemala

4294 (© **11/4865-9102;** www.cecym. org.ar). It specializes in sexual violence against women, but not all of the staff members speak English. The group also conducts arts programs, discussions, and other events related to the feminist movement within Argentina.

Single women, or women whose partners refuse to dance, who want to take advantage of the tango scene can contact **Tanguera Tours** (www.tangomina.com. ar/tanguera/index.htm), which offers specialized tango tours for groups of women. The tango scene in general, with its strict rules, combining both chauvinism and chivalry, is a safe option for single women to try their hand at dancing. Nothing more than a dance is expected of a woman who accepts an invitation on the dance floor. In spite of tango's brothel roots, misbehavior among men is frowned upon in tango settings today.

Check out the award-winning website **Journeywoman** (www.journeywoman. com), a "real life" women's travel information network where you can sign up for a free e-mail newsletter and get advice on everything from etiquette and dress to safety; or the travel guide *Safety and Security for Women Who Travel,* by Sheila Swan and Peter Laufer (Travelers' Tales, Inc.), offering common-sense tips on safe travel.

JEWISH TRAVELERS

Buenos Aires is one of the world's greatest Jewish centers, with an estimated Jewish population of more than 250,000. The historical foci of the community are the neighborhoods of **Once** and **Abasto.** They developed that way in the beginning of the 20th century after immigration of both Ashkenazi Jews from Eastern Europe escaping pogroms and Sephardic Jews who emigrated after the breakup of the Ottoman Empire at the end of World War I. Ironically, after World War II, Argentina welcomed Eastern European Jewish refugees while also allowing the entry of former Nazis. While the communities have generally dispersed to the suburbs, replaced by other immigrants, the area is still home to kosher restaurants, Jewish businesses, and various synagogues. The **Abasto Shopping Center** food court also has the only kosher McDonald's (p. 193) in the world outside of Israel. With subsequent generations, assimilation and intermarriage have also meant that few Buenos Aires Jews maintain traditions, except at holiday times.

In 1992, there was a bomb attack on Buenos Aires's Israeli Embassy, killing 29 people, and in 1994, an attack on the Jewish community group **Asociación Mutual Israelita Argentina (AMIA)** killed 85 people. However, in spite of these attacks engineered by outsiders, most Argentine Jews feel little discrimination. Argentines of all faiths responded to the attacks by massive candlelight vigils. Visit AMIA's website at www.amia.org.ar for more information.

One company that leads Jewish tours of Buenos Aires is **Travel Jewish** (*C* 949/307-9231 in the U.S.; www.traveljewish.com; info@traveljewish.com), a company owned by Deborah Miller, an American who has lived in Buenos Aires. Travel Jewish can plan your trip, including flights and hotels, from beginning to end, or you can take their simple, Jewish-themed day tours once you are in Buenos Aires. Freelance Jewish tour guides include Gabriel Blacher, who can be reached at *C* **11/15-5240-4915** or by e-mail at gblacher@hotmail.com, as well as Susana Alter, who can be reached at *C* **11/4555-7297** or by e-mail at alters usana@yahoo.com.ar.

KIDS & TEENS

Argentines love and pamper their children in every way possible. Buenos Aires's kids are also trained from an early age to stay up late in this nocturnal city. Don't be surprised to find yourself passing a playground full of kids and their parents on the swing sets at 2am when you're trying to find your way back to your hotel. There are restaurant chains, such as **Garbis** (p. 114), that have indoor playgrounds, and several museums have been created just for kids, such as the **Museo de los Niños** (p. 145) in Abasto Shopping Center and the **Museo Participativo de Ciencias** (p. 146) in the Centro Cultural Recoleta. Teens will love the concentration of movie theaters, video arcades, and inexpensive eateries on the pedestrianized **Calle Lavalle** (p. 155). The area can be rough at night however. Be aware that, with a drinking age of only 18, unsupervised minors who look older than they actually are might have easy access to alcohol.

That said, your children might find it hard to see other children begging on the streets in large cities throughout the country and helping their *cartonero* (homeless parent) by looking for discarded paper to sell to recyclers for a very desperate living. The peso crisis has enacted a heavy toll on many Argentine children, creating a young, homeless class of beggars. It might be a good idea to explain to your child the inequities within Argentina, and the rest of Latin America for that matter, if he or she comments on this. In theory, your visit to Argentina, in the long run, will improve the economy and the plight of these homeless children. It might be tempting to give money to these sad kids, but nutritious, wrapped food or school supplies will do them more good in the long run. The nonprofit **Voluntario Global** (p. 166) allows tourists to do charity work on vacation in Buenos Aires, which might be ideal for helping children understand the poverty in Argentina in a constructive way.

STUDENT TRAVELERS

Student discounts are very common in Argentina, but usually only if one has appropriate ID. **STA Travel** (*C* **800/781-4040** in the U.S., 020/7361-6144 in the U.K., or 1300/360-960 in Australia; www.statravel.com) specializes in affordable airfares, bus and rail passes, accommodations, insurance, tours, and packages for students and young travelers, and issues the **International Student Identity Card (ISIC).** This is the most widely recognized proof that you really are a student. As well as getting you discounts on a huge range of travel, tours, and attractions, it comes with a 24-hour emergency help line and a global voice/fax/e-mail messaging system with discounted international telephone calls. Available to any full-time student older than 12, it costs $21 (£15).

Buenos Aires is a very fun city for college students on vacation. The legal drinking age in Argentina is 18, but underage drinking is common, although rarely in the excesses found in North America. There are places to drink and socialize all over Buenos Aires. The bars around Plaza Serrano (see chapter 10), in Palermo Soho, offer inexpensive beers on tap and pitchers of sangria. This is often served up with inexpensive snacks and live music, which means that having fun won't break a student budget.

9 PACKAGES FOR THE INDEPENDENT TRAVELER & ESCORTED GENERAL-INTEREST TOURS

These days, so many people plan their trips via websites and e-mail that it's easy to forget that a computer can never replace the knowledge a good travel agent can have of a region and its offerings. Maybe you want to be in a special hotel for a romantic night or a honeymoon. Buenos Aires's tango history is a major component of its draw, but how do you know the difference from one show to the other or what *milonga* (tango salon) would be the best for a beginner? You might also have time for a few side trips, but is Iguazú Falls better, or should you try a beach destination? And what about the kids? What hotels will make them happiest, and how do you keep them interested while you enjoy the shopping and nightlife?

I answer most of these questions with special tips throughout this book, but nothing can replace the human touch. If you have a special agent whom you have used for years, ask him or her for advice, or try some of the following specialists who are based in the U.S. and Argentina. See also the above sections for gay and lesbian travelers, women travelers, travelers with disabilities, and senior travelers

for even more specially tailored vacation needs when visiting Buenos Aires.

RECOMMENDED U.S.-BASED AND OTHER OPERATORS The following U.S.-based tour companies offer solid, well-organized tours in various price categories, and they are backed by years of experience. All can arrange tours of Buenos Aires, the surroundings, and other parts of Argentina and South America.

• **Borello Travel & Tours,** 7 Park Ave., Ste. 21, New York, NY 10016 (✆ **800/405-3072** or 212/686-4911; www.borellotravel.com; info@borellotravel.com), is a New York–based travel firm specializing in upscale travel to South America. The owner, Sandra Borello, has run her company for nearly 20 years and is a native of Buenos Aires. Prices can vary, depending on the season, options, and hotel. Offering excellent, tailored client service, they also maintain an additional office in Buenos Aires that can be reached at ✆ **11/5031-1988.**

• **Travel Dynamics International,** 132 East 70th St., New York, NY 10021 (✆ **800/257-5767;** 212/517-0076; www.traveldynamicsinternational.com), is a luxury cruise operator that specializes in educational enrichment programs aboard small cruise ships. TDI voyages include expert guided land tours and on-board lectures by distinguished scholars and guests. They cater to the traveler with an intellectual interest in history, culture, and nature. Operating for almost 40 years, this company offers voyages with destinations in South America and Antarctica. Their journeys to Antarctica usually begin with an overnight stay in Buenos Aires.

- **Limitless Argentina,** 135 Willow St., #907, Brooklyn, NY 11201 (© **202/ 536-5812;** www.limitlessargentina. com; info@limitlessargentina.com), is a boutique travel company dedicated to designing authentic, personalized journeys for the discerning traveler. Founder Vanessa Guibert Heitner returned home to Buenos Aires after attending college and earning her Ph.D. in the United States to lead the company's Argentine operations. Itineraries often include fine arts, regional culture and history, food and wine, the great outdoors, and shopping. Her work with families, honeymooners, individual travelers, and small groups has earned her the distinction of top travel specialist for Argentina 2006 from Condé Nast's *Traveler* magazine.

RECOMMENDED BUENOS AIRES–BASED OPERATORS
Even if you have arranged things at home, once you're in Buenos Aires, there are always last-minute changes or new things you would like to see. The following companies are all excellent and have English-speaking staff members. All can also provide trips to other cities in Argentina outside of Buenos Aires, as well as South America.

- **Say Hueque Tourism,** Viamonte 749, Office 601, 1053 Buenos Aires (© **11/ 5199-2517,** -2518, -2519, and -2520;

www.sayhueque.com), is a highly recommended small company with knowledgeable, friendly service and attention to personalized client care. The company began by catering to the young and adventurous on a budget, but has begun to deal with a more upscale, yet independent-thinking clientele. Various tour themes include Literary Buenos Aires, Biking Buenos Aires, and Tango Buenos Aires, among many others. They also offer adventure tours within the vicinity of Buenos Aires such as to the Tigre Delta. Outside of Buenos Aires, they specialize in Patagonia and Iguazú, finding special, out-of-the-way places for their clients. Based on their very personal service, this is among my favorites of the operators within Buenos Aires.

- **Euro Tur,** Viamonte 486, 1053 Buenos Aires (© **11/4312-6077;** www.eurotur. com), is one of the largest and oldest travel companies in Argentina, specializing in inbound travel, but they can also help walk-ins to accommodate travelers' needs directly while in Buenos Aires. They can arrange basic city tours and trips of all kinds throughout Argentina and South America.

- **Les Amis,** Maipú 1270, 1005 Buenos Aires (© **11/4314-0500;** www.lesamis. com.ar), is another large Argentine tour company, with offices throughout Buenos Aires and Argentina. They can arrange trips while you are in town for Buenos Aires, Argentina, and many other parts of South America.

- **Dine At Home–Home Hosted Dinners Tours,** Av. Las Heras, 4A, 1127 Buenos Aires (© **11/4801- 3182** or 11/15-6051-9328 or 11/15- 5564-9846; www.dineathome.com.ar). Edward Goedhart is the owner of this interesting company offering tours based on dinners at home with Buenos Aires residents. The meals can be accommodated for diabetics, vegetarians, kosher, seniors, fashionistas, gay

Frommers.com: The Complete Travel Resource

Planning a trip or just returned? Head to **Frommers.com,** voted Best Travel Site by *PC Magazine.* We think you'll find our site indispensable before, during, and after your travels—with expert advice and tips; independent reviews of hotels, restaurants, attractions, and preferred shopping and nightlife venues; vacation giveaways; and an online booking tool. We publish the complete contents of more than 135 travel guides in our **Destinations** section, covering more than 4,000 places worldwide. Each weekday, we publish original articles that report on **Deals and News** via our free **Frommers.com Newsletters.** What's more, **Arthur Frommer** himself blogs 5 days a week, with cutting opinions about the state of travel in the modern world. We're betting you'll find our **Events** listings an invaluable resource; it's an up-to-the-minute roster of what's happening in cities everywhere—including concerts, festivals, lectures, and more. We've also added weekly **podcasts, interactive maps,** and hundreds of new images across the site. Finally, don't forget to visit our **Message Boards,** where you can join in conversations with thousands of fellow Frommer's travelers and post your trip report once you return.

groups, and many others. Tours must be booked through your own agent, but call Edward for more information or visit the site. He also offers other kinds of services through his company, as well as trips to Córdoba in the west of Argentina.

- **South America Travel Advisor** (☎ 11/5275-5280 or 11/15-3232-8600 and in Brazil ☎ 21/9469-8367) is not a travel agency but works as a travel advisor for Argentina, Brazil, Uruguay, Chile, and Peru. Travelers can contact them with a tentative plan and a budget, and after a question-and-answer session, they suggest possible itineraries or travel combinations until getting to a final desired product. They provide accurate information on airfare, transportation, excursions, accommodations, restaurants, bars, shopping, and/or any other requested service, as well as discounted prices they may know about. Their aim is to let clients get the best-value full-customized vacation, charging

a flat fee per person per week of travel, currently of $50 (£36). The service is run by Buenos Aires native Marcos Wolff, who has worked for many travel companies and has an enthusiastic love of the city. If clients are not pleased with the advice after their trip, they refund their fee.

PRIVATE TOUR GUIDES   It's easy to hire guides through your hotel or any travel agency in Buenos Aires. You may also want to contact **AGUITBA (Asociación de Guías de Turismo de Buenos Aires),** Carlos Pellegrini 833, 6th floor C, Buenos Aires (☎ **11/4322-2557;** aguitba@sion. com), a professional society of tour guides that has tried to promote licensing and other credentials legislation to ensure the quality of guides. Its offices are open Monday to Friday from 1 to 6pm. Take a look also in our section on themed tours in chapter 7, Exploring Buenos Aires (p. 163).

Additionally, private guides I recommend include Buenos Aires–based **Marta**

Pasquali (☎ 11/15-4421-2486; marpas@ uolsinectis.com.ar) and **Monica Varela** (☎ 11/15-4407-0268; monyliv@hotmail. com or varmonica@gmail.com). Both have conducted tours for several years in Buenos Aires. They offer high-quality specialized tours and often work with corporations. I highly recommend them for their specialized knowledge of the city,

which goes far beyond what many other tour guides know.

Another excellent tour guide to consider is **Francisco Martoccia,** who gives private, personalized tours, one-on-one or with small groups. He knows the city well and has been doing tours on various themes for many years (☎ 011/4803-0950; franmarto@hotmail.com).

---

10 STAYING CONNECTED

TELEPHONES

The country code for Argentina is **54.** The area code for Buenos Aires, called a *caracteristica,* is 011, but is not needed within the city and surrounding area. Phone numbers in Buenos Aires have 8 digits.

When making domestic long-distance calls in Argentina, make sure to include the 0 in the area code, which can have from 4 to 5 digits. Provincial phone numbers can have from 5 to 7 digits.

For international calls, add 00 before the country code. If dialing into Argentina, drop the 0 when combining from overseas with Argentina's country code, 54. The number 15 in front of a number indicates a cellular phone. This will need the addition of the 011, if you're calling into Buenos Aires.

Public phones take either phone cards (sold at kiosks on the street) or coins (less common). Local calls cost 20 centavos to start and charge more the longer you talk. *Telecentro* or *locutorio* offices—found everywhere in Buenos Aires—offer private phone booths where calls are paid when completed and cost about a peso a minute to Europe and North America. Most hotels offer fax services, as do all *telecentro* offices. Dial ☎ **110** for directory assistance (most operators speak English) and ☎ **000** to reach an international operator.

Direct dialing to North America and Europe is available from most phones. International, as well as domestic, calls are

expensive from hotels (rates fall 10pm– 8am). Holders of AT&T credit cards can reach the money-saving **USA Direct** from Argentina by calling toll-free ☎ **0800/555-4288** from the north of Argentina or 0800/222-1288 from the south. Similar services are offered by **MCI** (☎ **0800/555-1002**) and **Sprint** (☎ **0800/555-1003** from the north of Argentina, or 0800/222-1003 from the south).

CELLPHONES

Cellular phones become complicated dialed from overseas. Dial the international code you need from your country (011 from the U.S. and Canada), then 54 for Argentina, then 9 to indicate a cellphone, then the area code of the cellphone, and then the number, without the 15. To call Buenos Aires cellphones from the U.S., you would dial 011-54-9-11 and then the eight-digit number. There are new cellphones in Buenos Aires, which no longer need the 15, but always ask for clarification.

You can buy or rent prepaid cellphones from phone stores all over Calle Florida. You can buy low-cost ($11/£7.80) chips or SIM cards for cellphones that are usable overseas and use a prepaid system that runs about 1 or 2 pesos a minute for local calls. If your phone won't work overseas, you can buy a low-cost phone for about $40 (£28) that also uses the prepaid system. Sprint, AT&T, and other services

Online Traveler's Toolbox

- **Foreign Languages for Travelers** (www.travlang.com)
- **Events in Buenos Aires** (www.bue.gov.ar)
- **Maps** (www.mapquest.com)
- **Restaurants in Buenos Aires** (www.guiaoleo.com.ar)
- **Nightlife in Buenos Aires** (www.bsasinsomnio.com.ar)
- **Visa ATM Locator** (www.visa.com), **MasterCard ATM Locator** (www.mastercard.com)

should, in theory, work on a U.S. or Canadian phone in Argentina, but the service is not reliable and may mean having to make the call several times. Locals also may not want to dial your phone because of the cost. Your best option is a local SIM card or phone. Reception is good on most local cellular services, but can vary in the suburbs and rural regions popular with tourists, such as Tigre and the *estancia* region around San Antonio de Areco.

VOICE-OVER INTERNET PROTOCOL (VOIP)

If you have Web access while traveling, consider a broadband-based telephone service (in technical terms, **Voice-over Internet Protocol,** or **VoIP**) such as Skype (www.skype.com) or Vonage (www.vonage.com), which allow you to make free international calls from your laptop or in a cybercafe. Neither service requires the people you're calling to also have that service (though there are fees if they do not). Check the websites for details.

INTERNET & E-MAIL

Travelers have any number of ways to check their e-mail and access the Internet on the road. Of course, using your own laptop—or even a PDA (personal digital assistant) or electronic organizer with a modem—gives you the most flexibility.

But even if you don't have a computer, you can still access your e-mail and even your office computer from cybercafes and restaurants, a few of which now offer free Wi-Fi, especially in Palermo Viejo. Most hotels have Wi-Fi, regardless of the price category.

With Your Own Computer

More and more hotels, resorts, airports, cafes, and retailers are going **Wi-Fi** (wireless fidelity), becoming "hotspots" that offer free high-speed Wi-Fi access or charge a small fee for usage. Most laptops sold today have built-in wireless capability. To find public Wi-Fi hotspots in Buenos Aires, go to **www.jiwire.com**; its Hotspot Finder holds the world's largest directory of public wireless hotspots.

For dial-up access, most business-class hotels throughout the world offer dataports for laptop modems, and most now offer free high-speed Internet access.

Wherever you go, bring a **connection kit** of the right power and phone adapters, a spare phone cord, and a spare Ethernet network cable; or find out whether your hotel supplies them to guests.

To find cybercafes in Buenos Aires, check **www.cybercaptive.com** and **www.cybercafe.com**. Most major airports have **Internet kiosks** that provide basic Web access for a per-minute fee that's usually higher than cybercafe prices.

Suggested Itinerary

After a few days, most tourists wish they could spend a lifetime in Buenos Aires. Of course, that's not realistic for most people! Here, we highlight the most important sites in various neighborhoods so you can plan your trip, no matter the length. Then we suggest a 5-day itinerary, which you can easily tailor for a day or a week, by picking and choosing the highlights from each neighborhood.

THE NEIGHBORHOODS IN BRIEF

Buenos Aires is an enormous metropolis, with nearly 12 million inhabitants in the city and its suburbs. Most of what you'll be interested in, however, is in a compact area near the center of the city's historical core, around Plaza de Mayo. Below I list the neighborhoods you'll most likely see as a tourist, including each neighborhood's general boundaries. Keep in mind, though, that even in Buenos Aires, some people and maps call the same areas by different names, so keep these descriptions only as a general guide.

Plaza de Mayo Area This is not so much a district as the historical and political heart of the city, laid out by Don Juan de Garay in 1580 during the second founding of the city. The plaza is surrounded by city and national government buildings and the **Metropolitan Cathedral,** which dates to the late colonial era. The plaza's main defining feature is the **Casa Rosada (Presidential Palace),** home to Evita's famous balcony. It still remains the main point for political demonstrations and also serves as a shelter area for the homeless and the *piqueteros* (demonstrators) who often camp out here at night. The most important ongoing political demonstration that occurs here is that of the **Madres de la Plaza de Mayo.** The demonstrators are made up of the mothers and grandmothers of citizens who disappeared during the 1976 to 1982 dictatorship in what was known as the **Dirty War.** This demonstration occurs every Thursday beginning at 3:30pm and is a must-see for understanding the country (see p. 129 for more information). Other than the drastically altered **cathedral,** which was remodeled in 1836, the **Cabildo** (old city hall) is the only other remaining colonial building on the plaza. That, too, however, has been severely altered from its original dimensions, chopped away as Avenida de Mayo and Diagonal Sud were created.

Puerto Madero This area sits to the east behind the Plaza de Mayo. Once a dilapidated port, the area is now filled with an abundance of restaurants in renovated warehouses. New construction has also placed offices, high-rise residences, and luxury hotels into this neighborhood. The district can feel cold and antiseptic by day because of both its vast expanses and its new construction, so you might want to come at sunset when the water in the port glows a fiery red and the city skyline is silhouetted. This is also perhaps the only neighborhood in a major world city where all its streets are named for women. One of its major highlights here is also the **Bridge of Woman,** designed by Santiago Calavatra. Puerto Madero's other unique feature is its **Ecological Reserve,** an area of open space created by natural forces in revolt against man's abuses. Sediment has collected on construction debris dumped into the river here, and wild plants and birds have slowly settled onto the reclaimed land. The closest *subte* to the neighborhood is Alem, on the B line, and a new tourist train runs the length of Puerto Madero, but walking is faster.

Microcentro No doubt you'll spend plenty of time in this part of Buenos Aires, the city's busy downtown core. The Microcentro is home to many of the hotels, banks, services, and everything else that makes the city tick. The area's defining feature is the pedestrianized **Calle Florida,** which runs from Avenida de Mayo to Plaza San Martín. It's crowded by day with shoppers and businesspeople. At night, sidewalk shows by performance artists thrill tourists and locals alike. The most important shopping center in this district is **Galerías Pacífico,** at the intersection of Calle Córdoba. **Plaza San Martín** on its northern border provides a restful respite from this very compact center. On its edge sits **Retiro Station,** once among the most important points of entry into Buenos Aires from the provinces.

Monserrat This neighborhood sometimes gets thrown in with many people's descriptions of San Telmo, but it's actually a proper district of its own, though it shares a similar history and a border with San Telmo. Also, technically, San Telmo is part of Monserrat, not the other way around. Sitting between San

Telmo and the Plaza de Mayo, Monserrat is home to some of the city's oldest churches. Additionally, many government buildings have been constructed here. Some are beautiful old Beaux Arts structures; others, built in the mid-20th century, exemplify South American fascist architecture, with their smooth massive walls of dark polished marble and granite and heavy, pharaonic bronze doors that never seem to open. Many unions have headquarters here so that they can more easily speak with government officials (and try to influence their views). Though busy during the day, parts of Monserrat are desolate and possibly dangerous at night. To some Porteños (residents of Buenos Aires), Monserrat extends up the historic **Avenida de Mayo** toward Congreso. Others call this area **San Cristóbal.**

San Telmo If you think of tango, romance, and a certain unexpressed sensual sadness when you think of Buenos Aires, then you're thinking of San Telmo. This is one of the city's oldest neighborhoods, once the home of the very wealthy until the 1877 outbreak of yellow fever caused many to flee to newly developing areas north of the city center. The heart of San Telmo is **Plaza Dorrego,** the city's second-oldest plaza (after the Plaza de Mayo). A few of the buildings on its edges still date from the colonial period. There is a decayed grace here, and travelers who have been to Habana Vieja in Cuba will experience a certain déjà vu. This neighborhood is my favorite, and I like it most during sunset to twilight when the buildings glow gold and their ornamental tops become silhouetted against the sky.

Tango-themed bars make up much of the entertainment in San Telmo, in addition to the restaurants and cafes that have been in operation for almost

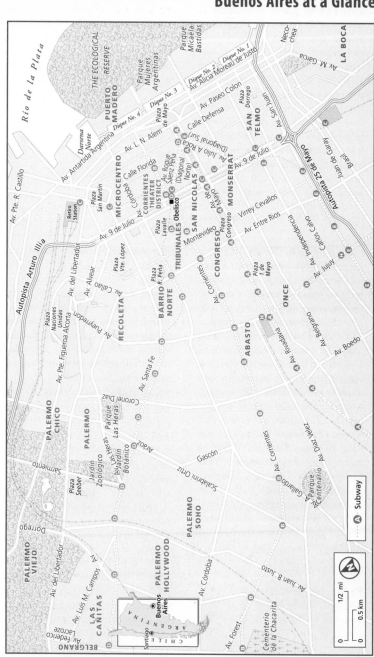

150 years. **Calle Defensa,** lined with antiques stores, runs from north to south and is the area's main street. It takes its name from the route Argentina's colonial army used to defend itself from a British invasion in the early 1800s. If you have only 1 day to visit this neighborhood, do it on a Sunday when the San Telmo Antiques Fair (p. 192) is in full swing, complete with tango dancers. The event generally runs from 11am to 5pm, and it's become so popular that vendors have set up on side streets. Many Porteños still think of the neighborhood as dangerous, based on crime dating back to the 1990s, but rapid gentrification has changed the area completely. Still, take caution at night, just as you should wherever you are.

La Boca Historically, La Boca is Buenos Aires's Little Italy, the main point of entry for Italians at the end of the 19th and beginning of the 20th centuries. Literally, *La Boca* means "the mouth," taking its name from a natural harbor formed by a twist in the Río Riachuelo, a tributary that feeds into the Río de la Plata. Many of the immigrants here settled into haphazardly built boarding houses with metal sheeting called *conventillos.* These were decorated with whatever paint was left over on the docks, creating a mishmash of colors on each building. The main focal point of La Boca is **El Caminito,** a touristy pedestrianized roadway with plaques and statues explaining neighborhood history, which are surrounded by stores selling T-shirts and souvenirs. Buildings on this street are painted in bold and brilliant colors as a reminder of the area's past. La Boca is my least favorite neighborhood because it overdoes its efforts to draw in tourists to the point where it has nothing authentic to offer. Many will be shocked at this assessment, but if you are short on time, I don't think it's a bad idea to either skip

this neighborhood or give it very little attention on your visit. Be aware that the area is considered exceedingly dangerous at night. When the shops close up, you should head out. There is no convenient subway access to La Boca.

Recoleta The name of this neighborhood comes from an old Spanish word meaning "to remember." Its history dates to the late colonial period and the establishment of a convent where Recoleta Cemetery, Evita's final resting place, now sits. Once on the edge of Buenos Aires, Recoleta is now one of its most exclusive shopping and residential neighborhoods. Marble buildings reminiscent of Paris and green leafy streets make up the main impression of this area. **Avenida Alvear,** crowned by the city's most famous hotel, the **Alvear Palace,** is lined with luxurious showrooms (some are in buildings that were once the homes of the city's wealthiest residents) from the most impressive designers. The **Polo Ralph Lauren** store is particularly worth a venture inside. There is no convenient subway access to this neighborhood.

Barrio Norte This neighborhood borders Recoleta, and many consider Barrio Norte to be part of Recoleta. However, while the two are physically similar, Barrio Norte is busier and more commercialized, with shops primarily aimed at a middle- and upper-middle-class clientele. If anyone ever describes to you a place in Recoleta with convenient subway access, it really means they are in this neighborhood. Its main defining feature is Avenida Santa Fe (serviced by the D subway line), where most of these shops are located. This area was also historically home to much of the city's gay population and services, but that is changing over time as these venues spread across the city, especially into San Telmo.

Palermo You might think that half of Buenos Aires is in Palermo, as it's a catchall term for a rather nebulous and large chunk of northern Buenos Aires. The area encompasses **Palermo** proper, with its park system and expensive homes; **Palermo Chico,** which is within Palermo proper; **Palermo Viejo,** which is further divided into **Palermo Soho** and **Palermo Hollywood;** and **Las Cañitas,** which is just to the side of the city's world-famous polo field.

Palermo is a neighborhood of parks filled with magnolias, pines, palms, and willows, where families picnic on weekends and couples stroll at sunset. You might want to think of this part as Palermo Nuevo when compared to Palermo Viejo, described below, though some locals also call the area Alto Palermo. Designed by French architect Charles Thays, the parks of Palermo take their inspiration from London's Hyde Park and Paris's Bois de Boulogne. The **Botanical Gardens** and the **Zoological Gardens** are both off of **Plaza Italia.** Stone paths wind their way through the botanical gardens, and flora from throughout South America fills the garden, with more than 8,000 plant species from around the world represented. Next door, the city zoo features an impressive diversity of animals, and the eclectic and kitschy architecture, with some buildings designed as exotic temples, is as much of a delight as the animals themselves.

Palermo Chico, part of Palermo proper, is an exclusive neighborhood of elegant mansions off of Avenida Alcorta. Other than the beauty of the homes and a few embassy buildings, this small set of streets, tucked behind the **MALBA** museum, has little of interest to the average tourist. Plus, there is no subway access to this neighborhood.

Palermo Viejo, once a run-down neighborhood full of warehouses, factories, and tiny, decaying stucco homes few cared to live in as recently as 15 years ago, has been transformed into the city's chicest destination. Once you walk through the area and begin to absorb its charms—cobblestone streets, enormous oak-tree canopies, and low-rise buildings giving a clear view to the open skies on a sunny day—you'll wonder why it had been forsaken for so many years. Palermo Viejo is further divided into **Palermo Soho** to the south and **Palermo Hollywood** to the north, with railroad tracks and Avenida Juan B. Justo serving as the dividing line. The center of Palermo Soho is **Plazaleto Jorge Cortazar,** better known by its informal name, **Plaza Serrano,** a small oval park at the intersection of Calle Serrano and Calle Honduras. Take note that on some maps, Serrano is also called Calle Borges. Young people gather in the plaza late at night for impromptu singing and guitar sessions, sometimes fueled by drinks from the myriad of funky bars and restaurants that surround the plaza. Palermo Soho is known for both its restaurants and its chic designer shops. Palermo Hollywood, a quieter, slightly less gentrified area, got its name because many Argentine film studios were initially attracted to its once-cheap rents and easy parking. Both areas were historically where Middle Eastern immigrants originally settled, and this presence is still apparent in the businesses, restaurants, and community centers that remain.

Las Cañitas was once a favored neighborhood of the military powers during the dictatorship period of 1976 to 1982. A military training base, hospital, high school, and various family housing units still remain and encircle the neighborhood, creating an islandlike sense of safety on the neighborhood's streets. Today, however, the area is far better known among the hip, trendy, and nouveau riche as the place to dine out, have a drink, party, and be seen in the fashionable venues built into converted low-rise former houses on Calle Báez; though with Palermo Viejo's rise on the scene, it is becoming overshadowed. The polo field where the International Championships take place is also in the neighborhood and is technically part of the military bases. The polo field's presence makes the neighborhood bars and restaurants great places for enthusiasts to catch polo champions celebrating their victories in season.

Congreso The western end of the Avenida de Mayo surrounds the massive Congreso building overlooking Plaza Congreso. Though this has been an important area for sightseeing for many years, the whole neighborhood seems to have a run-down feeling to it. Things are beginning to change, however, and numerous hotels have opened in this area, though they are not as well known as those in some of the more glamorous parts of the city. An important feature of this neighborhood, hinting at the area's former glory, is the Café del Molino at the northwest corner of Rivadavia and Callao. An Art Nouveau masterpiece, it was the informal meeting place of politicians and the powerful until shutting its doors in the 1990s. Walking to the north along Callao, you'll also come across blocks of decaying marble and stucco neoclassical buildings that have an almost imperial sense and call to mind Buenos Aires's glory days and Argentina's desire to rise as a global power.

Corrientes Theater District The Obelisco at the intersection of Corrientes and Avenida 9 de Julio is the defining feature of this part of the city, but while it's nice to look at, this white stone structure won't keep you entertained for long. The neighborhood surrounding it will, however. Corrientes was widened in the 1930s, on both sides of Avenida 9 de Julio, and it is lined with the city's most important live theaters and movie palaces. The world-famous Teatro Colón sits a block away from Corrientes in this district, the whole neighborhood acting as Buenos Aires's answer to New York's Broadway. Billboards and big names in bright lights are all over the street here. You should take the time to see a production, even though most are in Spanish only. Though most of the action is at night, some theaters are worth wandering into during the day as well, in particular the Teatro San Martín, which always has ongoing exhibits. On either side of Corrientes, adjacent streets also have smaller production houses, and numerous used-book shops specialize in hard-to-find Spanish-language literature. Starry-eyed hopefuls from the provinces still come into the area hoping for fame, just as Evita once did (her first Buenos Aires apartment was in this district). There are bits of sleaze on Corrientes, because, just as on New York's Broadway, there's a broken heart for every marquee light bulb.

Abasto On first glance, this working- and middle-class neighborhood seems to have little of interest to tourists. However, it is steeped in Buenos Aires history and is where tango crooner Carlos Gardel grew up and lived as an adult. Vestiges of that time period include the **Abasto Shopping Center** on Calle Corrientes, which was once an open-air market, where Gardel sang to the vendors as a child and first became famous. The tango show palace **Esquina**

Carlos Gardel was built over a bar he frequented, and his home on Calle Jean Jaures is now a museum.

Once The name of this neighborhood is short for **Once de Septiembre,** and it takes its name from a train station that honors the death of Domingo Faustino Sarmiento, President of Argentina from 1868 to 1874. Once borders Abasto (see above) and has a similar history and feel. It is most important as a historically Jewish neighborhood. Calle Tucumán, in particular, still retains many Jewish businesses and kosher restaurants. While the community is no longer as large as it once was, and most Jews have scattered to the suburbs, the importance of this community in Buenos Aires after World War I is evidenced by the variety of Art Deco buildings that Jewish merchants built here. It is a style not as common in other parts of the city and is the best remaining physical evidence of the community's economic impact on the growth of Buenos Aires.

Tribunales The defining feature of this neighborhood is the **Argentine Supreme Court,** from which the area takes its name. This massive building overlooks **Plaza Lavalle** and is currently undergoing repair. The court is not generally open to the public, but if you can sneak in, it's worth a look. For tourists, the most important feature of this neighborhood is what sits across the plaza, **Teatro Colón,** the city's supreme cultural center, also in the midst of a serious and terribly delayed overhaul. Other important buildings also overlook the plaza, including the **Roca School,** the Spanish Imperial–style **Teatro Cervantes,** and the synagogue **Templo Libertad,** which contains the **Jewish History Museum.**

Belgrano You'll probably be on a very long trip to Buenos Aires before you venture out to Belgrano, a well-to-do neighborhood in the north of the city, beyond Palermo. It's full of private homes and modern apartments with underground garages and residents who hide behind porter-controlled doors. Its main feature is its *barrancas,* a series of hills in the center of the neighborhood and an enormous waterfront park, which is an extension of those in Palermo. While tiny, this is where you'll find Buenos Aires's Chinatown, near the intersection of Arribeños and Mendoza, close to the Belgrano train station. The Chinese Lunar New Year parade is held here on the closest Sunday to its date, usually in February.

1 BUENOS AIRES IN 5 DAYS

No length of time ever seems like enough in a city as wonderful as Buenos Aires. This itinerary takes you through 5 days in the capital—ideally a Wednesday to a Sunday. The route guides you through the best features of various neighborhoods—from the Microcentro and Palermo Viejo to Recoleta and San Telmo. You'll eat several great meals, go shopping, and take in some breathtakingly beautiful sites. I've scheduled in plenty of downtime, too, in case you want to tango all night long and take it easy the following day (Buenos Aires, like New York, is a city that doesn't sleep).

SUGGESTED ITINERARY

4

BUENOS AIRES IN 5 DAYS

Day 1
1. Galerías Pacífico
2. Plaza de Mayo
3. Cabildo
4. Metropolitan Cathedral
5. Casa Rosada
6. Cabaña las Lilas

Day 2
7. Congreso
8. Café Tortoni
9. Plaza de Mayo
10. Palacio Español

Day 3
11. Recoleta Cemetery
12. La Biela
13. Centro Cultural Recoleta
14. La Bourgogne

Day 4
15. Plaza Italia
16. Zoological Gardens
17. Museo Nacional de Bellas Artes
18. Casa Cruz

Day 5
19. Plaza Dorrego
20. San Telmo antiques fair
21. Bar El Federal
22. Galería El Solar de French
23. El Viejo Almacén

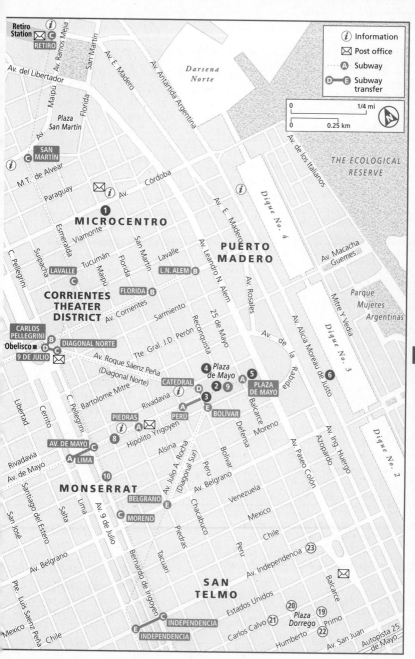

Legend:
- (i) Information
- ⊠ Post office
- (A) Subway
- (D)—(E) Subway transfer

0   1/4 mi
0   0.25 km

Retiro Station • RETIRO
Av. del Libertador
San Martín
Av. Ramos Mejía
Av. E. Madero
Av. Antártida Argentina
Darsena Norte
THE ECOLOGICAL RESERVE

Maipú
Florida
Plaza San Martín
SAN MARTÍN
M.T. de Alvear
Paraguay
Córdoba
Av.
Av. de los Italianos
Dique No. 4

MICROCENTRO

Esmeralda
Viamonte
Tucumán
Maipú
Florida
San Martín
Lavalle
Av. Leandro N. Alem
Av. E. Madero

PUERTO MADERO

Av. Macacha Guemes

C. Pellegrini
Suipacha
LAVALLE
FLORIDA 8
L.N. ALEM B
Av. Rosales

CORRIENTES THEATER DISTRICT
Av. Corrientes
Sarmiento
Tte. Gral. J.D. Perón
Reconquista
25 de Mayo
Av. de la Rabida
Parque Mujeres Argentinas
Dique No. 3

CARLOS PELLEGRINI
DIAGONAL NORTE
Obelisco
9 DE JULIO
Av. Roque Sáenz Peña (Diagonal Norte)
Bartolomé Mitre
Rivadavia
CATEDRAL (i)
PIEDRAS
PERÚ
BOLÍVAR
Plaza de Mayo 4
2 9
5 PLAZA DE MAYO
6
Balcarce
Defensa
Moreno
Av. Alicia Moreau de Justo
Av. Ing. Huergo
Dique No. 2

Libertad
Cerrito
C. Pellegrini
AV. DE MAYO
LIMA
Rivadavia
Av. de Mayo
Hipólito Yrigoyen
Alsina
Av. Julio A. Rocha (Diagonal Sur)
Bolívar
Perú
Av. Belgrano
Azopardo
Av. Paseo Colón

Santiago del Estero
San José
MONSERRAT
Salta
Lima
Av. 9 de Julio
10
BELGRANO
MORENO
Venezuela
Chacabuco
Mexico
Chile

Pte. Luís Sáenz Peña
Mexico
Chile
Bernardo de Irigoyen
Tacuarí
Piedras
Perú
Av. Independencia
23
Balcarce

SAN TELMO
Estados Unidos
Carlos Calvo 21
20 Plaza Dorrego 19
22
Humberto Primo
Av. San Juan
Autopista 25 de Mayo

INDEPENDENCIA
INDEPENDENCIA

Day ❶: Relaxing & Settling In

More than likely, you've arrived early in the morning after an all-night flight. Before you head out for the day, make reservations at **Cabaña las Lilas** ★★★ (p. 89) for dinner tonight. Afterwards, head to Calle Florida, checking out the shops at **Galerías Pacífico** (p. 194), and have a snack at **Il Gran Caffe** ★ (p. 94). Wander down to **Plaza de Mayo** (p. 129) and take a look at historic sites such as the **Cabildo** (p. 123), Buenos Aires's original city hall, the **Metropolitan Cathedral** ★★ (p. 129), and the **Casa Rosada** ★★★ (p. 126), with Evita's famous balcony. Head back to the hotel for a much-needed nap before heading out to Cabaña las Lilas for dinner. Certainly you've admired the view of **Puerto Madero** (p. 154) from your table, so have a wander dockside.

Day ❷: Historical Buenos Aires

I highly recommend exploring the historic center of Buenos Aires with a professional guide, such as **Borello Travel & Tours** (✆ 800/405-3072 or 212/686-4911; p. 44), **Say Hueque Tours** (✆ 11/5199-2517; p. 45), or private tour guides **Marta Pasquali** (✆ 11/15-4421-2486) or **Monica Varela** (✆ 11/15-4407-0268). As the guides lead you through the historic center of Buenos Aires, passing the **Plaza de Mayo** (p. 129) and the turn-of-the-20th-century marvel **Avenida de Mayo** to **Congreso,** they'll explain how architecture, history, and the lost glory of a powerful Argentina are reflected in the streets of Buenos Aires. Ride the **A line subway's** (p. 123) wooden trains down to station Avenida de Mayo. Have a coffee and *medialunas* at **Café Tortoni** ★★★ (p. 126), one of the city's most historic and scenic cafes, and try to catch the conversation of Buenos Aires locals discussing the latest issues. At 3:30pm, head back to Plaza de Mayo for the **Madres of Plaza de Mayo,** a weekly protest held by the mothers of the 30,000 young people who disappeared during the military regime between 1976 to 1982. Head back and take a nap at the hotel. In the evening, have dinner in the glorious gilded dining hall of **Palacio Español** ★★ (p. 98).

Day ❸: A Day in Recoleta

Sleep in and have a late breakfast at your hotel. Have your hotel make dinner reservations at **La Bourgogne** ★★★ (p. 101), a fine French restaurant in the **Alvear Palace Hotel** ★★★ (p. 72). Then head to **Recoleta Cemetery** ★★★ (p. 136), in the Recoleta neighborhood. Pay homage to the most famous tomb of all, Evita's. Make sure to wander around and see many of the other tombs, all glorious works of art. Around the corner from the cemetery, head to the **Centro Cultural Recoleta** ★ (p. 214) and check out the newest art exhibit. If you've brought the kids along or you're feeling young at heart, don't forget to visit the children's section inside, with its interactive science exhibits. Afterwards, head across **Plaza Francia** and take a coffee at **La Biela** ★★★ (p. 104), one of the most famous cafes in the city. After this much-needed break, it's time to do some shopping along **Avenida Alvear,** stopping into such stores as **Polo Ralph Lauren** (p. 204), built into a grand mansion. If you've been shopping for hours, you're just in time for your reservation at La Bourgogne.

Day ❹: Palermo

After breakfast, head to **Plaza Italia** and take a brief walk around, enjoying the contrast of the green trees against the white-marble buildings lining this part of Avenida Santa Fe. Head to the **Zoological Gardens** ★ (p. 156) and check out all the animals, after buying special food for them at the entrance. Afterwards, stroll down Avenida Libertador and wander among the parks, heading to **Museo Nacional de Bellas Artes** ★★ (p. 148). It's a long walk, but beautiful all along the way. Head back to the hotel, freshen up, and head for dinner to **Casa Cruz** ★★ (p. 108), in Palermo Viejo, one of the city's best places to be seen on a night out.

Day ⑤: San Telmo & Tango

Head to **Plaza Dorrego** (p. 130) for the Sunday **San Telmo antiques fair** ★★★ (p. 192), one of the most enjoyable highlights of Buenos Aires. In this open-air bazaar, you can buy small antiques and souvenirs to bring home, and watch live tango performances. (Keep an eye on your pockets while you watch.) Then, grab a late lunch at the atmospheric **Bar El Federal** ★★ (p. 99). Head up **Calle Defensa** to take a look at more antiques in the numerous shops lining the street, such as **Galería El Solar de French** (p. 197). Head back to the hotel and freshen up. You're having dinner tonight at **El Viejo Almacén** (p. 225). Watching their show is a great way to end your 5-day stay in Buenos Aires.

5

Where to Stay

You love Buenos Aires and so does everyone else. With the massive influx of tourists to Buenos Aires and international tourism increasing as much as 20% each year, the famous bargains at the city's hotels are much harder to find now. Many of the rates are almost 30% higher than a couple of years ago. Still, bargains can be found, especially at four-star or off-the-beaten-path hotels, and at locally owned rather than international hotel chains. Of course, every traveler knows never to accept the first room rate offered. Always ask if there is a better rate, or if your AAA card, student ID, or other discounts might also apply.

Hotels in Buenos Aires fall into a range of categories, from the most humble hostels to the newest, most luxurious five-star properties. As tourism continues to flourish throughout the city, new hotels are opening quite rapidly. Older ones are being renovated or bought by international companies hoping to cash in on the volume of people coming to Buenos Aires. There are many more boutique hotels than ever before, especially in Palermo. Hotels here often fill up in high season, so you should book ahead, even if it is only for your first night or two. Then, if you're not happy with your choice, you can always poke around and change your accommodations once you're on the ground.

Hotel websites (provided in each hotel's listing) frequently offer special rates or packages, so it's worth tooling around online before booking. Also, no matter what the rack rate is, always inquire about a hotel's best rate, as many proprietors are willing to come down in price, especially when they fear a room may be left empty.

Most five- and four-star hotels in Buenos Aires provide in-room safes, 24-hour room service, cable TV, direct-dial phones with voice mail, in-room modem access or Wi-Fi, and many other amenities. The competition between the hotels on this level can be intense, so they often renovate and add amenities to add value. Many—especially the five-stars—also have superb health clubs, pools, and spas, which might be an important factor depending on your interests. Even if you are usually on a budget, I recommend splurging for maybe 1 or 2 nights of your trip if you find a five-star property you really like.

To save money, you will need to compromise, as not all three- or two-star hotels have the above-mentioned amenities (though air-conditioning and even lobby-based Wi-Fi access have become virtually standard in all hotels in Buenos Aires, no matter the category). When dealing with some of the less expensive hotels, your best option is usually to ask to see the available room, or a few of them. This will ensure the room will be up to your standards and can help you choose the best room available. Many recently renovated hotels often have internal variations, with huge rooms and small rooms sometimes for exactly the same price.

Local hotels, especially if they are family-run, have a certain charm that is rarely met by four- and five-star properties. Be aware, however, that while many people in Buenos Aires's travel industry speak English, fewer will at the less expensive or family-run hotels. Also, while a room might not have a particular amenity, such as a hair dryer, iron, or coffeemaker, it might still be available upon request at the concierge. The same applies for safes, which might not be in the room, but at the front desk instead. Always ask for a receipt when trying to secure valuable items at the front desk, or at least find out the name of the person who locked them, and if keys for access are only available during certain hours of the day or 24 hours.

Finally, hostels are shared bunk-bed-filled rooms, usually booked by the young, budget-minded, and adventurous. However, some also have private rooms with attached bathrooms for one person as well as for groups, so ask before you decide a hostel isn't for you. All the hostels listed in this chapter provide sheets and towels and have 24-hour access, with no shutout periods.

As for choosing a location, it's a matter of deciding what is best for you and what you want out of your Buenos Aires vacation. In this chapter, I have tried to give you a range of hotels based on both location and price. I have also given a brief description of each neighborhood where I've listed hotels. For a more thorough discussion of neighborhoods, however, see "The Neighborhoods in Brief" in chapter 4.

Prices listed below are for rack rates in high season and include the 21% tax levied on hotel rooms. Discounts are almost always available for weekends at business-oriented hotels, low season for all hotels, and may even be available in high season. Web packages and specials can also be found on various hotel sites. Most hotels charge for valet parking or are close to self-parking facilities they can recommend. You should avoid parking long-term on the street. Few hotels have separate tour desks, but all concierges and front desks can arrange tours, offer advice, and rent cars, bicycles, and other things you might need on your trip.

I give exact prices for hotels below and place them within general price categories by neighborhood. **Very Expensive** refers to hotels costing $300 (£213) or more nightly. Keep in mind that some hotels in this category do not serve free breakfasts, which can increase your costs even more. **Expensive** hotels run roughly in the general range of $175 to $299 (£124–£212) per night. **Moderate** hotels will run from about $50 to $174 (£36–£124) per night. **Inexpensive** hotels are $49 (£35) per night and less, and include hostels, which can run as little as $8 (£5.70) per person for a bed space. Quality and offerings vary considerably in this price category. All prices listed are rack rates in high season for doubles and include taxes, but the actual price varies depending on circumstances.

Also, for long-term stays, I have added a section on apartment rental services. Prices will vary by company, location, and length of stay, but are generally cheaper than staying in a hotel.

1 PUERTO MADERO

Puerto Madero is home to some of the newer, more expensive hotels in Buenos Aires. But it's also off the beaten path, so you'll need to use taxis as your mode of transportation. There is a sense of isolation in being cut off from the rest of the city in Puerto Madero. This might be a benefit for people on business trips or those who like the sense of being whisked from one scene to another or slipping away peacefully to bed when the day is over. The hotels here are near the restaurants of Puerto Madero's historic dock district, so you'll never want for places to dine at night. The sunset from hotel rooms in Puerto Madero is a magnificent sight. The water in the port turns a fiery red, and the city's skyline is magically silhouetted, adding a touch of romance to an area that by day can seem clinical and desolate.

Alvear Palace Hotel **2**
Amerian Buenos Aires Park Hotel **17**
Art Hotel **8**
The Axel Hotel **27**
Claridge Hotel **19**
The Cocker **33**
Dazzler Hotel Libertad **9**
El Lugar Gay **32**
Esplendor **16**
Faena Hotel and Universe **29**
Four Seasons Hotel **4**
The Golden Tulip Savoy **10**
Grand Boulevard Hotel **28**
Hilton Buenos Aires **23**
Hostel Carlos Gardel **31**
Hotel Castelar **24**
Hotel Emperador **5**
Hotel Ibis **11**
Hotel Reconquista Plaza **18**
Howard Johnson Florida Street **14**
InterContinental Hotel Buenos Aires **25**
Lafayette Hotel **20**
Lina's Tango Guesthouse **30**
Loi Suites **1**
Marriott Plaza Hotel **13**
Moreno **26**
NH Florida **15**
Pan Americano **22**
Park Hyatt Buenos Aires **3**
The Recoleta Hostel **7**
Sheraton Buenos Aires Hotel and Convention Center **12**
Sofitel **6**
V&S Hostel **21**

Alem on the B Line is the only metro stop close to the neighborhood, but in general there is not good *subte* access. For a map of the hotels listed in this section, see the "Where to Stay in Central Buenos Aires" map on p. 62.

VERY EXPENSIVE

Faena Hotel and Universe ★★★   This hotel designed by Philippe Starck is built into El Porteño, an old grain silo, and feels like a resort within the city. In the public spaces, old Edwardian elegance combines with country chic. In the rooms, midcentury classical meets modern—with white Empire-style furnishings in modern surroundings, and cut-glass mirrors reminiscent of colonial Mexico. White and red are key color elements throughout the oversize rooms, with interesting touches such as heavy velvet curtains controlled electronically. Each room has a home entertainment center. Bathrooms are enormous, completely mirrored, outfitted with oversize tubs. Some of the rooms facing the city skyline and the port have incredible vistas; others overlook the nearby Ecological Reserve and the Río de la Plata. The spa is spacious and unique, using the round shapes of the silos to great effect, with Turkish-style hammam baths and a special stone Incan-style sauna shaped like an igloo. A business center with secretarial services is on the premises.

Martha Salotti 445 (at Av. Juana Manso), 1107 Buenos Aires. ✆ **11/4010-9000.** Fax 11/4010-9001. www.faenahotelanduniverse.com. 103 units. From $600 (£426) double; from $865 (£614) suite. Rates include continental breakfast. AE, MC, V. Parking $24 (£17). No metro access. **Amenities:** 3 restaurants; 3 bars; free airport transfers; concierge; large health club and spa w/extensive treatments; Internet in business center; outdoor heated pool; room service. *In room:* A/C, TV/DVD, CD player, hair dryer, minibar, Wi-Fi.

Hilton Buenos Aires ★★   The Hilton opened in mid-2000 as the first major hotel and convention center in Puerto Madero. Within easy walking distance of some of the best restaurants in Buenos Aires, it's an excellent choice for steak and seafood connoisseurs. The strikingly contemporary hotel—a sleek silver block hoisted on stilts—features a seven-story atrium and more than 400 well-equipped guest rooms. The spacious rooms have multiple phone lines, walk-in closets, and bathrooms with separate showers and tubs. Those staying on the executive floors enjoy complimentary breakfast and have access to a private concierge. The lobby restaurant El Faro serves California cuisine with a focus on seafood. The hotel has the largest in-hotel convention center in the city, along with a business center with secretarial services.

Av. Macacha Güemes 351 (at Malecón Pierina Dealessi), 1106 Buenos Aires. ✆ **800/445-8667** in the U.S. or 11/4891-0000. Fax 11/4891-0001. www.buenos.hilton.com. 418 units. From $265 (£188) double; from $568 (£403) suite. AE, DC, MC, V. Parking $24 (£17). No metro access. **Amenities:** Restaurant; bar; babysitting; concierge; exercise room; Internet in business center; outside pool; room service. *In room:* A/C, TV, hair dryer, minibar, free Wi-Fi.

2 MICROCENTRO

The Microcentro is an ideal place to stay if you want to be close to Buenos Aires's shopping and most of the *subte* lines that converge in this region. Theater buffs will also appreciate this location, because most performance spaces, including Teatro Colón, are within walking distance of the hotels here. The Microcentro will also give you easy access to the majority of local travel agencies that seem to cluster in this area, which can be convenient for making a last-minute change of plans or for adding a day trip outside the city to your itinerary. Low-cost Internet and telephone centers are everywhere too, so

For a map of the hotels listed in the section, see the "Where to Stay in Central Buenos Aires" map on p. 62.

VERY EXPENSIVE

Marriott Plaza Hotel ★★   As the grande dame of Buenos Aires for most of the 20th century, the historic Plaza has maintained much of its original splendor, its lobby decorated in Italian marble, crystal, and Persian carpets. All the rooms are spacious and well appointed. Twenty-six rooms overlook Plaza San Martín, providing dreamlike views of the green canopy of trees in spring and summer. The **Plaza Grill** (p. 93) remains a favorite spot for a business lunch and offers a reasonably priced multicourse dinner menu as well. The **Plaza Bar** (p. 220) is among the most famous bars in the city. The hotel's enormous health club is one of the city's best, with specialized dance and aerobics rooms. Guests whose rooms are not ready can rest and shower in the health club lounge. The exterior of the hotel, with its historic landmark facade, recently underwent a cleaning and restoration. The intimate lobby is a virtual revolving door of Argentine politicians, foreign diplomats, and business executives. The hotel also provides excellent, free historical tours of Buenos Aires.

Calle Florida 1005 (at Santa Fe, overlooking Plaza San Martín), 1005 Buenos Aires. ✆ **11/4318-3000** or 888/236-2427 in the U.S. Fax 11/4318-3008. www.marriott.com. 325 units. $296 (£210) double; from $400 (£284) suite. Rates include breakfast buffet. AE, DC, MC, V. Valet parking $16 (£11). Metro: San Martín. **Amenities:** 2 restaurants; cigar bar; concierge; extensive health club; Internet in business center; outdoor pool; room service; sauna; free Wi-Fi in lobby. *In room:* A/C, TV, hair dryer, Internet ($16 £11 daily), minibar.

Sofitel ★★★   This classy French hotel near Plaza San Martín comprises two seven-story buildings joined to a 20-story neoclassical tower dating from 1929. They're linked by a glass atrium lobby that resembles an enormous gazebo, with ficus trees, a giant iron-and-bronze chandelier, an Art Nouveau clock, and Botticcino and black San Gabriel marble filling the space. The guest rooms vary in size, mixing modern French decor with traditional Art Deco; ask for one of the "deluxe" rooms or suites if you're looking for more space. Beautiful marble bathrooms have separate showers and bathtubs and feature Roger & Gallet amenities. Rooms above the eighth floor enjoy the best views, and the 17th-floor suite, *L'Appartement,* covers the whole floor. Adjacent to the hotel lobby is an elegant French restaurant, **Le Sud** (p. 93), and the early-20th-century-style Buenos Aires Café. Many of the Sofitel's staff members speak Spanish, English, and French.

Arroyo 841/849 (at Juncal), 1007 Buenos Aires. ✆ **11/4131-0000.** Fax 11/4909-1452. www.sofitel.com. 144 units. From $556 (£395) double; from $684 (£486) suite. AE, DC, MC, V. Valet parking $20 (£14). Metro: San Martín. **Amenities:** Restaurant; cafe; bar; concierge; fitness center; Internet in business center; indoor pool; room service. *In room:* A/C, TV, hair dryer, Internet, minibar.

EXPENSIVE

Amerian Buenos Aires Park Hotel ★★ (Finds)   One of the best four-star hotels in the city, the modern Amerian is a good bet for tourists as well as business travelers. The warm atrium lobby looks more like California than Argentina, and the highly qualified staff offers personalized service. Soundproof rooms are elegantly appointed with wood, marble, and granite. All boast comfortable beds, chairs, and work areas. This Argentine-owned hotel is just blocks away from Calle Florida, Plaza San Martín, and the Teatro Colón.

Reconquista 699 (at Viamonte), 1003 Buenos Aires. © **11/5032-5100.** Fax 11/5032-5101. www.amerian. com. 152 units. $175 (£124) double; from $250 (£178) suite. Rates include breakfast buffet. AE, DC, MC, V. Parking $12 (£8.50). Metro: Florida. **Amenities:** Restaurant; bar; concierge; exercise room; Internet in business center; room service; sauna. *In room:* A/C, TV, Internet, minibar.

Esplendor ★★ Esplendor is built into the Galerias Pacifico shopping gallery, in a spectacularly renovated space that once housed a hotel. If you want a stylish boutique hotel, you don't have to sacrifice a convenient location close to everything. Rooms have a cool decor, mixing neutral tones with splashes of color and interesting fabrics by the Tramando Design House of Martin Churba. The high ceilings are punctuated by light fixtures that are themselves often made from interesting fabrics. Beds are very comfortable and the lobby has a restaurant, Rouge, and a gift shop full of design-based items. Double-insulated windows keep out the noise and many rooms also have balconies; bathrooms are very large.

San Martin 780, btw. Viamonte and Cordoba, 1004 Buenos Aires. © **11/5256-8800.** Fax 11/5256-8800. www.esplendorbuenosaires.com. 51 units, including 25 suites and 3 VIP suites. $232 (£162) double; from $252 (£179) suite. Rates include breakfast buffet. Parking $12 (£8.50). AE, MC, V. Metro: San Martín. **Amenities:** Restaurant; bar; babysitting; bikes; concierge; health club; Internet in business center; room service; sauna. *In room:* A/C, TV, Internet, minibar.

Hotel Reconquista Plaza ★ Near busy Calle Florida, this hotel is a good option for business travelers who do not need full services and want a convenient central location and clean, modern amenities. All rooms have enormous, rounded windows looking out onto the street. Desks provide a workspace. Suites are merely oversize rooms partially separated by a large wardrobe unit with a sleeper couch. Some suites have enormous terraces, with views overlooking the Microcentro. All rooms have tub/shower combinations, but the tubs are small in standard rooms. Suite bathrooms are equipped with whirlpools. Double-glazing on the windows blocks out noise, an important consideration in this area. Staff is exceptionally friendly and helpful.

Reconquista 602 (at Tucumán), 1003 Buenos Aires. © **11/4311-4600.** Fax 11/4311-3302. www. reconquistaplaza.com.ar. 60 units. From $181 (£129) double; from $291 (£207) suite. Rates include breakfast buffet. AE, MC, V. Parking $10 (£7.10). Metro: Florida. **Amenities:** Restaurant; bar; concierge; small health club; Internet in business center; room service; sauna. *In room:* A/C, TV, hair dryer, Internet ($8/£5.70 per day), minibar.

Lafayette Hotel ★ (Kids) Popular with European and Brazilian travelers, the Lafayette Hotel has spacious rooms, some even large enough to accommodate an entire family. Street-side rooms are great for people-watching in the Microcentro, though you should expect some noise. Back rooms are quieter, but afford limited views. All rooms have desks. Bathrooms are hit-or-miss—some are large, others seem like jammed-together afterthoughts. The location is ideal for Microcentro's Lavalle and Calle Florida shopping, and the *subte* is only a few blocks away. The breakfast buffet is generous and varied, with made-to-order omelets on request. The hotel is built in two parts with two different elevator bays, so if you're staying with friends or family, request rooms in the same division of the hotel.

Reconquista 546 (at Viamonte), 1003 Buenos Aires. © **11/4393-9081.** Fax 11/4322-1611. www.lafayette hotel.com.ar. 83 units. From $168 (£119) double; from $300 (£213) suite. Rates include breakfast buffet. AE, DC, MC, V. Parking (offsite) $12 (£8.50). Metro: Florida. **Amenities:** Restaurant; bar; concierge; exercise room; Internet in business center; room service; sauna. *In room:* A/C, TV, hair dryer, minibar, Wi-Fi.

Pan Americano ★★ An enormous hotel, the Pan Americano faces both the Obelisco and the Teatro Colón, allowing convenient access to tourist sites as well as the *subte* lines that converge on this part of town. Once part of the American Crowne Plaza chain, it's now independent. The South Tower rooms are a good size, but the North Tower rooms are even larger and better appointed. Bathrooms are also larger, with whirlpool tubs and separate shower units, and marble counters and floors. All rooms in both towers come with desks, extra side chairs, and ample closet space. The health club and spa, in a three-story glass rooftop structure, give the sense of floating above Avenida 9 de Julio. The health club restaurant becomes a sushi bar at night. Two other restaurants located in the lobby serve international, Argentine, and Italian cuisine.

Carlos Pelligrini 551 (at Corrientes), 1009 Buenos Aires. (℃ **11/4348-5115** or 800/227-6963 in the U.S. Fax 11/4348-5250. www.panamericano.us. 386 units. $217 (£154) double; from $300 (£213) suite. Rates include breakfast buffet. AE, DC, MC, V. Free valet parking. Metro: Lavalle, Diagonal Norte. **Amenities:** 3 restaurants; babysitting; concierge; large health club and spa; Internet in business center; indoor/outdoor pool; room service. *In room:* A/C, TV, hair dryer, Internet, minibar.

Sheraton Buenos Aires Hotel and Convention Center ★ Across from Retiro train station and the British Clock Tower, the Sheraton has an ideal location for both business travelers and tourists. Rooms are large, and all have new Sheraton Suite Sleeper bedding. A new, interactive game-and-business center off the lobby, called Link@ Sheraton, was installed in 2006. The hotel boasts four restaurants that it shares with the Park Tower, including Crystal Garden, serving refined international cuisine in an atrium dining room overlooking Alem; El Aljibe, cooking Argentine beef from the grill; Cardinale, offering Italian specialties; and Café Express, a fast-food and pastry shop off the lobby. The hotel's "Neptune" pool and fitness center are among the best in the city. The entire pool and spa complex is set in a garden, giving the sense of being in a resort, rather than in the heart of the city. One of the pools also contains a pressurized current to boost your workout during your swim.

Av. San Martín 1225, at Leandro N. Alem, 1104 Buenos Aires. (℃ **11/4318-9000.** Fax 11/4318-9346. www.sheraton.com. 742 units. $247 (£175) double; from $660 (£469) suite. AE, DC, MC, V. Valet parking $20 (£14). Metro: Retiro. **Amenities:** 3 restaurants; piano bar; babysitting; concierge; health club and spa; Internet in business center; 2 outdoor pools; room service; 2 lighted tennis courts. *In room:* A/C, TV, hair dryer, Internet, minibar.

MODERATE

Claridge Hotel ★ The Claridge is living testimony to the once-close ties between England and Argentina. The grand entrance, with its imposing Ionic columns, mimics a London terrace apartment. Guest rooms are spacious, tastefully decorated, and equipped with all the amenities expected of a five-star hotel. The restaurant has a hunting-themed, wood-paneled interior—a registered city landmark—and a menu of inexpensive, carefully prepared international food. Because it occasionally hosts conventions, the Claridge can become very busy. The rates at this hotel can go down significantly when booking promotions via the website.

Tucumán 535 (at San Martín), 1049 Buenos Aires. (℃ **11/4314-7700.** Fax 11/4314-8022. www.claridge.com.ar. 152 units. $125 (£89) double; from $176 (£125) suite. Rates include breakfast buffet. AE, DC, MC, V. Valet parking $20 (£14). Metro: Florida. **Amenities:** Restaurant; bar; concierge; health club and spa; Internet in business center; heated outdoor pool; room service. *In room:* A/C, TV, Internet, minibar.

Howard Johnson Florida Street ★★ (Value) Having taken over the property from Courtyard by Marriott, this Howard Johnson is an excellent choice for travelers who don't require many special services. It has a great location off Calle Florida near Plaza San Martín, with access through a shopping-and-restaurant gallery on the ground level. Guest rooms come equipped with sleeper chairs (in addition to the bed), large desks and dressers, and well-appointed bathrooms. Room size is above average in this category. Each room has two phones, with free local calls and Internet use—a rarity in Buenos Aires. There's a small, airy cafe and bar in the lobby, with additional food served in the gallery below. Four small, budget-priced function rooms off the lobby are available for business and social events, and business services are available. The hotel advertises as gay-friendly and patrons can receive the Argentine native rate by booking through Daniel Porce Producciones (© **15/5817-3041**; www.dpproducciones.com.ar).

Calle Florida 944 (at Alvear), 1005 Buenos Aires. © **11/4891-9200.** Fax 11/4891-9208. www.hojoar.com. 77 units. $157 (£111) double. Rates include breakfast buffet. AE, DC, MC, V. Parking $12 (£8.50). Metro: San Martín. **Amenities:** Restaurant; bar; Internet in business center; room service. *In room:* A/C, TV, hair dryer, Internet (free), minibar.

NH Florida This is a simple, well-located, four-star hotel less than a block away from the Galerías Pacífico. Views are not the focus at NH Florida, surrounded by buildings of the same size, but the rooms are larger than most in this price category. Most have wood floors with small carpets, adding a simple elegance to the modern decor, and all rooms have a good workstation. Suites are much larger, with large doors separating the guest areas from the sitting room. The hotel provides many good services, but its main disadvantage, compared to other accommodations in this category, is its lack of a gym or pool. However, for a fee ($10/£7.10 per day), clients can access nearby facilities. Eleven rooms are equipped for those with special needs, but I recommend calling and asking specific questions about your needs before booking here. With its Microcentro location, this is among the most accessible hotels, for all travelers, in Buenos Aires.

San Martín 839 (at Córdoba), 1004 Buenos Aires. © **11/4321-9850.** Fax 11/4321-9875. www.nh-hotels. com. 148 units. $156 (£111) double; from $170 (£121) suite. Rates include breakfast buffet. AE, DC, MC, V. Valet parking $12 (£8.50). Metro: San Martín. **Amenities:** Restaurant; bar; babysitting; concierge; Internet in business center; room service. *In room:* A/C, TV, hair dryer, Wi-Fi (free), minibar.

INEXPENSIVE

V&S Hostel ★★ (Finds) Privately owned, but part of an Argentine network of hostels, V&S provides exceptionally friendly service in a convenient Microcentro location. The hostel is in a gorgeous turn-of-the-20th-century apartment building, with lavish touches such as molded plaster, curved doorway entries, stained-glass ornamentation, and balconies. Five private bedrooms with attached shower-stall bathrooms are also available. A kitchen for preparing meals is on the premises. Guests can mingle in the quiet library, TV sitting room, or patio. Several computers are also available for Internet access. This place is a great value, with air-conditioning throughout the rooms, though an electricity fee ($1–$3/70p–£2.15) is charged per person, depending on the room. Except for same-day reservations, the hostel prefers reservations requests by e-mail at reservas@hostelclub.com.

Viamonte 887 (at Suipacha), 1053 Buenos Aires. © **11/4322-0994.** www.hostelclub.com. 60 bed spaces, 10 with attached bathroom. From $15 (£11) bed; $78 (£55) private room. Rates include continental breakfast. No credit cards. Metro: Lavalle. **Amenities:** Concierge; Internet in lobby. *In room:* A/C, hair dryer, Wi-Fi (select rooms).

The neighborhood of Monserrat borders San Telmo and is more easily accessed by subway. There are also more four- and five-star hotels here, so staying in Monserrat might be a compromise for people who want San Telmo's romance, but a more convenient location for subways and shopping in the Microcentro. Monserrat is distinguished by old, turn-of-the-20th-century buildings similar to those in San Telmo, as well as enormous midcentury, Fascist-style government buildings where it borders the Plaza de Mayo. While Monserrat, like San Telmo, is rapidly gentrifying, parts of it can be desolate and a little dangerous at night, so use caution near your hotel and avoid empty streets.

For a map of the hotels listed in this section, see the "Where to Stay in Central Buenos Aires" map on p. 62.

EXPENSIVE

InterContinental ★★★ This luxurious tower hotel built in one of the city's oldest districts is decorated in the Argentine style of the 1930s. The marble lobby has handsome carved-wood furniture and antiques inlaid with agates and other stones. Guest rooms continue the 1930s theme, with elegant black woodwork, comfy king-size beds, marble-top nightstands, large desks, and black-and-white photographs of the city. Marble bathrooms have separate showers and bathtubs, and extensive amenities. The lobby's small Café de las Luces sometimes has evening tango performances. The InterContinental is the only five-star hotel in walking distance to the San Telmo tango district. The **Restaurante y Bar Mediterráneo** (p. 98) serves healthful, gourmet Mediterranean cuisine on an outdoor patio under a glassed-in trellis. Stop by the Brasco & Duane wine bar for an exclusive selection of Argentine vintages.

Moreno 809 (at Piedras), 1091 Buenos Aires. ℂ **11/4340-7100.** Fax 11/4340-7119. www.buenos-aires. interconti.com. 312 units. $217 (£154) double; from $435 (£309) suite. AE, DC, MC, V. Parking $20 (£14). Metro: Moreno. **Amenities:** Restaurant; 2 bars; concierge; health club; Internet in business center; indoor pool; room service; sauna. In room: A/C, TV, hair dryer, Internet, minibar.

Moreno ★ This all-suite hotel says it is located in San Telmo, but it's really in Monserrat, on the border of the two neighborhoods. It opened in 2007 and is an incredible reuse of a 1920s Art Deco building. Inside, you'll find fantastic preserved details such as stained-glass windows. The suites are huge, with modern decor featuring dark woods and light accents, and they're graced with Art Deco furniture. The extra-large suites all have chaise longues and are some of the largest rooms at hotels in this category. Large rooms are about 39 sq. m (420 sq. ft.), and the big lofts are about 67 sq. m (721 sq. ft.). Loft rooms also come with Jacuzzis. A rooftop lounge has a Jacuzzi and views to the dome of the nearby San Francisco church, and is where the small gym sits. A new restaurant and theater/tango lounge are also under construction, due to open in mid-2009.

Moreno 376, btw. Balcarce and Defensa, 1091 Buenos Aires. ℂ **11/6091-2000.** Fax 11/6091-2001. www. morenobuenosaires.com. 39 units. $169 (£120) suite; from $375 (£266) loft. AE, DC, MC, V. Parking $8 (£5.70). Metro: Bolivar, Catedral, Plaza de Mayo. **Amenities:** Restaurant; bar; babysitting; concierge; exercise room; Internet in business center; room service. In room: A/C, TV, hair dryer, minibar, Wi-Fi.

MODERATE

Grand Boulevard Hotel ★ Value The Grand Boulevard has a location similar to the InterContinental (see above) at a much lower price, while still providing convenient services for both business and leisure travelers. Double-glazed windows lock out noise from Avenida 9 de Julio while allowing incredible views of that street and the river from higher floors. All rooms have desks and large closets, and some have limited wheelchair accessibility. Subway access is easy. With the *autopista* (highway) nearby, this is also the city's closest four-star hotel to the airport. A small, glassed-in meeting-room space sits on the roof of the building, with beautiful views of the city. The restaurant/bar is open 24 hours, serving both international cuisine and lighter fare.

Bernardo de Irogoyen 432 (at Belgrano), 1072 Buenos Aires. (©) **11/5222-9000.** www.grandboulevard hotel.com. 85 units. $121 (£86) double; from $175 (£124) suite. AE, DC, MC, V. Free parking. Metro: Moreno. **Amenities:** Restaurant; bar; babysitting; concierge; small health club w/personal trainer; free Internet in business center; room service; sauna. *In room:* A/C, TV, hair dryer, free Internet in some rooms, minibar, free Wi-Fi in some rooms.

Hotel Castelar The Hotel Castelar was a popular stopping point for Spanish-language literary stars during Argentina's golden years as an intellectual center in the 1930s. The former room of playwright Federico García Lorca is preserved as a kitschy minimuseum. The dining area was once a *confitería* (cafe) as culturally important as the Café Tortoni (p. 126). The Castelar's spa in the hotel's basement, free for guests, is enormous and built in the Turkish style. It's worth paying the nonguest entrance fee ($15/£11) just to see it. Renovations in all units were completed in 2005, but the 1920s wooden touches, speckled glass, and tiled bathroom floors have been retained. The rooms are not very large, but the setup—a small antechamber with the bedroom to one side, the bathroom to the other—adds a sense of privacy to the spaces, even when shared by a couple. Suites are similar, with an added living area. For guests with special needs, some units have wider spaces and grip bars in the bathroom.

Av. de Mayo (at Lima and Av. 9 de Julio), 1152 Buenos Aires. (©) **11/4383-5000.** Fax 11/4383-8388. www. castelarhotel.com.ar. 151 units. $150 (£107) double; $225 (£160) suite. Rates include breakfast buffet. AE, DC, MC, V. Parking $12 (£8.50). Metro: Lima. **Amenities:** Restaurant; bar; small health club; room service; extensive spa; Wi-Fi (free in lobby). *In room:* A/C, TV, free Internet, minibar.

4 SAN TELMO

I find San Telmo both romantic and the most authentic of all the touristy neighborhoods in Buenos Aires. San Telmo is rapidly becoming gentrified, so it's nowhere near as dangerous as in the past, but you still need to be more cautious here at night than in other parts of the city. This is, after all, where the Bush twins were supposedly robbed during their 2006 visit, even with the Secret Service all around them. Most hotels here are hostels, B&Bs, or boutique hotels. If you can live without certain luxuries, focusing more on absorbing the extreme Porteño flavor of the area, I highly recommend staying here. The area is accessed by stations for *subte* C running along Avenida 9 de Julio, and these can be a slightly long walk away from some of San Telmo's accommodations.

For a map of the hotels listed in this section, see the "Where to Stay in Central Buenos Aires" map on p. 62.

EXPENSIVE

The Axel Hotel ★★ Part of a Spanish chain, this is a hotel for gays, which bills itself as "hetero-friendly." Most of its clientele are glamorous gay men from around the world, with the rest lesbians and heterosexuals, usually from the fashion world. The hotel also bills itself as a five-star, but in reality it's a high-quality four-star, and the only one in San Telmo, which makes it ideal no matter what your orientation. Naturally, style is important. The chic, but small rooms look like space-station pods with their interior portholes and bathrooms set in glass cubes. The hotel has two pools, one set in an outdoor garden, with its own bar. Most unique is the glass-bottom pool set on the top floor of the building inside the combination sauna and lounge—you can watch people swimming from below within the combination atrium and lobby. The dining area is called Kitchen, and even if you don't stay here, it's worth coming to dine or for socializing in the bar.

Venezuela 649, btw. Peru and Chacabuco, 1095 Buenos Aires. © **11/4136-9393.** Fax 11/4136-9396. www.axelhotels.com. 48 rooms. $150–$300 (£107–£213) double. Rates include continental breakfast. AE, MC, V. Parking $12 (£8.50). Metro: Belgrano. **Amenities:** Restaurant; 2 bars; exercise room; Internet in business center; Jacuzzi, indoor and outdoor pools, room service, sauna. *In room:* A/C, TV, minibar, Wi-Fi.

MODERATE

The Cocker ★   Tucked away in an unassuming part of San Telmo, this boutique hotel is a fantastic Art Nouveau house and takes its name from the former owners' cocker spaniel. The structure has 16-foot-high ceilings and a variety of public spaces, including a sitting room graced by a piano, and a rooftop garden with a fantastic view. The decor in each of the five rooms varies—some are modern and stark while others have French touches. If you are looking for romance, choose the rooftop room with its own private patio. Guests can use the shared kitchen in the hotel. Be aware that the staircases throughout this hotel make it a difficult choice for people with limited mobility.

Av. Juan de Garay 458, btw. Defensa and Bolivar, 1153 Buenos Aires. © **11/4362-8451.** www.thecocker. com. 5 units. $90–$105 (£64–£75) double. Rates include continental breakfast. No credit cards. No parking. Metro: Constitución. *In room:* A/C, Wi-Fi.

INEXPENSIVE

El Lugar Gay ★   This is Buenos Aires's first exclusively gay hotel, inside a historical turn-of-the-20th-century building less than a block from Plaza Dorrego, the heart of San Telmo. With its century-old interior and industrial chic, it has a homey feel. Nestor and Juan, the gay couple who own the building, run a friendly staff, but most don't speak much English. Ask for the rooms in the back with the beautiful views of the Church of San Telmo, which is next to the building. Rooms are small and sparse. Some share bathrooms with adjacent rooms, but one group has a Jacuzzi. Some rooms have small desks or tables for use as workstations. Several flights of narrow stairs leading to the hotel's lobby and rooms might be a problem for people with limited mobility. The hotel becomes a de facto gay community center at times, with its small cafe and Sunday-evening tango lessons conducted by the gay tango group La Marshall, which are open to the public.

Defensa 1120 (at Humberto I), 1102 Buenos Aires. © **11/4300-4747.** www.lugargay.com.ar. 7 rooms (some with shared bathrooms). $35–$55 (£25–£39) double. Rates include continental breakfast. No credit cards. No parking. Metro: Independencia. **Amenities:** Restaurant; bar; free Internet in business center. *In room:* A/C, TV, Internet, no phone.

Hostel Carlos Gardel ★   If you can't get enough of Gardel in the tango clubs, then stay here, where a red wall full of his pictures is the first thing to greet you. This hostel is built into a renovated old house, and though it has been severely gutted, a few charming elements, such as marble staircases, wall sconces, and stained-glass windows, still remain. Two rooms with private bathrooms are available in this location and are reasonably priced, but with few amenities. The staff is friendly, and a large TV room off the concierge area allows for chatting with them and other patrons. A shared kitchen and an *asado* on the rooftop terrace provide more spaces for interacting and sharing stories of your adventures in Buenos Aires. Towels and sheets are provided for guests, along with in-room lockers; but of all the hostels, this seems to have the fewest bathrooms for the number of guests.

Carlos Calvo 579 (at Perú), 1102 Buenos Aires. © **11/4307-2606.** www.hostelcarlosgardel.com.ar. 45 bed spaces (10 in 2 private rooms with bathroom). From $22 (£16) per bed; $50 (£36) for room. Rates include continental breakfast. No credit cards. Metro: Independencia. **Amenities:** Concierge; free Internet.

Lina's Tango Guesthouse ★★★ (Finds) If you want to immerse yourself in the tango scene, this is the place to stay. Owner Lina Acuña, who hails from Colombia, is a tango dancer and has created a charming little spot for the tango community from around the world. As a woman-owned space, it's also great for women traveling alone, and Lina often accompanies her guests on informal trips to the *milongas,* offering a unique inside view. Lina has painted the rooms and patio in kitschy La Boca colors, and vines and trees add to the Porteño atmosphere. Guests and Lina's friends gather on the patio for conversation, help with each other's dance techniques, and *asados* on holidays and weekends. Three of the eight guest rooms share bathrooms. Rooms come in different sizes, but all are big enough to share. Guests can use the small kitchen and a washing machine. The TV is in the shared living room.

Estados Unidos 780 (at Piedras), 1011 Buenos Aires. © **11/4361-6817** and 11/4300-7367. www.tango guesthouse.com.ar. 8 units, 5 with bathroom. $40–$70 (£28–£50) double, additional 20% charge for 1-night stays. Rates include continental breakfast. No credit cards. Metro: Independencia. *In room:* Wi-Fi.

5 RECOLETA

Most of the best hotels are found in Recoleta, a very scenic, Parisian-style part of the city. But if you stay here, you'll probably find yourself spending more money on cabs; the area is not accessible by any of the metro *(subte)* lines, except in areas bordering nearby Barrio Norte. Even though taxis don't cost very much in Buenos Aires, using them several times a day can add up. Of course, if you can afford to stay in Recoleta, then the extra cost of taxis might not be an issue for you! Public transportation aside, Recoleta is exceedingly beautiful, and staying here puts you close to the Recoleta Cemetery and Evita's grave, as well as the parks and museums of nearby Palermo, which are best accessed by cab to begin with, no matter where you are coming from in the city.

There are no convenient metro stops in this neighborhood. For a map of the hotels in this section, see the "Where to Stay in Central Buenos Aires" map on p. 62.

VERY EXPENSIVE

Alvear Palace Hotel ★★★ In the center of the upscale Recoleta district, the Alvear Palace is the most exclusive hotel in Buenos Aires and one of the top hotels in the world, with an illustrious guest list. A gilded classical confection full of marble and bronze, the Alvear combines Empire- and Louis XV-style furniture with exquisite French decorative arts. The historically important facade was restored in 2004 to its original glory. Guest rooms combine modern conveniences with luxurious comforts, such as chandeliers, Egyptian cotton linens, and silk drapes. All rooms come with personal butler service, cellphones activated on demand, fresh flowers and fruit baskets, and daily newspaper delivery. Large marble bathrooms contain Hermès toiletries, and most have Jacuzzi baths. The formal hotel provides sharp, professional service. The Alvear Palace is home to one of the best restaurants in South America (**La Bourgogne;** p. 101) and serves an excellent Sunday brunch and afternoon tea in L'Orangerie. Kosher eating and dining is also available at the Alvear.

Av. Alvear 1891 (at Ayacucho), 1129 Buenos Aires. *(C)* **11/4808-2100.** Fax 11/4804-0034. www.alvear palace.com. 200 units (100 palace rooms and 100 suites). From $478 (£339) double; from $539 (£383) suite. Rates include breakfast buffet. AE, DC, MC, V. Valet parking $24 (£17). No metro access. **Amenities:** 2 restaurants; bar; concierge; health club and spa; Internet in business center; room service. *In room:* A/C, TV, hair dryer, minibar, Wi-Fi.

Four Seasons Hotel ★★★ (Kids) This landmark hotel consists of two parts—the 12-story "Park" tower housing the majority of the guest rooms, and the 1916 French-style "La Mansión," with seven elegant suites and a handful of private event rooms. A French-style garden and a pool separate the two buildings. The spa is named Pachamama and some treatments use wine and other Argentine ingredients. The hotel's restaurant, **Le Mistral** (p. 102), serves excellent Mediterranean cuisine in a casual environment. Spacious guest rooms provide atypical amenities such as walk-in closets, wet and dry bars, stereo systems, and cellphones. Large marble bathrooms contain separate water-jet bathtubs and showers. Guests on the executive Library Floor enjoy exclusive amenities. While new competition has opened up around the corner at the new Park Hyatt Buenos Aires, the Four Seasons holds its own with celebrities, and it wins top honors from *Condé Nast Traveler, Travel + Leisure,* and other magazines.

Posadas 1086–88 (at Av. 9 de Julio), 1011 Buenos Aires. *(C)* **11/4321-1200** or 800/819-5053 in the U.S. and Canada. Fax 11/4321-1201. www.fourseasons.com. 165 units. $545 (£387) double; from $750 (£533) suite; $3,500 (£2,485) mansion suite. Rates include breakfast. AE, DC, MC, V. Valet parking $24 (£17). No metro access. **Amenities:** Restaurant; bar; babysitting; concierge; health club and spa; Internet in business center; heated outdoor pool; room service. *In room:* A/C, TV/DVD, hair dryer, minibar, Wi-Fi.

Loi Suites ★★ Part of a small local hotel chain, the Loi Suites Recoleta is a contemporary hotel with spacious rooms and personalized service. A palm-filled garden atrium and covered pool adjoin the lobby, which is bathed in various shades of white. Breakfast and afternoon tea are served in the "winter garden." Management uses the term "suites" rather loosely to describe rooms with microwaves, sinks, and small fridges. However, the hotel does offer some traditional suites in addition to its more regular studio-style rooms. Loi Suites lies just around the corner from Recoleta's trendy restaurants and bars, and the staff will provide information on city tours upon request.

Vicente López 1955 (at Ayacucho), 1128 Buenos Aires. *(C)* **11/5777-8950.** Fax 11/5777-8999. www.loi suites.com.ar. 112 units. From $300 (£213) double; from $450 (£320) suite. Rates include breakfast buffet. AE, DC, MC, V. Parking $12 (£8.50). No Metro access. **Amenities:** Restaurant; exercise room; Internet in business center; indoor pool; room service; sauna. *In room:* A/C, TV, CD player, hair dryer, Internet (free), kitchenette (in some), minibar.

Park Hyatt Buenos Aires ★★★ This luxurious hotel opened in 2006 and comprises a modern tower connected to the Palacio Duhau, a former mansion. The spacious mansion rooms mix modern and classical details. Some tower rooms have breathtaking views of the Río de la Plata. Bathrooms in both buildings are enormous; suites have extra bathrooms for use during business meetings. The Oak Bar, masculine and gothic, with a fine selection of liquors, is one of the few bars in Buenos Aires with smoke filtration. The Gioia restaurant serves modern Italian cuisine, and the Duhau offers international food with French touches. The layered garden, with lily pools, is a pleasant place for a drink. A wine-and-cheese bar stocks about 45 artisanal cheeses produced in Argentina, along with wine to enhance the selection. The spa, called Ahin, offers a range of treatments

ab

from $120 (£85) to $400 (£284). Breakfast, a huge multicourse spread, runs about $20 (£14) per day.

Av. Alvear 1661 (at Montevideo), 1014 Buenos Aires. ✆ **11/5171-1234.** Fax 11/5171-1235. www.buenos aires.park.hyatt.com. 165 units. $575 (£408) double; from $756 (£537) suite; from $1,119 (£794) select suites. AE, DC, MC, V. Valet parking $24 (£17). No metro access. **Amenities:** 3 restaurants; bar; concierge; health club and spa; Internet in business center; heated indoor pool; room service. *In room:* A/C, TV/VCR, CD player, hair dryer, minibar, Wi-Fi ($12/£8.50 per day).

EXPENSIVE

Hotel Emperador ★★   Located on Avenida Libertador, this Spanish-owned hotel is on the border of Retiro and Recoleta—a few blocks from the Patio Bullrich shopping center, near the train station complex. The theme here is "Empire with a modern update." Behind the main restaurant, the lobby opens onto a large overgrown patio with a gazebo and outdoor seating. The English-hunting-lodge-style lobby bar is a place for ladies who lunch and businesspeople who gather for informal discussions. The imperial theme continues in the spacious rooms. Royal-blue carpets with wreath patterns, and elegant furnishings with rich veneers, brass fittings, and gold velvet upholstery await the visitor. The suites, with their walls, multiple doors and entrances, and extra sinks, are ideal for doing business without infringing on the sleeping quarters. All bathrooms are oversize, with cream-and-green marble. Wheelchair-accessible rooms are available. An indoor pool has modern columns that give the impression of a Roman bath.

Av. del Libertador 420 (at Suipacha), 1001 Buenos Aires. ✆ **11/4131-4000.** Fax 11/4131-3900. www. hotel-emperador.com.ar. 265 units. $250 (£178) double; from $400 (£284) suite; $1,000 (£710) nuptial suite. Breakfast buffet $24 (£17). AE, DC, MC, V. Valet parking $20 (£14). Metro: Retiro. **Amenities:** Restaurant; bar; babysitting; concierge; exercise room; Internet in business center; indoor heated pool; room service; sauna. *In room:* A/C, TV, hair dryer, minibar, Wi-Fi ($12/£8.50 per day).

INEXPENSIVE

The Recoleta Hostel ★ (Finds)   This is a great inexpensive choice for young people who want to be in a beautiful neighborhood close to everything, but can't ordinarily afford such a location. Accommodations are simple, with 22 bunk bed–filled rooms for 8 to 12 people each. Two double rooms with private bathrooms can also be rented, but they have bunk beds, too, so lovers wishing to cozy up will have to get really cozy. Rooms are simple, with bare floors and walls, beds, and a small wooden desk in the private rooms. The decor is reminiscent of a convent. Public areas have high ceilings, and there is a shared public kitchen, a TV room, laundry service, lockers, and an outdoor patio. The hostel is also a Wi-Fi hotspot.

Libertad 1216 (at Juncal), 1012 Buenos Aires. ✆ **11/4812-4419.** Fax 11/4815-6622. www.trhostel.com. ar. 75 bed spaces, including 4 in 2 bedrooms with bathroom. From $11 (£7.80) per bed; $45 (£32) per private room. Rates include continental breakfast. No credit cards. Metro: Lavalle. **Amenities:** Concierge; Wi-Fi (free); *In room:* Hair dryer.

6 BARRIO NORTE

Barrio Norte borders Recoleta, though some people—especially real estate agents and many hotels—say it is actually a part of it. However, the area is distinctly busier and more commercialized, with more of a middle-class feel than in the upscale Recoleta. Its main boulevard is busy Santa Fe, full of shops, restaurants, and cafes. This can make staying in

Barrio Norte noisier than Recoleta, but still less so than the Microcentro. You also have easy metro access in this neighborhood.

For a map of the hotels listed in the section, see the "Where to Stay in Central Buenos Aires" map on p. 62.

MODERATE

Art Hotel ★ This was one of the first of the boutique hotels to open in Buenos Aires in 2004 during the tourism boom, and the owners have maintained the historical nature of the property. You'll find high ceilings, rich wood details on the doors, and even "Viva Perón" etched into the mirrors of the 100-year-old elevator. Some rooms are on the small side, but all have such interesting details as polished concrete floors with embedded ornamental tiles and comfy linens in neutral tones and wicker accents on the furniture. Bathrooms are on the small side, with showers only. The public areas on each floor are spacious. A rooftop solarium also has great views, and two guest rooms are located here as well. There are no rooms for people with disabilities, and the extensive stairs throughout make it difficult for anyone with limited mobility. The hotel describes itself as being in Recoleta, but it is truly in Barrio Norte.

Azcuénaga 1268, btw. Beruti and Arenales. 1115 Buenos Aires. © **11/4821-4744.** Fax 11/4821-6248. www.arthotel.com.ar. 36 units. $95–$195 (£67–£138) double. Rates include breakfast buffet. AE, MC, V. Parking (offsite) $12 (£8.50). Metro: Puerreydon. **Amenities:** Babysitting; concierge; Internet in business center; room service. *In room:* A/C, TV, hair dryer, minibar, Wi-Fi.

7 CONGRESO

Congreso is a historic district that surrounds the building Congreso, at the western terminus of the Avenida de Mayo. In addition to Congreso, the neighborhood contains other grand and imposing buildings, some almost imperial in scale and design. While there is a lot to see in the area, it can seem desolate and seedy at night, especially in the Congreso Plaza, which serves as a hangout for the homeless. The intense government police presence in the area, however, means that, in spite of appearances, it is relatively safe at night. With increased tourism to Buenos Aires, more hotels and other establishments are beginning to move into this neighborhood.

For a map of the hotels listed in the section, see the "Where to Stay in Central Buenos Aires" map on p. 62.

MODERATE

The Golden Tulip Savoy The Dutch-owned Golden Tulip, opened in the faded but historic hotel Savoy, has a distinctly European clientele. The original hotel opened in 1910, with largely Art Nouveau elements, as part of the glamorous rebuilding of Avenida Callao following the opening of the nearby Congreso. The company has renovated the hotel completely, maintaining original details, such as gorgeous molding and stained-glass decoration. The rooms are very large, in keeping with the old grandeur, and each is entered through its own antechamber. Rooms facing the street have tiny French balconies, but half of the hotel faces an interior courtyard with no views. All rooms are soundproofed. Suite bathrooms include a whirlpool bathtub. The hotel's Madrigales restaurant serves Argentine cuisine with interesting Latin American fusion elements. There is no pool, sauna, or gym here, but the hotel provides access to a nearby establishment.

Av. Callao 181 (at Juan Perón), 1022 Buenos Aires. ✆ **11/4370-8000.** Fax 11/4370-8020. www.gtsavoy hotel.com.ar. 174 units. From $145 (£103) double; $242 (£172) suite. Rates include breakfast buffet. AE, DC, MC, V. Parking $12 (£8.50). Metro: Congreso. **Amenities:** Restaurant; bar; concierge; access to nearby health club; Internet in business center; room service. *In room:* A/C, TV, hair dryer, minibar, Wi-Fi.

Hotel Ibis ★★ Ⓚids Ⓥalue   The Ibis is well located on Plaza Congreso, and all rooms have street views, many facing the plaza. Double-glazed windows lock out noise in this busy location. Rooms are a good size for this price range, all with an identical color pattern. They are all doubles, but an extra bed is available, for a few dollars more. Some rooms also connect, which is an ideal option for a family or group of friends. Three rooms can accommodate travelers with disabilities. Bathrooms are bright and clean, all with showers and no tubs. Safes and hair dryers are available at the concierge. The basic Argentine restaurant is an incredible value at about $10 (£7.10) for a prix-fixe dinner. Breakfast is not included in the rates, but is about $5 (£3.55). The hotel is naturally popular with French tourists, and most of the staff speaks Spanish, English, and French. You'll find lots of college-age backpackers here.

Hipólito Yrigoyen 1592 (at Ceballos), 1089 Buenos Aires. ✆ **11/5300-5555.** Fax 11/5300-5566. www. ibishotel.com. 147 units. From $62 (£44) double. AE, DC, MC, V. Parking $10 (£7.10) in a nearby garage. Metro: Congreso. **Amenities:** Restaurant; bar; concierge; Internet in business center. *In room:* A/C, TV, Wi-Fi.

8 TRIBUNALES

Tribunales encompasses the area surrounding the Supreme Court building and Teatro Colón, which borders the Corrientes theater district. It's full of government and other important buildings and is close to the Microcentro's shopping, but is far less noisy. Its most important feature is Plaza Lavalle.

For a map of the hotels listed in the section, see the "Where to Stay in Central Buenos Aires" map on p. 62.

MODERATE

Dazzler Hotel Libertad ★   This hotel is virtually unknown to the North American market, with the majority of its clients from South America. All staff members speak English. It is conveniently situated overlooking Plaza Libertad, set against Avenida 9 de Julio, a few blocks from Teatro Colón (p. 136). Front rooms have excellent views, but can be noisy, as there is no double glazing on the windows. All rooms are on the small side, but they're exceptionally bright, with floor-to-ceiling windows, making rooms feel larger. Ask about connecting rooms if you're traveling in a group or with family. Large closets and a combination desk and vanity space round out the rooms. Lights and air-conditioning are controlled by a single panel over the bed. The lobby has a staircase leading to the large and bright restaurant, where breakfast is served.

Libertad 902 (at Paraguay), 1012 Buenos Aires. ✆ **11/4816-5005.** www.dazzlerhotel.com. 88 units. From $115 (£82) double. Rates include breakfast buffet. AE, MC, V. Valet parking $18 (£13). Metro: Tribunales. **Amenities:** Restaurant; bar; concierge; small health club; Internet in business center; room service; sauna. *In room:* A/C, TV, hair dryer, minibar.

Palermo Viejo is divided into two sections: Palermo Soho and Palermo Hollywood, with Juan B. Justo as the dividing line. This is the trendiest part of Buenos Aires right now, yet it still retains a small-neighborhood feel with its old low-rise houses, cobblestone streets, and oak-tree-shaded sidewalks. Subway access is not the best in this area, however. Being trendy, it's also where the newest and most fashionable boutique hotels are located. Some of those mentioned here opened in just the past couple of years. For the young and chic, this area can be a great place to stay.

For a map of the hotels listed in the section, see the "Where to Stay & Dine in Palermo" map on p. 110.

EXPENSIVE

Bo-Bo ★★ Bo-Bo is short for Bourgeois Bohemian, whatever that contradictory term is supposed to mean. This little boutique hotel is high on charm and feels like a step back in time. The rooms have mostly modern touches, though, with bold colors and white surfaces. Some have terraces, some have carpeted floors, and others have polished wood. Each room has a different theme and name, such as the Angelina Room, with a Jacuzzi and balcony. One room is also available for travelers with disabilities and, though this is a turn-of-the-20th-century building, an elevator has been added for the convenience of all. Children under 14 are generally not allowed. The restaurant serves excellent cuisine, overseen by Chef Adrian Sarkassian. You might also just want to come by for drinks at the bar, an enjoyable place to meet before going to dinner in other restaurants in Palermo.

Guatemala 4882, btw. Borges and Thames. 1425 Buenos Aires. ☏ **11/4774-0505.** Fax 11/4774-9600. www.bobohotel.com. 7 units. From $200–$236 (£142–£168) double. Rates include buffet breakfast. AE, MC, V. Free parking. Metro: Plaza Italia. **Amenities:** Restaurant; bar; bikes; concierge; Internet (in lobby); room service. *In room:* A/C, TV, hair dryer, Wi-Fi.

The Glu ★ Taking its name from the family that owns it—the Glusmans—this is one of the newest boutique hotels in Palermo, opened at the end of 2008. The hotel is very simple in its decor, with a masculine mix of neutral and dark tones, hardwood floors, and then a splash of color via a floral wall pattern in each room. Rooms, while not technically suites, are oversize, and all have king-size beds, balconies, microwaves, and L'Occitane toiletries. What makes the hotel special, in addition to service, is how quiet it is compared to other boutique hotels in Palermo Soho, which strive to be social centers. Walls and windows are specially insulated, so when you're done with having your fun on the town, the Glu will be a quiet respite, even if near plenty of the action. The fantastic rooftop lounge has a Jacuzzi and swimming pool.

Godoy Cruz 1733, btw. Gorriti and Honduras, 1414 Buenos Aires. ☏ **800/405-3072** or 11/4831-4646. Fax 11/4831-4646. www.thegluhotel.com. 11 units. From $242 (£172) double. Rates include breakfast buffet. AE, MC, V. No parking. Metro: Palermo. **Amenities:** Concierge; health club and spa; Internet in business center; Jacuzzi; outdoor pool; room service. *In room:* A/C, TV/DVD, hair dryer, minibar, Wi-Fi.

Home ★★★ This is among the nicest of the boutique hotels in Palermo, due to the young couple that built the place, Argentine Patricia O'Shea and her British husband Tom Rixton. She grew up a few blocks from here and he is a former DJ, giving the place both anchor and soul. On Fridays, there's a DJ in the lobby bar, and it's a great place for drinks, even if you're not staying here. There's a real backyard, with grass and an outdoor heated pool, with an ironic suburban edge. Rooms are high design with blonde woods and white linens—it has a modern feel, but with '60s mod accents. Bathrooms are large and some suites come with Jacuzzis and have kitchens. One room is available for travelers with disabilities. A two-level apartment is attached to the property with its own entrance. Home has an excellent spa sunken into its courtyard, open to the public, with day-rate packages running about $200 (£142), which includes breakfast and lunch.

Honduras 5860, btw. Carranza and Ravignani. 1414 Buenos Aires. ⓒ **11/4778-1008.** Fax 11/4779-1006. www.homebuenosaires.com. 21 units. From $143 (£102) double; from $460 (£327) suite; $330 (£234) apt. Rates include breakfast buffet. AE, MC, V. Free parking. Metro: Palermo. **Amenities:** Restaurant; bar; babysitting; bikes; concierge; health club and spa; heated outdoor pool; Internet in business center; room service. *In room:* A/C, TV, hair dryer, kitchen (in some), minibar.

Soho All Suites ★★★   Chic is the word that sprang to mind when I first stepped into this new boutique hotel. The lobby is modern and clean and the staff in all-black uniforms is immediately attentive. The fashionable lobby bar and its adjacent patio lounge are often the sites of parties and special events for Buenos Aires's young media crowd. The majority of the hotel's clients fall within the age range of 25 to 45 years old. All rooms have kitchens and complete apartment accessories, from dishes and microwaves to irons. Guest rooms are different sizes, with extra bedrooms or terraces, so ask when booking. They all have a clean, modern feeling, with their large leather sofas, bar stools, and high design. All bathrooms have tub/shower combinations. There is a rooftop solarium with a wonderful view of the neighborhood.

Honduras 4762, btw. Malabia and Armenia, 1414 Buenos Aires. ⓒ **11/4832-3000.** www.sohoallsuites. com.ar. 21 units. From $175–$411 (£124–£292). Rates include breakfast buffet. AE, DC, MC, V. Parking $8 (£5.70). Metro: Palermo, Ortiz. **Amenities:** Restaurant; bar; concierge; room service; spa. *In room:* A/C, TV, hair dryer, kitchenette, minibar, Wi-Fi.

MODERATE

Five Cool Rooms ★   The name of this hotel is somewhat misleading—there are actually 16 rooms—with the five referring to the number of owners. It's a little hard to find—look for the small metal sign saying FIVE COOL ROOMS, and be mindful of the address. There are no restaurants or bars inside, but breakfast is served on the delightful rooftop terrace. The terrace also has an *asado* and the owners periodically barbecue for hotel patrons. Their lobby—called the living room—has modern leather sofas, artwork on walls, and leads to an outdoor patio garden with tiny patches of bamboo. Overall, for a small hotel, there is a lot of public space. The rooms can be on the small side, but are filled with light, making them feel larger. Bohemian chic characterizes the design throughout this place. Bathrooms have basin bowl sinks, and some rooms have Jacuzzis. The hotel lacks a pool or gym. One room is available for travelers with disabilities.

Honduras 4742, btw. Malabia and Armenia, 1414 Buenos Aires. ⓒ **11/5235-5555.** Fax 11/4833-3600. www.fivebuenosaires.com. 126 units. From $120 (£85) double. Rates include breakfast buffet. AE, MC, V. Parking (offsite) $12 (£8.50). Metro: Palermo, Ortiz. **Amenities:** Bikes; children's programs; concierge; Internet (in lobby); room service. *In room:* A/C, TV, hair dryer, minibar, Wi-Fi (free).

La Otra Orilla ★★   The name of this tranquil B&B comes from a Julio Cortazar story and means "The Other Side" or "The Other Bank" of a river. The neoclassical building itself dates from 1937, but opened as a hotel in 2003. There is a shady, vine-covered, flower-filled back garden that serves as a wonderful retreat when you've returned from exploring the city. All of the guest rooms—large for a B&B—have different styles, some French Provincial, some country rustic, others Shaker-style. All are full of light, and most have balconies. If you want to be near Palermo's shopping, convenient to the center, and also have a tranquil end of your day, this is a great place to stay.

Julian Alvarez 1779, btw. El Salvador and Costa Rica, 1414 Buenos Aires. ✆ **11/4867-4070** or 11/4863-7426. www.otraorilla.com.ar. 7 units, 2 with shared bathroom. From $40–$169 (£28–£120). Rates include breakfast buffet. AE, MC, V. No parking. Metro: Scalabrini Ortiz. **Amenities:** Concierge; Internet in business center. In room: A/C, TV, Wi-Fi.

INEXPENSIVE

Casa Jardín ★   Owner Nerina Sturgeon wanted to create an "artist hostel" in the heart of Palermo Viejo, and she has succeeded in doing so. Built into an old house, this intimate hostel boasts high ceilings—all the better to display Nerina's paintings, as well as the artwork of others, throughout the space. The gallery atmosphere is furthered by exhibitions held here periodically, complete with rooftop parties on the garden-wrapped terrace overlooking the street. There are 15 bed spaces, nine in shared spaces, and six in three private rooms. All rooms share public bathrooms and have lockers. As a woman-owned-and-run business, it's an ideal location for young women travelers. Take note that, while the atmosphere is the same, the hostel has moved across the street from its old location into an equally charming house. No breakfast is served, but a 24-hour cafe sits across the street, and there is a shared kitchen. The living room has an Internet station with Wi-Fi capability.

Charcas 4422 (at Scalabrini Ortiz), 1425 Buenos Aires. ✆ **11/4774-8783** or 11/15-4028-9063. Fax 11/4891-9208. www.casajardinba.com.ar. 15 bed spaces, 3 private rooms. $15 (£11) per bed; $20 (£14) single room; $33 (£23) double room; $50 (£36) triple room. No credit cards. Metro: Plaza Italia. **Amenities:** Concierge. In room: Wi-Fi.

10 ABASTO

The Abasto neighborhood lies outside of the main center of the city, along Corrientes, but beyond the theater district. In general, it's a working- and middle-class area—busy, but not distinct architecturally. Historically, it's associated with singer Carlos Gardel, the country's greatest tango star of the 1920s and 1930s. The area, along with the bordering Once neighborhood, is also the historic home of Buenos Aires's Jewish communities, though most have long since moved to the suburbs. This neighborhood is anchored by the enormous Abasto Shopping Center, which is home to many things of interest to families with kids, such as the Museo de los Niños (p. 145).

For a map of the hotels listed in the section, see the "Abasto & Once" map on p. 119.

EXPENSIVE

Abasto Plaza Hotel ★   This hotel is a block away from the Abasto Shopping Center and Esquina Carlos Gardel—both locations built over sites related to the tango crooner. The hotel takes this to heart, with a unique tango shop, free tango lessons and shows on Thursday evenings, and a daily tango show in the restaurant. The rooms are a good size, with rich dark woods and deep-red carpets, though so-called thematic suites take their special decor from tango. Superior rooms come with whirlpool bathtubs. The restaurant, Volver, named for a Gardel song, is brilliantly sunny and decorated in a funky design.

The small heated outdoor pool sits on the rooftop with access through a small gym. One wheelchair-accessible room is available. For Jewish travelers, this is the closest full-service hotel to Once and Abasto's historic Jewish sites.

Av. Corrientes 3190 (at Anchorena), 1193 Buenos Aires. ℂ **11/6311-4465.** Fax 11/6311-4465. www. abastoplaza.com. 126 units. From $157 (£111) double; from $266 (£189) suite. Rates include breakfast buffet. AE, DC, MC, V. Parking $12 (£8.50). Metro: Carlos Gardel. **Amenities:** Restaurant; bar; concierge; small health club; free Internet in business center; heated outdoor pool; room service. *In room:* A/C, TV, hair dryer, minibar, Wi-Fi.

11 APARTMENT SERVICES IN BUENOS AIRES

Hotels are not for everyone, and maybe you want a place where you can come and go as you please. Or you might want more space to throw parties while in town. Maybe you're independent-minded and want a better idea of what it feels like to live in Buenos Aires as a local, especially if you're thinking of making the big leap and living here like tens of thousands of expats. Apartments allow you the opportunity do all of that. Most apartment services provide apartments with Internet access, in great locations throughout Buenos Aires, though the majority are located in the residential high-rises of Barrio Norte and Recoleta. Most apartment-rental companies also provide maid service. Contact each company directly for exact terms, prices, payments, and services. A few words of caution are in mind. Recently, crime targeting foreign apartment renters has gone up, especially coming from the airport, as most apartment-rental companies demand a huge amount of cash up front. If you can work out payment by credit card, PayPal, or in installments, it is a good idea. Also, keep in mind that hotels have concierges and guards, and many buildings, unless they have a doorman, do not, so there is a certain amount of vulnerability to renting an apartment. That said, apartment living is a great window into living like a local.

BA Apartments A full-service rental company with apartments in many neighborhoods throughout Buenos Aires. Paraguay 2035, btw. Ayacucho and Junin. ℂ **11/4864-8084.** www.baapartments.com.ar.

Best Rentals Buenos Aires This service is run out of the El Firulette youth hostel in downtown Buenos Aires. It offers inexpensive long-term and short-term rentals, many with an eye to the budget-conscious. Some of their prices are significantly lower than those offered by other companies, but the sizes of apartments will differ. Maipu 208, at Peron. ℂ **11/5031 2215** in Buenos Aires, and 646/502-8605 in the U.S. and Canada. www.best rentalsba.com.

ByT Argentina This apartment service has apartments all over Buenos Aires. It offers a large selection within Palermo Viejo, one of the hottest sections of Buenos Aires. ℂ **11/4821-6057.** www.bytargentina.com.

Friendly Apartments This apartment service concentrates on Barrio Norte, catering to gay North Americans and Europeans, hence the name Friendly—indicating gay-friendly. Facundo Yebne, the manager of the company, describes it as "short-term rentals with hotel services." It offers concierge and almost-daily maid service in buildings where it owns a lot of apartments. The company also represents foreigners purchasing apartments as investments. **Temporary Apartments,** listed below, is the same company, but

Tips **Expat Living in Buenos Aires**

Apartments are a great way to see how locals live, but if you want to live long-term cheaply, check out ads in **Clarin, El Pais, Pagina 12,** and other local news-papers. As for Americans living in Buenos Aires, the estimates range wildly from 25,000 to 50,000, along with a nearly equal number of Brits, and a smaller num-ber of Canadians, Australians, and New Zealanders. There are also some great websites out there for connecting with other expats and finding out about local parties. Here are just a few of them: www.baexpats.org, www.expat-argentina.blogspot.com, www.discoverbuenosaires.com, www.yanquimike.blogspot.com, www.everydayinbuenosaires.com, www.movingtoargentina.typepad.com, www.gaysawayinba.multiply.com, and www.expat-connection.com, run by Martin Frankel of the Sugar bar. Technically, the vast majority of expats live here illegally on tourist visas, but as long as you leave the country every 3 months, even with a day trip to Colonia, Uruguay, no one seems to mind. If you plan to set up a busi-ness or buy property, it's a good idea to check with your local Argentine Embassy or Consulate for proper paperwork.

their nongay face. Callao 1234, at Juncal in the Concord Building. © **11/4816-9056,** 11/4811-0279 in Buenos Aires, or 619/841-0054 in the U.S. and Canada. www.friendlyapartments.com.

Loft & Arte   This is a boutique apartment hotel complex just off Avenida de Mayo. Apartments range from tiny efficiencies to double-level apartments. Many have balconies and washing machines, as well as other amenities. As a hotel/apartment combo, this complex provides breakfast each day, cleaning service, and a concierge for your questions and for added general safety. There is also a pleasant central patio. Hipólito Yrigoyen 1194, btw. Cerrito (Nueve de Julio) and Libertad © **11/4381-3229** or 11/4115-1770. www.loftyarte.com.ar.

Temporary Apartments   The mainstream face of Friendly Apartments, the build-ings, offerings, and prices are the same. Callao 1234, at Juncal in the Concord Building. © **11/4816-9056,** 11/4811-0279 in Buenos Aires, or 619/841-0054 in the U.S. and Canada. www.temporaryapartments.com.ar.

Where to Dine

Buenos Aires offers world-class dining and cuisine at a variety of Argentine and international restaurants. With the collapse of the peso, fine dining in Buenos Aires now is also marvelously inexpensive.

Nothing matches the meat from the Pampas grass–fed Argentine cows, and that meat is the focus of the dining experience throughout the city, from the humblest *parrilla* (grill) to the finest business-class restaurant. Empanadas, dough pockets filled with minced meat and other ingredients, are also an Argentine staple, sold almost everywhere.

In this chapter, I'll go over what you can expect to find in Buenos Aires's different restaurants and where certain types of food are found within the city's various neighborhoods.

Buenos Aires's most fashionable places for eating out are all found in Palermo. Palermo Hollywood and Palermo Soho, the two divisions of this neighborhood, are full of trendy hot spots combining fine dining with a bohemian atmosphere in small, renovated, turn-of-the-20th-century houses. These restaurants have attracted some of the city's top chefs, many of whom have received their training in France and Spain. Some of the most exquisite and interesting cuisine in the city is available in the restaurants in Palermo Viejo. The only issue in this trendy area is that many places come and go quite quickly. Both Palermo Viejo and Las Cañitas, another division of Palermo well known for dining and nightlife, are near the D subway line, but the best restaurants are often a long walk from metro stations. That and the 11pm closing of the subway stations means you are best off with cabs to and from these restaurants.

Puerto Madero's docks are lined with more top restaurants, along with a mix of chains and hit-or-miss spots. The Microcentro and Recoleta offer many outstanding restaurants and cafes, some of which have been on the map for decades. Buenos Aires's cafe life, where friends meet over coffee, is as sacred a ritual to Porteños as it is to Parisians. Excellent places to enjoy a *cafe con leche* (coffee with milk) include **La Biela** in Recoleta, across from the world-famous Recoleta Cemetery, and **Café Tortoni,** one of the city's most beautiful and traditional cafes, on Avenida de Mayo close to Plaza de Mayo. These are two places you should not miss if you want to experience Buenos Aires's cafe life.

Porteños eat breakfast until 10am, lunch between noon and 4pm, and dinner late—usually after 9pm, though some restaurants open as early as 7pm. If you are an early bird diner in the North American and British style, wanting to eat from 5pm on, look for restaurants in my listings that remain open between lunch and dinner. If you can make a reservation, I highly recommend doing so. If you do not want to commit, go to a restaurant at the typical 8pm opening time, when you will almost always arrive to a nearly empty restaurant. However, as the clock hits 9pm, virtually every table at the best restaurants will suddenly become completely filled.

Executive lunch menus (usually fixed-price three-course meals) are served at many restaurants beginning at noon, but most dinner menus are a la carte. There is sometimes a small "cover" or "service" charge for bread and other items placed at the table. In restaurants that serve pasta, the pasta and its sauce are sometimes priced separately. Standard tipping is 10% in Buenos Aires, more for exceptional

Bares y Cafés Notables

If you want to dine in an atmosphere recalling the glory days of Buenos Aires's past, choose one from the list of nearly 40 *bares y cafés notables,* historic restaurants, cafes, and bars that have been specially protected by a law stating that their interiors cannot be changed. Known as Law No. 35, this special protection granted by the city of Buenos Aires was passed in 1998 and updated in 2002. I list many of these special establishments in this chapter, including Café Tortoni, La Biela, and Bar El Federal. Naturally, based on age, these *notables* cluster in Monserrat, Congreso, La Boca, and San Telmo, the city's oldest areas. Ask the tourism office for the map *Bares y Cafés Notables de Buenos Aires,* which lists them all and includes photographs of their interiors. If you really like the atmosphere in these unique spots, you can bring a part of them home with you, as they all sell a coffee-table book with photos from these wonderful places.

service. When paying by credit card, you will often be expected to leave the *propina* (tip) in cash, since many credit card receipts don't provide a place to include the tip. Many restaurants close between lunch and dinner, and some close on Sunday or Monday completely, or only serve dinner. In late December, January, and February, many restaurants have limited hours and service, or close for vacations, as this is the traditional time when Porteños flee the city to the beach resorts. It's a good idea to call ahead of time during these months to make sure you don't make a trip out, only to become disappointed by a closed and locked door.

Though Buenos Aires is a very cosmopolitan city, it is surprisingly not a very ethnically diverse place, at least on the surface. However, the influences of Middle Eastern and Jewish immigrants who came to this city in the wake of World War I are reflected in a few areas. Middle Eastern restaurants are clustered in Palermo Viejo, near the *subte* station Scalabrini Ortiz, and also on Calle Armenia. Because Once and Abasto were the traditional neighborhoods for Jewish immigrants, you'll find many kosher restaurants along Calle Tucumán in particular. And, because many Buenos Aires Jews are Sephardic or of Middle

Eastern descent, you'll also find Arabic influences here.

As there are almost as many Italian last names as Spanish ones, it's hard to call those of Italian descent a specific ethnic group within Argentina as you can in the United States, Canada, or Australia. As such, Buenos Aires's Italian food is Argentine food in essence, and pastas and other Italian dishes are usually folded in with traditional Argentine offerings such as grilled beef. La Boca is Buenos Aires's historic Little Italy, the place where Italian immigrants first settled in the late 19th and early 20th centuries. The atmosphere in these restaurants plays on this past and caters to tourists, but this is not where the city's best Italian food is served. Instead, it is usually found in old, simple *parrillas* that have operated for decades and include pastas on their menus. Throughout this chapter, most of these are in the "Inexpensive" or "Moderate" categories all over the city. Though on the pricey side, check out **Piegari** in Recoleta's La Recova restaurant area, which has some of the best northern Italian cuisine in the city.

Asians only make up a tiny portion of Buenos Aires's population and, as a whole, have had little effect on cuisine offerings. Still, in keeping with international trends,

(Tips) **Wine Tasting**

Part of what makes a meal in Buenos Aires so good is the fine wine selection, specially chosen to complement beef, chicken, fish, and other items on the menu. Most Argentine wine comes from the Mendoza district, bordering the Andean mountains. Malbecs make up most of the best, with cabernets, champagnes, and even grappas on the menus in the humblest restaurants. If you know nothing about wine, you may want to take a wine-tasting class, to make sense of the selections and suggestions offered by the waiter or sommelier. One of the city's best is run by the **Hotel Alvear's Cave de Vines,** which will run you about $50 (£36) per person. You'll get about an hour with a sommelier, who will explain the grape-growing process, the harvest, and how the wine is actually produced as you sample different wines and taste with various appetizers from different regions of Argentina. Like fine diamonds, wine is judged by color and clarity, and you'll learn what to look for in every glass, as well as how to pair wines with food. Other points include discerning taste and scent points, as well as how to hold a glass of wine without damaging its contents with your hand's own body heat.

you'll find sushi bars and other restaurants with Japanese and Chinese influences throughout Buenos Aires. All over the city, you will find sushi fast-food-chain restaurants as well. For Asian authenticity, I also point you to Belgrano's very tiny and little-known Chinatown district. Many Peruvian restaurants have opened up, such as **Ceviche,** which combine Japanese influences.

If you are looking through these listings and still cannot decide what you want to eat, three areas are so loaded with restaurants of all types, one after another, that you are bound to find something that pleases you. Puerto Madero's historic dock buildings are one such place, and it's a bonus that many of the restaurants here are a bargain. Calle Báez in the Las Cañitas area of Palermo is another such area and is also one of the most happening restaurant scenes in the whole city. Finally, restaurants and bars that serve food surround Plaza Serrano in Palermo Hollywood, with many a good choice for the young, funky, and bargain-minded. All of these areas also have plenty of nearby places for heading out for after-dinner drinks and dancing, so

you won't have to move all over the city to spend a night out.

If you still can't make up your mind and want some second opinions, check out **www.restaurant.com.ar.** It provides information in English and Spanish on restaurants in Buenos Aires and other major cities, and allows you to search by neighborhood as well as cuisine type. Also check out www.guiaoleo.com.ar. Though only in Spanish, it provides a similar excellent service. Finally, look to www.gastronomique.com.ar, which also provides a great overview of Argentine cuisine. For great bar/restaurant combos, many with exceptionally good prices, see section 3 of chapter 10.

Once in Buenos Aires, look for the **De Dios** map company's excellent restaurant map in bookstores everywhere, or order it ahead of time at www.dediosonline.com. Many Palermo Viejo restaurants are on a special Palermo Viejo dining map available at most of the restaurants listed in this neighborhood. Many other neighborhoods, such as San Telmo, also have similar maps.

I list exact prices for main courses and group restaurants into general price categories. One change from our last edition is that many restaurants have gone up significantly in price, jumping categories. However, it's all relative, as in many cases, prices overlap within categories, and sometimes a single menu item, such as lobster, might push an ordinarily "Inexpensive" restaurant into a "Very Expensive" category. In short, take a look at the specific prices, which are expressed in a range. With the current exchange rates, it is difficult to overspend on food in Argentina and you rarely go wrong anywhere you eat in this city. Inexpensive restaurants have main courses ranging from under $3 (£2.15) to about $8 (£5.70). Moderate restaurants have prices ranging from around $5 to $12 (£3.55–£8.50). Expensive restaurants have main courses at about $10 to $20 (£7.10–£14). Very Expensive restaurants range from about $15 to $50 or more (£11–£36). Remember that in all restaurants, lunch is usually cheaper, and that there may also be Executive or Tourist menus, which afford a very reasonably priced, three-course meal. Tips, drinks, desserts, other menu items, as well as table service and the unavoidable charge for bread and spreads, will add to your costs. Keep in mind also that, while English is becoming more and more prevalent in Buenos Aires, less expensive restaurants tend to have fewer English speakers on staff.

1 RESTAURANTS BY CUISINE

American
McDonald's Kosher ★★ (Abasto, $, p. 118)

Argentine
Barbería (La Boca, $$, p. 120)
Bar El Federal ★★ (San Telmo, $$, p. 99)
Bien Porteño ★ (Congreso, $, p. 107)
Cabaña las Lilas ★★★ (Puerto Madero, $$$, p. 89)
Café de la Ciudad (Microcentro, $$, p. 94)
Café Literario (Microcentro, $, p. 96)
Café Retiro ★★ (Microcentro, $, p. 96)
Café Tortoni ★★ (Microcentro, $, p. 97)
Campo Bravo ★★ (Palermo, $$, p. 113)
Clásica y Moderna ★★ (Barrio Norte, $$, p. 105)
Cluny ★★★ (Palermo, $$$, p. 109)
Confitería del Botánico (Palermo, $, p. 116)

El Galope ★ (Once, $$, p. 118)
El General ★★★ (Monserrat, $$, p. 97)
El Obrero ★★★ (La Boca, $, p. 120)
Gardel de Buenos Aires ★ (Abasto, $, p. 117)
Gran Victoria ★ (Plaza de Mayo area, $$, p. 88)
Inside Resto-Bar ★ (Congreso, $$, p. 105)
La Americana ★★ (Congreso, $, p. 107)
La Brigada ★ (San Telmo, $$, p. 100)
La Cabaña ★ (Recoleta, $$$$, p. 101)
La Cabrera ★★ (Palermo, $$$, p. 109)
La Chacra ★ (Microcentro, $$, p. 95)
La Clac ★ (Congreso, $$, p. 106)
La Coruña ★★ (San Telmo, $$, p. 100)
La Perla (La Boca, $, p. 120)
Las Choclas ★★ (Palermo, $, p. 116)
Las Nazarenas ★ (Microcentro, $$, p. 95)

Key to Abbreviations: $$$$ = Very Expensive $$$ = Expensive $$ = Moderate $ = Inexpensive

La Vieja Rotisería ★★ (San Telmo, $$, p. 100)

Meridiano 58 ★★ (Palermo, $$, p. 115)

Pappa Deus ★ (San Telmo, $$, p. 100)

Plaza Asturias ★★ (Congreso, $$, p. 106)

Plaza del Carmen (Congreso, $$, p. 106)

Richmond Cafe ★★ (Microcentro, $$, p. 96)

Rio Alba ★ (Palermo, $$$, p. 112)

T-Bone Bar & Grill ★ (Palermo, $$, p. 115)

36 Billares ★★ (Congreso, $$, p. 106)

Asian

Asia de Cuba ★ (Puerto Madero, $$, p. 89)

Empire ★ (Microcentro, $$, p. 94)

Sudestada ★ (Palermo, $$$, p. 112)

Tandoor ★ (Barrio Norte, $$, p. 105)

Cafe/Confitería

Bar El Federal ★★ (San Telmo, $$, p. 99)

Bien Porteño ★ (Congreso, $, p. 107)

Café de la Ciudad (Microcentro, $$, p. 94)

Café de Madres de Plaza de Mayo ★ ★ (Congreso, $, p. 107)

Café Literario (Microcentro, $, p. 96)

Café Retiro ★★ (Microcentro, $, p. 96)

Café Tortoni ★★★ (Microcentro, $, p. 97)

Café Victoria ★ (Recoleta, $$, p. 103)

Confitería del Botánico (Palermo, $, p. 116)

Gran Victoria ★ (Plaza de Mayo area, $$, p. 88)

Il Gran Caffe ★ (Microcentro, $$, p. 94)

La Biela ★★★ (Recoleta, $, p. 104)

La Coruña ★★ (San Telmo, $$, p. 100)

La Moncloa ★ (Congreso, $, p. 108)

La Perla (La Boca, $, p. 120)

Malouva (Palermo, $, p. 116)

Maru Botana ★ (Recoleta, $, p. 104)

Petit Paris Café ★ (Microcentro, $, p. 97)

Plaza del Carmen (Congreso, $$, p. 106)

Richmond Cafe ★★ (Microcentro, $$, p. 96)

Chilean

Los Chilenos ★ (Microcentro, $$, p. 95)

Chinese

Buddha BA ★ (Belgrano, $$$, p. 121)

French

Brasserie Petanque ★★ (San Telmo, $$$, p. 98)

La Bourgogne ★★★ (Recoleta, $$$$, p. 101)

Le Sud ★★ (Microcentro, $$$, p. 93)

Ligure ★★ (Microcentro, $$, p. 95)

Te Mataré Ramírez ★★★ (Palermo, $$$, p. 133)

Indian

Tandoor ★★ (Barrio Norte, $$, p. 105)

International

Bar Uriarte ★★★ (Palermo, $$$, p. 108)

Bien Porteño ★ (Congreso, $, p. 107)

Casa Cruz ★★ (Palermo, $$$$, p. 108)

Clark's ★ (Recoleta, $, p. 103)

Cluny ★★★ (Palermo, $$$, p. 109)

Inside Resto-Bar ★ (Congreso, $$, p. 105)

Limbo Club ★ (Palermo, $$, p. 114)

Lola ★ (Recoleta, $$$, p. 102)

Mamá Jacinta ★★ (Once, $$, p. 118)

Maru Botana ★ (Recoleta, $, p. 104)

Meridiano 58 ★★ (Palermo, $$, p. 115)

Milion ★★ (Barrio Norte, $$$, p. 104)

Mute (Palermo, $$$, p. 112)

Novecento ★★★ (Palermo, $$, p. 115)

Pappa Deus ★ (San Telmo, $$, p. 100)

Plaza Grill ★★ (Microcentro, $$$, p. 93)

Prologo ★ (Palermo, $, p. 116)

Puerto Cristal ★ (Puerto Madero, $$, p. 92)

647 Club ★★ (San Telmo, $$$, p. 99)

T-Bone Bar & Grill ★ (Palermo, $$, p. 115)

Te Mataré Ramírez ★★★ (Palermo, $$$, p. 113)

Italian

Barbería (La Boca, $$, p. 120)

Bar Uriarte ★★★ (Palermo, $$$, p. 108)

Broccolino ★ (Microcentro, $$, p. 94)

Casa Cruz ★★ (Palermo, $$$$, p. 108)

El Obrero ★★★ (La Boca, $, p. 120)

Filo ★ (Microcentro, $, p. 97)

Gardel de Buenos Aires ★ (Abasto, $, p. 117)

Il Fiume (Puerto Madero, $$$, p. 89)

Il Gran Caffe ★ (Microcentro, $$, p. 94)

La Americana ★★ (Congreso, $, p. 107)

La Baita ★★ (Palermo, $$$, p. 109)

La Vieja Rotisería ★★ (San Telmo, $$, p. 100)

Ligure ★★ (Microcentro, $$, p. 95)

Mamá Jacinta ★★ (Once, $$, p. 118)

Piegari ★★ (Recoleta, $$$$, p. 102)

Plaza Asturias ★★ (Congreso, $$, p. 106)

Sorrento del Puerto ★★ (Puerto Madero, $$$, p. 92)

Sottovoce ★★ (Puerto Madero, $$$, p. 92)

Japanese

Asia de Cuba ★ (Puerto Madero, $$, p. 89)

Ceviche ★ (Palermo, $$$, p. 109)

Kandi (Palermo, $$, p. 114)

Morizono ★ (Microcentro, $$, p. 95)

Sushi Club (Palermo, $, p. 117)

Kosher

El Galope ★ (Once, $$, p. 118)

Mamá Jacinta ★★ (Once, $$, p. 118)

McDonald's Kosher ★★ (Abasto, $, p. 118)

Mediterranean

Bio ★★ (Palermo, $$, p. 113)

De Olivas i Lustres ★★ (Palermo, $$, p. 113)

Le Mistral ★★ (Recoleta, $$$, p. 102)

Le Sud ★★ (Microcentro, $$$, p. 93)

Restaurante y Bar Mediterráneo ★★ (Monserrat, $$, p. 98)

647 Club ★★ (San Telmo, $$$, p. 99)

Mexican

Lupita ★★ (Palermo, $$, p. 115)

Middle Eastern

El Galope ★ (Once, $$, p. 118)

Garbis ★★ (Palermo, $$, p. 114)

Mamá Jacinta ★★ (Once, $$, p. 118)

Viejo Agump ★ (Palermo, $, p. 117)

Parrilla

Campo Bravo ★★ (Palermo, $$, p. 113)

Desnivel ★ (San Telmo, $$, p. 99)

El Estanciero ★ (Palermo, $$, p. 114)

El Galope ★ (Once, $$, p. 118)

El Mirasol ★★ (Recoleta, $$, p. 103)

El Obrero ★★★ (La Boca, $, p. 120)

Juana M ★★ (Recoleta, $$, p. 103)
La Bisteca ★★ (Puerto Madero, $$, p. 92)
La Brigada ★ (San Telmo, $$, p. 100)
La Cabaña ★ (Recoleta, $$$$, p. 101)
La Cabrera ★★ (Palermo, $$$, p. 109)
La Chacra ★ (Microcentro, $$, p. 95)
La Clac ★ (Congreso, $$, p. 106)
Las Choclas ★★ (Palermo, $, p. 116)
La Vieja Rotisería ★★ (San Telmo, $$, p. 100)
Mamá Jacinta ★★ (Once, $$, p. 118)
Rio Alba ★ (Palermo, $$$, p. 112)
T-Bone Bar & Grill ★ (Palermo, $$, p. 115)

Peruvian
Ceviche ★ (Palermo, $$$, p. 109)

Pizza
Filo ★ (Microcentro, $, p. 97)
Prologo ★ (Palermo, $, p. 116)

Scandinavian
Olsen ★★ (Palermo, $$$, p. 112)

Seafood
Ceviche ★ (Palermo, $$$, p. 109)
Dora ★★ (Microcentro, $$$, p. 93)

Kandi (Palermo, $$, p. 114)
Los Chilenos ★ (Microcentro, $$, p. 95)
Olsen ★★ (Palermo, $$$, p. 112)
Puerto Cristal ★ (Puerto Madero, $$, p. 92)

Spanish
Dora ★★ (Microcentro, $$$, p. 93)
La Tasca de Plaza Mayor ★★ (Recoleta, $$$, p. 102)
Palacio Español ★★ (Monserrat, $$, p. 98)
Plaza Asturias ★★ (Congreso, $$, p. 106)

Thai
Empire ★ (Microcentro, $$, p. 94)
Sudestada ★ (Palermo, $$$, p. 112)

Uruguayan
Medio y Medio ★ (San Telmo, $, p. 101)

Vegetarian
Bio ★★ (Palermo, $$, p. 113)

Vietnamese
Sudestada ★ (Palermo, $$$, p. 112)

2 PLAZA DE MAYO AREA

For a map of the restaurants listed in this section, see the "Where to Dine in Central Buenos Aires" map on p. 90.

MODERATE

Gran Victoria ★ CAFE/ARGENTINE Watch the political world of Argentina pass by your window at this great cafe overlooking Plaza de Mayo. This cafe sits in the middle of one of the country's most important historic areas, with stunning views of the Cabildo, Plaza de Mayo, Casa Rosada, and the Metropolitan Cathedral. It's also an excellent spot for people-watching. Food is basic Argentine, with Italian touches, and a great dessert selection. I'd recommend coming here for a break after sightseeing in the area. What's more, the waitresses have a pleasant sense of humor.

Hipólito Yrigoyen 500 (at Diagonal Sur). © **11/4345-7703.** Main courses $5–$12 (£3.55–£8.50). AE, MC, V. Mon–Sat 7am–9pm. Metro: Bolívar.

3 PUERTO MADERO

Not all of Puerto Madero has convenient metro stops, but all restaurants are, at most, a 20-minute walk from a metro station.

For a map of the restaurants listed in this section, see the "Where to Dine in Central Buenos Aires" map on p. 90.

EXPENSIVE

Asia de Cuba ★ ASIAN/JAPANESE Though not associated with the other Asia de Cubas around the world, this place is an exciting environment in which to dine. The space is chic, with gilded carved columns decorated in lotuses, and a golden reclining Buddha over the bar. In the back, there's a sushi bar and a VIP lounge. It's very glamorous at dinner time, but lunch is a more casual, businesslike affair. A table sushi menu, with 110 different items, is about $175 (£124). Dinner comes with all kinds of exotic entertainment, such as Arabian belly dancers. Asia de Cuba is also one of the most important clubs in the Puerto Madero area, ideal for an older crowd because a large portion of its clientele is over the age of 40. Dancing begins at about 1am Tuesday to Saturday and there is no admission charge if you're already dining. If you do not eat here, admission ranges from $15 to $20 (£11–£14), depending on the day.

P. Dealessi 750 (at Guemes, on Dique 3). © **11/4894-1328** or 11/4894-1329. www.asiadecuba.com.ar. Reservations recommended. Main courses $10–$20 (£7.10–£14). AE, MC, V. Daily 1pm–5am, often later Sat–Sun. No metro access.

Cabaña las Lilas ★★★ ARGENTINE Widely considered the best *parrilla* in Buenos Aires, Cabaña las Lilas is always packed. The menu pays homage to Argentine beef, which comes from the restaurant's private *estancia* (ranch). The table "cover"—which includes dried tomatoes, mozzarella, olives, peppers, and delicious garlic bread—nicely whets the appetite. Clearly, you're here to order steak: The best cuts are the rib-eye, baby beef, and thin skirt steak. Order sautéed vegetables, grilled onions, or Provençal-style fries separately. Service is hurried, but professional; ask your waiter to match a fine Argentine wine with your meal. The enormous eatery has both indoor and outdoor seating. In spite of its high prices, it's casual and informal; patrons come in suits or shorts. There's also a large and very good salad bar, so even vegetarians can be happy here.

Alicia Moreau de Justo 516 (at Villaflor, in Dique 3). © **11/4313-1336.** Reservations recommended. Main courses $10–$30 (£7.10–£21). AE, DC, V. Sun–Thurs noon–12:30am; Fri–Sat noon–1am. Metro: L. N. Alem.

Il Fiume ITALIAN This Italian restaurant has a great location, with a combination of indoor and outdoor seating, directly on the Puerto Madero waterfront, in the newer sections on the eastern bank of the port. You'll find scaloppini, rabbit Genovese with portobello mushrooms and cherry tomatoes, *pollo* (chicken) de Capri, cod Venetian-style, and other creative Italian dishes and several kinds of risotto. Desserts are decadent, from vanilla *panna cotta (cream custard),* to *baba au rhum* (yeast cake in rum) with gelato. Sometimes, there is also live modern Italian music and jazz in the outdoor dining area.

Olga Cossetini 1651 (at Ezcurra, in Dique 1). © **11/5787-3097.** Main courses $12–$20 (£8.50–£14). AE, DC, V. Daily 12:30pm–1am. No metro access.

WHERE TO DINE

6

PUERTO MADERO

Asia de Cuba **43**
Bar El Federal **61**
Bien Porteño **24**
Brasserie Petanque **54**
Broccolino **36**
Cabaña las Lilas **44**
Café de la Ciudad **39**
Café de Madres de Plaza
  de Mayo **25**
Café Literario **38**
Café Retiro **26**
Café Tortoni **47**
Café Victoria **4**
Clark's **5**
Clásica y Moderna **19**
Desnivel **57**
Dora **33**
El General **53**
El Mirasol **9**
Empire **32**
Filo **34**
Gran Victoria **46**
Il Fiume **64**
Il Gran Caffe **35**
Inside Resto-Bar **20**
Juana M **13**
La Americana **22**
La Biela **1**
La Bisteca **58**
La Bourgogne **2**
La Brigada **59, 6**
La Cabaña **7**
La Chacra **37**
La Clac **49**
La Coruña **62**
La Moncloa **23**
La Tasca de Plaza Mayor **12**
La Vieja Rotiseria **60**
Las Nazarenas **28**
Le Mistral **11**
Le Sud **15**
Ligure **16**
Lola **3**
Los Chilenos **30**
Maru Botana **14**
Medio y Medio **55**
Milion **18**
Morizono **31**
Palacio Español **48**
Pappa Deus **63**
Petit Paris Café **29**
Piegari **8**
Plaza Asturias **51**
Plaza del Carmen **21**
Plaza Grill **27**
Puerto Cristal **45**
Restaurante y Bar
  Mediterráneo **52**
Richmond Café **40**
647 Club **56**
Sorrento del Puerto **10, 42**
Sottovoce **41**
Tandoor **17**
36 Billares **50**

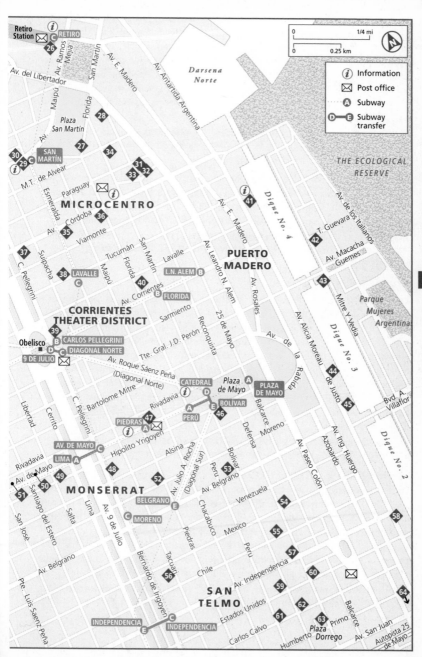

Retiro Station
(i) RETIRO
26
Av. del Libertador
Av. Ramos Mejía
San Martín
Av. E. Madero
Av. Antártida Argentina
Darsena Norte

THE ECOLOGICAL RESERVE

(i) Information
⊠ Post office
A Subway
D—E Subway transfer

Maipú
Florida
28
Plaza San Martín
Av.
27
34
30 29 C SAN MARTÍN
(i)
M.T. de Alvear
31 32
33
Paraguay
⊠ (i)
Esmeralda
MICROCENTRO
Córdoba
36
35
Viamonte
37
Tucumán
Lavalle
Av. E. Madero
(i) 41
Dique No. 4

Suipacha
C. Pellegrini
38 LAVALLE C
San Martín
Florida
Maipú
Av. Corrientes
40 B
B FLORIDA
L.N. ALEM B
Av. Leandro N. Alem
PUERTO MADERO
T. Guevara de los Italianos
42
Av. Macacha Guemes
43
Parque Mujeres Argentinas

CORRIENTES THEATER DISTRICT
39 B CARLOS PELLEGRINI
Obelisco
D C DIAGONAL NORTE
9 DE JULIO ⊠
Av. Roque Sáenz Peña
(Diagonal Norte)
Sarmiento
25 de Mayo
Reconquista
Tte. Gral. J.D. Perón
Av. de la Rabida
Dique No. 3
44
45
Bvd. A. Villaflor
Av. Ing. Huergo
Av. Alicia Moreau de Justo
Mitre y Vedia

Libertad
Cerrito
C. Pellegrini
Bartolome Mitre
Rivadavia
CATEDRAL
(i)
Plaza de Mayo A
A D
PERÚ E
BOLÍVAR
46
PLAZA DE MAYO
Balcarce
Defensa
Moreno

PIEDRAS 47 ⊠
(i) A
AV. DE MAYO C
LIMA A
Rivadavia
Av. de Mayo
49
50
51
Santiago del Estero
Hipólito Yrigoyen
48
Alsina
52
Av. Julio A. Rocha (Diagonal Sur)
Bolívar
Perú
53
Av. Belgrano
Venezuela
Chacabuco
Azopardo
Av. Paseo Colón
Dique No. 2
54
58

MONSERRAT
BELGRANO E
C MORENO
San José
Salta
Lima
Av. 9 de Julio
Bernardo de Irigoyen
Piedras
Tacuarí
Mexico
Perú
55
57
60
⊠

Pte. Luis Sáenz Peña
Av. Belgrano
56
Chile
Av. Independencia
59
62
SAN TELMO
Estados Unidos
61
63
Plaza Dorrego
Humberto
Carlos Calvo
Balcarce
Primo
Av. San Juan
64
Autopista 25 de Mayo
INDEPENDENCIA E
C INDEPENDENCIA

0   1/4 mi
0   0.25 km

Sorrento del Puerto ★★ ITALIAN   When the city decided to reinvigorate the port in 1995, this was one of the first five restaurants opened (today, you'll find more than 50). The sleek modern dining room boasts large windows, modern blue lighting, and tables and booths decorated with white linens and individual roses. The outdoor patio accommodates only 15 tables, but the inside is enormous. People come here for two reasons: great pasta and even better seafood. Choose your pasta and accompanying sauce: seafood, shrimp scampi, pesto, or four cheeses. The best seafood dishes include trout stuffed with crabmeat, sole with a Belle Marnier sauce, Galician-style octopus, paella Valenciana, and assorted grilled seafood for two. A three-course menu with a drink costs $12 (£8.50).

Av. Alicia Moreau de Justo 430 (at Guevara, on Dique 4). ✆ 11/4319-8731. Reservations recommended. Main courses $10–$25 (£7.10–£18). AE, DC, MC, V. Mon–Fri noon–4pm and 8pm–1am; Sat 8pm–2am. Metro: L. N. Alem.

Sottovoce ★★ ITALIAN   One of the city's best Italian restaurants, Sottovoce provides great dining with a view to the port. Look for various *lomos*, rabbit dishes, saltimbocca, shrimp with a curry red-wine sauce, and more than 17 kinds of pasta dishes. The wine list, with local, French, and Italian vintages, is more than 10 pages long.

Alicia M. De Justo 176 (at Tucuman, on Dique 4). ✆ 11/4313-1199. www.sottovoceristorante.com.ar. Main courses $12–$25 (£8.50–£18). AE, MC, V. Daily noon–4pm; Mon–Thurs 8pm–midnight; Fri–Sat 8pm–1am. Metro: L. N. Alem.

MODERATE

La Bisteca ★★ Value PARRILLA   La Bisteca offers a wide range of meal choices at incredible value for the money. This is an all-you-can-eat establishment, locally called a *tenedor libre*. A three-course lunch is about $12 (£8.50), and dinner ranges from $12 to $20 (£8.50–£14). If you've come to Argentina for beef, definitely stop here. The high quality of the meat is surprising, considering the price and bottomless portions. There really was no limit to the number of times I could fill my plate at the various grills in the restaurant. For vegetarians, there is also a diverse salad bar. In spite of the restaurant's large size, the lighting and seating arrangements work to create small, intimate spaces. At lunchtime, the place is full of businesspeople, while at night you'll find a mix of couples, friends, and families.

Av. Alicia Moreau de Justo 1890 (at Peñaloza, on Dique 1). ✆ 11/4514-4999. Main courses $5–$7 (£3.55–£4.95). AE, DC, MC, V. Daily noon–4pm and 8pm–1am. No metro access.

Puerto Cristal ★ INTERNATIONAL/SEAFOOD   The menu here has everything, but fish is why patrons choose this restaurant among all the others in Puerto Madero. The place is enormous, with friendly hostesses and theatrical waiter service; a constant flurry of fresh silverware and dishes will cross your table between courses, befitting a much pricier establishment. Windows overlooking the port and glassed-in central garden amid the dining area lend tranquillity to the industrial-chic design. Great lunch specials are part of the draw here; the executive menu runs about $15 (£11) and usually includes a glass of champagne (though other drinks and the table cover will be additional).

Av. Alicia Moreau de Justo 1082 (at Villaflor, in Dique 3). ✆ 11/4331-3669. www.puerto-cristal.com.ar. Main courses $6–$20 (£4.25–£14). AE, MC, V. Sun–Fri 6:30am–midnight; Sat 6:30am–2am. No metro access.

For a map of the restaurants listed in this section, see the "Where to Dine in Central Buenos Aires" map on p. 90.

EXPENSIVE

Dora ★★ SPANISH/SEAFOOD   Dora has been open since the 1940s, run by the same family (the third generation is now in charge), but it has moved recently from its former location. It's still loud, noisy, crazy, and chaotic—an odd mix of businesspeople from nearby offices and casually dressed older locals who have been regulars for decades. The specialty is fish, with a few beef, chicken, and pasta dishes thrown in almost as an afterthought. The Cazuela Dora is the specialty—a casserole of fish, shellfish, and shrimp thrown into one pot. It's expensive for Buenos Aires; appetizers alone run from $4 to $14 (£2.85–£9.95), though some of the starters are made with caviar. The dessert menu includes a surprisingly varied choice of light fruits in season. Because it serves so much fish, Dora has one of the city's largest white-wine selections.

Reconquista 1076 (at Paraguay). © **11/4311-2891.** Main courses $12–$25 (£8.50–£18). V. U.S. dollars accepted. Mon–Thurs noon–1am; Fri–Sat noon–2am. Metro: San Martín.

Le Sud ★★ FRENCH/MEDITERRANEAN   Executive Chef Thierry Pszonka earned a gold medal from the National Committee of French Gastronomy and gained experience at La Bourgogne before opening this gourmet restaurant in the new Sofitel Hotel. His simple, elegant cooking style embraces spices and olive oils from Provence, to create delicious entrees such as stewed rabbit with green pepper and tomatoes, polenta with Parmesan and rosemary, and spinach with lemon ravioli. Le Sud's dining room is as sophisticated as the cuisine: The design is contemporary, with chandeliers and black-marble floors, tables of Brazilian rosewood, and large windows overlooking Calle Arroyo. After dinner, consider a drink in the adjacent wine bar.

Arroyo 841/849 (at Suipacha, in the Sofitel Hotel). © **11/4131-0000.** Reservations recommended. Main courses $15–$25 (£11–£18). AE, DC, MC, V. Daily 6:30–11am, 12:30–3pm, and 7:30pm–midnight. Metro: San Martín.

Plaza Grill ★★ INTERNATIONAL   For nearly a century, the Plaza Grill dominated the city's power-lunch scene, and it remains the first choice for government officials and business executives. The dining room is decorated with dark-oak furniture and tables are well spaced, allowing for intimate conversations. Order a la carte from the international menu or off the *parrilla*—the steaks are perfect Argentine cuts. Marinated filet mignon, thinly sliced and served with gratinéed potatoes, is superb. Another interesting choice is venison with crispy apple sauce, served during the November and December holiday season, though seemingly incongruous in the heat of Buenos Aires's summer. The "po parisky eggs" form another classic dish—two poached eggs in a bread shell topped with a rich mushroom-and-bacon sauce. The restaurant's wine list spans seven countries, with the world's best Malbec from Mendoza.

Marriott Plaza Hotel, Calle Florida 1005 (at Santa Fe, overlooking Plaza San Martín). © **11/4318-3070.** Reservations recommended. Main courses $12–$25 (£8.50–£18). AE, DC, MC, V. Daily noon–4pm and 7pm–midnight. Metro: San Martín.

MODERATE

Broccolino ★ ITALIAN   The name of this restaurant doesn't mean little broccoli; it's a corruption of Italian immigrant slang for New York's biggest and once most heavily Italian borough (notice the Brooklyn memorabilia filling the walls and the mural of Manhattan's skyline). This casual trattoria near Calle Florida is popular with North Americans, including Robert Duvall. Three small dining rooms are decorated in quintessential red-and-white-checkered tablecloths, and the smell of tomatoes, onions, and garlic fills the air. The restaurant is known for its spicy pizzas, fresh pastas, and, above all, its sauces (*salsas* in Spanish). The restaurant also serves 2,000 pounds per month of baby calamari sautéed in wine, onions, parsley, and garlic.

Córdoba 820 (at Esmeralda). ℂ **11/4322-9848.** Reservations recommended. Main courses $5–$15 (£3.55–£11). No credit cards. Daily noon–4pm and 7pm–1am. Metro: Lavalle.

Café de la Ciudad CAFE/ARGENTINE   The city's only restaurant with outdoor dining directly overlooking the Obelisco, Café de la Ciudad opened 40 years ago on one of the six corners around the landmark, on Avenida 9 de Julio. It's like Buenos Aires's Times Square, where you can watch the myriad flashing electronic ads for Japanese and American companies. Sure, it's noisy, and, sure, you're a target for beggars, but you'll be dining under the symbol of the city. The food comes in large portions; sandwiches, pizzas, and specially priced executive menus are made fast, so it's a great stop if you're short on time. Other Argentine basics, such as beef, chicken, and pasta, round out the menu. The cafe is also a 24-hour place, so you can stop by after clubbing or a show at one of the nearby theaters, and watch the parade of Porteños passing by.

Corrientes 999 (at Carlos Pellegrini, Av. 9 de Julio). ℂ **11/4322-8905** or 11/4322-6174. Main courses $3–$12 (£2.15–£8.50). AE, DC, MC, V. Daily 24 hr. Metro: Carlos Pellegrini.

Empire ★ ASIAN/THAI   This restaurant is interesting, but it's in a surprisingly desolate part of the Microcentro—steps away from the action, on a very small street that gets little foot traffic, but was recently pedestrianized. Enter this dark space, with paintings of elephants and mosaic decorations made from broken mirrors on the columns, and you'll feel as though you've stepped into some kind of funky club. For vegetarians seeking a break from the meat offerings everywhere else, it's an ideal stop, with many all-vegetable or noodle offerings. Many patrons come for drinks alone and sit at the large bar. Empire's advertising symbol is the Empire State Building, but there's nothing New York–like about it. It's also one of the city's most popular restaurants among gay locals.

Tres Sargentos 427 (at San Martín). ℂ **11/5411-4312** or 11/5411-5706. empire_bar@hotmail.com. Main courses $6–$10 (£4.25–£7.10). AE, MC, V. Mon–Fri noon–1am; Sat 7:30pm–3am. Metro: San Martín.

Il Gran Caffe ★ CAFE/ITALIAN   As its name implies, this largely Italian restaurant sells an extensive selection of pastries, pastas, and panini, as well as more traditional Argentine fare. On a busy corner across the street from Galerías Pacífico, it is also one of the best perches from which to watch the crowds passing by on Calle Florida. A covered canopy on the Córdoba side also provides further outdoor seating, rain or shine. The people-watching is so good, in fact, that the restaurant charges about 10% more for outdoor dining. If that bothers the budget-conscious spy in you, the best compromise is to sit inside, on the upper-floor level, with its bird's-eye view of the street and the Naval Academy, one of the city's most beautiful landmarks. Mixed drinks start at about $5 (£3.55) each. There's an excellent Italian pastry menu; the Neapolitan *sfogliatella* is especially good.

Calle Florida 700 (at Córdoba). ✆ **11/4326-5008.** Main courses $8–$15 (£5.70–£11). AE, MC, V. Daily

7am–2am. Metro: Florida.

La Chacra ★ ARGENTINE/PARRILLA   Your first impression from outside this place will be either the stuffed cow begging you to go on in and eat some meat, or the open-fire spit grill glowing through the window. Professional waiters clad in black pants and white dinner jackets welcome you into what is otherwise a casual environment, with deer horns and wrought-iron lamps adorning the walls. Dishes from the grill include sirloin steak, T-bone with red peppers, and tenderloin. Barbecued ribs and suckling pig call out from the open-pit fire, as do a number of hearty brochettes. Steaks are thick and juicy. Get a good beer or an Argentine wine to wash it all down.

Av. Córdoba 941 (at Carlos Pelligrini, on Av. 9 de Julio). ✆ **11/4322-1409.** Main courses $5–$12 (£3.55–£8.50). AE, DC, MC, V. Daily noon–1:30am. Metro: San Martín.

Las Nazarenas ★ ARGENTINE   This is not a restaurant, an old waiter will warn you; it's an *asador*. More specifically, it's a steakhouse with meat on the menu, not a pseudo-*parrilla* with vegetable plates or some froufrou international dishes for the faint of heart. You have two choices: cuts grilled on the *parrilla* or meat cooked on a spit over the fire. Argentine presidents and foreign ministers have all made their way here. The two-level dining room is handsomely decorated with cases of Argentine wines and abundant plants. Service is unhurried, allowing you plenty of time for a relaxing meal. The location near several high-rise office complexes means it is very busy during lunch.

Reconquista 1132 (at Leandro N. Alem). ✆ **11/4312-5559.** www.lasnazarenas.com.ar. Main courses $6–$12 (£4.25–£8.50). AE, DC, MC, V. Daily noon–1am. Metro: San Martín.

Ligure ★★ (Finds) FRENCH/ITALIAN   Painted mirrors look over the long rectangular dining room, which, since 1933, has drawn ambassadors, artists, and business leaders by day and a more romantic crowd at night. A nautical theme prevails, with fishnets, dock ropes, and masts decorating the room; captain's wheels substitute for chandeliers. Portions are huge and meticulously prepared—an unusual combination for French-inspired cuisine. Seafood options include the Patagonian tooth fish sautéed with butter, prawns, and mushrooms, or the trout glazed with an almond sauce. The chateaubriand is outstanding, and the *bife de lomo* (filet mignon) can be prepared seven different ways (pepper sauce with brandy is delightful, made at your table).

Juncal 855 (at Esmerelda). ✆ **11/4393-0644** or 11/4394-8226. Reservations recommended. Main courses $6–$10 (£4.25–£7.10). AE, DC, MC, V. Daily noon–3pm and 8pm–midnight. Metro: San Martín.

Los Chilenos ★ SEAFOOD/CHILEAN   A taste of the long country next door is what you'll find here, and because of that, this restaurant is popular with Chileans who live here or are visiting. It's a simple place, with a home-style feeling. The dining room has long tables where everyone sits together, and it's decorated with posters of Chilean tourist sites and draped with Chilean flags. Fish is one of the restaurant's fortes, and one of the most popular dishes is abalone in mayonnaise.

Suipacha 1024 (at Santa Fe). ✆ **11/4328-3123.** Main courses $3–$10 (£2.15–£7.10). V. Mon–Sat noon–4pm and 8pm–1am. Metro: San Martín.

Morizono ★ (Value) JAPANESE   A casual Japanese restaurant and sushi bar, Morizono offers such menu items as dumplings stuffed with pork, shrimp and vegetable tempuras, salmon with ginger sauce, and a variety of sushi and sashimi combination platters.

Reconquista 899 (at Paraguay). ✆ **11/4314-0924.** www.morizonosushi.com.ar. Reservations recommended. Main courses $5–$15 (£3.55–£11). AE, DC, MC, V. Mon–Fri 12:30–3:30pm and 8pm–1am; Sat 8pm–1am. Metro: San Martín.

Richmond Cafe ★★ CAFE/ARGENTINE   Enter this place and find the pace and atmosphere of an older Buenos Aires. The Richmond Cafe, a *café notable,* is all that is left of the Richmond Hotel, which once catered to the elite. The cafe sits in the lobby of the former hotel. The menu here is traditionally Argentine, and there is a *confitería,* or cafe, section in the front, serving as a cafe and fast-food eatery. You'll find locals of all kinds here, from workers to well-dressed seniors who recall Calle Florida's more elegant heyday. The decor is that of a gentlemen's club, full of wood, brass, and red-leather upholstery. Patrons can still let loose downstairs, in a bar area full of billiard tables. The menu of high-quality pastries is extensive. The restaurant serves hearty basics such as chicken, fish, and beef. The a la carte choices tend to be expensive, but three-course executive menus with a drink are a good bargain, running about $20 (£14).

Calle Florida 468 (at Corrientes). ✆ **11/4322-1341** or 11/4322-1653. www.restaurant.com.ar/richmond. Main courses $6–$10 (£4.25–£7.10). AE, MC, V. Mon–Sat 7am–10pm. Metro: Florida.

INEXPENSIVE

Café Literario CAFE/ARGENTINE   This quiet little cafe takes advantage of its location next-door to the birthplace of Argentine literary great Jorge Luis Borges. With a literature theme, the cafe hosts readings and art events on an irregular basis. A range of publications lie on shelves and racks for patrons to peruse while they eat. The owners' plan was to have a place where people could come to read and eat and be more relaxed than in a library. Fare includes light items such as sandwiches, snacks, desserts, and Argentine steak. The building is modern, but opens into the patio of the adjacent YWCA (Tucumán 844; ✆ **11/4322-1550**), inside a gorgeous early-20th-century building. Café Literario serves as the cafeteria for the YWCA. Stop in for information on plays, art shows, other events aimed at the general public, and exercise programs strictly for women.

Tucumán 840 (at Suipacha). ✆ **11/4328-0391.** Main courses $2–$5 (£1.40–£3.55). No credit cards. Mon–Fri 8am–6pm. Metro: Lavalle.

Café Retiro ★★ (Finds) CAFE/ARGENTINE   This cafe is part of the Café Café consortium and, as such, there is nothing spectacular about the food, but it is high quality, consistent, and inexpensive. You'll find a great range of coffees and teas, as well as desserts and sandwiches, perfect for a quick bite before catching a train. The main point of dining here is to enjoy the restored elegance of the original cafe, which was part of Retiro Station when it was built in 1915. It is now one of the *cafés notables,* the interiors of which are considered historically important to the nation. The marble has been cleaned, the bronze chandeliers polished, and the stained-glass windows have been restored, allowing a luminescent light to flow in. This cafe is ideal if you are taking a train from here to other parts of Argentina and the province, such as Tigre, or if you've come to admire the architecture of Retiro and the other classical stations, or the nearby English Clock Tower that sits in the plaza just outside. The staff is friendly and full of advice on things to do in town.

Ramos Meija 1358 (at Libertador, in the Retiro Station lobby). ✆ **11/4516-0902.** Main courses $2–$6 (£1.40–£4.25). No credit cards. Daily 6:30am–10pm. Metro: Retiro.

Café Tortoni ★★★ (**Moments**) CAFE You cannot come to Buenos Aires without visiting this Porteño institution, the city's artistic and intellectual hangout since 1858. Wonderfully appointed in woods, stained glass, yellowing marble, and bronzes, the place itself
exudes history. It's the perfect place for a coffee or a small snack after wandering along
Avenida de Mayo. Twice-nightly tango shows are held in a cramped side gallery. The
recent explosion in tourism has taken out some of the authenticity of the venue, with
tour buses pulling up and filling the venue with gawkers. Try to visit in the morning, or
very late at night. Do not, however, expect great service: Sometimes, the only way to get
attention is to jump up and down, even if your server is a few feet from you. Management sometimes limits who can gain entry. All told, it's a beautiful place, but service and
treating people well has never been the Tortoni's forte.

Av. de Mayo 825 (at Esmeralda). ℂ **11/4342-4328.** Main courses $2–$10 (£1.40–£7.10). AE, DC, MC, V.
Mon–Thurs 8am–2am; Fri–Sat 8am–3am; Sun 8am–1am. Metro: Av. de Mayo.

Filo ★ (**Finds**) ITALIAN/PIZZA Popular with young professionals, artists, and anyone
looking for cause to celebrate, Filo presents its happy clients with pizzas, more kinds of
pasta than you can imagine, salads with an Italian touch, and potent cocktails. The color-
fully decorated and crowded bar hosts occasional live music, and tango lessons take place
downstairs a few evenings per week.

San Martín 975 (at Alvear). ℂ **11/4311-0312.** www.filo-ristorante.com. Main courses $4–$10 (£2.85–
£7.10). AE, MC, V. Daily noon–4pm and 8pm–2am. Metro: San Martín.

Petit Paris Café ★ CAFE Marble-top tables with velvet-upholstered chairs, crystal
chandeliers, and bow-tie-clad waiters give this cafe a European flavor. Large windows
look directly onto Plaza San Martín, placing the cafe within short walking distance of
some of the city's best sights. The menu offers a selection of hot and cold sandwiches,
pastries, and special coffees and teas. Linger over your coffee as long as you like—nobody
will pressure you to move on.

Av. Santa Fe 774 (at Esmeralda). ℂ **11/4312-5885.** Main courses $3–$8 (£2.15–£5.70). AE, DC, MC, V.
Daily 7am–2am. Metro: San Martín.

6

WHERE TO DINE

MONSERRAT

---

5 MONSERRAT

For a map of the restaurants listed in this section, see the "Where to Dine in Central
Buenos Aires" map on p. 90.

MODERATE

El General ★★★ (**Moments**) ARGENTINE This restaurant dedicated to the memory
of Argentina's most famous couple, the Peróns. The owners knew Perón personally and
opened this restaurant intending to inform young Argentines and tourists about the
historical couple. Authentic and important artwork and memorabilia fill the place,
including a rare portrait of Juan Perón. Tango shows on Saturdays are at special prices
with dinner included. In spite of the kitsch, the food and the service are excellent and
authentically Argentine. Try the Chorizo El General, a slab of beef large enough for two
people, served with Pastel de Papa, a potato dish that was Perón's favorite. In addition,
there is a large fish selection, and interesting chicken recipes, such as Provencial- and
Portuguese-style. While there are tourists here, you'll be surprised by the large number

of locals. For a Peronist restaurant, the setup is somewhat formal, with Chippendale furniture.

Av. Belgrano 561 (at Perú). ✆ **11/4342-7830.** Main courses $5–$12 (£3.55–£8.50). AE, DC, MC, V. Mon–Sat 8am–2am. Metro: Moreno.

Palacio Español ★★ SPANISH This restaurant has one of the most magnificent dining rooms in Buenos Aires. It's in the Club Español, one of the grandest buildings along Avenida 9 de Julio. An orgy of brass, marble, agate lighting fixtures, carved oak bas-reliefs, and molded plaster ornaments surround you, along with Spanish paintings. Despite the restaurant's architectural grandeur, the atmosphere is surprisingly relaxed and often celebratory; don't be surprised to see a table of champagne-clinking Argentines. Tables have beautiful silver place settings, and tuxedo-clad waiters provide friendly but formal service. The menu is a tempting sample of Spanish cuisine—including paella and Spanish omelets—but the fish dishes are best. Special salads are meals in themselves; a few include calamari. The long wine list has a large selection of whites to complement the fish dishes. Bills include a table service of $1.50 (£1.05).

Bernardo de Yrigoyen 180 (at Alsina). ✆ **11/4334-4876.** Reservations recommended. Main courses $5–$12 (£3.55–£8.50). AE, DC, MC, V. Daily noon–4pm and 8pm–midnight, sometimes until 1am Fri–Sat. Metro: Lima.

Restaurante y Bar Mediterráneo ★★ MEDITERRANEAN The InterContinental Hotel's exclusive Mediterranean restaurant and bar are built in colonial style, resembling the city's famous Café Tortoni. The downstairs bar, with its hardwood floor, marble-top tables, and polished Victrola playing tango, takes you back to Buenos Aires of the 1930s. A spiral staircase leads to the elegant restaurant, where subdued lighting and well-spaced tables create an intimate atmosphere. Mediterranean herbs, olive oil, and sun-dried tomatoes are among the chef's usual ingredients. Dishes might include carefully prepared shellfish bouillabaisse; black hake served with ratatouille; chicken casserole with morels, fava beans, and potatoes; or duck breast with cabbage confit, wild mushrooms, and sautéed apples. Express menus (items ready within minutes) are available at lunch.

Moreno 809 (at Piedras, in the InterContinental Hotel). ✆ **11/4340-7200.** Reservations recommended. Main courses $8–$15 (£5.70–£11). AE, DC, MC, V. Daily 7–11am, 11:30am–3:30pm, and 7pm–midnight. Metro: Moreno.

6 SAN TELMO

For a map of the restaurants listed in this section, see the "Where to Dine in Central Buenos Aires" map on p. 90.

EXPENSIVE

Brasserie Petanque ★★ Ⓜ️oments FRENCH While the Swiss-born owner of this restaurant, Pascal Meyer, insists this is a brasserie and not a bistro . . . well, it's almost the same thing and certainly looks like one. Newly made with the intention of looking old, the walls are in soft yellow, with old advertising posters and other decorations, such as French flags, politely tucked into corners. The stunning tile floor was redone in a turn-of-the-20th-century style. The menu is in French and Spanish, and offers such specialties as steak tartare, lemon chicken, trout with almonds, and beef bordelaise. Chef Sebastian

Fouillade once worked with Alain Ducasse. Smaller children's portions of select main menu items are available for about $10 (£7.10).

Defensa 596 (at corner with Mexico). © 11/4342-7930. www.brasseriepetanque.com. Main courses $10–$25 (£7.10–£18). AE, DC, MC, V. Sun–Fri 12:30–3:30pm; Tues–Sun 8:30pm–midnight. Metro: Independencia.

647 Club ★★ Ⓜoments INTERNATIONAL/MEDITERRANEAN Tucked away in an obscure part of San Telmo, 647 Club is among the most romantic of restaurants in Buenos Aires. Crystal chandeliers, red walls, and marbleized, gold-flecked mirrors give a retro, nightclub atmosphere. The cuisine is a mix of European influences, heavy on French and Italian touches. Look for such creative starters as the pastry confection duck strudel layered with brie cheese, and smothered in a molasses sauce, or goat sweetbreads drizzled in truffle oil with tomato chimichurri. Main dishes are elaborate, with such ingredients as a risotto made from corn, held together with mascarpone and dotted with sautéed portobello mushrooms, beans and broccoli; or veal ravioli with toasted almonds. Argentine standbys, such as rib-eye steak, are reinvented as kabobs with a special sauce. You might just come for drinks, however, to check out the atmosphere.

647 Tacuari (at Chile). © 11/4331-3026. www.club647.com. Reservations recommended. Main courses $15–$20 (£11–£14). AE, V. Mon–Sat 8pm–1am, later Sat–Sun. Metro: Independencia.

MODERATE

Bar El Federal ★★ Ⓜoments ARGENTINE/CAFE This bar and restaurant, on a quiet corner in San Telmo, presents a beautiful step back in time. Fortunately, as another *bar notable,* it will stay that way forever. The first thing that strikes you is the massive, carved-wood and stained-glass ornamental stand over the bar area. Local patrons sit at the old tables whiling away their time, chatting, or sitting with a book and drinking tea or espresso. The original tile floor remains, and old signs, portraits, and small antique machines decorate this space. In business since 1864, Bar El Federal is among the most Porteño of places in San Telmo, a neighborhood with more of these establishments than any other area. Some of the staff has been here for decades on end, and proudly so. Food is a collection of small, simple things, mostly sandwiches, steaks, *lomos* (sirloin cuts), with a very large salad selection. High-quality pastries are also served to complement the menu.

Corner of Perú and Carlos Calvo. © 11/4300-4313. Main courses $3–$10 (£2.15–£7.10). AE, MC, V. Sun–Thurs 7am–2am; Fri–Sat 7am–4am. Metro: Independencia.

Desnivel ★ PARRILLA This place brings new meaning to the term "greasy spoon." Everything in here has an oily sheen—from the slippery floor to the railings, glasses, and dishes. Even the walls and the artwork seem to bleed grease. Thankfully, the food more than makes up for the atmosphere: Serving mostly thick, well-cooked, and fatty steaks, this is one of San Telmo's best *parrillas.* A flood of locals and tourists, often lined up at the door, keeps the place hopping. On Sunday or when a game is on television, especially large crowds come to watch and eat under the blaring TV screen suspended over the dining area. The decor in this two-level restaurant is unassuming, home-style, and full of mismatched wooden chairs, tablecloths, and silverware. Unlike many other local restaurants that have inflated their prices in recent years, this *parrilla* has maintained its reasonably priced menu.

Defensa 858 (at Independencia). © 11/4300-9081. Main courses $5–$8 (£3.55–£5.70). No credit cards. Daily noon–4pm and 8pm–1am. Metro: Independencia.

La Brigada ★★★ ARGENTINE/PARRILLA   Known as one of the best *parrillas* in San Telmo, La Brigada is reminiscent of the Pampas, with gaucho memorabilia filling the restaurant. White-linen tablecloths and tango music complement the atmosphere. An upstairs dining room faces an excellent walled wine rack. The best choices include the *asado* (short rib roast), *lomo* (sirloin steak, prepared with a mushroom or pepper sauce), baby beef (an enormous 850g/30 oz., served for two), and the *mollejas de chivito al verdero* (young goat sweetbreads in a scallion sauce). The Felipe Rutini merlot goes perfectly with baby beef and chorizo. The waiters are exceedingly nice and professional, but I found the management to be suspicious of the tourism press. It was explained to me that tourists had driven away locals from this San Telmo favorite, but with prices now set to capture the tourism market—in some cases tripled—this no longer seems a concern.

Estados Unidos 465 (at Bolívar). ✆ **11/4361-5557.** Reservations recommended. Main courses $4–$25 (£2.85–£18). AE, DC, MC, V. Daily noon–3pm and 8pm–midnight. Metro: Constitución.

Pappa Deus ★ INTERNATIONAL/ARGENTINE   You'll find basic beef dishes, with some creatively fused in a Mediterranean-Italian style, and a large selection of hearty salads, an unusual find in Buenos Aires. An interesting menu every day of the week, live music shows, folkloric dancing, and jazz and blues on Friday and Saturday nights make this place one of the best alternatives to tango venues along Dorrego Plaza. This restaurant has moved around the corner from its old location. It still has a loft area for a more secluded dinner.

Humberto Primo 499 423 (at Bolivar). ✆ **11/4307-1751.** Main courses $7–$13 (£4.95–£9.25). AE, DC, MC, V. Sun–Thurs 9am–2am; Fri–Sat 9am–4am, often later. Metro: Independencia.

INEXPENSIVE

La Coruña ★★ ⓜoments CAFE/ARGENTINE   This extremely authentic old cafe and restaurant bar, another of the *cafés notables* protected by law, is the kind of place where you'd expect your grandfather to have eaten when he was a teenager. This neighborhood hub draws young and old alike, who catch soccer games on television or quietly chat away as they order beer, small snacks, and sandwiches. The quality of food is great and pastas are made with special care. The TV seems to be the only modern thing in here. Music plays from a wooden table-top radio that must be from the 1950s, and two wooden refrigerators, dating from who knows when, are still used to store food. José Moreira and Manuela Lopéz, the old couple who own the place, obviously believe that if it ain't broke, there's no reason for a new one.

Bolívar 994 (at Carlos Calvo). ✆ **11/4362-7637.** Main courses $2–$4 (£1.40–£2.85). No credit cards. Daily 9am–10pm. Metro: Independencia.

La Vieja Rotisería ★★ ⓥalue PARRILLA/ITALIAN/ARGENTINE   The slabs of meat sizzling at this *parrilla* are so huge that you hope the cook doesn't drop one on his foot, which would put him out of commission and deprive you from eating at one of the best *parrillas* in San Telmo. Following the rule "simple is best," this place concentrates on the food, not the decor, and prices are reasonable. Mismatched vinyl tablecloths and old tacky prints and mirrors in baroque frames are part of the visual disorder here, but keep your eyes on the food. Steaks are thick and well prepared, with interesting twists on the meat, such as *lomo* (sirloin) in tasty sauces. Pastas, salads, fish, and boneless chicken are served here, too. The place gets very crowded at night, so make reservations if you're coming after 9pm. While the food is excellent as ever, a recent renovation has relegated the grill to the back of the restaurant, so you can no longer watch as your order is prepared.

Defensa 963 (at Estados Unidos). ✆ **11/4361-7019.** Reservations recommended. Main courses $2–$8 (£1.40–£5.70). No credit cards. Mon–Tues and Thurs noon–4:30pm and 8pm–12:30am; Fri–Sat noon–4pm and 8pm–1am; Sun noon–5:30pm and 8pm–12:30am. Metro: Independencia.

Medio y Medio ★ URUGUAYAN   This place serves Uruguayan *chivitos*, which are *lomo* (steak) sandwiches. *Lomo* takes on a different meaning in Uruguay than in Argentina. In Argentina, it is only a cut of beef; in Uruguay, it can be steer, pork, or chicken, cut flat as a filet, served as a hot sandwich with a slice of ham, cheese, and an egg, with a garnish of tomatoes and lettuce. This is a crowded, busy place, especially at night when patrons sit outside, under a canopy, at tables painted with *fileteado*, an Italian art of painted filigree borders, which has become quintessentially Argentine. Live entertainment in the form of Spanish and folkloric music and tango is available at lunchtime on Monday, Tuesday, and Wednesday, and night on Thursday through Sunday.

Chile 316 (at Defensa). ✆ **11/4300-7007.** Main courses $4–$10 (£2.85–£7.10). No credit cards. Mon–Tues noon–2am; Wed noon–3am; Thurs noon–4am; Fri noon–8am; Sat 24 hr. Metro: Independencia.

7 RECOLETA

There are no convenient metro stops in this neighborhood. For a map of the restaurants listed in this section, see the "Where to Dine in Central Buenos Aires" map on p. 90.

VERY EXPENSIVE

La Bourgogne ★★★ FRENCH   As the only Relais Gourmand in Argentina, Chef Jean Paul Bondoux serves the finest French and international food in the city here. *Travel + Leisure* magazine rated La Bourgogne the number-one restaurant in South America, and *Wine Spectator* called it one of the "Best Restaurants in the World for Wine Lovers." Decorated in elegant pastel hues, the formal dining room serves the city's top gourmands. To begin your meal, consider a warm foie gras scallop with honey-wine sauce, or perhaps the succulent *ravioli d'escargots* (ravioli with snails). Examples of the carefully prepared main courses include *chateaubriand béarnaise* (steak with béarnaise sauce) and lamb with parsley-and-garlic sauce. The kitchen's fresh vegetables, fruits, herbs, and spices originate from Bondoux's private farm. Downstairs, **La Cave** offers a less formal experience, with a different menu. Wine tastings are held in the restaurant's wine-cellar area called **Cave de Vines.**

Av. Alvear 1891 (at Ayacucho, in the Alvear Palace Hotel). ✆ **11/4805-3857.** www.alvearpalace.com. Reservations required. Jacket and tie required for men. Main courses $20–$35 (£14–£25). AE, DC, MC, V. Free valet parking. Mon–Fri noon–3pm; Mon–Sat 8pm–midnight. Closed Jan. No metro access.

La Cabaña ★ ARGENTINE/PARRILLA   This is the second incarnation of one of the most legendary Buenos Aires eateries. The food here—all about the beef—is strictly Argentine, but the decor is very British, complete with plaids and dark woods. Kitschy touches include stained-glass windows with cow heads, saddles over the staircase, and gaucho cartoon drawings. A computer lets you track where your beef came from, even the date the cow was killed (creepy or kitschy, depending on your taste). Steaks are excellent, but the service can be slow. It took about an hour for my steak to arrive. The restaurant is huge, with more than 170 seats, including a rooftop terrace. The staff is knowledgeable about wine and there's an excellent bar. Besides beef—served in portions as large as a kilogram (2.2 lbs.)—there's chicken, fish, and a large selection of salads. This place is often confused with its main competitor, Cabaña las Lilas, but is far more formal at similar prices.

Rodríguez Peña 1967 (btw. Posadas and Alvear, next to the Park Hyatt). ☎ **11/4814-0001.** www.la cabanabuenosaires.com.ar. Main courses $14–$50 (£9.95–£36). AE, DC, MC, V. Daily noon–4pm and 7pm–midnight. No metro access.

Piegari ★★ ITALIAN   You would not expect to find such a fine restaurant under a highway overpass in a part of Recoleta dubbed "La Recova," meaning poultry business. Piegari has two restaurants across the street from each other; the more formal one focuses on Italian dishes, while the other (Piegari Vitello e Dolce) is mainly a *parrilla*. Both restaurants are excellent, but visit the formal Piegari for outstanding Italian cuisine, with an emphasis on seafood and pastas. Homemade spaghetti, six kinds of risotto, pan pizza, veal scallops, and black salmon ravioli are just a few of the mouthwatering choices. Huge portions are made for sharing, and an excellent eight-page wine list accompanies the menu. If you decide to try Piegari Vitello e Dolce instead, the best dishes are the short rib roast and the leg of Patagonian lamb.

Posadas 1042 (at Av. 9 de Julio, in La Recova, near the Four Seasons Hotel). ☎ **11/4328-4104.** Reservations recommended. Main courses $25–$45 (£18–£32). AE, DC, MC, V. Daily noon–3:30pm and 7:30pm–1am. No metro access.

EXPENSIVE

La Tasca de Plaza Mayor ★★ SPANISH   We list the full name of this restaurant, but most people just call it Plaza Mayor, named for Madrid's main square. Decorations on the rough brick walls, such as Spanish fans in glass casements, let you know you have entered into the mother country. The waitstaff in aprons gives old-fashioned service. Highlights of the menu include *pollo Plaza Mayor* (chicken in a wine sauce), several kinds of paella, and lots of steak and pastas as you'd find all over Argentina. There are plenty of exotic fruits of the sea, from octopus to crabs, and an excellent Bacalao a la Gallega.

Posadas 1052 (at Av. 9 de Julio in La Recova, near the Four Seasons Hotel). ☎ **11/4393-5671.** www. grupoplazamayor.com. Reservations recommended. Main courses $15–$30 (£11–£21). AE, MC, V. Daily noon–1am, sometimes later Sat–Sun. No metro access.

Le Mistral ★★ MEDITERRANEAN   Formerly known as Galani, this elegant but informal restaurant in the Four Seasons Hotel serves Mediterranean cuisine with Italian and Asian influences. It has been completely redesigned from its previous incarnation, paying homage to Argentine materials such as leather and native woods. The executive lunch menu includes an antipasto buffet with seafood, cold cuts, cheese, and salads followed by a main course and dessert. From the dinner menu, the aged Angus New York strip steak makes an excellent choice. All grilled dishes come with béarnaise sauce or *chimichurri* (a thick herb sauce) and potatoes or seasonal vegetables. Organic chicken and fresh seafood join the menu, along with terrific desserts. Live harp music often accompanies meals, and tables are candlelit at night. Enjoy an after-dinner drink in Le Dôme, the split-level bar. The Sunday brunch is one of the best in Buenos Aires.

Posadas 1086 (at Av. 9 de Julio, in the Four Seasons Hotel). ☎ **11/4321-1234.** Reservations recommended. Main courses $12–$25 (£8.50–£18). Sun brunch $35 (£25). AE, DC, MC, V. Daily 7–11am, noon–3pm, and 8pm–1am. No metro access.

Lola ★ INTERNATIONAL   Among the best-known international restaurants in Buenos Aires, Lola recently completed a makeover, turning its dining room into one of the city's brightest and most contemporary spots. Caricatures of major personalities adorn the walls, and fresh plants and flowers give Lola's dining room a springlike atmosphere.

A French-trained chef prepares creative dishes such as chicken fricassee with leek sauce, grilled trout with lemon-grass butter and zucchini, and beef tenderloin stuffed with Gruyère cheese and mushrooms. The chef will prepare dishes for those with special dietary requirements as well.

Guido 1985 (at Junin). © 11/4804-5959. www.lolarestaurant.com. Reservations recommended. Main courses $10–$20 (£7.10–£14). AE, DC, MC, V. Daily noon–4pm and 7pm–1am. No metro access.

MODERATE

Café Victoria ★ CAFE Perfect for a relaxing afternoon in Recoleta, the cafe's outdoor patio is surrounded by flowers and shaded by an enormous tree. Sit and drink a coffee or enjoy a complete meal. The three-course express-lunch menu offers a salad, main dish, and dessert, with a drink included. Afternoon tea with pastries and scones is served daily from 4 to 7pm. The cafe remains equally popular in the evening, with excellent people-watching opportunities, when live music enlivens the patio. It's a great value for the area—the Recoleta Cemetery and cultural center are next-door.

Roberto M. Ortiz 1865 (at Quintana). © 11/4804-0016. Main courses $6–$12 (£4.25–£8.50). AE, DC, MC, V. Daily 7:30am–11:30pm. No metro access.

Clark's ★ INTERNATIONAL The dining room here is an eclectic mix of oak, yellow lamps, live plants, and deer antlers. A slanted ceiling descends over the English-style bar with a fine selection of spirits; in back, a 3m-high (9³/₄-ft.) glass case showcases a winter garden. Booths and tables are usually occupied by North Americans. Specialties include tenderloin steak with goat cheese, sautéed shrimp with wild mushrooms, and sole with a sparkling wine, cream, and shrimp sauce. A number of pasta and rice dishes are served as well. A large terrace attracts a fashionable crowd in summer.

Roberto M. Ortiz 1777 (at Quintana). © 11/4801-9502. Reservations recommended. Main courses $8–$14 (£5.70–£9.95). AE, DC, MC, V. Daily noon–3:30pm and 7:30pm–midnight. No metro access.

El Mirasol ★★ PARRILLA One of the city's best *parrillas,* this restaurant serves thick cuts of fine Argentine beef. Like Piegari (see above), El Mirasol is also located in La Recova, but this glassed-in dining area full of plants and trellises gives the impression of dining outdoors. Your waiter will guide you through the selection of cuts, among which the rib-eye, tenderloin, sirloin, and ribs are most popular. A mammoth, 1.1kg (2¹/₂ lb.) serving of tenderloin is a specialty, certainly meant for sharing. El Mirasol is part of a chain that first opened in 1967. The best dessert is an enticing combination of meringue, ice cream, whipped cream, *dulce de leche* (caramel sauce), walnuts, and hot chocolate sauce. The wine list pays tribute to Argentine Malbec, syrah, merlot, and cabernet sauvignon. El Mirasol, frequented by business executives and government officials at lunch and a more relaxed crowd at night, remains open throughout the afternoon.

Posadas 1032 (at Av. 9 de Julio in La Recova, near the Four Seasons Hotel). © 11/4326-7322. www.el-mirasol.com.ar. Reservations recommended. Main courses $8–$40 (£5.70–£28). AE, DC, MC, V. Daily noon–2am. No metro access.

Juana M ★★ (Value) PARRILLA This *parrilla* is hard to find but worth the effort and remains one of my favorite dining spots in the city. A family-owned affair, it takes its name from its chic matriarch owner and is known almost solely to Porteños who want to keep this place all to themselves. This neoclassical building has a cavernous, industrial-chic space that can seat more than 200 patrons. Art covers one of the walls lining the waiter stations. At night, when the space is lit only by candlelight, trendy young people flood in, chattering the night away. The menu is simple, high quality, and inexpensive, with a free unlimited salad bar. A new light menu with fish and chicken options has been added recently, along with other healthy options. The restaurant may move to a new location by 2010, but will remain in Recoleta through 2009.

In the basement at Carlos Pellegrini 1535 (at Libertador, across from the La Recova area). © **11/4326-0462.** Main courses $5–$13 (£3.55–£9.25). AE, MC, V. Sun–Fri noon–5pm and 7:30pm–1am; Sat 8pm–2am. No metro access.

INEXPENSIVE

La Biela ★★★ CAFE   Originally a small sidewalk cafe opened in 1850, La Biela earned its distinction in the 1950s as the rendezvous choice of race-car champions. Black-and-white photos of these Argentine racers decorate the huge dining room. Today artists, politicians, and neighborhood executives (as well as a very large number of tourists) all frequent La Biela, which serves breakfast, informal lunch plates, ice cream, and crepes. The outdoor terrace sits beneath an enormous 19th-century gum tree opposite the church of Nuestra Señora del Pinar and the adjoining Recoleta Cemetery. This place ranks among the most important cafes in the city, with some of the best sidewalk viewing anywhere in Recoleta. You might just feel like you're in Paris when you come here. La Biela is a protected *bar notable*.

Av. Quintana 596 (at Alvear). © **11/4804-0449.** www.labiela.com.ar. Main courses $3–$12 (£2.15–£8.50). V. Daily 7am–3am. No metro access.

Maru Botana ★ CAFE/INTERNATIONAL   A pleasant little cafe on a small out-of-the-way street in Recoleta, Maru Botana is owned by an Argentine television cooking-show personality. In spite of her fame, the cafe is unpretentious and quiet, with only a few nods to its celebrity-chef owner. You'll find a small inside seating area where you can sip tea and have excellent baked goods or such light items as salads and sandwiches. It's also near the Israeli Embassy Monument, commemorating the fatal 1992 bombing, so it makes a great place to stop and quietly contemplate what you have just seen.

Suipacha 1371 (at Arroyo). © **11/4326-7134.** www.marubotana.com.ar. Main courses $3–$7 (£2.15–£4.95). AE, MC, V. Mon–Fri 9am–8pm. Metro: San Martín.

8 BARRIO NORTE

For a map of the restaurants listed in this section, see the "Where to Dine in Central Buenos Aires" map on p. 90.

EXPENSIVE

Milion ★★ Finds INTERNATIONAL   This is one of the most stunningly situated restaurants in Buenos Aires, and yet, though around for a decade, it remains hard to find. You must pass through the marble-lined, former carriage entrance of a beautiful Belle Epoque mansion, and then make the choice of dining in the garden or upstairs in a room with dark-wood-paneled walls with bronze sconces and beveled-glass windows. Beef is served in large, hearty portions, and lighter menu items include fish, especially in the summer months, as well as creative salads and tapas. Many people come here just for drinks and socializing, which spreads to all the floors of the five-level mansion. If you hear about any of the local art or media parties that sometimes happen here, be sure to find a way to get invited.

Parana 1048 (at Santa Fe). ℂ **11/4815-9925.** www.milionargentina.com.ar. Main courses $10–$15 **105** (£7.10–£11). AE, MC, V. Mon–Wed noon–2am; Thurs noon–3am; Fri noon–4am; Sat 8pm–4am; Sun 8pm–2am. Metro: Callao.

MODERATE

Clásica y Moderna ★★ (Finds) ARGENTINE   This restaurant represents an interesting way to save an important bookstore from extinction—by opening a restaurant inside. The bookstore opened in this location in 1938, but in 1988, books were relegated to the back to make way for diners. This is one of the best bookstores for English-speaking tourists in the city. You'll find Buenos Aires photo and history books, as well as Argentine short-story collections, all translated into English. While this is a protected *café notable,* the interior has been completely stripped down to the exposed brick, giving the place a dark, industrial feel. However, it is a pleasant, relaxed space. There are many light, healthful choices, such as salads and soy burgers. Mixed drinks start at $5 (£3.55). Events of all kinds are held here, from literary readings to dance shows. Shows are held Wednesday to Saturday at 10pm, and sometimes after midnight.

Callao 892 (at Córdoba). ℂ **11/4812-8707** or 11/4811-3670. Reservations recommended for shows. Main courses $5–$15 (£3.55–£11). AE, MC, V. Daily 8am–1am. Bookstore hours: Mon–Sat 9am–1am; Sun 5pm–1am. Metro: Callao.

Tandoor ★ (Finds) ASIAN/INDIAN   If you're looking for an overdone, Bollywood-inspired dining experience, you won't find it at Tandoor. You will, however, enjoy fine dining in an elegant French neoclassical building. Owners Shahrukh and Belli are Indian expats; Shahrukh had originally come to Argentina to tango in 2004, and then opened Tandoor in 2007. All of the menu items come mildly spiced, but you can have anything spiced to taste. The philosophy behind the restaurant is to have various regional dishes, many cooked in styles as families do at home. Choose such staples as the classic Tandoori curry chicken dish, *tikka masala,* or *KuKuPak,* chicken in curry and coconut milk, based on a family recipe. Shahrukh recommends lamb Biryani, cooked the old-fashioned way in a sealed pot for a few hours. Several kinds of *naan* (flatbread) can accompany the meal. Finish with basmati rice pudding, mango ice cream, or a fusion dessert.

Laprida 1293 (at Charcas). ℂ **11/4821-3676.** www.tandoor.com.ar. Main courses $8–$15 (£5.70–£11). AE, MC, V. Daily noon–4pm, 8pm–1am, sometimes later. Metro: Aguero.

9 CONGRESO

For a map of the restaurants listed in this section, see the "Where to Dine in Central Buenos Aires" map on p. 90.

MODERATE

Inside Resto-Bar ★ INTERNATIONAL/ARGENTINE   This place is very popular with a largely gay clientele, though anyone is welcome. The waitstaff and owners provide great, attitude-free service here; in fact, the two co-owners work along with their staff, with Diego serving and Matias cooking. There is a low-key red-and-black decor, with dim moody lighting, and a second level of tables that open up when it gets crowded. The food is a mix of French and Italian influences and is very flavorfully prepared. This is also a good place to go just for drinks at the small bar, where many locals gather for conversation. On weekends, there are special tango shows and male strippers, too, after 12:30am. Reservations are accepted and recommended for weekends. Ask about return coupons, with great discounts for people who come back during slow nights early in the week. The owners plan to sell the restaurant in 2009, which might change the atmosphere.

Bartolomé Mitre 1571 (at Montevideo). ✆ **11/4372-5439.** Main courses $5–$15 (£3.55–£11). No credit cards. Daily 7pm–2am, later Sat–Sun, depending on the crowds. Metro: Congreso.

La Clac ★ PARRILLA/ARGENTINE   If you're looking for a fun, kitschy place with a lot of local color, this is the right spot. This is a theater restaurant, decorated with all manner of things on the walls and ceiling, from pictures of 1960s Argentine comedians, to currency from all over the country, to bottles of all kinds and some things indescribable. As you're eating, you may begin to notice lines forming all around you, but people aren't gathered to keep an eye on your table manners. The basement of the restaurant plays host to unusual plays and comedy routines, usually starting at 9pm. Food is basic Argentine, from steaks to salads, sandwiches, and pastas.

Av. de Mayo 1156 (at Salta). ✆ **11/4382-6529** or 11/4115-3510. Main courses $8–$10 (£5.70–£7.10). MC. Daily 8am–2am, sometimes later Sat–Sun. Metro: Lima.

Plaza Asturias ★★ (Finds) SPANISH/ITALIAN/ARGENTINE   This decades-old place on Avenida de Mayo is about as authentic as it gets, packed mostly with only Porteños who want to keep this place to themselves. It's all about the food here, with touches of Italian, Argentine, and most importantly, authentic Spanish cuisine. They are so busy and have to keep so much food on hand here that legs of cured ham literally hang from the rafters over the diners' heads. Steaks are as thick as the crowds waiting to get into this place, and among the specialties are Spanish casseroles and lots of food with various sauces. Fish is also a big highlight. Be warned: The staff is so busy yelling out orders to the kitchen and bringing food to the tables that you can get hurt trying to find the bathroom.

Av. de Mayo 1199 (at San José). ✆ **11/4382-7334.** Main courses $6–$10 (£4.25–£7.10). No credit cards. Daily noon–3am. Metro: Sáenz Peña.

Plaza del Carmen CAFE/ARGENTINE   This is part of a chain, slightly sterile and clean. However, the best part of this cafe is not inside, but the view outside from this corner overlooking Congreso. The cafe is generally open 24 hours, but no matter what time of day, you can find people having nothing more than croissants and coffee here. Weekdays, the outdoor seating area is a little overwhelming, since there is a huge amount of traffic flowing by this corner. But inside, protected from the noise and bus and car fumes, everything is just fine. Wait until the weekends, when the sidewalk is less busy, and the outdoor area becomes more ideal. This restaurant serves standard Argentine cuisine, in addition to a healthy choice of salads and diet and other light food. Pizzas, pastas, and other Italian items round out the menu.

Rivadavia 1795 (at Callao). ✆ **11/4374-8477.** Main courses $5–$8 (£3.55–£5.70). AE, MC, V. Daily 24 hr. Metro: Congreso.

36 Billares ★★ ARGENTINE   This restaurant opened in 1894, but was reborn in 2005 into a more exciting version of itself. Originally a restaurant that was part of a gambling and gaming hall (*billares* is Spanish for billiards), it has been revamped with new food and nightly entertainment, ranging from tango to flamenco. Most patrons are old-time Porteños who even sing along to the music. Some of the best nights are Thursdays, when there's a spontaneous tango show. As a historic bar, it has a rich and beautiful interior of oak paneling with marquetry details, and a Movado clock from the 1920s. Below ground, the billiards-and-games hall remains, with some of the oldest equipment around still in use. The dishes are reasonably priced, with large portions. Try the Lomo de la Avenida, a steak with Patagonian mushrooms, or any of the chicken or pasta dishes. There's no charge for the show, held every night except Monday.

Av. de Mayo 1265 (btw. Libertad and Talcahuano). © **11/4381-5696.** www.los36billares.com.ar. Main courses $3.50–$10 (£2.50–£7.10). AE, DC, MC, V. Mon–Thurs 8am–1am; Fri–Sat 8am–5am; Sun 3pm–midnight. Metro: Lima.

INEXPENSIVE

Bien Porteño ★ CAFE/INTERNATIONAL/ARGENTINE   Known largely to Argentines who tango, this small cafe, opened in 2006, has an old-time atmosphere with its exposed-brick walls. The food is basic Argentine staples, such as grilled-beef *picadas* (tartlets), enhanced with sandwiches and salads, and many people come just for coffee to while away the time and chat. The main highlight of the restaurant is its emphasis on tango and folkloric shows on Friday and Saturday, which sometimes means a small entry fee of about $8 to $12 (£5.70–£8.50), or sometimes none at all. Ask about the schedule of tango classes also held on Monday, Wednesday, and Friday. Owner Ceferina de Jesus Orzuza speaks English, and with her piercing green-hazel eyes, is an engaging woman with whom to hold a conversation. The name of the restaurant is an expression meaning "very Buenos Aires," and it is to the core.

Rivadavia 1392 (at Uruguay). © **11/4383-5426.** www.bienporteno.com. Main courses $2–$6 (£1.40–£4.25). AE, MC, V. Daily Mon–Fri noon–9:30pm without show, until 2am or later with show. Sat–Sun hours depend on show times. Metro: Saenz Peña.

Café de Madres de Plaza de Mayo ★★ (Moments) CAFE   Officially named Café Literario Osvaldo Bayer, this cafe is inside the lobby of the headquarters of the Madres de Plaza de Mayo, just off Plaza Congreso. It's special for its location and left-wing political atmosphere. In few other places can you so easily speak with people whose family members disappeared during Argentina's military dictatorship, or with young students who have come to study and seek justice in this cause. The Madres bookstore is full of books and newspapers on liberal causes from throughout Latin America, with a large collection of books on Che Guevara. An Argentine native, he is a personal hero to many of the Madres, and his image adorns the building walls. The restaurant has expanded, with waitress service and an outdoor seating area added—a side effect of the smoking ban. New items include simple pasta dishes and a selection of Italian pastries.

Hipólito Yrigoyen 1584 (at Ceballos). © **11/4382-3261.** Main courses $3–$8 (£2.15–£5.70). No credit cards. Mon–Fri 8:30am–10:30pm; Sat (and some Sun) 11am–5pm. Metro: Congreso.

La Americana ★★ ARGENTINE/ITALIAN   This place calls itself "La Reina de las Empanadas" (the Queen of Empanadas), and that indeed it is. It serves an enormous range of empanadas, all made with a very light dough and slightly burnt edges; they're never heavy or greasy. The place is busy and loud, with the constant din of conversation bouncing off the tile-and-stone walls and the glass-plate windows looking out over Callao. There are tables, as well as a takeout section and an area for standing and eating. The place looks like many of the fast-food-chain empanada emporiums, but this is the only one of its kind. Waiters are frantic, and you may have to keep reminding them of what you ordered; the place is just too busy for normal humans to keep up with the pace. Italian specialties such as calzones and pizzas round out the menu choices. Deliveries can be made to nearby hotels.

Callao 83 (at Bartolomé Mitre). © **11/4371-0202.** Main courses $1–$7 (70p–£4.95). No credit cards. Sun–Thurs 7am–2am; Fri–Sat 7am–3am. Metro: Congreso.

La Moncloa ★ (Value) CAFE   The surrounding trees provide a sense of calm to side-walk eating in normally a busy area on a street just off Plaza Congreso. La Moncloa takes its name from a famous Spanish palace. Basic Argentine fare, such as empanadas, steaks, and salads, is served, along with croissant sandwiches and an extensive dessert menu. There is also a large selection of pork dishes, including the tempting pork in white-wine sauce. Still, for the diet-conscious, there is also a low-calorie menu with vegetarian offerings. Whatever you order, I recommend taking time for a break in this restaurant's park-like setting. Coffee runs about $1 (70p) and mixed drinks start at $3 (£2.15). Flavored and alcoholic coffees, another of the specialties, are about $5 (£3.55). If you don't have time to eat, stop by and grab a menu, as they'll deliver to local hotels.

Av. de Mayo 1500 (at Sáenz Peña). ℂ **11/4381-3357** or 11/4382-7194. Main courses $3–$9 (£2.15–£6.40). AE, DC, MC, V. Daily 7:30am–2am. Metro: Sáenz Peña.

10 PALERMO

For a map of the restaurants listed in this section, see the "Where to Stay & Dine in Palermo" map on p. 110.

VERY EXPENSIVE

Casa Cruz ★★ (Finds) ITALIAN/INTERNATIONAL   Opened in December 2004, Casa Cruz is one of the city's chicest restaurants. With its enormous polished-brass doors and lack of a sign on the door, it feels like you are entering a nightclub, and inside the dark modern interior maintains the theme. The impressive round bar, always decorated with fresh flower arrangements, is the first thing you'll see before entering the spacious dining area full of polished woods and red upholstery. The place takes its name from its owner, Juan Santa Cruz. This is his first venture into restaurants, and with the attention this restaurant has received in the national and international press, he has done exceedingly well. The menu here is eclectic and interesting, overseen by Germán Martitegui, the same chef who oversees the kitchen at Olsen. Rabbit, sea bass, Parma ham rolls, and other interesting and exotic ingredients go into the many flavorful dishes.

Uriarte 1658 (at Honduras). ℂ **11/4833-1112.** www.casa-cruz.com. Reservations highly recommended. Main courses $25–$45 (£18–£32). AE, MC, V. Mon–Sat 8:30pm–3am. No metro access.

EXPENSIVE

Bar Uriarte ★★★ INTERNATIONAL/ITALIAN   This restaurant is another of the city's hippest places to eat. It serves many creative dishes, from veal ravioli to saffron risotto to skirt steak with olives and thyme, in a kitchen overseen by one of the few female star chefs in Buenos Aires, Julieta Oiolo. Such basics as *parrilla*, pasta, and salads round out the menu for the less experimental. There's a long bar with moody pink lights on the walls, and lounge areas to sit and chat with friends either for 5 to 8pm tea or 8 to 10:30pm happy hour. The place has an industrial-chic design with a polished concrete floor and interesting wooden art. Choose a table in the patio garden and dine in the open air. Other unique touches here include a *horno de barro* at the bar, where they bake bread and cook with wood for special flavor. The main kitchen seen through the front window is immaculate from so much attention by onlookers. A special brunch is served on weekends.

Uriarte 1572 (btw. Honduras and Gorritti). ℂ **11/4834-6004.** www.baruriarte.com.ar. Reservations highly recommended. Main courses $9–$30 (£6.40–£21). AE, MC, V. Daily noon–2am, later Sat–Sun. Metro: Plaza Italia.

Ceviche ★★ JAPANESE/PERUVIAN/SEAFOOD   A trend has developed in Buenos Aires, which some say came out of the sushi trend and combined with an increase in the Peruvian population living in the city following the tourism boom. Peruvian restaurants have sprouted, with Japanese-Argentine chefs working as the stars bringing the cuisine together. Ceviche is among the newest and most elegant of the locations, with exposed blood-red brick walls and antique posters, and a hint of the Andean nation with its Peruvian textile accents. The sushi bar sits at the front of the restaurant, with the dark, moody, candlelit dining area towards the back, and an open-air patio decorated with cactus and other desert plants. Chef Roberto Nishida oversees the menu and preparation, from the sushi to the *ceviche* to an array of other seafood dishes. Desserts are a highlight as well, from Peruvian flan to *dulce de leche* (caramel) cheesecake.

Costa Rica 5644 (at Fitzroy). ℂ **11/4776-7373.** www.ceviche.com.ar. Reservations recommended. Main courses $12–$15 (£8.50–£11). AE, DC, MC, V. Mon–Fri 12:30–3pm and 8pm–1am; Sat 8pm–1am. Metro: Palermo.

Cluny ★★★ INTERNATIONAL/ARGENTINE   Cluny is casual but elegant, looking more like a modernist living room than a dining room. A loft space is excellent for hiding away for private conversations or romance. Some choose to dine outside in the patio garden in the restaurant's front space. Sinatra tunes and bossa nova music from the 1960s add to the soft, casual atmosphere. The food, overseen by the new chefs, is the highlight, with an emphasis on fish and fowl, from prawn risotto to spider crabs and duck magret. There are many salmon and codfish dishes, and the interestingly named "Lamb cooked in two different ways." Beef seems to be a second thought, unlike in other Argentine restaurants, though it is well prepared. The extensive wine list runs more than eight pages, noting the finest Argentine vintages from Catena Zapata to French imports at more than $250 (£178) a bottle. In the afternoon, there's a fine British tea service.

El Salvador 4618 (at Malabia). ℂ **11/4831-7176.** Reservations highly recommended. Main courses $15–$20 (£11–£14). AE, MC, V. Mon–Sat 12:30–4pm, 4–7:30pm for tea time, and 8pm–1am, sometimes later. Metro: Plaza Italia.

La Baita ★★ ITALIAN   This is one of the best Italian restaurants you'll find in Palermo Viejo. It's upscale and yet very family-style, so much so that manager Guido Bioloi often has his grandchildren in his arms as he leads you to your seat. Traditional home-made pastas and sauces, seafood of the day, and *Saltimbocca alla Romana* are served in the Pompeian red interior space. Wine is served by the glass and the bottle, and an upstairs loft has seating under a skylight. This restaurant is often exceedingly crowded, but with good reason.

Thames 1603 (at Honduras). ℂ **11/4832-7234.** www.labaita-restaurante.com.ar. Main courses $10–$15 (£7.10–£11). AE, MC, V. Tues–Fri noon–3pm; Mon–Fri 8pm–2am; Sat–Sun noon–2am, sometimes later. Metro: Plaza Italia.

La Cabrera ★★ (Finds) ARGENTINE/PARRILLA   This restaurant has become so well known among tourists visiting Buenos Aires, that the owners have also opened another branch up the street for spillover patrons, called **La Cabrera Norte** at Cabrera 5127 (ℂ **11/4832-5754**). The place and its branch deserve their very worthy reputations. The meat is excellent and comes in such huge portions that it's impossible to finish it. One of the specialties is also Pamplona, a roll made of various meats and sauces, or try their pork ribs with a sauce of dried tomatoes and pesto. All meals come with a spread of olives, sauces, breads, and other appetizers, which is a meal in itself. The restaurant sits

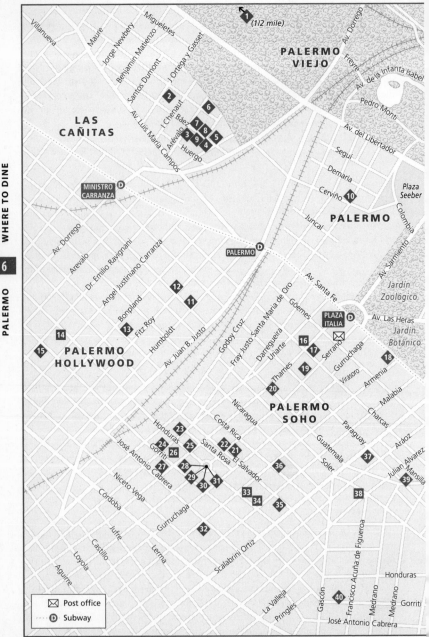

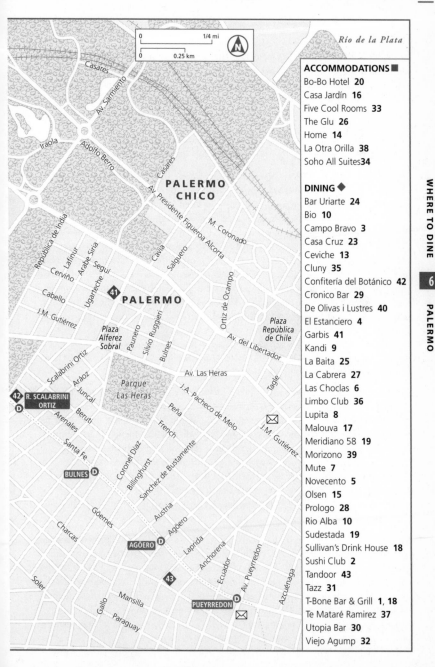

Río de la Plata

ACCOMMODATIONS ■
Bo-Bo Hotel **20**
Casa Jardín **16**
Five Cool Rooms **33**
The Glu **26**
Home **14**
La Otra Orilla **38**
Soho All Suites **34**

DINING ◆
Bar Uriarte **24**
Bio **10**
Campo Bravo **3**
Casa Cruz **23**
Ceviche **13**
Cluny **35**
Confitería del Botánico **42**
Cronico Bar **29**
De Olivas i Lustres **40**
El Estanciero **4**
Garbis **41**
Kandi **9**
La Baita **25**
La Cabrera **27**
Las Choclas **6**
Limbo Club **36**
Lupita **8**
Malouva **17**
Meridiano 58 **19**
Morizono **39**
Mute **7**
Novecento **5**
Olsen **15**
Prologo **28**
Rio Alba **10**
Sudestada **19**
Sullivan's Drink House **18**
Sushi Club **2**
Tandoor **43**
Tazz **31**
T-Bone Bar & Grill **1, 18**
Te Mataré Ramirez **37**
Utopia Bar **30**
Viejo Agump **32**

WHERE TO DINE

6

PALERMO

on a corner and is a beautiful setting for outdoor dining, or you can eat inside in the charming dining room with exposed brick walls and antique posters.

Cabrera 5099 (at Thames). ✆ **11/4831-7002.** Main courses $8–$18 (£5.70–£13). AE, DC, MC, V. Wed–Sun 12:30–4pm; Sun–Thurs 8:30pm–1am, later Sat–Sun. No metro access.

Mute INTERNATIONAL   Open from late breakfast until the wee hours, Mute has dining on two levels in its dark, chic space. The place really comes alive at night though, when a DJ spins Electronica. Technically there's no dancing, but people have been known to shake around while eating. The selection is varied, from Argentine beef staples to fish to a vegetarian selection and different pastas. Top it off with interesting desserts, such as ice cream with ginger sauce, or risk their huge chocolate volcano, a multilayered confection.

Baez 243 (btw. Arguibel and Arevalo). ✆ **11/4776-6883.** www.mute.com.ar. Main courses $12–$17 (£8.50–£12). AE, MC, V. Mon–Tues 10am–3am; Wed–Sat 10am–5am. Metro: Carranza.

Olsen ★★ SCANDINAVIAN/SEAFOOD   A bit of Scandinavia has landed in Argentina. Built into a former warehouse, Olsen soars to churchlike proportions, with a mezzanine overlooking the main dining area. The interior, complete with a central round metal fireplace, has a 1960s feel, with blond woods, straight lines, and funky dish settings. A patio garden with a metal sculpture fountain is an extremely tranquil space. Olsen is very popular with tourists and locals alike, and most of the extremely attractive staff members speak English. Starters are fun and meant to be shared, such as an excellent selection of bagels, tiny pancakes, smoked salmon, smoked herring, caviar, and flavored cheeses and butters. Fish is the main point of this place, and a few of the meat dishes, though flavorful, tend to be on the dry side. Many people come just for the bar, and there is an enormous vodka selection kept in special super-cold freezers. Sunday brunch is at 10am.

Gorriti 5870 (at Carranza). ✆ **11/4776-7677.** restaurantolsen@netizon.com.ar. Reservations recommended. Main courses $12–$25 (£8.50–£18). AE, MC, V. Tues–Thurs noon–1am; Fri–Sat 12:30pm–2:30am, sometimes later if busy; Sun 10am–1am. No metro access.

Rio Alba ★ PARRILLA/ARGENTINE   Tucked away in the neighborhood behind La Rural, this great high-end *parrilla* is easy to overlook. Its neighborhood makes it a favorite of the embassy crowd. There's a certain old-fashioned flavor to the place, with its white-linen tablecloths, rustic chairs, yellow walls, wheat-stalk bouquets in its columns, and legs of ham hooked to the rafters, mixing a touch of elegance with a touch of the countryside. Cuts of meat are massive and juicy, from the *ojo de bife* to the *lomo*. Or choose pork, chicken, or fish, all in hefty portions. Wine from 10 different bodegas is served, and there's a great selection of desserts to top it all off.

Cerviño 4499 (at Oro). ✆ **11/4773-5748.** Main courses $12–$25 (£8.50–£18). AE, DC, MC, V. Daily noon–4pm and 8pm–1am. Metro: Plaza Italia.

Sudestada ★ VIETNAMESE/ASIAN/THAI   Inside this simply decorated restaurant, a Zen-like white and black, you'll find some of the best Asian cuisine in Buenos Aires. Sudestada is a mix of Vietnamese, Thai, and other Oriental cuisine. Look for the special wok menu, or choose pork with lemon grass, rabbit with rice and vegetables, or interesting desserts such as lychee pie. Argentine beef is great, but if you're looking for a night out with something different, this will be a wonderful change.

Guatemala 5602 (at Fitzroy). ✆ **11/4776-3777.** Main courses $12–$20 (£8.50–£14). AE, MC, V. Mon–Sat noon–3:30pm; Mon–Thurs 8pm–midnight; Fri–Sat 8pm–1am. Metro: Palermo.

Te Mataré Ramírez ★★★ (Finds) INTERNATIONAL/FRENCH   This is perhaps **113**
the most interesting and creative dining experience in Buenos Aires. Its symbol, an
aroused fork with an extended and upright prong, hints at the erotic nature of the restaurant, whose name ("I am going to kill you, Ramírez)" comes from playful arguments
the owner had with a friend who was a Casanova. The food has sensual combinations,
such as garlic and sun-dried tomatoes, mixed with sweet elements and poured over sautéed or marinated meats with deeply embedded flavor. This emphasis on contrasts creates
some of the most flavorful cooking in town. The ceilings are decorated with paintings of
naked men and women with naughty cherubs. Erotic art hangs on the walls and the
lighting is boudoir red. Black-clothed actors perform playfully racy shows on a small
stage here. Slow, soft music, such as jazz and bossa nova, plays as you eat, adding to the
mood for love.

Paraguay 4062 (at Scalabrini Ortiz). ✆ 11/4831-9156. www.tematareramirez.com. Reservations recommended. Main courses $10–$20 (£7.10–£14). AE, MC, V. Sun–Wed 9pm–midnight; Thurs–Fri 9pm–1am;
Sat 9pm–2am. Metro: Scalabrini Ortiz.

MODERATE

Bio ★★ (Finds) VEGETARIAN/MEDITERRANEAN   In a nation where meat reigns
supreme, finding an organic vegetarian restaurant is nearly impossible. Bio, opened in
2002, is the exception. The "meat" is made on the premises from wheat, then marinated
to add more flavor, making for an elevated, tasty variation on a hamburger. All the ingredients are organic, grown or produced strictly in Argentina. Piles of organic cheese line
the counters near the chefs, who explain the processes by which they work. Quinoa, the
ancient Incan grain, is used in many dishes, some described as Mediterranean-Asian
fusion. Try the quinoa risotto, one of the restaurant's specialties, though everything here
is simply delicious and fresh. A small shop sells organic chips, teas, cheeses, and even
organic wine, and it's a great place for veg-heads to buy snacks. You can also get takeout—a delight if you want to bring something home with you.

Humboldt 2199 (at Guatemala). ✆ 11/4774-3880. Main courses $8–$10 (£5.70–£7.10). No credit cards.
Mon 9am–5pm; Tues–Sun 9am–1am, often later Sat–Sun. No metro access.

Campo Bravo ★★ (Value) PARRILLA/ARGENTINE   This place serves as the virtual
center of the Las Cañitas dining scene. It's relaxed during the day, but insane at night.
Dining on the sidewalk here, you'll get a great view of the glamorous crowds emerging
from taxis to kick off their night in this exciting neighborhood. The *parrilla* serves up
basic Argentine cuisine, and its enormous slabs of meat are served on wooden boards. A
large, efficient waitstaff will take care of you, but there's a long wait for an outside table
on weekends—sometimes 40 minutes to an hour—and they don't accept reservations. So
do as the locals do on Saturday night: Get a glass of champagne and sip it on the street
amid what looks like a well-dressed and overage frat party. A limited wine selection and
imported whiskeys are also part of the drink selection, and the place doesn't close
between lunch and dinner.

Báez 292 (at Arévalo). ✆ 11/4514-5820. Main courses $6–$11 (£4.25–£7.80). AE, MC. Mon 6pm–4am;
Tues–Sun 11:30am–4am, often later Sat–Sun, depending on crowds. Metro: Carranza.

De Olivas i Lustres ★★ MEDITERRANEAN   This magical restaurant opened in
Palermo Viejo several years ago, setting the trend for the gastronomic paradise the neighborhood would soon become. The dining room displays eccentric antiques, olive jars,
and wine bottles. The reasonably priced menu celebrates Mediterranean cuisine, with
light soups, fresh fish, and sautéed vegetables as its focus. The breast of duck with lemon

and honey is mouthwatering; there are also *tapeos*—appetizer-size dishes. Best of all: For about $15 (£11) a person, you and your partner can share 15 sensational small plates brought out individually over the course of a couple of hours. What I find most unique in the restaurant beyond the Mediterranean fare is the use of native and Incan ingredients in various dishes. If you have ever wanted to try alligator or llama, this is the place to do it.

Gorriti 3972 (at Medrano). ☎ **11/4867-3388.** Reservations recommended. Main courses $6–$15 (£4.25–£11). AE, MC, V. Mon–Sat 7:30pm–1:30am. Metro: Scalabrini Ortiz.

El Estanciero ★ (Finds) PARRILLA   In most of the restaurants in the Las Cañitas section of Palermo, it's all about the glamour. Here, however, in the *parrilla* El Estanciero, it's all about the beef, arguably the best in the neighborhood. The portions are not the largest, but the cuts are amazingly flavorful, with just the right mix of fat to add tenderness. If you order the steak rare *(jugoso),* it won't be served nearly raw. The restaurant is in two levels, with sidewalk seating at the entrance and a covered open-air terrace above. Both floors have a subtle, gaucho-accented decor that does not overwhelm the senses with kitsch. Never as crowded as the other restaurants lining the street, it's a great option when the lines are too long at nearby hot spots.

Báez 202 (at Arguibel). ☎ **11/4899-0951.** Main courses $3–$12 (£2.15–£8.50). AE, MC, V. Daily noon–4pm and 8pm–1am (to 2am Sat–Sun). Metro: Ministro Carranza.

Garbis ★★ (Kids) MIDDLE EASTERN   If you're looking for great Middle Eastern food at reasonable prices or a spot to entertain the kids, Garbis has the answer. Kabobs, falafel, lamb, and other Middle Eastern mainstays are all on the menu, along with great, friendly service. The desert decor—in the form of tiled walls and brilliant colors—makes you think you've wound up far away from Argentina. A children's entertainment center will keep the kids happy while you dine. Tarot card readings on select days add fun for the adults. Call to find out the mystic's schedule. This is a chain, with additional restaurants in Belgrano and Villa Crespo.

Scalabrini Ortiz 3190 (at Cerviño). ☎ **11/4511-6600.** www.garbis.com.ar. Main courses $5–$15 (£3.55–£11). AE, MC, V. Daily 11am–3pm and 7–11:30pm. Metro: Scalabrini Ortiz.

Kandi JAPANESE/SEAFOOD   You'll find great sushi and other seafood at this dinner-only sushi bar built in the style of a funky '70s club, with curved wooden decor and psychedelic orange wallpaper. The menu has a mix of other items, from hamburgers and Spanish tapas to small pizzas, chicken salads, and bar food, so you can always bring landlubber friends along. The large wine list notes a broad array of whites, perfect for the cuisine. On weekends, after dining, the decor is enhanced with a DJ playing electronic dance music.

Baez 340 (btw. Arevalo and Chenaut). ☎ **11/4772-2453.** Main courses $10–$15 (£7.10–£11). AE, DC, MC, V. Sun and Tues–Thurs 8pm–2am; Fri–Sat 8pm–5am. Metro: Carranza.

Limbo Club ★ INTERNATIONAL   More a bar than a restaurant, this place has an international menu of finger food, tapas, salads, sandwiches, and other quick eats. With the ambience of a lounge, it's a great place to pop in for conversations with friends. The front area is open to the sidewalk and has outdoor seating, so you're in the open air no matter where you sit, great for Palermo people-watching. The club serves Happy Hour specials, and, though there is no dancing, a DJ rules the night, with a mix of jazz, electronic, Latin pop, and other music to while away the evening hours.

Costa Rica 4588 (btw. Armenia and Malabia). ☎ **11/4831-0459.** Main courses $5–$12 (£3.55–£8.50). MC, V. Tues–Fri 6pm–4am; Sat–Sun noon–4am, sometimes later. Metro: Plaza Italia.

Lupita ★★ MEXICAN   Modern Mexican cuisine awaits at Lupita, an almost religious experience with its giant image of the Virgin of Guadalupe (hence the name) overlooking the bar. This dinner-only restaurant has nine kinds of guacamole, various combination platters, and delicious gourmet tacos and quesadillas. Desserts are a riot of creativity from pastries mixing peaches and corn to chocolate flan with banana topping. At night, the restaurant's two levels are lit throughout by candles. The menu of alcoholic drinks comes on a board with crazy decorations glued all over it—more Virgins and plastic Day of the Dead skeletons and tiny sombreros—and it lists the enormous tequila collection, among other liquors. Owner Diego Sicoli has worked at nearby Novecento and uses his skills to great effect here.

Baez 227 (btw. Arguibel and Arevalo). ✆ **11/5197-5149.** www.lupitaweb.com.ar. Main courses $7–$9 (£4.95–£6.40). AE, MC, V. Sun–Tues 8pm–1am; Wed 8pm–2am; Thurs–Sat 8pm–3am. Metro: Carranza.

Meridiano 58 ★★ (Finds) ARGENTINE/INTERNATIONAL   This moody Argentine restaurant has an aura of Zen chic. During the day, you'll notice its Argentine touches, such as Salta Indian designs, leather lounge sofas, and tables with dark leather placemats. At night, when the staircase is lit with candles and the water fountain is on, you're in a new romantic world. The restaurant has three levels, plus a torchlit terrace, all overseen by waiters in gauzy outfits with Nehru collars. In spite of these slightly Asian touches, the food is strictly Argentine. It is "elaborado," or ornate Argentine, with many of the meats marinated, such as the beef with mushrooms and herbs. Desserts are worth a trip here, especially the chocolate mousse with passion fruit or the orange flan with ginger and coconut. Prix-fixe lunch and dinner menus run from $12 to $15 (£8.50–£11), Monday to Thursday. The restaurant's refers Buenos Aires's location on the globe, Meridian 58.

J.L. Borges 1689 (at El Salvador). ✆ **11/4833-3443.** Main courses $7–$12 (£4.95–£8.50). AE, DC, MC, V. Daily noon–1am, later Sat–Sun. Metro: Plaza Italia.

Novecento ★★★ INTERNATIONAL   With a sister restaurant in New York's Soho, Novecento is a pioneer restaurant in Palermo's Las Cañitas neighborhood. Fashionable Porteños pack the New York–style bistro by 11pm, clinking wine glasses under a Canal Street sign or opting for the busy outdoor terrace. Waiters rush to keep their clients happy, with dishes such as salmon carpaccio and steak salad. The pastas and risotto are mouthwatering, but you may prefer a steak au poivre or a chicken brochette. Other wonderful choices include filet mignon, grilled Pacific salmon, and penne with wild mushrooms. Top it off with an Argentine wine. At night, by candlelight, Novecento makes a romantic choice for couples. A large, separate, but slightly sterile side room is available for spillover patrons or to rent for private parties.

Báez 199 (at Arguibel). ✆ **11/4778-1900.** www.bistronovecento.com. Reservations recommended. Main courses $8–$15 (£5.70–£11). AE, DC, MC, V. Daily noon–4pm and 8pm–2am; Sun brunch 8am–noon. Metro: Ministro Carranza.

T-Bone Bar & Grill ★ PARRILLA/INTERNATIONAL/ARGENTINE   If you want authentic Argentine meat by *parrilla* experts who have worked for more than 20 years, then come here, where huge portions weigh in at 500 grams, more than a pound of meat. T-Bone has two restaurants in Palermo, combining modern ambience and unique sightseeing with specialties from land and sea. Interesting starters include grilled provolone cheese with oregano, olive oil, tomato slices and arugula, and fresh sashimi salmon. T-Bone's signature steak and Patagonian rack of lamb are accompanied by rustic potatoes. The table service includes homemade bread, sauces, and an ice cream shot. More than 60 wines are on the wine list. The original Armenia Street restaurant has a warm, urban feel, while its new branch, overlooking the lakes next to the golf course in Palermo Park, has a terrace with a gardenlike atmosphere. (Av. Tornquist 6385 and Olleros; ℂ **11/4775-8866**).

Armenia 2479 (at Av. Santa Fe). ℂ **11/4833-6565**. www.tbone.com.ar. Reservations recommended. Main courses $8–$12 (£5.70–£8.50). AE, MC, V. Daily 8am–1 am. Metro: Plaza Italia.

INEXPENSIVE

Confitería del Botánico CAFE/ARGENTINE   Stop here after visiting the nearby zoo or Botanical Gardens. It's on a pleasant corner of busy Avenida Santa Fe, but the green spaces of the gardens and Plaza Siria give it a more tranquil feel. Enormous windows seem to bring the park inside. Continental breakfast here is inexpensive, and you can also order from the entire menu anytime of day (omelets from the dinner menu make a hearty breakfast). Lunch specials run $3 to $4 (£2.15–£2.85). They also do takeout, which makes a great picnic for the park or zoo.

Av. Santa Fe (at República Siria). ℂ **11/4833-5515**. Main courses $2–$4 (£1.40–£2.85). AE, MC, V. Sun–Fri 6:30am–midnight; Sat 6:30am–2am. Metro: Plaza Italia.

Las Choclas ★★ ARGENTINE/PARRILLA   Rustic tables, a casual atmosphere, inexpensive, wonderful food, and a great corner location combine in this Las Cañitas restaurant. The main emphasis is on beef, and tons of it, with *bife de chorizo, ojo de bife,* and other beef cuts served in large proportions. Filled with the scent of charred wood used in the ovens, the place is always very busy and doesn't close between lunch and dinner, so it's a great choice for getting your *parrilla* fix any time of day.

Arce 306 (at Arevolo). ℂ **11/4899-0094**. Main courses $3–$8 (£2.15–£5.70). No credit cards. Sun–Thurs noon–1am; Fri–Sat noon–2am. Metro: Carranza.

Malouva CAFE   This is a great location anytime, but it's best late at night when you have the munchies after barhopping in Palermo Viejo. Malouva is open 24 hours and was here long before the neighborhood around it got trendy. As such, you're not here for sophistication, but rather for the simple menu and the drink selection. Cheap items include salads, pastries, sandwiches, and pizzas. On the downside, service can be slow, and there's not enough staff for both the indoor and outdoor seating sections. Nevertheless, lots of young local people come here, making weekends especially crowded, with kids conversing over large bottles of Quilmes beer. If you're not staying nearby, don't worry about getting a cab from here: It's across the street from a gas station where taxi drivers clean and fuel up, so it's always easy to get a cab. In fact, the table next to yours may be full of taxi drivers taking a break from their long days.

Charcas 4401 (at Thames). ℂ **11/4774-0427**. Main courses $3–$9 (£2.15–£6.40). No credit cards. Daily 24 hr. Metro: Plaza Italia.

Prologo ★ PIZZA/INTERNATIONAL   Whether you're looking for a bar or a great place to eat inexpensively, Prologo's theme is "Let it Beer," and there are more than 70 local and international beers on the menu. To go along with that is a great selection of food, from breakfast omelets, to heavy German sandwiches, homemade pastas, hamburgers, salads, and Argentine staples such as beef from the grill. There's even a children's menu. Walls are covered with all sorts of bric-a-brac and posters, and there are tiny booths with high wooden backs, so you can sit cozily with friends and chat away, forgetting the world around you. Upstairs, dine with a view to Plaza Serrano and the exciting nightlife of Palermo Soho.

Serrano 1580 (at Borges, on Plaza Serrano). (C) **11/4833-0447.** Main courses $3–$8 (£2.15–£5.70). No credit cards. Sun–Thurs 8:30am–4am; Fri–Sat 24 hr. No metro access.

Sushi Club JAPANESE   This restaurant is part of a very popular chain, with many locations throughout the city, but this is one of its nicest outlets. It serves sushi and other Japanese cuisine in a modern, clublike interior, with orange, black, and metallic elements. Fish is a big highlight of the menu, as is beef with Japanese seasonings. The sushi-roll selection is enormous and creative, with different ingredients from international cuisine.

Ortega Y Gasset 1812 (at Arce). (C) **810/222-SUSHI** (222-78744; toll-free). Main courses $4–$8 (£2.85–£5.70). AE, DC, MC, V. Daily noon–5pm and 8pm–3am. Metro: Carranza.

Viejo Agump ★ (Finds) MIDDLE EASTERN   In the heart of the old Armenian section of Buenos Aires, owner Elizabeth Hounanjian provides authentic Middle Eastern cuisine and a new hub for her compatriots ("agump" means "club" or "meeting place" in Armenian), in the shadows of the Armenian church and the community center. The exposed-brick interior of the old house adds a touch of comfort to the dining area, where mainstays include kabobs and baklava. Sidewalk seating on this tree-lined street is a delight in warm weather. A special menu is offered for about $12 (£8.50), including an entree and a drink. On weekends, Arabic belly-dancing and coffee-bean readings heighten the exotic atmosphere. To arrange a reading, contact the mystic Roxana Banklian and schedule an appointment ((C) **11/15-4185-2225** [cell]; roxanabanklian@arnet.com.ar).

Armenia 1382 (at José Antonio Cabrera). (C) **11/4773-5081.** www.viejoagump.com.ar. Main courses $4–$8 (£2.85–£5.70). No credit cards. Mon–Thurs 8am–midnight; Fri 8am–2am; Sat 11am–2am. Metro: Scalabrini Ortiz.

11   ABASTO & ONCE

ABASTO
For a map of the restaurants listed in this section, see the "Abasto & Once" map on p. 119.

Inexpensive
Gardel de Buenos Aires ★ ARGENTINE/ITALIAN   You won't see tango here, but this cafe celebrates Carlos Gardel, the famous tango singer, in other ways. A clock with his face at the 12 o'clock position overlooks the dining area and his photos adorn red walls like icons in a Russian church. A papier-mâché mannequin of Gardel's likeness juts out from one of the walls, and his songs play nonstop from loudspeakers. It's a cute diversion, and in spite of the overwhelming kitsch, the food is good. The menu lists Argentine standards such as beef and empanadas, salads, pastas, desserts, sandwiches, pizzas, and other Italian specialties. The house specialty is *fugazzata*—a kind of stuffed pizza. Service is fast and friendly, so this is a great place for grabbing a quick coffee or a sandwich. It's

open 24 hours Friday and Saturday, so come by and toast Gardel, after a night on the town, with a drink from the extensive liquor selection. They also have a takeout menu.

Entre Ríos 796 (at Independencia). ✆ **11/4381-4170.** Main courses $3–$10 (£2.15–£7.10). AE, MC, V. Sun–Thurs 6am–2am; Fri–Sat 24 hr. Metro: Entre Ríos.

McDonald's Kosher★★ (Finds) AMERICAN/KOSHER   Certainly you didn't come all this way to eat at McDonald's. I wouldn't ordinarily tell a traveler to eat here on vacation, but this franchise is clearly unique: This is the only kosher McDonald's outside of Israel in the world, underscoring Buenos Aires's reputation as one of the world's greatest Jewish centers. Rabbi supervision makes sure that kosher rules are strictly followed here. It's typical McDonald's fare—burgers, fries, salads, fish sandwiches—except that no dairy at all is served here. They also sell souvenir mugs and other items to bring home. Locals of all kinds, Jewish or not, patronize the place. If you only come here to gawk and just can't stand a Big Mac without cheese, fret not: It's in the Abasto Shopping Center's Food Court, so all you have to do is turn around and walk to the regular McDonald's on the other side.

Abasto Shopping Center Food Court, Av. Corrientes 3247 (at Agüero). ✆ **11/4959-3709** or 0800/777-6236 for McDonald's Argentina information hot line. Main courses $1–$3 (70p–£2.15). No credit cards. Sun–Thurs 10am–midnight; Fri 10am–2pm; Sat 9pm–midnight, but times vary seasonally depending on sunset and Jewish holidays. Metro: Carlos Gardel.

ONCE

For a map of the restaurants listed in this section, see the "Abasto & Once" map on p. 119.

Moderate

El Galope ★ ARGENTINE/PARRILLA/MIDDLE EASTERN/KOSHER   This place is best described as an Argentine *parrilla,* with Middle Eastern accents and the added twist of being kosher. It's in what was once the main area of Buenos Aires's Jewish community. The *parrilla* serves wonderfully juicy and kosher slabs of beef (my experience in the U.S. has always been that beef plus kosher equals dry, but not here). This is one of Buenos Aires's most popular kosher restaurants. The interior is simple, wood-paneled, and home-style. The family that owns the restaurant oversees its operations; sometimes they argue right in front of you. The menu also features a selection of kosher Argentine wines, and you can take a bottle home with you. Middle Eastern fare—such as pitas and hummus as starters or sides, and baklava desserts—is also on hand, as well as fast food such as pastrami sandwiches and salads. Service is very low-key, but the food more than makes up for it.

Tucumán 2633 (at Pueyrredón). ✆ **11/4963-6888.** Main courses $3–$12 (£2.15–£8.50). No credit cards. Sun–Fri noon–3pm; Sun–Thurs 8pm–1am; Sat 9pm–midnight, but times vary seasonally depending on sunset and Jewish holidays. Metro: Pueyrredón.

Mamá Jacinta ★★ (Finds) INTERNATIONAL/ITALIAN/KOSHER/MIDDLE EASTERN/PARRILLA   Owner José Mizrahi opened this restaurant in 1999 and named it in honor of his Syrian Sephardic grandmother. His idea was to bring to the public the kind of food he remembers eating while growing up, updating it with the international influences that are all the rage in Argentina. He does much of the cooking himself, and chicken dishes are his favorite thing to make. After that, he recommends his

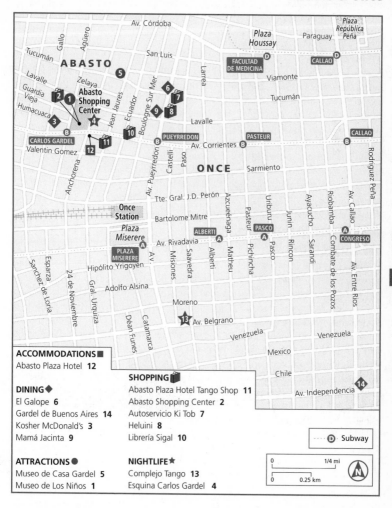

ACCOMMODATIONS ■
Abasto Plaza Hotel **12**

DINING ◆
El Galope **6**
Gardel de Buenos Aires **14**
Kosher McDonald's **3**
Mamá Jacinta **9**

ATTRACTIONS ●
Museo de Casa Gardel **5**
Museo de Los Niños **1**

SHOPPING 🛍
Abasto Plaza Hotel Tango Shop **11**
Abasto Shopping Center **2**
Autoservicio Ki Tob **7**
Heluini **8**
Librería Sigal **10**

NIGHTLIFE ★
Complejo Tango **13**
Esquina Carlos Gardel **4**

········ Ⓓ ····· Subway

0   1/4 mi
0   0.25 km

WHERE TO DINE

6

ABASTO & ONCE

fish and rice salad dishes, served in large enough portions for a table full of patrons to share and enjoy together. French, Japanese, and Italian sausages are grilled on the *parrilla* and can be sampled as starters. Pasta lovers can choose from a wide selection, all custom-made in the restaurant. Try also the *kibbe,* a kind of meat-filled dumpling.

Tucumán 2580 (at Paso). 🕾 **11/4962-9149** or 11/4962-7535. mamajacintakosher@hotmail.com. Main courses $3–$12 (£2.15–£8.50). No credit cards. Mon–Thurs noon–3:30pm and 8–11:30pm; Fri noon–3:30pm; Sat 1 hr. after sunset until midnight; Sun noon–3:30pm, but times vary seasonally depending on sunset and Jewish holidays. Metro: Pueyrredón.

For a map of the restaurants listed in this section, see the "La Boca" map on p. 121.

MODERATE

Barbería ARGENTINE/ITALIAN   This is a La Boca institution, with a very colorful interior, old-style banisters, and a waitstaff that prides itself on its Italian La Boca heritage. It's very touristy, though, just steps away from El Caminito's flood of out-of-town visitors and tacky souvenir stands. The owners, Nancy and Gustavo, are often around visiting the diners and will tell you that members of the La Boca Juniors often pop in for a meal. Tango, folkloric, and even drag shows run from noon until 5pm on the sidewalk dining area in front of the cafe, which overlooks the harbor. The prices are reasonable, especially for such a tourist-driven area, and the show is included in the price. Pastries, such as the Neapolitan *sfogliatella,* a local tradition, are always available. Every dish is served with a generous helping of history, and the staff is friendly.

Pedro de Mendoza 1959 (at Caminito). ✆ **11/4303-8256.** Main courses $3–$9 (£2.15–£6.40). No credit cards. Daily 11am–6pm, later in summer if busy. No metro access.

INEXPENSIVE

El Obrero ★★★ **Kids** PARRILLA/ITALIAN/ARGENTINE   Two old brothers from Barcelona started this wonderful institution several decades ago in a remote, hard-to-find part of La Boca. Here, you'll dine on thick, juicy, perfectly cooked steaks. Italian food, fish, and chicken are also served. You can order one-half and one-quarter portions of many items, which is great because they give you so much and you can bring the kids along without wasting food. La Boca Juniors and other sports memorabilia hang on the walls. This is one of the only places I recommend for serious eating in La Boca, but tables fill up rapidly at 9pm, so reserve or come earlier. You should arrive here by cab and have the restaurant call a cab for you when you leave at night. El Obrero is one of the best restaurants in Buenos Aires and should not be missed. However, though I've never had a problem in La Boca, it's considered a dangerous neighborhood to wander at night.

Agustin R. Caffarena 64 (at Caboto). ✆ **11/4362-9912.** Main courses $3–$8 (£2.15–£5.70). No credit cards. Mon–Sat noon–4pm and 8:30pm–midnight, sometimes later, depending on crowds. No metro access.

La Perla CAFE/ARGENTINE   This ancient cafe and bar is one of Buenos Aires's *cafés notables.* It dates from 1899 and has a beautiful interior, loaded with photos of the owners mingling with important visitors from around the world, who have come to visit La Boca and this important stop on the tourist circuit. Bill Clinton is among the luminaries, and his image is among those most highlighted. Pizzas, *picadas* (tartlets), and different coffees and drinks are served. If you're in La Boca, it's a good place to have a drink and soak up some atmosphere. Ironically, inflationary pressures throughout Buenos Aires mean that this is now a reasonably priced venue, and large numbers of locals often come now in a way they didn't before, adding authenticity to the bar.

Pedro de Mendoza 1899 (at Caminito). ✆ **11/4301-2985.** Main courses $3–$8 (£2.15–£5.70). No credit cards. Daily 7am–9pm. No metro access.

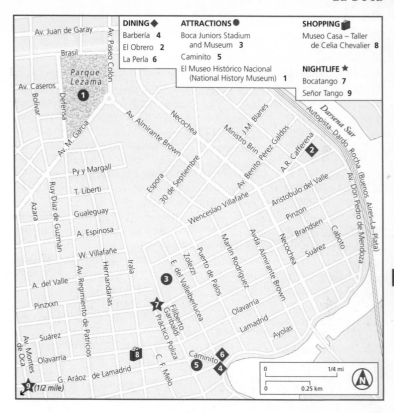

DINING ◆
Barbería 4
El Obrero 2
La Perla 6

ATTRACTIONS ●
Boca Juniors Stadium and Museum 3
Caminito 5
El Museo Histórico Nacional (National History Museum) 1

SHOPPING 🛍
Museo Casa – Taller de Celia Chevalier 8

NIGHTLIFE ★
Bocatango 7
Señor Tango 9

WHERE TO DINE

6

BELGRANO

13 BELGRANO

EXPENSIVE

Buddha BA ★ CHINESE   In the heart of Belgrano's Chinatown, this very elegant, two-level Chinese teahouse and restaurant is built into a house, with an adjacent garden and art gallery selling fine Asian art and antiques. The interesting and creatively named menu includes items such as Dragon Fire, a mix of spicy chicken and curried *lomo* (sirloin); or Buddha Tears, squid in a soy-and-chicken broth sauce with seasoned vegetables. The atmosphere is very welcoming and makes a great rest stop if you're exploring this neighborhood in depth.

Arribeños 2288 (at Mendoza). ℭ **11/4706-2382.** www.buddhaba.com.ar. Main courses $8–$15 (£5.70–£11). MC, V. Wed–Sun 8:30–11:30pm; Sat–Sun 12:30–3:30pm; tea service Wed–Sun 4–7:30pm. Metro: Juramento.

7

Exploring Buenos Aires

The beauty of Buenos Aires is evident the moment you set foot on her streets. You'll find yourself compelled to walk for hours, the alluring architecture and atmosphere pulling you along. The city's most impressive historical sites surround Plaza de Mayo, although you will certainly experience Argentine history in other neighborhoods, such as La Boca and San Telmo, too. You should also be sure not to miss a walk along the riverfront in Puerto Madero or an afternoon among the plazas and cafes of Recoleta or Palermo. Sidewalk cafes offer respite for weary feet, and there's good public transportation to carry you from neighborhood to neighborhood.

Your first stop should be one of the city tourism centers (see "Visitor Information," in chapter 3) to pick up a city map and get advice. You can also ask at your hotel for a copy of *The Golden Map* and *QuickGuide Buenos Aires* to help you navigate the city and locate its major attractions. Various neighborhoods have their own special maps, so ask at the centers or at local businesses.

Though no longer as cheap as just a few years ago, Buenos Aires is still less expensive than a North American or European vacation. This is a huge change from before the 2001 peso crisis, when it was Latin America's most expensive city. It's a legacy from long ago: When exploring Buenos Aires, it's important to remember that for almost the entire first half of the 20th century, this was one of the wealthiest cities in all the world. Many of the buildings described in this chapter testify to that extreme wealth, though following revolutions, crisis after crisis, and the fall

of the peso, little of that wealth now remains. In particular, buildings and monuments constructed between the 1880s National Unification and the 1910 Independence Centennial celebrations were meant to also represent Argentina's self-conscious hopes of becoming a superpower, and the desire to rival the United States as the preeminent power in the Americas.

With the pending 2010 Bicentennial, the capital has tried to renovate its wealth of architecture. With so many projects delayed, renovation continues behind schedule on many monuments, the Teatro Colón in particular. If you're in doubt, or there's scaffolding around a building you've planned to see, call ahead to find out if renovations have altered schedules.

Under the Spanish Empire, Buenos Aires was an unimportant backwater, with other Argentine cities, such as Córdoba, being more significant and culturally sophisticated. With the 1880 movement of the capital to Buenos Aires, however, the city sought to overcome its inferiority complex with grand architectural plans. Within the descriptions of these sites, I include, where possible, the philosophy behind their impressive beauty and their role in what the city hoped to achieve. They are not mere baubles; they are the physical remnants of a lost opportunity for glory on the world stage. Maybe you're in Buenos Aires because you've heard of its beauty or are curious about the prices. Regardless of your reason, no matter what areas of the city you explore, you are certain to be impressed by all that Buenos Aires has to offer.

A Line Subte ★★★ (Kids) (Moments)   This was the first subway line opened in Buenos Aires, and it still retains its original cars. The line was opened in 1913 and is the 13th-oldest subway system in the world, the oldest in South America, and the fourth-oldest in the Americas as a whole (after New York, Boston, and Philadelphia). This line runs under Avenida de Mayo, beginning at Plaza de Mayo, running through Congreso, which was its original terminus, though it now continues on to Primera Junta thanks to a later extension. Trains are wooden, old, and rickety, and as they proceed along the bends underground, you can watch the whole car shimmy and shake. The cars' wooden side panels are made to bend and slip into each other, which is fun or scary depending on how you look at it. Windows are still wooden, with leather pulls to open and close them. Rings, now plastic, are also held by leather straps. Unlike those on the cars of the other four subway lines, the doors on this line do not always open and close automatically, something to be aware of when you reach your station. The system has begun adding new cars to this line, meaning fewer of these wooden trains are running, but about every third car passing will be one of these historical treasures. It's worth the few minutes' wait to ride one.

The stations between Plaza de Mayo and Congreso still retain most of their ornamentation from the very beginning, but the best station of all is Perú. Here, mock turn-of-the-20th-century ads and ornamental kiosks painted cream and red recall the very beginning of underground transport on this continent. The Congreso station has a minimuseum inside some glass display cases, with revolving exhibitions related to the history of the Congreso building. Well-worn old wooden turnstiles throughout this line remain in use for exiting and still have the old token slots, which are no longer operational. I know of no other place in the world where you can experience firsthand how magical a subway must have been when it was the highest form of transportation technology at the turn of the 20th century. With the system approaching 100 years, the A Line stations have been renovated, and the line itself extended, but in keeping with an eye to the past. The renovations, however, have removed the old painted-glass station signs that once adorned the entrances at street level, replacing them with colorful and garish plastic signs that ruin the once romantic notion of stepping into another era underground.

The A Line begins at Plaza de Mayo and travels along Av. de Mayo to Congreso and beyond. www.subte. com.ar. Admission 25¢ (18p).

Cabildo ★   This small, white, colonial-style building with a central bell tower was the original seat of city government established by the Spaniards. The building was completed in 1751, but parts of it were demolished to create space for Avenida de Mayo and Diagonal Sur in the late 1800s and early 1900s. The remainder of the building was restored in 1939 and is worth a visit. The small informal museum displays paintings and furniture from the colonial period, and its ledges and windows allow some of the best views of the Plaza de Mayo. The Cabildo is the only remaining public building dating back to colonial times still existing on the Plaza de Mayo. Many people come here just for the changing of the guard in front every hour (which happens at a few other spots around town as well). On Thursday and Friday from 11am to 6pm, the Cabildo's back patio is home to a crafts fair.

Bolívar 65 (at Rivadavia). (✆ **11/4334-1782.** Admission $3 (£2.15). Tues–Fri 12:30–7pm; Sun 2–6pm. Metro: Bolívar, Catedral, or Plaza de Mayo.

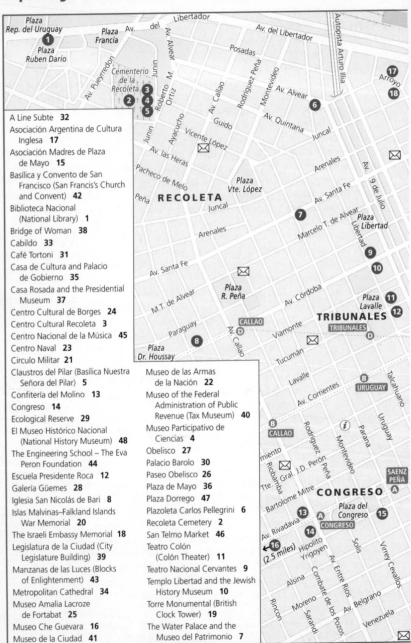

A Line Subte **32**

Asociación Argentina de Cultura Inglesa **17**

Asociación Madres de Plaza de Mayo **15**

Basílica y Convento de San Francisco (San Francis's Church and Convent) **42**

Biblioteca Nacional (National Library) **1**

Bridge of Woman **38**

Cabildo **33**

Café Tortoni **31**

Casa de Cultura and Palacio de Gobierno **35**

Casa Rosada and the Presidential Museum **37**

Centro Cultural de Borges **24**

Centro Cultural Recoleta **3**

Centro Nacional de la Música **45**

Centro Naval **23**

Circulo Militar **21**

Claustros del Pilar (Basílica Nuestra Señora del Pilar) **5**

Confitería del Molino **13**

Congreso **14**

Ecological Reserve **29**

El Museo Histórico Nacional (National History Museum) **48**

The Engineering School – The Eva Peron Foundation **44**

Escuela Presidente Roca **12**

Galería Güemes **28**

Iglesia San Nicolás de Bari **8**

Islas Malvinas–Falkland Islands War Memorial **20**

The Israeli Embassy Memorial **18**

Legislatura de la Ciudad (City Legislature Building) **39**

Manzanas de las Luces (Blocks of Enlightenment) **43**

Metropolitan Cathedral **34**

Museo Amalia Lacroze de Fortabat **25**

Museo Che Guevara **16**

Museo de la Ciudad **41**

Museo de las Armas de la Nación **22**

Museo of the Federal Administration of Public Revenue (Tax Museum) **40**

Museo Participativo de Ciencias **4**

Obelisco **27**

Palacio Barolo **30**

Paseo Obelisco **26**

Plaza de Mayo **36**

Plaza Dorrego **47**

Plazoleta Carlos Pellegrini **6**

Recoleta Cemetery **2**

San Telmo Market **46**

Teatro Colón (Colón Theater) **11**

Teatro Nacional Cervantes **9**

Templo Libertad and the Jewish History Museum **10**

Torre Monumental (British Clock Tower) **19**

The Water Palace and the Museo del Patrimonio **7**

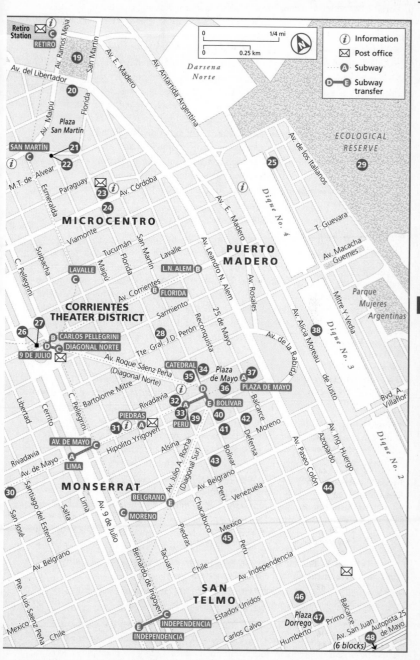

Café Tortoni ★★★ (Moments) You cannot come to Buenos Aires and not visit this important Porteño institution. I mention this cafe in the dining chapter, but at the risk of being repetitive, it is a must-see no matter if you plan to dine there or not. This historic cafe has served as the artistic and intellectual heart of Buenos Aires since 1858, with guests such as Jorge Luis Borges, Julio de Caro, Cátulo Castillo, and José Gobello. Wonderfully appointed in woods, stained glass, yellowing marble, and bronzes, the place tells more about its history by simply existing than any of the photos on its walls. This is the perfect place for a coffee or a small snack when wandering along Avenida de Mayo. Twice-nightly tango shows in a cramped side gallery, where the performers often walk through the crowd, are worth seeing. What makes the Tortoni all the more special is that locals and tourists seem to exist side-by-side here, one never overwhelming the other. Do not expect great service, however: Sometimes only jumping up and down will get the staff's attention, even when they are just a few feet from you. I've recently found that when the cafe is overwhelmed with visitors, they no longer allow tourists to come in for a quick peek. If that happens, make a plan to come back either very early in the day, or very late at night.

Av. de Mayo 825 (at Piedras). ✆ **11/4342-4328.** www.cafetortoni.com.ar. Mon–Thurs 8am–2am; Fri–Sat 8am–3am; Sun 8am–1am. Metro: Av. de Mayo.

Casa de Cultura & Palacio de Gobierno ★★ These are two separate buildings, but tours will take you to parts of both. On a street lined with impressive structures meant to give the Champs-Elysées a run for its money, these two buildings are standouts that should not be missed. The Palacio de Gobierno, on the corner of Rivadavia and San Martín, is the new City Hall. The working office of the mayor of Buenos Aires, it is a white neoclassical building directly fronting the Plaza de Mayo on the block opposite the Cabildo, the old city hall. The original construction was between 1891 and 1902, and it was expanded 10 years later.

The adjoining Casa de Cultura, a sumptuous gray granite building with bronze ornamentation and a series of sinuous lanterns protruding along its facade facing the Avenida de Mayo, is the former home of the newspaper *La Prensa,* which was at one time the most important and prestigious paper in Argentina. The paper was started by the Paz family, the former owners of the palace on San Martín now occupied by the Círculo Militar (p. 138). The Casa de Cultura is topped by a statue representing freedom of the press (which was commonly suppressed in Argentina under many regimes). Most of the clientele of the paper were among the wealthy oligarchs, and the beauty of this building reflects this. The dark lobby even has extremely ornate payment-window stands. Etched glass, dark carved woods, and heavy plaster ornamentation make up the bulk of what is seen here. The most impressive room is the Salón Dorado, a French neoclassical masterpiece of gilded columns, painted ceilings, an ornate parquet floor, and a performance stage. Tours take visitors through this room and others throughout the building, but you should also ask for schedules of the various functions hosted here in the evenings, which are usually free. The building is now the headquarters of the city's Office of Culture, and there's no finer home for it in the city.

Av. de Mayo 575 (at San Martín, near Plaza de Mayo). ✆ **11/4323-9669.** Free guided tours Sat 4 and 5pm; Sun every hour 11am–4pm. Metro: Catedral, Bolívar, or Plaza de Mayo.

Casa Rosada & the Presidential Museum ★★★ Perhaps the most photographed building in Buenos Aires, the Casa Rosada is the main presence on the Plaza de Mayo. The Argentine president does not live here, contrary to what many tourists think, but she does work here. (She lives in the suburbs in a mansion in Los Olivos, north of the city, with her husband, the former president.) It is from a balcony of the north wing of this building that Eva Perón addressed adoring crowds of Argentine workers. Hoping for some star-quality glamour for his term of office, former President Carlos Ménem allowed Madonna to actually use it for the 1996 movie, to the shock of many Porteños. Most Argentines, however, associate the balcony with the announcement of military dictator Leopoldo Galtieri's ill-fated declaration of war in 1982 against the United Kingdom over the Falkland Islands, known here as the Islas Malvinas. Girl power aside, the color pink has nothing to do with a female president either. Two theories explain the color. One is political—two warring parties, one represented by the color red, the other by white, created a truce by painting the building a color combining both shades. The other, rather revolting theory is more practical: In days past, the building was painted with cow blood that later dried in the sun to a deep pink color.

You can watch the changing of the guard in front of the palace every hour on the hour. To the side of the palace, at the *subte* (subway) entrance, you'll find the Presidential Museum, with information on the history of the building and items owned by various presidents over the centuries. Portions of the museum extend underground into basements of former buildings. Make sure to step outside to look at excavations on the customs house and port area, which existed along the Río de la Plata at this point until landfill projects pushed the shore farther east. You should also ask about the periodic tours of the Casa Rosada itself. These tours are free, but must be reserved ahead of time by asking about the schedule and signing up at the museum's front desk. If you're going on one, bring identification and expect to have personal items X-rayed to help ensure the security of the president. The tour will take you through ornate chambers, many overseen by marble busts of past presidents. You won't, however, be allowed to visit the famous balcony, no matter how much you cry for Argentina.

Casa Rosada overlooking Plaza de Mayo on Calle Balcarce, at intersection with Yrigoyen. Museum entrance at Yrigoyen 219. ℂ **11/4344-3802.** Free admission. Mon–Fri 10am–6pm. Metro: Plaza de Mayo.

Legislatura de la Ciudad (City Legislature Building) ★

This striking neoclassical building houses exhibitions in several of its halls. Ask about free tours, offered on an informal basis by the guide Alejandra Javier in English or Spanish, Monday through Friday. She will take you into the impressive bell tower that, according to legend, was made as high as it is so that the city could keep an eye on the nearby president in the Casa Rosada. Portions of the building were also built around an old mansion that once faced the Plaza de Mayo. The view from the corner balcony of this part of the building calls to mind how powerful, wealthy families, at one time, could oversee the entire town from their living-room window before the city grew so rapidly. In front of the Legislatura, you'll see a bronze statue of Julio A. Roca. He is considered one of Argentina's greatest generals, but one of his legacies is the slaughtering of tens of thousands of Indians in the name of racial purity within the province of Buenos Aires. It's because of him that Argentina, unlike most of Latin America, is a largely white, rather than mestizo, society.

Calle Perú and Hipólito Yrigoyen. ℂ **11/4338-3167** or 11/4338-3212. www.legislatura.gov.ar. Free admission. Mon–Fri 10am–5pm. Metro: Bolívar.

Manzanas de las Luces (Blocks of Enlightenment) ★★

Manzana is an old name for a city block (as well as modern Spanish for an apple), and the name "las Luces" refers to this area being the intellectual center, or "light," of the city in the 17th and 18th centuries. This land was granted in 1616 to the Jesuits, who built **San Ignacio**—the city's

> **Fun Facts** **Men in Uniform—The Changing of the Guard**
>
> Watching the changing of the guard throughout historical sites in Buenos Aires is part of the fun of visiting. Many tourists take particular delight in photographing these men in early-19th-century military clothing parading through Plaza de Mayo on their way to their next station. But did you know there is more than one kind of guard? *Granaderos* guard national monuments such as the San Martín Mausoleum and the Casa Rosada. *Patricios* guard Buenos Aires city-owned buildings, such as the Municipal Palace and the Cabildo. Both dress in historical costumes dating from the beginning of the 1800s Napoleonic era. The Patricios represent the oldest branch of the military and were originally formed before the country's independence, in response to British attacks on Buenos Aires. Granaderos were formed after independence. If they're not in front of a building, you can also tell the difference between the guards by the pants they wear: white for Patricios, and blue for Granaderos. The Islas Malvinas–Falkland Islands Monument in Plaza San Martín is guarded by the three branches of the military, the Navy, Air Force, and the Army. Wearing a mix of historical and contemporary uniforms, each branch rotates, holding the honor for a 2-week cycle.

oldest church—still standing at the corner of calles Bolívar and Alsina. San Ignacio has a beautiful altar carved in wood with baroque details. It was renovated in 2007 after years of neglect, and it was also nearly destroyed in the revolution that took Perón out of power in 1955 when he sought to reduce the power of the Catholic Church. Also located here is the **Colegio Nacional de Buenos Aires (National High School of Buenos Aires).** Argentina's best-known intellectuals have gathered and studied here, and the name "block of lights" honors the school's graduates and their work in achieving Argentina's independence in the 19th century.

Tours in English are usually led on Saturday and Sunday at 3 and 4:30pm and include a visit to the Jesuits' system of underground tunnels, which connected their churches to strategic spots in the city (admission $2/£1.40). Speculation remains as to whether the tunnels also served a military purpose or funneled pirated goods into the city when it was a smuggling center in the colonial period. The full extent of the tunnels is still unknown and various military dictators, including Perón, added to them in case they needed to flee the nearby Casa Rosada in the event of unexpected coups (which he did, escaping to Paraguay). *Ratearse,* the Argentine slang for playing hooky, which literally means becoming a rat, comes from the tunnels, as this is where students from the Colegio hid when they didn't want to go to class. In addition to weekend tours, the Comisión Nacional de la Manzana de las Luces organizes a variety of cultural activities, including folkloric dance lessons, open-air theater performances, art expositions, and music concerts.

Calle Perú 272 (at Moreno). (C) **11/4342-6973** for tours, or 11/4331-9534 for cultural events. Metro: Bolívar.

Metropolitan Cathedral ★★   The original structure of the Metropolitan Cathedral was built in 1745; it was given a new facade with carvings telling the story of Jacob and his son Joseph and was designated a cathedral in 1836. The look of the cathedral was changed from a traditional Spanish colonial look to a Greek-revival style at that time, with a pediment and colonnade in front, though the sides, back, and exterior dome remain similar to the original. Inside lies an ornate mausoleum containing the remains of General José de San Martín, the South American liberator regarded as the "Father of the Nation." (San Martín fought successfully for freedom in Argentina, Peru, and Chile alongside the better-known Simón Bolívar.) His body was moved here in 1880 to become a rallying symbol of Argentina's unification and rise to greatness when Buenos Aires became the capital of Argentina at the end of a long civil war. The tomb of the unknown soldier of Argentine independence is also here, and an eternal flame burns in remembrance. Among the chapels of note is the one on the east side of the cathedral with a statue of Jesus with the notation, "Santo Cristo del Gran Amor," or the Holy Christ of Great Love. It was donated in 1978 by an Argentine soccer player whose family had disappeared. He swore he would donate a statue to the church if they were ever found, and they were. While Argentina is a strongly Catholic nation, it is not very big on ritual. However, the most important midnight Mass in Argentina occurs in this church. Called the "Noche Buena," it is held every December 24, generally at 10pm, but call the cathedral to make sure of the exact time.

San Martín, at Rivadavia, overlooking Plaza de Mayo. ✆ **11/4331-2845.** Metro: Bolívar, Catedral, or Plaza de Mayo.

Plaza de Mayo ★★ (Kids)   Juan de Garay founded the historic core of Buenos Aires, the Plaza de Mayo, upon the city's second founding in 1580. The plaza's prominent buildings create an architectural timeline: the Cabildo, or Old City Hall, and Metropolitan Cathedral are vestiges of the colonial period (18th and early 19th c.), while the Pirámide de Mayo (Pyramid of May) and the buildings of the national and local government reflect the styles of the late 19th and early 20th centuries. In the center of the plaza, you'll find palm trees, fountains, and benches. Though many of these facilities are in need of an upgrade, the plaza is still full of local people at lunchtime, chatting and eating takeout food. Surrounding the government and union offices are structures built in the mid-20th century that are less interesting. However, they typify the severe Fascist style popular in South America at the time, with their smooth surfaces and enormous Roman-style metal doors.

Plaza de Mayo remains the political heart of Buenos Aires, serving as a forum for protests with many camping out here overnight. The mothers of the *desaparecidos,* victims of the military dictatorship's campaign against leftists, known as the Dirty War, have demonstrated here since 1976. An absolute must-see for understanding Argentina's recent history, you can watch them march, speak, and set up information booths every Thursday afternoon at 3:30pm (p. 134 has more information).

Mass demonstrations are very common here, and most protests begin in front of the **Casa Rosada** (now separated from the crowds by permanent barricades) and proceed up **Avenida de Mayo** toward **Congreso.** For the most part, these demonstrations are peaceful, usually led by people who have suffered the economic consequences of the peso crisis, known as *piqueteros.* However, at times, protests have broken into violence, so be aware when demonstrations are occurring and leave immediately if things seem to be

> **Fun Facts   A City of Murals**
>
> You'll definitely see the writing on the wall when you're in Buenos Aires, but on top of graffiti, there are also tons of murals painted all over the city walls. The majority of them are in the southern portions of the city, particularly La Boca, San Telmo and in Monserrat. Most celebrate Porteño culture, with tango and sports as a major theme. Gardel, Maradona and numerous other icons beam from formerly blank walls and make great backgrounds for an only-in-Buenos-Aires shot.

getting out of hand. A major renovation of this Plaza was presented to the public in 2007, which would have severely altered pedestrian traffic flow and removed seating, largely to prevent people from gathering here, though that was never the stated reason. The plan, which was to have commenced in 2008 in time for the 2010 Bicentennial, has not however been enacted as of this writing.

Plaza de Mayo begins at the eastern terminus of Av. de Mayo and is surrounded by calles Yrigoyen, San Martín, Rivadavia, and Balcarce. Metro: Bolívar, Catedral, or Plaza de Mayo.

MONSERRAT, SAN TELMO & LA BOCA

Centro Nacional de la Música ★   This sumptuous building belies its location on a quiet, almost run-down block in San Telmo. Its main exhibition hall boasts an intricate stained-glass ceiling within a cast-iron dome, held up by four oversize and graceful female goddesses and other angel-like figures. The building hosts various lectures, art exhibits, and musical recitals during the day, but the building itself is the true star. This was the site of the National Library before it was moved to Palermo.

México 564 (at Perú). © **11/4300-7374.** www.cultura.gov.ar. Admission varies depending on exhibition; up to $5 (£3.55). Metro: Independencia.

Plaza Dorrego ★★   Originally the site of a Bethlehemite monastery, this plaza, the second-oldest square in the city, is also where Argentines met to reconfirm their declaration of independence from Spain. On Sunday from 10am to 5pm, the city's best **antiques market ★★★** takes over. You can buy leather, silver, handicrafts, and other products here along with antiques, all while tango dancers perform on the square. The tall, darkly handsome dancer nicknamed El Indio is the star of this plaza. Sundays here are absolutely not to be missed, if you're here on a weekend, and even locals come to enjoy themselves. The local restaurants also have outside seating here, but whether dining or watching the entertainment, keep a very close eye on personal belongings.

Plaza Dorrego, at the intersection of Defensa and Humberto I. Metro: Independencia.

San Telmo Market ★★ **(Moments)**   Though this is definitely a place to shop, the building is also worth seeing on its own. The San Telmo market opened in 1897, and it is a masterpiece not just for its soaring wrought-iron interior, but for the atmosphere you find here. Half of the market is made up of things that locals need—butchers, fresh-fruit-and-vegetable grocers, and little kiosks selling sundries and household items. This part looks like the kind of place where your grandmother probably shopped when she was a child. I recommend chatting with the staff in these places, who seem to have all the time in the world. The other half is more touristy, but never overly so, with various antiques and vintage-clothing shops. There are several entrances to this large market; it's almost a block in size and squeezed between several other historical buildings.

961 Defensa or Bolívar 998 (both at Carlos Calvo). Daily 10am–8pm, but each stand will have individual hours. Metro: Independencia.

The Engineering School—The Eva Perón Foundation   This imposing building takes up an entire block. It was once the headquarters for the Eva Perón Foundation, a foundation Evita established to distribute funds to needy children and families, as well as, some say, siphon funds for personal use. Today there is little to mark the former use of the building, miraculously saved by the subsequent military regime, which felt it was too important and expensive a building to demolish as had been the case with other sites associated with Evita. Only a tiny plaque, affixed to a lobby column in 2002, explains the relationship—though someone has vandalized the sign, stealing the image of Evita with it. Nevertheless, this is a grand 1940s classical building, reserved in style, with simple Doric columns fronting Paseo Colón. It is decorated with sumptuous multicolored marble on all the floors and walls throughout the structure. As an engineering school, it is brimming with students, but it still maintains a hushed atmosphere of quiet academic pursuits. The dean's office was once Evita's own. As a public building, anyone can enter it, but the school offers no information or tours based on its former use and discourages random wanderers.

Paseo Colón, at México. Metro: Independencia.

Caminito (Overrated)   This is the main attraction in La Boca, Buenos Aires's original Little Italy. A pedestrianized street a few blocks long with a colorful, kitschy collection of painted houses known as *conventillos* (flimsily built houses that immigrants lived in), it's lined with art displays explaining the history of the area. Untold numbers of tacky T-shirt and souvenir vendors and artists set up stalls here and cater strictly to tourists. To be honest, I find this area repulsive and insulting to visitors to Buenos Aires. The history of La Boca is very important to Buenos Aires and the development of the tango. However, what remains here today has little to do with any of that. Even the touristy name of the street "Caminito" has nothing to do with Buenos Aires at all. It's from a song about a flower-filled remote rural village, not an intensely urban neighborhood where Italian-immigrant gangsters, prostitutes, and sailors once roamed the streets committing crimes and other acts of mayhem. To top it all off, in the summertime, the stench from the polluted port can also simply be overwhelming.

I am not saying you shouldn't come to La Boca, because that would be a shame—the neighborhood has real value, but the Caminito does not do it justice. More interesting are the areas a few blocks from here where artists have set up studios such as **Museo Casa—Taller de Celia Chevalier** (see chapter 9), or take a visit to the **Boca Juniors Stadium and Museum** (see below), which give you an idea of the psyche of Argentina. It's best to talk to locals off the all-too-beaten tourist track, rather than those along the Caminito who attempt to harass you into buying overpriced items or give you flyers with directions to Italian restaurants. Come to Caminito if you must, and if you're on a tour, you will anyway. However, if you are on a very short stay in Buenos Aires, skip La Boca. For true authenticity and a flavor of old Buenos Aires, choose to see San Telmo instead. In anticipation of Argentina's 2010 Bicentennial, the city had planned to redevelop the southern portion of Buenos Aires, which is where La Boca is situated, and extend a tourist train through the district. As of this writing, the plans fell apart, and though tracks were cleared, the train goes no farther than nearby Puerto Madero.

Caminito, at Av. Pedro de Mendoza, La Boca. No metro access.

Boca Juniors Stadium & Museum ★   This stadium overlooks a desolate garbage-strewn lot at the corner of calles Del Valle Iberlucea and Brandsen. But go on game day, when street parties and general debauchery take over the area, and it is another story. This is the home of the *fútbol* (soccer) club Boca Juniors, the team of Argentine legend Diego Maradona, who, like his country, went from glory to fiery collapse rather quickly. For information on *fútbol* games, see the *Buenos Aires Herald* sports section. Wealthy businessman Mauricio Macri, the former president of the Boca Juniors Fútbol Club, opened the **Museo de la Pasión Boquense** in the stadium, part of his bid to eventually woo Porteños into electing him the city's mayor, which worked. This glitzy showstopper is full of awards, TV screens showing important events that happened on the field, and more things related to this legendary team.

Brandsen 805 (at Del Valle Iberlucea). ⓒ **11/4362-1100.** www.museosdeportivos.com. Free admission. Tues–Sun 10am–9pm; holidays 10am–7pm. No metro access.

CONGRESO AREA

Congreso ★★   Opened in 1906, after nearly 9 years of work, and built in a Greco-Roman style with strong Parisian Beaux Arts influences, Congreso is the most imposing building in all of Buenos Aires. One of the main architects was Victor Meano, who was also involved in designing the Teatro Colón (p. 136), but he was murdered before completion of either building. Congreso is constructed of Argentine gray granite, with walls more than 1.75m (5³⁄₄ ft.) wide at their base. At night, its copper dome is lit through its tiny windows, creating a dramatic vista point down Avenida de Mayo from the Plaza de Mayo. Congreso is also the best example of the self-conscious Argentine concept of taking architectural elements of the world's most famous buildings and reinterpreting them. For instance, it resembles the U.S. Capitol, with a central dome spreading over the two wings holding the bicameral legislative chambers. In addition, the ornamental bronze roofline calls to mind Garnier's opera house and the central pediment is topped by a Quadriga or Triumph carried by four horses, the whole appearance of which directly echoes the Brandenburg Gate in Berlin. This sculpture was designed in Venice by artist Victor de Pol, took more than 4 years to make, weighs 20 tons, and was cast in Germany.

Tours take visitors through the fantastic chambers, which are adorned with bronze, statues, German tile floors, Spanish woods, and French marbles and lined with Corinthian columns. The horseshoe-shaped Congressional chamber is the largest, with the Senatorial chamber an almost identical copy but at one-fifth the size. The power of the Catholic Church is also evident in both chambers—the archbishop has his own seat next to the president of either section of Congress and, though he has no voting power, is allowed to preside over all of the sessions. The old seats for representatives and senators have a form of electronic whoopee cushion—simply by sitting down, attendance is taken based on the pressure of a politician's buttocks against his or her chair. The tour also takes you to the very pink Salón Rosado, now called the Salón Eva Perón. She opened this room after women received the right to vote, so that women politicians could sit without men around them to discuss feminist issues. Upon her death, Evita's body was temporarily placed under Congreso's central rotunda so that citizens could view her during the 2-week mourning period in 1952.

The building faces the Plaza Congreso, with its enormous fountain called the Dos Congresos. This multilevel confection of statues, horses, lions, condors, cherubs, and other ornaments has stairs leading to a good spot for photographing the Congreso. Unfortunately, the park had become quite run-down over the years, with homeless encampments and graffiti. It was renovated in 2007 as part of the city's refurbishment in anticipation of the 2010 Bicentennial Independence celebrations, with new paving and cleaning and restoration of the fountain and other monuments. Near the fountain, on the southeast corner of the intersection of Callao with Rivadavia, is Argentina's **National AIDS Monument.** It is a tiny concrete stub with a Lucite plaque and a red ribbon.

For more information on Congreso, visit the Congressional Library across the street and request the book *El Congreso de la Nación Argentina* by Manrique Zago, which provides rich detail on the building and its history in English and Spanish. Though both English and Spanish tours of Congreso are available, they are often subject to cancellation, depending on functions occurring in the building. Plus, English-speaking tour guides aren't always available, in spite of the schedule. Entrance is usually through the Rivadavia side of the building, but can switch to the Yrigoyen doors, so arrive early and let the guards know that you are there for a visit. The tour guide will not be called down unless he/she knows people are waiting. This is an incredible building and worth the confusion. Its beauty also speaks for itself, even if you have to take the Spanish tour and do not know a word of Spanish.

Entre Ríos and Callao, at Rivadavia. ✆ **11/4370-7100** or 11/6310-7100, ext. 3725. Free guided tours in English on Mon–Tues and Thurs–Fri 11am and 4pm. Spanish tours Mon–Tues and Thurs–Fri 11am, and 4 and 5pm. Metro: Congreso.

Asociación Madres de Plaza de Mayo ★★★ (Moments) I have already highly recommended that you visit Plaza de Mayo on Thursday afternoon to see the Madres speak about their missing children in front of the Casa Rosada (p. 126). Here at their headquarters, on Plaza Congreso, you can learn even more about them. This complex contains the office of the Madres, the Universidad Popular Madres de Plaza de Mayo, the Librería de las Madres, the Café Literario Osvaldo Bayer, and the Biblioteca Popular Julio Huasi, among other facilities. At this busy center of activity, you will find the Madres themselves, now mostly very old women, surrounded by young people who come to work and take university classes with a decidedly leftist bent. Many lectures, video conferences, and art exhibitions are held throughout the space. The bookstore has perhaps the largest collection of books anywhere in the world on Che Guevara, a Madres personal hero, though he was killed long before their movement began. The large library of reference books on liberal causes is decorated with depictions of events around the world in which people have sought justice from their governments. On Friday, Saturday, and Sunday from 11am to 6pm, there is a market held on Plaza Congreso, in front of the building, which serves as a fundraiser for the Madres. This is also good for children, because it is next to the part of the park with the merry-go-round and other rides. The fair has antiques, crafts, food, and a few interesting book vendors. There is also live music on occasion.

Hipólito Yrigoyen 1584 (at Ceballos). ✆ **11/4383-0377** or 11/4383-6340. www.madres.org. Various hours, but building is generally open Mon–Fri 10am–10pm; Sat 10am–9pm. Metro: Congreso.

The Madres: A Union of a Mother's Pain

The Madres de Plaza de Mayo was formed in 1976, with the concept in mind that even the cruelest man can identify with a mother's pain in trying to find her missing child. The military government that came into power that year, after the fall of Perón's third wife Isabel's administration, began what it called a reorganization of society based largely on making up lists of suspected social-ist dissidents and making them essentially disappear. Estimates range from 13,000 to 30,000 *desaparecidos,* or disappeared ones, mostly young people who were kidnapped, tortured, and murdered during this era. Many of the bodies were thrown naked into the Atlantic rather than buried so that they could never be found or identified. The children of the dead were given out as gifts to military families who had none of their own. This era of murdering people for their political beliefs was called the *Guerra Sucia* (Dirty War). It did not end until the collapse of the military government upon Argentina's loss of the Islas Malvinas/Falkland Islands War in June of 1982.

It is easy to think of the dead as statistics and the mothers as simply a curios-ity for tourists and history buffs, but this terrible chapter of Argentina's history is far from closed. Unfortunately, both young Argentines who have no recollec-tion of this period as well as old Argentines involved in the murders wish the mothers would simply go away. Still, though many of the original mothers have died, their work goes on.

Their work was extremely dangerous, and the mothers were themselves threatened. The first gatherings of the Madres in Plaza de Mayo took place on Saturdays in April 1977. However, since there weren't many people around the

Palacio Barolo ★ (Finds)   Among the most impressive buildings in Buenos Aires, and once the tallest in South America, this oddly decorated building with a central tower is a showstopper among all those on Avenida de Mayo. Its eclectic design can be called many things, among them Art Nouveau, neo-Gothic, neo-Romantic, and Asian Indian revival. The design of the building is based on Dante's *Inferno.* Opened in 1923, it was the work of eccentric Italian architect Mario Palanti, who largely used materials imported from his home country. The entrance is supposed to be Hell, and the patterned medal-lions on the floor here simulate fire. The interior gallery at this level is decorated with grotesque dragons, and if you look closely, you will notice that those on the east side are female, those on the west are male. Floors 1 through 14 represent Purgatory and 15 to 22 represent Heaven. The interior is significantly less interesting than the exterior and lobby. However, tours take you to the rooftop lighthouse, meant to represent God and Salvation. The views up and down Avenida de Mayo, and especially to Congreso, are unparalleled. The building is also designed so that at 7:45pm on July 9, Argentine Inde-pendence Day, the Southern Cross directly lines up over the tower.

Palanti had hoped that Italy would allow Dante's ashes to be brought here, and he designed a statue of him with a receptacle for his ashes for that purpose. Though Dante's ashes were never brought here, the statue remained in the lobby until 1955 when it was

plaza on weekends, they changed their meeting day to Thursday. It was only then that other citizens started becoming aware of what was going on. Realizing the power the Madres began to wield, the government started arresting them.

Eventually they were told by the government they could march so long as they spoke to no one. This tradition continues today with the silent main march around the Pirámide de Mayo, called "La Marcha de la Resistencia." *Pañuelos* (handkerchiefs) are painted in a circle surrounding the Pirámide. Mothers write the names of their children on the handkerchiefs and wear them on their heads, in the hopes someone would know their children's whereabouts.

After the military regime fell out of power in 1982, with the loss of the Islas Malvinas/Falkland Islands War with the U.K., little was done to bring the murderers to justice. In fact, under President Ménem during the 1990s, immunity was granted to many and there were few investigations. Still, the Madres never stopped marching. With Néstor Kirchner's winning of the presidency in 2003, the Madres have found new hope, and investigations have been reopened. He also removed immunity for politicians who tortured and murdered dissidents. There are different schools of thought regarding the mothers. Even they argue about whether economic reparations, monuments, and museums will bring an end to the dispute, or if they should push to continue investigations to ensure that the murderers are finally brought to trial. Yet no matter what is each mother's ultimate goal, the fight goes on for all of them.

stolen during the revolution that deposed Perón. The building has been renovated in 2008, and there are plans as part of the process to recreate the missing statue and ask, once again, for the ashes. Palanti designed a similar version of this building in Montevideo, as well as the Hotel Castelar a few blocks down Avenida de Mayo. Miqueas Tharigen, the nephew of the building manager, runs building tours part-time in English and Spanish, using his uncle's administrative office, preserved from the 1920s, for his work. In addition to the tour, where he also explains the secret Masonic symbols, he offers wine tastings, using a special Palacio Barolo wine label, produced in Mendoza. Tours are scheduled as listed below, but if you contact Miqueas, he will make other arrangements as well as do evening tours. Be aware that elevators and passages are tiny in the building, and groups of more than 10 people will have time delays for a usually 40-minute tour. Palacio Barolo is also home to one of the most stunningly situated stores in all of Buenos Aires, **Tango Moda** (© **11/4381-4049**), on the 16th floor (p. 211). The store has an enormous rooftop terrace overlooking the Congreso where patrons sometimes break into tango as the sun sets behind them. It's one of the wonders of Buenos Aires.

Av. de Mayo 1370 (at San José, Administrative office, 9th floor, desks 249–252). © **11/4383-1065,** 11/4383-1063, or 15/5027-9035. www.pbarolo.com.ar. Admission $3.35 (£2.40). Tours Mon and Thurs on the hour 2–7pm, or by arrangement. Metro: Sáenz Peña.

7

Recoleta Cemetery ★★★ (Kids)(Moments) Open daily from 8am to 6pm, this is the final resting place of many of the wealthiest and most important Argentine historical figures. Weather permitting, free English-language tours are held every Tuesday and Thursday at 11am. Ask for information at the small office between the cemetery gate and the church with the sign Junín 1790 on it. The door is sometimes closed and locked during office hours, but you can still peek into the windows and ask the staff questions. If you can't take a tour or want to explore on your own, cemetery maps are also for sale at the gate for 4 pesos each, with proceeds going to the Friends of Recoleta Cemetery, a private group that helps with upkeep.

Once the garden of the adjoining church, the cemetery was created in 1822 and is among the oldest in the city. You can spend hours here wandering the grounds that cover 4 city blocks, full of tombs adorned with works by local and international sculptors. More than 6,400 mausoleums form an architectural free-for-all, including Greek temples and pyramids. The most popular site is the tomb of Eva "Evita" Perón, which is always heaped with flowers and letters from adoring fans. To prevent her body from being stolen, as it had been many times by the various military governments installed after her husband's fall from grace in 1955, she was finally buried in a concrete vault 8.1m (27 ft.) underground in 1976. Many other rich or famous Argentines are buried here as well, including a number of Argentine presidents whose tomb names you'll recognize because they match some of the streets of the city.

Most tourists who come here visit only Evita's tomb and leave, but among the many, two are worth singling out and should not be missed while exploring here. One is the tomb of the Paz family, who owned the newspaper *La Prensa,* as well as the palatial building on Plaza San Martín now known as the Círculo Militar (p. 138). It is an enormous black stone structure covered with numerous white marble angels in turn-of-the-20th-century dress. The angels seem almost to soar to the heavens, lifting up the spirit of those inside with their massive wings. The sculptures were all made in Paris and shipped here. Masonic symbols such as anchors and pyramidlike shapes adorn this as well as many other Recoleta tombs.

Another tomb I recommend seeing while here is that of Rufina Cambaceres, a young woman who was buried alive in the early 1900s. She had perhaps suffered a coma, and a few days after her interment, workers heard screams from the tomb. Once opened, there were scratches on her face and on the coffin from trying to escape. Her mother then built this Art Nouveau masterpiece, which has become a symbol of the cemetery. Her coffin is a Carrara marble slab, carved with a rose on top, and it sits behind a glass wall, as if her mother wanted to make up for her mistake in burying her and make sure to see her coffin if she were ever to come back again. The corner of the tomb is adorned by a young girl carved of marble who turns her head to those watching her; she looks as if she is about to break into tears, and her right hand is on the door of her own tomb.

Calle Junín 1790 (at Plaza Francesa). Administrative office next door at Calle Junín 1760. ✆ 11/4804-7040 or 11/7803-1594. Free admission. Free English-language tours, weather permitting, Tues and Thurs 11am. No metro access.

TRIBUNALES

Teatro Colón (Colón Theater) ★★★ (Moments) Buenos Aires's golden age of prosperity gave birth to this luxurious opera house. It's one of the crowning visual delights of Avenida 9 de Julio, though its true entrance faces a park on the opposite side of the

(Kids) Recoleta's Living Residents

The dead are not the only residents in Recoleta Cemetery. About 84 cats also roam among the tombs. The cats are plumper than most strays because a dedicated group of women from the area comes to feed and provide them with medical attention at 10am and 4pm. Normally, the cats hide away from visitors, but at these times, they gather in anticipation at the women's entrance. This is a good time to bring children who might otherwise be bored in the cemetery. The women, who are not official to the cemetery, pay for these services out of their own pocket and welcome donations of cat food.

building. Over the years, the theater has been graced by the likes of Enrico Caruso, Luciano Pavarotti, Julio Bocca, Maria Callas, Plácido Domingo, Arturo Toscanini, and Igor Stravinsky. Work began in 1880 and took close to 18 years to complete, largely because the first two architects died during the building process. The majestic building opened in 1908 and combines a variety of European styles, from the Ionic and Corinthian capitals and stained-glass pieces in the main entrance to the Italian marble staircase and French furniture, chandeliers, and vases in the Golden Hall. In the main theater—which seats 3,000 in orchestra seats, stalls, boxes, and four rises—an enormous chandelier hangs from the domed ceiling painted by Raúl Soldi in 1966 during a previous renovation. The theater's acoustics are world-renowned. In addition to hosting visiting performers, the Colón has its own philharmonic orchestra, choir, and ballet company. Opera and symphony seasons last from February to late December.

Unfortunately, while the building represents the glory of Argentina's golden period, its current renovation represents everything that is wrong with Argentina today. A multimillion-dollar renovation was announced to much fanfare in 2004, with plans to finish by May 25, 2008—its 100th anniversary—for a revival of *Aida,* the opera's first production. As of this writing, the building remains in scaffolding, unfinished, its interior partly exposed to the elements because windows have been removed. Without pointing any fingers, somehow much of the money went missing and the building is certainly not in a state to function in any capacity. Rumor has it that some of the opera's extensive collection of props and outfits has also been pilfered. Work should be completed by 2010, according to a new schedule, but no work appears to be in progress at the time of this writing. Hourly **guided tours,** currently suspended, would allow you to view the main theater, backstage, and costume and underground stage-design workshops. These had taken place between 11am and 3pm weekdays, and from 9am to noon Saturday. Call © **11/4378-7130** for more information and to see if any tours will eventually take place, which depends on the progress, if any, of the renovation. As of this writing, the ticket office is only intermittently open, but performances that would ordinarily take place here are scattered in other venues throughout the city. The website, www.teatrocolon.org.ar, may provide more information in the future, but is itself not currently up to date. For those who love Buenos Aires, and love opera, what has happened to Teatro Colón is a tragedy worthy of a production itself.

Calle Libertad 621 (or Calle Toscanini 1180, at Tucaman). © **11/4378-7132** (ticket office) or © 11/4378-7344. www.teatrocolon.org.ar. Prior tour admission fee $2.50 (£1.80). Seating for events $2–$45 (£1.40–£32). Metro: Tribunales.

Escuela Presidente Roca ★   Workers in this building say that people often mistake it for the Teatro Colón, which sits next-door, across the street. Opened in 1904 and designed as a Greek temple, it's easy to see why, and it is one of the most impressive buildings on Plaza Libertad. Though it's not technically open to the public, polite curious visitors will be allowed into the courtyard with its Doric colonnade and may be able to have a glimpse inside. The upstairs areas, which include a theater and activity center for the school's children, have beautiful fresco ceilings with Greek decoration.

Libertad and Tucumán, overlooking Plaza Libertad next to Teatro Colón. Metro: Tribunales.

PLAZA SAN MARTIN AREA

Círculo Militar ★★★   You're certain to notice this grand marble building overlooking Plaza San Martín. The Círculo Militar is one of the most beautiful buildings in all of Buenos Aires, and it seems to have been plucked out of France's Loire Valley. It was built as the mansion of the Paz family, the owners of the newspaper *La Prensa,* whose original office was on Avenida de Mayo and is now the Casa de Cultura (p. 126). The Paz family was one of the wealthiest and most powerful families in the whole country, and some will still call this building by its two old names—Palacio Paz and Palacio Retiro. But it is now officially called the Círculo Militar, named for the society of retired military officers who bought the building in 1938, when the economics of the Depression made such a building impossible to keep. It was built in stages spanning from 1902 to 1914, under the direction of the French architect Louis H. M. Sortais. The commissioner of the project, family patriarch José Clemente Paz, died in 1912 and never saw its completion. (If you go to Recoleta Cemetery [p. 136], don't miss his tomb, among the most impressive.) Marble and other materials throughout the building were imported from all over Europe.

Most rooms are reminiscent of Versailles, especially the bedrooms and the gold-and-white music hall with an ornate parquet floor and windows overlooking the plaza. Other rooms are in the Tudor style, and the Presidential Room, where men would retreat for political conversation, is the most unusual. Very masculine and dark, it is lit by strange chandeliers decorated with naked hermaphrodite characters with beards and breasts, whose faces contort as they are lanced through their private parts. It is unknown why this was the decorative theme of a room intended for politics. The six elevators are original to the building and the overall height of the building is eight stories, though with their high ceilings, there are only four levels to the building. The most impressive room is the round Hall of Honor, which sits under an interior rotunda and even has a balconied second level overlooking a stage. It was a private mini–opera house, covered in multicolored marble and gilded bronze, used now for conferences.

Av. Santa Fe 750 (at Maipú, overlooking Plaza San Martín). ✆ **11/4311-1071.** www.circulomilitar.org. Admission $1.35 (95p). Tours Mon–Fri 11am, 3 and 4pm, and sometimes in English Wed–Thurs 3pm. Metro: San Martín.

Islas Malvinas–Falkland Islands War Memorial ★★   In many English-speaking countries (which most of the readers of this book are likely from), the notion of a country like Argentina challenging a major world power like Great Britain to war is almost ridiculous—and when it actually happened, it was treated as such by English-language media. This short war lasted from April to June 1982, and it remains an extremely touchy and serious subject among Argentines, with the Monday near April 2, the date of Argentina's taking of the Islands, as a national holiday. Regardless of your personal opinion on the logic of Argentina declaring war on Great Britain, any

conversation with locals on the topic must be treated very delicately. The war came **139**
during a period of rapid inflation and other troubles when the Argentine military government, under the leadership of General Leopoldo Galtieri, was looking for a way to distract attention from its failed economic policies. Argentina lost the war and suffered more than 700 casualties, sparking the government collapse that Galtieri was exactly trying to avoid. Democracy returned to Argentina, and the 6-year Dirty War, under which 30,000 political opponents were tortured and murdered, finally ended. The United States had tried to balance itself and serve as a diplomatic channel between the two countries during the war, but it generally sided with Great Britain, in technical violation of the Monroe Doctrine.

The legal basis of Argentina's claim to the Falkland Islands, known here as Las Islas Malvinas (and you'd better use that term, not the British one, while you're here), is due to their being a portion of Argentina's territory when it was still ruled by Spain. However, as a fledgling nation after independence, Argentina could do little to prevent Great Britain from setting up a fishing colony and base there. This colonization by Britain of the islands, however, spurred Argentina to explore and populate its Patagonia region to prevent losing even more land to the European power. To most Argentines, having lost the war does not mean that they have no rights to the islands, and diplomatic maneuvers continue with the ongoing dispute. The argument is over more than mere sovereignty: Oil reserves have been discovered in the area.

This monument contains Vietnam Memorial–like stark plaques with lists of names of the Argentines who died. An eternal flame burns over a metallic image of the islands, and the three main branches of the military, the Army, the Navy, and the Air Force, each guard the monument in 2-week rotations. The location of the monument, at the bottom of a gentle hill under Plaza San Martín, is itself a message. It faces the Torre Monumental, previously known as the British Clock Tower, a gift from British citizens who made a fortune developing the nearby Retiro railroad station complex. Like checkmate in a game of chess, the two sides, Argentina and Great Britain, stand facing each other, symbolically representing the dispute that has no end.

Av. Libertador, under Plaza San Martín, across from Retiro Station. Metro: San Martín or Retiro.

Torre Monumental (British Clock Tower) ★

This Elizabethan-style clock tower, which some call the Argentine Big Ben, was a gift from the British community of Buenos Aires after building the nearby Retiro railroad station complex. At the turn of the 20th century, Argentina had vast natural resources such as grain and cattle waiting to be exploited, but it was the British Empire that had the investment capability and technology to create Retiro and connect Buenos Aires to its hinterlands to get products to markets overseas. This, however, was always a sore point, and for years, many Argentines felt exploited by Great Britain. Recently, the tower was renamed the Torre Monumental, in response to the very common post–Islas Malvinas/Falkland Islands War renaming of anything associated with Great Britain, yet nearly all locals still call it the British Clock Tower (see "British Names Post–Islas Malvinas," below). The monument survived the war unscathed, but a few years later, during an anniversary memorial service, an angry mob attacked it. They destroyed portions of the base and also toppled a statue of George Canning, the first British diplomat to recognize the country's independence from Spain. (He's now safely kept at the British Embassy.) The Islas Malvinas–Falkland Islands War Memorial (p. 138) was purposely placed across the street as a permanent reminder of Britain's battle with Argentina. There is little to see inside the monument itself, save for a small museum of photographs. The main attraction here is the view: A free elevator ride

> **Fun Facts** — **British Names Post–Islas Malvinas**
>
> British influence was once visible all over Buenos Aires, but following the Islas Malvinas/Falkland Islands War, the city has made an effort to honor Argentines in places once named for British heroes. The person worst affected by this was George Canning, the British foreign secretary who recognized Argentina's independence from Spain. He once had a major Buenos Aires thoroughfare named after him (since changed to Scalabrini Ortiz), but the only remnant now is Salón Canning, a tango hall on that street. At subway station Malabia, under many layers of paint, you might find the old signs that once announced it as Station Canning. Worst hit, though, was the statue of Canning that was once part of the Torre Monumental, formerly known as the British Clock Tower. An angry mob tore down this statue during an Islas Malvinas/Falkland Islands War anniversary service. British citizens shouldn't be alarmed: You can still view the statue at the British embassy, where it is now well protected. And besides, Argentines speak more English now than they ever did before the war, keeping Canning's legacy alive, at least in the language.

will take you to the top floor with its wraparound view of the port, the trains, and the city of Buenos Aires itself. There is also a small Buenos Aires city tourism information center inside.

Av. Libertador 49 (across from Plaza San Martín, next to Retiro Station). 11/4311-0186. www.museos. buenosaires.gov.ar. Free admission. Thurs–Sun 11am–6pm. Metro: Retiro.

MICROCENTRO

Obelisco The Obelisco is one of the defining monuments of Buenos Aires. It was inaugurated in 1936 to celebrate the 400th anniversary of the first, and unsuccessful, founding of the city by Pedro de Mendoza. (The city was later reestablished in 1580.) It sits at the intersection of Corrientes and Avenida 9 de Julio, which is the heart of the city and the Theater District. The Obelisco is the focal point of the vista between Plaza de Mayo and Diagonal Norte, meant to mimic the vistas found in Paris around Place de la Concorde. The Obelisco sits in the oval Plaza de República, all of which was once the site of Iglesia de San Nicolás where the Argentine flag was first displayed on August 23, 1812, in Buenos Aires shortly after independence from Spain. This church, of course, was demolished to create the city's most iconic symbol, but an inscription on the north side of the Obelisco honors its noble sacrifice. As with Paris's Eiffel Tower, some criticized the project and considered it ugly, but the city has embraced the Obelisco as its main symbol.

When Argentines have something to celebrate, the Obelisco is where they head. If you're in town when Argentina wins an international event, you can be sure hundreds of people will gather around the Obelisco with flags in their hands, waving them at the cars that honk in celebration as they head past. The edges of the plaza have plaques that celebrate the various provinces that make up the country. Unfortunately, many had to be replaced with replicas when the Plaza was renovated in 2007, since the originals were stolen for the value of their copper in the years following the 2001 peso crisis. Certainly, the Obelisco would have a great vista, but it is not a structure built as a viewing spot. As the city's preeminent phallic symbol, it has periodically been graced with a very large condom on December 1, International AIDS Awareness Day. Though this has not been done in years, postcards of the event are available at kiosks.

Av. 9 de Julio, at Corrientes. Metro: Carlos Pellegrini, Diagonal Norte, or 9 de Julio.

Paseo Obelisco This shopping complex and underground pedestrian causeway (which you may have to pass through at some point on your trip anyway) is worth a short trip by itself. Paris, New York, London, and virtually every major city with a subway once had similar underground complexes, but this area under the Obelisco, where three subway lines converge, seems to have remained unchanged since the 1960s. The shops are nothing special—several barber shops, shoe-repair spots, and stores selling cheap clothing and other goods make up the bulk of them. Yet together, with their cohesive old signs, fixtures, and furnishings, they look like the setting for a movie.

Subway entrances surrounding the Obelisco, along Av. 9 de Julio. Metro: Carlos Pellegrini, Diagonal Norte, or 9 de Julio.

Galería Güemes ★★ (Finds) This is a sumptuous building, though its modern entrance on Calle Florida would make you think otherwise. Its back entrance on San Martín, however, still retains all of its original glory from its opening in 1915. This is a shopping gallery with a mix of stores without distinction and several kiosks that obscure the views, but look around at the walls and decorations. The architecture is a mix of Art Nouveau, Gothic, and neoclassical—all heavily ornamented—and was the creation of the architect who designed the now-closed Café del Molino next door to Congreso. Make sure to look also at the ornate elevator banks, which lead to the offices above. The building also houses the Piazzolla tango show (p. 226). The Art Nouveau theater in which it sits was closed for nearly 40 years and was only recently restored. Of all the tango show palaces in Buenos Aires, this is the most beautiful.

Calle Florida 165 (at Perón). Metro: Florida.

Centro Cultural de Borges ★★ You can shop all you want in Galerías Pacífico, but if it's culture you're after, you can find it there too. Inside of the shopping mall is this arts center named for Jorge Luis Borges, Argentina's most important literary figure. You'll find art galleries, lecture halls with various events, an art cinema, and art bookstore. There's also the **Escuela Argentina de Tango,** which offers a schedule of lessons tourists can take with ease (© **11/4312-4990;** www.eatango.org) and the ballet star **Julio Bocca's Ballet Argentino** performance space and training school full of young ballet stars and their not-to-be-missed performances, though he himself has since retired from public performances (© **11/5555-5359;** www.juliobocca.com).

Enter through Galerías Pacífico or at the corner of Viamonte and San Martín (the back of the Galerías Pacífico Mall). © **11/5555-5359.** www.ccborges.com.ar. Various hours and fees. Metro: San Martín.

OTHER SITES

Biblioteca Nacional (National Library) ★ Opened in 1992, though begun in the 1970s, this modern architectural oddity stands on the land of the former Presidential Residence where Eva Perón died. (The building was demolished by the new government so that it would not become a holy site to Evita's millions of supporters after her death.) It is a spectacular example of 1970s Brutalist architecture, which was extremely popular under the dictatorship. Built almost as a fortress, among its distinctions are its porthole windows at ground level, the raising of the actual structure off the ground, long approach ramps, moatlike berm landscaping, and the difficulty in determining where the actual entrance is. With its underground levels, the library's 13 floors can store up to five million volumes. Among its collection, the library stores 21 books printed by one of the earliest printing presses, dating from 1440 to 1500. Visit the reading room—occupying two stories at the top of the building—to enjoy an awe-inspiring view of Buenos Aires. The library also hosts special events in its exhibition hall and auditorium.

Calle Aguero 2502. ☎ 11/4807-0885. Free admission. Mon–Fri 9am–9pm; Sat–Sun noon–8pm. No metro access.

Bridge of Woman ★★ Looking for a romantic spot to share a kiss at sunset in Puerto Madero? This is the place. The Bridge of Woman (or Puente de La Mujer) is a white, sinewy structure resembling a plane taking flight, which was designed by Santiago Calatrava, the Spanish architect famed for his unusual approach to public architecture. It was opened in 2001 and crosses Dique 3, or port area 3. Calatrava is said to have listened to tango music while designing the bridge and intended it to be an abstraction of a couple dancing. The name of the bridge also refers to the naming pattern of the district of Puerto Madero, where all the streets are named for important women—the only major city in the world with such a neighborhood. A sign between Docks 2 and 3 explains the women.

Dique 3 (btw. Villafor and Güemes, connecting Dealissi with Alicia Moreau de Justo), Puerto Madero. Metro: Alem.

Plaza Serrano ★★ (Moments) This is the bohemian heart of Palermo Viejo. During the day, not much goes on here, but at night this plaza comes alive with young people gathering to drink, celebrate, sing, dance, play guitar, and just generally enjoy being alive. Many of the kids are dreadlocked Rastafarians, and it's easy to join and chat with any of them, many selling funky jewelry and other crafts while they gather together. The plaza is surrounded by numerous bars and restaurants, which I describe in chapters 6 and 10. On Saturday and Sunday from 11am to 6pm, there is an official but not-to-be-missed fair here with even more funky jewelry and arts and crafts. The true name of this plaza is Plazoleta Julio Cortazar, but few people will call it that. The plaza is at the intersection of Calle Serrano and Calle Honduras, but Calle Serrano is also named Calle Borges on some maps.

Plaza Serrano, at the intersection of Serrano/Borges and Honduras. www.palermoviejo.com. No metro access.

Plazoleta Carlos Pellegrini ★ This is one of the most beautiful of all the small plazas in Buenos Aires—not just for the plaza itself, but for what surrounds it. This is the most Parisian-appearing part of Recoleta, due in large part to the ornate Belle Epoque French Embassy presiding over it. The Brazilian Embassy, another beautiful building in a former mansion once owned by the Pereda family, also overlooks the plaza. A large statue of President Carlos Pellegrini sits in the center of the plaza. It was created in France by Félix Coutan and dedicated in 1914. A small fountain and a bench add to the relaxed environment. Nearby are several other mansions, including the Louis XIII–style "La Mansion," which is part of the Four Seasons, and the Palacio Duhau, which forms the entrance to the new Park Hyatt. The park is the terminus of the Avenida Alvear, the city's most exclusive shopping street, close to where it hits Avenida 9 de Julio. The collection of intact buildings here will give you an idea as to the beauty that was lost in Buenos Aires with the widening of Avenida 9 de Julio in the 1960s. In fact, demolition of the French

Embassy, which France refused, was originally part of the plan. Thankfully, that, at least, **143**
never happened.

Plazoleta Carlos Pellegrini, Av. Alvear at Cerrito (Av. 9 de Julio). No metro access.

The Israeli Embassy Memorial ★   In 1992, a bomb ripped through the Israeli
Embassy in Buenos Aires, located on a peaceful and seemingly out-of-the-way corner of
Recoleta at the intersection of calles Suipacha and Arroyo. Twenty-nine people lost their
lives in the tragedy, and—as with the 1994 attack on the Jewish community group, the
Asociación Mutual Israelita Argentina, which killed 85 people—the culprits are
unknown, but suspected to have been working with overseas groups. Under former
President Néstor Kirschner, investigations related to the bombings have been reopened.
The site is now a very tranquil place for contemplation, converted into a park graced by
22 trees and seven benches to represent the people who died in the embassy bombing.
The outline of the once-elegant building remains on the adjacent structure, like a ghost
speaking for the dead.

Calles Suipacha and Arroyo. www.amia.org.ar. Metro: San Martín.

Ecological Reserve ★★   The Ecological Reserve is an unusual and unexpected
consequence of highway construction throughout Buenos Aires during the mid-20th
century. Construction debris and the rubble of demolished buildings were unceremoni-
ously dumped into the Río de la Plata. Over time, sand and sediment began to build up,
and then grass and trees began to grow. The birds followed, and now the area is a preserve. Various companies will take people on biking and bird-watching tours of the area.
Ask your travel agent about it or see our list of tour companies (p. 163). Since there are
few genuine beaches in the Buenos Aires area, some people come here to sunbathe,
sometimes in the nude. Whatever you do, don't go into the water, since it is heavily polluted and still full of rough construction debris in some parts. The Costanera walkway,
extending from Puerto Madero, has been improved since 2007, with ice cream kiosks
and other services for the increasing amount of spillover wanderers from the port. In spite
of its being a preserve, development is slowly encroaching on it as the Puerto Madero
area grows. Though the police do have a patrol station here, some homeless people also
camp out here, meaning you should be cautious.

Along the Costanera near Puerto Madero. ℭ 11/4893-1588. Metro: N. Alem.

Quinta San Vicente & Juan Perón Mausoleum ★★★   *Quinta* is an Argentine
word meaning country home, and this was the one shared by Juan and Evita. They lived
here on weekends, escaping the routine of their work in Buenos Aires. It is the only home
they lived in that still exists and is also open to the public, though it is about 45 miles
from the center of Buenos Aires, beyond the Ezeiza Airport. The home dates from the
1940s, but the majority of furnishings are from the early 1970s, when Perón returned to
power and shared this house with his third wife, Isabelita. The complex is also called the
Museo de 17 de Octubre, named in honor of the date that Peronism began. The house
is tiny, and the complex also contains a museum explaining the history of Peronism,
which was curated by Gabriel Miremont, who also designed the Museo Evita (p. 147).
The interesting things displayed include a cross given by the city of Santiago, Spain, to
Evita during the famous Rainbow Tour of 1947. In addition, the colossal marble statues
of Juan, Evita, and a *Descamisado* (worker), originally intended for the never-built Evita
memorial planned for Avenida Libertador in front of the former Presidential Palace, are
also in the gardens. The statues of Juan and Evita are headless now, damaged in the 1955

revolution that deposed Juan Perón. According to speculation, the heads are somewhere offshore in the Río Riachuelo running through La Boca. (So as not to offend the workers, the head of the *Descamisado* was spared the same fate.)

An imposing mausoleum on the grounds now holds the remains of Juan Perón, moved here from Chacarita Cemetery in a chaotic and violent parade on October 17, 2006. A space exists for Evita, but her family will not allow her to be moved here from Recoleta Cemetery. The stark setting is ornamented with a mosaic produced by Lilian Lucía Luciano and the Azzurro group of artisans and is inspired by The Embrace, or El Abrazo, a famous photo of Evita and Juan taken by Pinelides Fusco on October 17, 1951, her last speech on this important date as she was dying of cancer. (You'll recognize it from the scene in Madonna's *Evita* movie.) The museum complex is 75¢ (55p) to enter, but it is only open on weekends and you should call to verify the closing time. Because it is hard to get to, it is best reachable by taxi from Buenos Aires, costing about $50 (£36).

Intersection of Lavalle and Av. Eva Perón, off Highway 58 in San Vicente ☎ **222/548-2260.** Sat–Sun and holidays only 10am–5:30pm fall and winter, until 7:30pm spring and summer, but call ahead to verify the hours.

2 MUSEUMS

Museo Amalia Lacroze de Fortabat ★　The newest museum to grace Buenos Aires, this gleaming low-rise structure hugs the banks of Puerto Madero and houses the private collection of Amalia Lacroze de Fortabat. It's best to look at it as the female version of the MALBA, started by a male real-estate mogul, but this time it's a grande dame, Amalia Lacroze de Fortabat, something of an Argentine Brooke Astor who opened this airy museum in October 2008. The museum contains an enormous collection of Argentine artists, as well as works by Warhol, Dalí, Chagall, the Breughels, and other well-known painters, as well as a collection of ancient art. Many of the paintings are of Amalia when she was a young, stunning beauty.

Olga Cossettini 141 (at Sanchez de Thompson). ☎ **11/4310-6600.** www.coleccionfortabat.org.ar. Admission $4 (£2.85). Tues–Fri noon–9pm; Sat–Sun 10am–9pm. Metro: Alem.

Museo Che Guevara　No longer technically a museum, but with the remnants of what had been the Museo Che Guevara until it ran into financial problems ironically around the 40th anniversary of Che's death, this store is unusual. Run by Eladio González, an extremely eccentric character with an amazing depth of knowledge, along with Irene Perpiñal, you'll find some of Che's clothes, explanatory signs from the original museum, as well as other items from his life. The rest of the place is a hodgepodge of used electrical parts, Evita sculptures, old dishes, and Halloween masks, adding to the odd atmosphere. English-fluent Eladio will beguile you with stories about Argentine-born Che, his place in the world, and how he continues to impact generations, along with his own visits to Cuba. It's a strange place, but worth a visit, and they hope by late 2009 to reopen the actual museum somewhere nearby in the Caballito neighborhood.

Rojas 129 (at Yerbal). ☎ **11/4903-3285.** www.museocheguevaraargentina.blogspot.com. Free admission. Mon–Fri 9am–7pm. Metro: San Martín.

Museo de las Armas de la Nación ★ (Kids)　This small museum in the impressive Círculo Militar overlooking Plaza San Martín is very helpful for gaining a better understanding of the Argentine side of the Islas Malvinas/Falkland Islands War. In Argentina that war is called the Guerra de las Islas Malvinas, using the name of the island chain from when it was part of the Spanish Empire, which is the basis for Argentina's dispute with Great Britain. Despite losing the war, Argentina still lays claim to the islands. Calling them by their English name is likely to cause an argument even with the most polite Argentine. The curator of the museum is Isidro Abel Vides, a veteran of the war. Among the items of note related to the war is a display about the sinking of the *General Belgrano,* where 323 Argentines perished—the greatest individual loss of life in a single event of the war. Other displays show uniforms of the time period. Children will like the huge collection of toy soldiers showing the history of military costume in Argentina and other countries up to the 1940s. There are also models of old forts from the Argentine frontier.

Gun collections show arms used in Argentina and other parts of the world. Most of these weapons were produced in the United States, demonstrating that, by the time of the U.S. Civil War, U.S. companies were the major suppliers of arms used throughout the Americas. Other items of note include rifles spanning 5 centuries, cannons, samurai suits, swords, and replicas of armored suits. The museum also contains a small library of military books and records and is of note for scholars looking for information on Argentina's various military dictatorships and the Islas Malvinas/Falkland Islands War. The Círculo Militar, located in the former mansion of the Paz family (p. 138), is a social club for retired members of the military. Here, there is also a private section of the museum containing more historical military documents and artifacts, which is not open to the general public. However, if you are a current or retired member of the military in your home country, they sometimes make exceptions.

Av. Santa Fe 702 (at Maipú overlooking Plaza San Martín). ✆ **11/4311-1071.** www.circulomilitar.org. Admission $3 (£2.15). Museum and library Mon–Fri noon–7pm. Metro: San Martín.

Museum of the Federal Administration of Public Revenue (Tax Museum)

Finds Numismatists, accountants, and others interested in the history of money and taxes will enjoy this small and unique museum, one of only three of its type in the world. Photographs, tax-record books, and other documents here tell the history of Customs and other forms of tax collection in Argentina. One room has also been set up as a re-creation of 1930s tax offices, complete with period machines. Though it has nothing to do with taxes, a highlight of the museum's collection is a desk used by Manuel Belgrano, the man who designed the Argentine flag. The museum has relocated from its former location on Avenida de Mayo into the main building of Administración Federal de Ingresos Públicos (AFIP) overlooking Plaza de Mayo.

Hipólito Yrigoyen 370 (at Defensa). ✆ **11/4347-2396.** www.afip.gov.ar. Free admission. Mon–Fri 11am–5pm. Metro: Bolivar, Plaza de Mayo.

Museo de Los Niños ★★★ Kids

This museum, really a play center, located in the Abasto Shopping Center, is a fun way for your kids to learn about different careers and learn a little about Buenos Aires too, since many of the displays relate to the city. (I wish I'd had one of these places when I was growing up.) First, for the city, they have miniature versions of the Casa Rosada, Congreso, and a street layout to demonstrate how traffic flows, so it's a great way to orient your kids to Buenos Aires. Various careers can be explored here with a miniature dentist's office, doctor's office, TV station with working cameras, gas station and refinery, working radio station, and newspaper office. The bank has interactive computers, too. Some of the displays have a corporate feel to them, like a McDonald's where kids can play in the kitchen and serve you for a change. Another is the post office imitating a branch of the private OCA mail service company. Here, kids can write out postcards, which they say get sent to the mayor of Buenos Aires. Even more fun is a giant toilet where kids learn what happens in the sewer system after they use the bathroom. Intellectual kids can also seek some solitude in the library, and budding dramatists can play dress-up onstage in a little theater, complete with costumes. A patio has small rides for little children too, when the big kids are too rambunctious. Don't worry if the kids wear you out—there are couches for weary parents to rest on, too. If you're here in a group at birthday-party time, have one here. While the museum says that kids 15 and younger will enjoy it, I think that after 12 years old, it may seem less of a fun a place to be.

Abasto Shopping Center Food Court, Av. Corrientes 3247. ☎ **11/4861-2325.** AE, DC, MC, V. Admission $4.50 (£3.20), family/group discounts available, free for seniors and kids younger than 3. Tues–Sun and holidays 1–8pm. Metro: Gardel.

Museo Participativo de Ciencias ★★ (Kids)

Okay, so you came to the Centro Cultural de Recoleta, adjacent to the Recoleta Cemetery, to see art and be sophisticated. Well, here's the place to bring the kids afterward, or let them wander in on their own. In this museum, unlike so many others, it's prohibited not to touch! There are two floors full of science displays where kids can touch, play, and see how electricity, gravity, and many other things work—all designed with fun in mind. Communications rooms, mechanical rooms, and wave and sound rooms all have various interactive stands that are aimed at kids of all ages. Sure, it's a noisy place, but if you can find a way to make learning fun, it's not a bad side effect.

Inside the Centro Cultural de Recoleta, adjacent to the Recoleta Cemetery. ☎ **11/4807-3260** or 11/4806-3456. www.mpc.org.ar. Admission $4.50 (£3.20). Daily 3:30–7:30pm. No metro access.

Museo de Casa Gardel ★

Carlos Gardel, the preeminent Argentine tango singer whose portraits you see all over the city and who is nicknamed Carlitos, bought this house in 1927 for his mother, with whom he lived when he was not traveling. The house dates from 1917 and, in keeping with tango history, it once served as a brothel. It served various functions after his mother's death in 1943—from a tailor shop to a tango parlor—until it reopened as a museum in his honor on June 24, 2003, the 68th anniversary of his death in a plane crash in Colombia. Visitors will find articles about him from the time, original musical notes, contracts, portraits of his singing partner José Razzano, records and sheet music from the period, as well as some of his clothing, including his signature fedora. His kitchen, bathroom, and ironing room remain almost untouched from the time he lived here. Most tours are in Spanish, but there are some in English on a periodic basis. This small, out-of-the-way museum is a must-see not only for tango lovers, but also to understand this important man in Argentine history, whose work brought tango to the world. A favorite phrase in Buenos Aires is that Carlos sings better every day, meaning as time passes, his music, the most Porteño thing of all, becomes more and more important to Argentines.

Jean Jaures 735 (at Tucumán). ☎ **11/4964-2071** and 11/4964-2015. www.museos.buenosaires.gov.ar. Admission $1.35 (95p). Mon and Wed–Fri 11am–6pm; Sat–Sun and holidays 10am–7pm. Metro: Carlos Gardel.

Templo Libertad & the Jewish History Museum ★

This impressive Byzantine-style temple is the home of the CIRA (Congregación Israelita de la República de Argentina). Sitting a block from the Teatro Colón, it is one of the stars of Plaza Libertad. The small building housing the temple's administrative office also contains the Jewish History Museum, known also as the Museo Kibrick after its founder. You'll find material related to the Jewish community in Buenos Aires, with both Sephardic and Ashkenazi items from their original homelands. Menorahs, altar cloths, spice holders, and various pieces of religious art make up the bulk of the collection. Special exhibits also relate the history of Jewish agricultural colonies in rural parts of Argentina.

Libertad 769 (at Córdoba, overlooking Plaza Libertad). ℂ **11/4123-0832.** www.judaica.org.ar. Admission $3 (£2.15). Tues–Thurs 3:30–6pm. Museum closes entirely Dec 15–Mar 15, but special requests might be honored. Metro: Tribunales.

Museo Evita ★★★ It is almost impossible for non-Argentines to fathom that it took 50 years from the time of her death for Evita, the world's most famous Argentine, to finally get a museum. The Museo Evita opened on July 26, 2002, in a mansion where her charity, the Eva Perón Foundation, once housed single mothers with children. The placement of the house here had been meant as a direct affront to the wealthy neighbors who hated Evita.

While the museum treats her history fairly, looking at both the good and the bad, it is quickly obvious to the visitor that each presentation has a little bit of love for Evita behind it, and indeed, members of the family are involved in the museum. Evita's grand-niece, the Buenos Aires Senator Cristina Alvarez Rodríguez, is president of the Evita Perón Historical Research Foundation, the group that runs the museum, and she is often in the building meeting with the staff. Gabriel Miremont, the museum's curator, is Argentina's preeminent expert on Evita history; he had become personally interested in Evita as a child, when he was forbidden from listening to lyrics from the Evita play. It was technically illegal at the time to do so while a military dictatorship ruled the country, following the collapse of Perón's second government in 1976, and he was punished by his father. Thus, while historically accurate, the museum has a close personal touch that sets it apart from most museums.

The museum displays divide Evita's life into several parts, looking at her childhood, her arrival in Buenos Aires to become an actress, her ascension to first lady and unofficial saint to millions, and finally her death and legacy. You will be able to view her clothes, remarkably preserved by the military government that took power after Perón's fall in 1955, along with adjacent photos of her wearing them. Other artifacts of her life include her voting card, as it was through Evita's work that Argentine women gained the right to vote in 1947. There are also toys and schoolbooks adorned with her image, given to children to indoctrinate them into the Peronist movement. The most touching artifact of all, though, is a smashed statue of Evita, hidden for decades by a farmer in his barn, despite the threat of being jailed for saving it. Whether you hate, love, or are indifferent to Evita, this is a museum that no visitor to Argentina should miss. Digesting the exhibits here will help you truly understand why she remains such a controversial figure within the Argentine psyche.

Calle Lafinur 2988 (at Gutierrez). ℂ **11/4807-9433.** www.museoevita.org and www.evitaperon.org. Admission $3.50 (£2.50). Nov–Apr Tues–Sun 11am–7pm; May–Oct Tues–Sun 1–7pm. Metro: Plaza Italia.

Museo Nacional de Arte Decorativo (National Museum of Decorative Arts) ★ French architect René Sergent, who designed some of the grandest mansions in Buenos Aires, also designed the mansion housing this museum. The building is itself a work of art, and it will give you an idea of the incredible mansions that once lined this avenue, overlooking the extensive Palermo park system, before high-rise construction was their demise. The building's 18th-century French design provides a classical setting for the diverse decorative styles represented within. Breathtaking sculptures, paintings, and furnishings make up the collection, and themed shows rotate seasonally. The **Museo de**

Arte Oriental (Museum of Eastern Art) displays art, pottery, and engravings on the first floor of this building.

Av. del Libertador 1902 (at Lucena). ℂ **11/4801-8248.** Admission $3 (£2.15). Mon–Fri 2–8pm; Sat–Sun 11am–7pm. No metro access.

Museo Nacional de Bellas Artes (National Museum of Fine Arts) ★★ This building, which formerly pumped the city's water supply, metamorphosed into Buenos Aires's most important art museum in 1930. The museum contains the world's largest collection of Argentine sculptures and paintings. It also houses European art dating from the pre-Renaissance period to the present day. The collections include notable pieces by Renoir, Monet, Rodin, Toulouse-Lautrec, and Van Gogh, as well as a surprisingly extensive collection of Picasso drawings.

Av. del Libertador 1473 (at Agote). ℂ **11/4803-0802.** Free admission. Tues–Sun 12:30–7:30pm. No metro access.

The Water Palace & the Museo del Patrimonio ★ ⓚⁱᵈˢ Many people pass by this massive, high Victorian structure on Avenida Córdoba in Barrio Norte and stop in wonder. This is Buenos Aires's Water Palace, a fantastic structure of more than 300,000 lustrous, multicolored faience bricks made by Royal Doulton and shipped from Britain. Its original interior engineering components were made in various countries, with Belgium as the largest contributor. Originally, the Water Palace was meant to be a humble building, constructed as a response to the yellow fever epidemic that hit San Telmo and other neighborhoods in Buenos Aires in 1877. In the days before plumbing, drinking water was held in collecting pools in individual homes, which helped to spread the disease. Alarmed, the city began looking for a spot to construct new, sanitary facilities to prevent another outbreak. As this was the highest point in the city, meaning water stored here could use gravity to flow down the pipes into residences, this location was chosen for the water tower.

However, two things happened that changed the plans, creating the 1887 building seen here now. First, Buenos Aires was made the capital of Argentina in 1880, and the city planners felt the building must not only serve a purpose but also reflect the glory of a new nation seeking its place in the world. (Still, Argentina did not have the technology, hence the need for foreign help in construction.) In addition, the yellow fever epidemic itself meant that the area surrounding this location was quickly filling up with new mansions for wealthy families fleeing San Telmo. The water purification building not only needed to fit in its surroundings, but also to outshine them.

The engineering works have been removed, and the building is now the headquarters of the water company Aguas Argentinas. It also contains one of the most unusual museums in the whole city, one kids will get a kick out of. Explaining the history of water sanitation in Argentina and the world, this museum is home to hundreds of toilets spanning the decades. Some are dissected, showing their interior workings. Others are multifunctional prison toilets with sink and toilet joined together, along with faucets, giant sewer pipes, and anything to do with waterworks. The museum also has an extensive library with plans, books, and other materials related to waterworks around the world, making it a worthwhile stop for students and engineers.

Av. Córdoba 1750 (at Riobamba). Entrance at Riobamba 750 (1st floor). ℂ **11/6319-1882** or 11/6319-1104. Admission $3 (£2.15). Mon–Fri 9am–1pm; guided tours in Spanish Mon, Wed, Fri at 11am. Metro: Facultad de Medicina.

Museo de la Ciudad   Like one big common attic for Buenos Aires, the Museo de la Ciudad is a kitschy collection of everything and anything related to the history of this city. It's built into an old pharmacy in Monserrat dating from 1894. Whether it's tango, Little Italy, bicycles, or a doll collection, this museum gives you a glimpse into the pride Porteños have for even the everyday aspects of their lives, no matter how disorganized the place feels.

Alsina 412 (at Bolívar). ℂ **11/4331-9855.** Admission $2 (£1.40). Mon–Fri 11am–7pm; Sat–Sun 3–7pm. Metro: Bolívar.

El Museo Histórico Nacional (National History Museum) ★★   Argentine history from the 16th through the 19th centuries comes to life in the former Lezama family home. The expansive Italian-style mansion houses 30 rooms with items saved from Jesuit missions, paintings illustrating clashes between the Spaniards and Indians, and relics from the War of Independence against Spain. The focal point of the museum's collection is artist Cándido López's series of captivating scenes of the war against Paraguay in the 1870s.

Calle Defensa 1600 (in Parque Lezama). ℂ **11/4307-1182.** Free admission. Tues–Sun noon–6pm. Closed Jan. Metro: Constitución.

MALBA-Colección Costantini ★★★   The airy and luminescent Museo de Arte Latinoamericano de Buenos Aires (MALBA) houses the private art collection of art collector Eduardo Costantini. One of the most impressive collections of Latin American art anywhere, temporary and permanent exhibitions showcase such names as Antonio Berni, Pedro Figari, Frida Kahlo, Cândido Portinari, Diego Rivera, and Antonio Siguí. Many of the works confront social issues and explore questions of national identity. Even the benches are modern pieces of art. The atrium allows access to the various floors under an enormous metal sculpture of a man doing pushups over the escalator bay. In addition to the art exhibitions, Latin films are shown Tuesday through Sunday at 2 and 10pm. This wonderful museum is located in Palermo Chico.

Av. Figueroa Alcorta 3415 (at San Martín). ℂ **11/4808-6500.** www.malba.org.ar. Admission $3 (£2.15). Free admission on Wed. Wed–Mon noon–8pm. No metro access.

3 NEIGHBORHOODS WORTH A VISIT

LA BOCA

La Boca, on the banks of the Río Riachuelo, originally developed as a trading center and shipyard. This was the city's first Little Italy, giving the neighborhood the distinct flavor it maintains today. La Boca is most famous for giving birth to the tango in the numerous bordellos, known as *quilombos,* that once served this largely male population.

The focus of La Boca is the **Caminito** (p. 131), a pedestrian walkway, named ironically after a tango song about a rural village. The walkway is lined with humorously sculpted statues and murals explaining its history. Surrounding the cobblestone street are corrugated metal houses painted in a hodgepodge of colors, recalling a time when the poor locals decorated with whatever paint was left over from ship maintenance in the harbor. Today, many artists live or set up their studios in these houses. Along the Caminito, art and souvenir vendors work side by side with tango performers. This Caminito "Fine Arts Fair" is open daily from 10am to 6pm. La Boca is, however, a victim of its own success, and it has become an obscene tourist trap. While the area is historically important, most of what you will find along the Caminito are overpriced souvenir and T-shirt shops and constant harassment from people trying to hand you fliers for mediocre restaurants. In summer, the smell from the heavily polluted river becomes almost over-bearable. Come to this area because you have to, but if you are short on time, don't let the visit take up too much of your day. What remains authentic in the area is off the beaten path, whether art galleries or theaters catering both to locals and to tourists, or the world-famous **Estadio de Boca Juniors (Boca Juniors Stadium and Museum;** p. 132).

Use caution in straying too far from the Caminito, however, as the less-patrolled sur-rounding areas can be unsafe. The police are here to protect the tourists, not the locals. When the shopkeepers go home, so do the police. Still, at dusk and away from the Caminito is where you will have the most interesting interactions with the neighborhood residents who quietly reclaim the streets and stroll along the waterfront. Most come not from Italy now, but from the poor interior provinces of the country. In anticipation of Argentina's 2010 Bicentennial, the city had planned to redevelop the southern portion of Buenos Aires, which is where La Boca is situated, and extend a tourist train through the district. As of this writing, the plans fell apart, and though tracks were cleared, the train goes no farther than nearby Puerto Madero. *Caution:* It's best to avoid La Boca at night.

SAN TELMO
One of Buenos Aires's oldest neighborhoods, San Telmo originally housed the city's elite. But when yellow fever struck in the 1870s—aggravated by substandard conditions in the area—the aristocrats moved north. Poor immigrants soon filled this neighborhood, and the houses were converted to tenements, called *conventillos.* In 1970, the city passed regulations to restore some of San Telmo's architectural landmarks. Still, gentrification has been a slow process, and the neighborhood maintains a gently decayed, very authen-tic atmosphere, reminiscent of Cuba's old Havana. It's a bohemian enclave, attracting tourists, locals, and performers 7 days a week on its streets. A victim of its own success in many ways, the area is home to a large number of English-speaking expats, and some-times you'll wonder if you're actually in South America when you sit at a cafe and realize many tables are engaged in conversations you can fully understand. The collapse of the peso has also meant that a glut of antiques, sold for ready cash, are available for purchase, though most of the best items have been picked through by now. The best shops and markets in San Telmo line **Calle Defensa.** After Plaza de Mayo, **Plaza Dorrego** is the second-oldest square in the city. For a description of the square, see p. 130.

San Telmo is full of tango clubs; one of the most notable is **El Viejo Almacén ★,** at Independencia and Balcarce. An example of colonial architecture, it was built in 1798 and was a general store and hospital before its reincarnation as the quintessential Argen-tine tango club. Make sure to make it here at night for a show (p. 225). If you get the urge for a beginner or refresher tango course while you're in San Telmo, look for signs advertising lessons in the windows of bars and restaurants.

PALERMO
Palermo ★★★ is a catchall for a rather nebulous and large chunk of northern Buenos Aires. It encompasses **Palermo** proper with its park system extending on Avenida Liber-tador and Avenida Santa Fe; **Palermo Chico; Palermo Viejo,** which is further divided into **Palermo Soho** and **Palermo Hollywood;** and **Las Cañitas,** which is just to the side of the city's world-famous polo field.

Palermo Chico is an exclusive neighborhood of elegant mansions off of Avenida Libertador, with prices that are seemingly unaffected by the peso crisis. Other than the beauty of the homes and a few embassy buildings, this small set of streets tucked behind the MALBA museum has little of interest to tourists.

Palermo proper is a neighborhood of parks filled with magnolias, pines, palms, and willows, where families picnic on weekends and couples stroll at sunset. Designed by French architect Charles Thays, the parks take their inspiration from London's Hyde Park and Paris's Bois de Boulogne. Take the metro to Plaza Italia, which lets you out next to the **Botanical Gardens** ★ (© 11/4831-2951; p. 156) and **Zoological Gardens** ★ (© 11/4806-7412; p. 156), open dawn to dusk, both good spots for kids. Stone paths wind their way through the Botanical Gardens. Flora from throughout South America fills the garden, with more than 8,000 plant species from around the world represented. Next-door, the city zoo features an impressive variety of animals.

Parque Tres de Febrero ★★, a 1,000-acre paradise of trees, lakes, and walking trails, begins just past the Rose Garden off Avenida Sarmiento. In summer, paddleboats are rented by the hour. The **Jardín Botánico,** located off Plaza Italia, is another paradise, with many South American plants specially labeled. It is famous for its population of abandoned cats, tended by little old ladies from the neighborhood, another delight for kids to watch. Nearby, small streams and lakes meander through the **Japanese Garden** ★★ (© 11/4804-4922; daily 10am–6pm; admission $1 [70p]; p. 157), where children can feed the fish (*alimento para peces* means "fish food") and watch the ducks. Small wood bridges connect classical Japanese gardens surrounding the artificial lake. A simple restaurant serves tea, pastries, sandwiches, and a few Japanese dishes such as sushi and teriyaki chicken. You'll also find notes posted here for various Asian events throughout the city.

Previous visitors to the parks within Palermo will notice security changes that do impact a visit here. As a result of vandalism and theft, driven both by increased poverty and the high value of metals, many statues and fountains are now surrounded by high gates, and sections of the park are locked at night. You can still look at the statues, of course, but it's impossible to get close to many of them.

Palermo Viejo, once a run-down neighborhood of warehouses, factories, and tiny decaying stucco homes in which few people cared to live as recently as 15 years ago, has been transformed into the city's chicest destination. Palermo Viejo is further divided into **Palermo Soho** to the south and **Palermo Hollywood** (sometimes also written as **Palermo Holywood**) to the north, with railroad tracks and Avenida Juan B. Justo serving as the dividing line. With real estate pressure and the need to always be trendy, many areas that are technically in Palermo Hollywood are now saying they are in Palermo Soho, considered the more upscale of the two areas, blurring this dividing line. The center of Palermo Soho is Plazaleto Jorge Cortazar, better known by its informal name, Plaza Serrano, a small oval park at the intersection of calles Serrano and Honduras. Young people gather here late at night for impromptu singing and guitar sessions, sometimes fueled by drinks from the myriad of funky bars and restaurants that surround the plaza. On weekends, there is a crafts festival, but you'll always find someone selling bohemian jewelry and leather goods no matter the day. Palermo Soho is well known for boutiques owned by local designers, with fancy restaurants and hotels mixed in. Palermo Hollywood is considerably quieter and less gentrified than Palermo Soho, which, in some ways, has become a victim of its own success, populated during the daytime by lost tourists with

Evita Perón: Woman, Wife, Icon

Maria Eva Duarte de Perón, known the world over as Evita, captured the imagination of millions of Argentines because of her social and economic programs for the working classes. An illegitimate child of a wealthy businessman, she was born in Los Toldos, deep in the province of Buenos Aires. At 15, she moved to the capital to pursue her dreams of becoming an actress. She achieved moderate success, but was known more for her striking beauty than for her talent. In 1944, she met Colonel Juan Perón, a rising figure in the Argentine government during a volatile period in the country's history. They married in 1945 and Evita became an important part of his presidential campaign.

Once Perón took office, she created the Eva Perón Foundation, which redirected funds traditionally controlled by Argentina's elite to programs benefiting hospitals, schools, homes for the elderly, and various charities. In addition, she raised wages for union workers, leading to the eventual growth of the Argentine middle class, and she succeeded in realizing women's right to vote in 1947. When Evita died of cancer on July 26, 1952, the working classes tried (unsuccessfully) to have her canonized. She is buried in the Recoleta Cemetery, in her father's family's tomb. She is one of only a few nonaristocratic figures in this most elite of final resting places.

You will find that even today there is considerable disagreement among Argentines over Evita's legacy. Members of the middle and lower classes tend to see her as a national hero, while many of the country's upper classes believe she stole money from the wealthy and used it to embellish her own popularity. Since the 50th anniversary of her death, the establishment of the Museo Evita (p. 147), and the return of the Peronist party to power, her role in the country's history has been revisited far less emotionally.

maps and guidebooks in hand. The neighborhood gained its name because many Argentine film studios were initially attracted to its once-cheap rents and easy parking.

Las Cañitas was once the favored neighborhood of the military powers during the dictatorship period of 1976 to 1982, and the area remains the safest and securest neighborhood of all the central Buenos Aires neighborhoods. A military training base, hospital, high school, and various family housing units still remain and encircle the neighborhood, creating an islandlike sense of safety on the area's streets. Today, the area is far better known among the hip, trendy, and nouveau riches as the place to dine out, have a drink, party, and be seen in the fashionable establishments built into converted low-rise former houses on Calle Báez. The polo field where the International Championships take place is also in the neighborhood and is technically part of the military bases. The polo field's presence makes the neighborhood bars and restaurants great places for enthusiasts to catch polo stars celebrating their victories in season. We place Las Cañitas into Palermo in this guidebook, though some refer to the area as a section of Belgrano or a location independent of any other neighborhood.

RECOLETA

The city's most exclusive neighborhood, La Recoleta has a distinctly European feel, and locals call it a piece of Paris transplanted. Here, tree-lined avenues lead past fashionable restaurants, cafes, boutiques, and galleries. Much of the activity takes place along the pedestrian walkway Roberto M. Ortiz and in front of the Cultural Center and Recoleta Cemetery. This is a neighborhood of plazas and parks, a place where tourists and wealthy Argentines spend their leisure time outside. Weekends bring street performances, art exhibits, fairs, and sports.

The **Recoleta Cemetery** ★★★ (p. 136), open daily from 8am to 6pm, pays tribute to some of Argentina's historical figures. Weather permitting, free English guided tours take place every Tuesday and Thursday at 11am from the cemetery's Doric-columned entrance at Calle Junín 1790.

Adjacent to the cemetery, the **Centro Cultural Recoleta** ★ (p. 214) holds art exhibits and theatrical and musical performances, and includes the **Museo Participativo de Ciencias** (p. 146). Next-door, the **Buenos Aires Design Recoleta** (p. 194) features shops specializing in home decor. Among the best is **Tienda Puro Diseño Argentino** (p. 205), which features high-quality items designed and manufactured only in Argentina. One word of caution about Recoleta: If you're a tourist staying in the area or visiting, there's an assumption that you're extremely wealthy and possibly naive. It's more likely here than in any part of the city that visitors might be given the runaround by taxi drivers who can't seem to find the location their passengers have requested. They assume that, if you can afford Recoleta, then you can afford a fraudulent fare, so be extra-vigilant in knowing your destination. Also, there are no special fees above what the meter says you owe.

PLAZA DE MAYO

Juan de Garay founded the historic core of Buenos Aires, the **Plaza de Mayo** (p. 129), in 1580. The plaza is the political heart of the city, serving as a forum for protests.

The mothers of the *desaparecidos,* victims of the military dictatorship's war against left-ists, have demonstrated here since 1976. You can see them march, speak, and set up information booths Thursday afternoons at 3:30pm. The circle of headscarves, known as *panuelos,* which surrounds the Pirámide de Mayo marks their demonstration route. The use of the headscarves as a symbol dates from a time when the military finally granted the mothers the right to march in protest, but forbid them from speaking to anyone. They wrote the names of their missing children on the scarves, with the hope that someone would see and later, in a safer space, tell them what had happened to their children.

The Argentine president goes to work at the **Casa Rosada** ★★★ (p. 126). It was from a balcony of this mansion that Eva Perón addressed adoring crowds of Argentine workers. You can watch the changing of the guard in front of the palace every hour on the hour, and around back is the **Presidential Museum** (p. 126) with information on the building's history and items owned by presidents over the centuries.

The original structure of the **Metropolitan Cathedral** ★★ (p. 129) was built in 1745 and given a new facade and designated a cathedral in 1836. The **Cabildo** ★ (p. 123), the original seat of city government established by the Spaniards, was completed in 1751 and restored in 1939. The **Legislatura de la Ciudad (City Legislature Building;** p. 127) features a striking neoclassical facade and houses exhibitions in several of its halls; ask about tours. Farther down Calle Perú are the **Manzanas de las Luces (Blocks of Enlightenment)** ★★ (p. 127), which served as the intellectual center of the city in the 17th and 18th centuries. **San Ignacio,** the city's oldest church, stands at the corner of calles Bolívar and Alsina, and has a beautiful altar currently under renovation. Also located here is the **Colegio Nacional de Buenos Aires (National High School of Buenos Aires),** where Argentina's best-known intellectuals have gathered and studied (p. 128). In addition to weekend tours, the Comisión Nacional de la Manzanas de las Luces (*©* 11/4331-9534) organizes a variety of cultural activities during the week.

PUERTO MADERO

Puerto Madero became Buenos Aires's second major gateway to trade with Europe when it was built in 1880, replacing in importance the port at La Boca. But by 1910, the city had already outgrown it. The Puerto Nuevo (New Port) was established to the north to accommodate growing commercial activity, and Madero was abandoned for almost a century. Urban renewal saved the original port in the 1990s with the construction of a riverfront promenade, apartments, and offices. Bustling and businesslike during the day, the area attracts a fashionable, wealthy crowd at night. It's lined with elegant restaurants serving Argentine steaks and fresh seafood specialties, and there is a popular cinema showing Argentine and Hollywood films, as well as dance clubs such as **Asia de Cuba.** The entire area is rapidly expanding, with high-rise luxury residences, making this a newly fashionable, if somewhat isolated and artificial, neighborhood to live in. Of note is that all of the streets in Puerto Madero are named for important women in Argentine history. Look for the Buenos Aires City Tourism brochure *Women of Buenos Aires* to learn more about some of them. A sign between Docks 2 and 3 explains these spectacular women. At sunset, take a walk along the eastern, modern part of the renovated area, and watch the water shimmer in brilliant reds with the city as backdrop.

As you walk out from the port, you'll also come across the **Ecological Reserve** ★★ (p. 143). This area is an anomaly for a modern city and exists as proof that nature can regenerate from an ecological disaster. In the 1960s and 1970s, demolished buildings and debris were dumped into the Río de la Plata after the construction of the *autopista* (highway system). Over time, sand and sediment began to build up, plants and grasses grew, and birds now use this space as a breeding ground. If you're interested, you can ask travel agents about bird-watching tours. In the summer, adventurous Porteños use it as a beach, but the water is too polluted to swim in and you must be careful of jagged debris and the homeless who set up camp here. In spite of limited protection, Puerto Madero development is slowly creeping onto the preserve. While the Ecological Preserve forms a sort of lung for the city, the height of the buildings in Puerto Madero has been blamed for blocking Río de la Plata winds, further decreasing air quality in downtown Buenos Aires. The focal point for the Puerto Madero area is Santiago Calatrava's **Bridge of Woman,** opened in 2001 (p. 142).

PLAZA SAN MARTÍN & THE SURROUNDING MICROCENTRO AREA

Plaza San Martín ★★★, a beautiful park at the base of Calle Florida in the Retiro neighborhood, is the nucleus of what's considered the city's Microcentro. In summer months, Argentine businesspeople flock to the park during their lunch hours, loosening their ties, taking off some layers, and sunning for a while amidst the plaza's flowering jacaranda trees. A monument to General José de San Martín towers over the scene. The park is busy at all hours, and even the playground will be teeming with kids and their parents out for a post-midnight stroll. Plaza San Martín was once the location of choice for the most elite Porteño families at the beginning of the 20th century. The San Martín Palace, now used by the Argentine Ministry of Foreign Affairs; the Círculo Militar, once the home of the Paz family who own the *La Prensa* newspaper; and the elegant Plaza Hotel testify to this former grandeur. The construction of the modern American Express building unfortunately destroyed this once completely classical area. Temporary art exhibits, usually with a social purpose, often occur within the Plaza, forcing you to stroll and take in each image and think about their connections. The Plaza was also recently renovated with improved sidewalks and paving, as well as brighter lighting.

Plaza San Martín cascades gently down a hill, at the base of which sits the **Islas Malvinas–Falkland Islands War Memorial** (p. 138), a stark circular wall engraved with the names of the nearly 750 killed in the war and an eternal flame, overseen by guards from the various branches of the military. The memorial directly faces the Elizabethan-style **British Clock Tower,** recently renamed the **Torre Monumental** (p. 139), though most locals still use the old name. It was a gift from the British who built and ran the nearby Retiro train station complex. Oddly, it remained unscathed during the war, but was attacked years later by a mob that also toppled an accompanying statue of George Canning, the British foreign secretary who recognized Argentina's independence from Spain. The tower is open to the public and provides a good view of the city and the river.

Calle Florida ★★★, the main pedestrian thoroughfare of Buenos Aires, is teeming with stores. The busiest section, extending south from Plaza San Martín to Avenida Corrientes, is lined with boutiques, restaurants, and record stores. It extends all the way through Avenida de Mayo to the south, turning into **Calle Perú,** where many international banks have retail branches. Day and night here, street performers walk on glass, tango, and offer comedy acts. You'll find the upscale **Galerías Pacífico** (p. 194) fashion center on Calle Florida, where it intersects Calle Viamonte. Most of the shopping on the street itself, however, is middle-of-the-road. Leather stores abound, so compare prices by stopping into a few and bargain before finalizing your purchase. Calle Florida intersects with **Calle Lavalle,** a smaller version of itself, which has even more stores, most of lesser quality, and some inexpensive *parrillas* worth visiting. The street is also home to numerous video- and electronic-game arcades, so it's a good place for teenagers to hang out while you shop around—though it might be easy for them to get into trouble as seedy characters do hang around this area. **Calle Reconquista,** parallel to Calle Florida, is also being repaved as a pedestrian causeway as of this writing, along with small adjacent streets.

Avenida Corrientes ★ is a living diary of Buenos Aires's cultural development. Until the 1930s, Avenida Corrientes was the favored hangout of tango legends. When the avenue was widened in the mid-1930s, it made its debut as the Argentine Broadway, and Evita lived in her first apartment here as she struggled to make herself famous. Today Corrientes, lined with Art Deco cinemas and theaters, pulses with cultural and commercial activity day and night. It is also home to many bookstores, from the chains that sell bestsellers and English-language guidebooks, to independent bargain outlets and rare booksellers. The **Obelisco,** opened in 1936 as Buenos Aires's defining monument to mark the 400th anniversary of the first (unsuccessful) founding of the city, marks the intersection of Corrientes with **Avenida 9 de Julio.** Whenever locals have something to celebrate, they gather here. It's exciting to come here when Argentina wins an international soccer match.

4 THE PALERMO GARDENS COMPLEX & ZOO

More than a neighborhood with a park in it, Palermo has the feel of a park where some people happen to live. This wide, miles-long expanse of green open space along the waterfront exists within the city because it was an enormous estate until the middle of the 1800s. While you'd need a long time to really see the entire complex fully, I have listed some must-see highlights below.

The park contains the Rose Gardens, the Planetarium, the Patio, several museums, jogging trails, and far too many monuments to count. The area expands out beyond Jorge Newberry, the domestic airport, into the neighboring district of Belgrano. Easy to get lost in, you'll never need to worry, as cabs cruise the boulevards that cut through the park.

Botanical Gardens ★★ (Kids)   The Botanical Gardens are a true delight, with a few acres of open space and a myriad of tree-lined walkways. A central greenhouse is often the location of rotating art shows, with young artists standing and sweating next to their artwork. Plants from all over the world are here, including many from Argentina and other parts of South America. They're signed with their local and Latin names, making for a fun lesson for kids as you walk along. Not all the paths are well maintained, however, so watch your step. If you're here without the kids, the gardens are also a romantic spot. Bring a picnic basket and share some quality time, as you'll easily see many of the locals doing.

Like the Recoleta Cemetery, this is another cat lover's dream, and you'll find plenty of women from the neighborhood coming to take care of these strays. The cats are also more playful and friendly here, and like to come up to visitors to be petted. Sit on a bench, and you'll very likely find one cuddling up next to you.

Av. Las Heras, at Plaza Italia, across from the subway entrance. ℂ **11/4831-2951.** Free admission. Daily 8am–6pm. Metro: Plaza Italia.

Zoological Gardens ★★★ (Kids)   The Buenos Aires city zoo features an impressive array of animals, including indigenous birds and monkeys, giant turtles, llamas, elephants, and a polar bear and brown bear habitat. The eclectic and kitschy buildings housing the animals, some designed as exotic temples, are as much of a delight as the inhabitants. A giant lake is close to the entrance of the zoo and is filled with pink flamingos hanging out near mock Byzantine ruins in the center of the lake. Overlooking the water is a building that resembles a Russian church, which contains monkey cages. Camels are surrounded by Moroccan-style architecture, and the kangaroo holding pens are painted with aboriginal designs. The lions, the kings of the jungle, are in a castle complex with its own moat. The most stunning building, however, is the Elephant House. Built to look like an Indian temple, it is overgrown with vines to make you feel as if you are a jungle explorer who has come across an elephant sanctuary. There are three elephants: two are African and one is Asian.

The Asian elephant, named Mara, was rescued by the zoo after years of abuse as a circus animal. Having been caged too tightly, she suffers from an emotional illness, standing in one place while she shakes her head back and forth. The other elephants, named Pupy and Kuki, seem to take care of her, and will try to prod her along at feeding time and massage their heads against her. It is sad and yet interesting to watch the social behavior of these magnificent and enormous creatures. I recommend making time to see them.

Make sure to also see the polar bears, whose habitat comes with an underwater viewing area. All the caretakers are great with kids throughout the zoo, but here especially they take the time, at least in Spanish, to teach about the bears. They also feed the bears, and kids can watch them retrieve food from the water. In the back of the zoo is an enclosed jungle habitat full of various plant species, which even has a waterfall with a rope bridge that a caretaker will lead you through. Giant bugs are also in display cases here. It's hot and steamy inside, just like the real jungle, and the interior is a labyrinth surrounded by plants, so keep an eye on kids because they can easily get lost.

Peacocks and some of the small animals are allowed to roam free, and feeding is allowed with special food for sale for $1 to $2 (70p–£1.40) at kiosks. Animals on the loose will flock to your kids, and many of the cages have special feeding chutes where the animals will line up to greet them. Boats can also be rented on the lake in the front of the zoo, but at the time of this writing, repairs were being made. The zoo is a must for anyone, but especially families with kids. I recommend at least half a day to explore and a full day if you have kids.

Av. Las Heras, at Plaza Italia across from the subway entrance. ☏ **11/4806-7412.** Admission $4.50 (£3.20), additional charges for boats, jungle habitat, and other extras; multi-amenity and family passes also available for purchase. V. Hours change throughout the year, but are generally Tues–Sun 10am–8pm. Metro: Plaza Italia.

Japanese Gardens & Cultural Center ★ (Kids) (Finds) Tucked in the midst of all the other Palermo gardens is this tiny gem opened in 1969 in honor of an official visit by one of the Japanese princes. Special landscaping, rock islands, and small red bowed bridges give the feeling of being in Japan as soon as you step through the gates here. Carp swim in the large central lake, a delight for children as well as adults. Beyond the lake lies the Cultural Center, with a small museum and various art exhibitions. Kids can also learn origami folding and many other Asian crafts. Asian fairs are held throughout the year in both the center and the park, so pick up one of the calendars while visiting, or check out the website below for more details.

Av. Figueroa Alcorta, at Av. Casares. ☏ **11/4807-7843.** www.jardinjapones.com. Admission $1.50 (£1.05) for gardens, $1 (70p) for Cultural Center. Daily 10am–6pm, though hours vary with exhibitions and fairs. Metro: Plaza Italia.

La Rural & Opera Pampa ★ The grand Belle Epoque stadium known as La Rural was built at the turn of the 20th century overlooking Plaza Italia. It served as the parade grounds for the Sociedad Rural Argentina, an association of wealthy landowners from all over the country founded in 1866. During their annual meetings in Buenos Aires, they would parade their most prized animals, along with their gaucho workers, and compete for awards. By promoting Argentina's agricultural resources, it was through this association that Argentina was able to become an important world economic force by the end of the 1800s. Their headquarters remain in Buenos Aires on the 400 block of Calle Florida. A modern exhibition hall has been added and is often the site of international expos, conferences, and other exhibitions. The United States Embassy is located behind this complex.

To get an idea of what the experience was like in the society's heyday, tourists should book a night with **Opera Pampa,** an event held in the old stadium. The show covers the at-times-violent history of Argentina, beginning with the Spanish conquest of the Indians, the 1810 Independence, Roca's slaughter of thousands of Indians in the province of Buenos Aires, through European immigration to Buenos Aires at the beginning of the 20th century. The scenes related to Indian history are exceedingly violent and sad, and

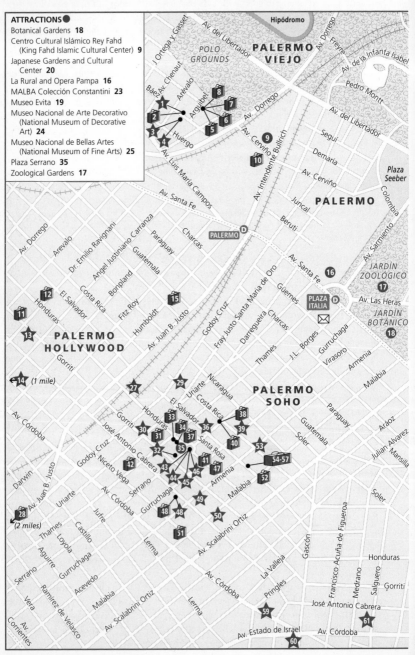

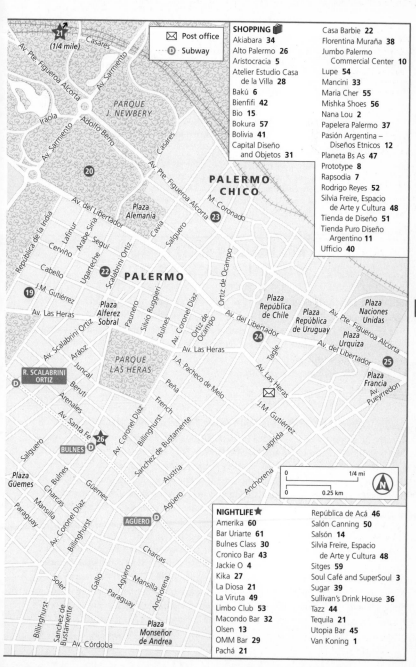

include the song "Fuera Fuera" ("Away, Away") as the Indians are forced to leave and one Indian remains behind, begging a soldier to let him stay. The most dramatic scenes are those relating to San Martín and the revolution, full of charging horses and simulated cannon fights. Cheerier portions include gaucho gatherings in *pulperías*, country bars where they would sing and dance after working on the *estancias* (farms). The *Zamba*, the national dance performed with white handkerchiefs, is featured in these scenes. (The tango, in spite of its fame and association with Argentina, is not the national dance.) The show is brilliantly choreographed and exciting to watch. Afterward, patrons are treated to an enormous all-you-can-eat *asado* (Argentine barbecue) in the stadium's dining hall. An evening here will give you a far better understanding of Argentina's history. I would recommend it for children because it is historically educational, but parents have to make a decision weighing that with the violence.

La Rural Stadium and Exhibition Hall on Av. Las Heras, at the intersection of Av. Santa Fe overlooking Plaza Italia. Opera Pampa office and information is at Av. Sarmiento, at Calle Paso. ℂ **11/4777-5557.** www.operapampa.com.ar. Sociedad Rural Argentina www.sra.org.ar. Tickets are $40 (£28) show only, $80 (£57) show and dinner. Showtimes Fri–Sat 8pm, dinner following. Metro: Plaza Italia for La Rural Stadium; Puerreydon for Opera Pampa office.

5 RELIGIOUS BUILDINGS WORTH CHECKING OUT

Iglesia San Nicolás de Bari ★★ Ⓚⁱᵈˢ   This is an exceedingly beautiful and impressive church built for a local Italian Roman Catholic community. Its interior is reminiscent of a mini–Saint Peter's, with its interior of Corinthian columns and white marble with colored accents. The block that surrounds it also has an array of exceptionally interesting buildings of various styles from the beginning of the 20th century, with a beauty not usually seen on most of Avenida Santa Fe. Take note of the Art Deco Casa de Teatro in particular.

Santa Fe 1364 (at Uruguay). ℂ **11/4813-3028.** Metro: Callao.

Centro Cultural Islámico Rey Fahd (King Fahd Islamic Cultural Center) ★
With its broad expanses, well-tended lawn, minarets, and palm trees, the Centro Cultural Islámico brings a little bit of the Middle East to Buenos Aires. Overlooking the polo grounds, this enormous structure, with its severely modern architecture that becomes simply radiant in strong sunlight, is the largest Islamic center and mosque in all of Latin America. At night, the two minarets are lit and are a striking contrast with the surrounding apartment complexes. The project began under the influence of former President Carlos Ménem, who (though Catholic at the time of his presidency) is of Syrian Muslim descent. Construction began in 1998, and it was opened in 2000. The center is open for free tours in Spanish and sometimes in English, Tuesday and Thursday at noon. Lasting 45 minutes, you will see the gardens, interior courtyard, library, and other spaces. Institutions can make special requests for tours at other times. The Centro offers classes in the Koran and Arabic language, and has a library open to the public daily from 10am to 5pm. Though the Centro is closed to the public on Muslim holidays, Muslim visitors to Buenos Aires are welcome to visit for activities. Estimates of the Islamic and Arabic community in Argentina run at about 750,000. Many Argentines call anyone of Arabic or

Muslim descent "Turcos," or Turks, regardless of their country of origin, based on the fact that the majority came here from places such as Syria, Armenia, and Lebanon, areas once controlled by the Ottoman Empire, the capital of which was situated in what is now modern-day Turkey.

Av. Bullrich 55 (at Libertador). © **11/4899-1144.** www.ccislamicoreyfahd.org.ar. Free tours Tues and Thurs at noon. Metro: Palermo.

Centro Cultural SGI (The Buddhist Center) This Buddhist temple and cultural center sits in two modern buildings spanning one block in the Belgrano neighborhood. There are several meeting and chanting spaces and a bookstore. The building is open to the public and is a peaceful respite in Buenos Aires. Various cultural and musical events, related to Buddhism and other Asian philosophies, are also held here.

Donado 2150 (at Juramento). © **11/4545-6000.** www.sgiar.org.ar. Daily 3–7:30pm; hours may differ based on events. Metro: Juramento.

Claustros del Pilar (Basílica Nuestra Señora del Pilar) ★★ This imposing white Spanish colonial church overlooks Recoleta Cemetery. While many visit inside to see the worship area, few take the time to discover the religious art museum within the former convent area, full of gorgeous pieces from Buenos Aires's early years. A step back in time, the convent retains the original flooring, stairs, walls, and other components from its 1732 construction. Most interesting are the windows with special panes, made from agate so that light could come into the structure, but the nuns would be hidden. Other highlights include the ecclesiastical wardrobes on display.

Junín 1904 (next to Recoleta Cemetery). © **11/4803-6793.** Admission $1 (70p). Tues–Sat 10:30am–6:15pm; Sun 2:30–6:15pm. No metro access.

Basílica y Convento de San Francisco (San Francis's Church & Convent) ★ The San Roque parish to which this church belongs is one of the oldest in the city. A Jesuit architect designed the building in 1730, but a final reconstruction in the early 20th century added a German baroque facade, along with statues of Saint Francis of Assisi, Dante, and Christopher Columbus. Inside, you'll find a tapestry by Argentine artist Horacio Butler, along with an extensive library.

Calle Defensa and Alsina. © **11/4331-0625.** Free admission. Hours vary. Metro: Plaza de Mayo.

---

6 ARCHITECTURAL HIGHLIGHTS

MUST-SEES FOR ARCHITECTURE BUFFS

Buenos Aires is full of architectural highlights. I have discussed many of the most important buildings throughout this chapter and in the walking tours in chapter 8. Here, are some particularly impressive standouts, not all of which are open to the public.

Centro Naval ★★ Inaugurated in 1914 and designed by the Swiss architect Jacques Dunant, this building is an incredible combination of Italian rococo elements and rustication, all executed in a high Beaux Arts style. The building is made of cast stone and is extremely well maintained. The ornate bronze doors feature shields, arrows, and other symbols of war, overseen by a nude bronze sea god in a Spanish galleon announcing triumph through a conch shell. Other bronze boats line the balustrades on the upper

---

(Kids) Especially for Kids

The following Buenos Aires attractions have major appeal to kids of all ages:

- Museo de Los Niños (p. 145)
- Museo Participativo de Ciencias (p. 146)
- Zoological Gardens (p. 156)
- The Water Palace and the Museo del Patrimonio (p. 148)
- Museo de las Armas de la Nación (p. 144)

In addition to the sights listed above, a number of playgrounds are of particular interest to kids. One of them, where you'll often see parents and their kids even after midnight, is in **Plaza San Martín.** A merry-go-round and swing sets are in **Plaza Congreso,** across from the headquarters of the Madres de Plaza de Mayo. You'll also find playgrounds in the **Botanical Gardens** (p. 156). Note that the Middle Eastern restaurant **Garbis** (p. 114) also has an indoor playground.

---

floors. The building is not open to the public, but at times people are allowed in the small lobby. There are also various events and functions held here, including weddings, so if you hear of any, find a way to get yourself invited.

Calle Florida 801 (at Córdoba, across from the Galerías Pacífico). Not usually open to the public. Metro: San Martín.

Confitería del Molino ★★   Unfortunately, not only will you not be able to enter this incredible masterpiece, but it is also rapidly crumbling away. Across the street from Congreso, this was once among the city's most important cafes, where politicians would mingle with well-to-do citizens and dignitaries from around the world. The cafe closed in 1997, and the building is now only rarely open to the public for events designed to raise consciousness of the need to restore the building before it disappears forever. (So bad is its condition that plants and moss are growing on the facade.) Primarily Art Nouveau, stained glass and ornate tile work were once part of the ornamentation here, and its main feature is the tower imitating a windmill. (Molino is Spanish for windmill.) The architect was Francesco Gianotti, an Italian who also designed Galería Güemes and its theater housing the Piazzolla tango show. These are open to the public if you want to get an idea of Molino's fabulous interior (p. 141).

Callao 10 (at Rivadavia, next to Congreso). Not open to the public. Metro: Congreso.

Teatro Nacional Cervantes ★★   One of the country's most important theaters, the architecture here puts on a show all its own. Built in Spanish Habsburg Imperial style, it overlooks Plaza Lavalle, only 2 blocks from the more famous Teatro Colón. The building was a gift from two Spanish actors who opened the theater in 1921. Within a few years, it went bankrupt and was taken over by the Argentine government. The interior is decorated with materials from Spain, including tapestries from Madrid and tiles from Valencia and Tarragona. The theater is open to the public for tours and has productions

Libertad 815 (at Córdoba, overlooking Plaza Lavalle). *(C* **11/4816-7212.** Guided tours Tues 2pm. Metro: Tribunales.

---

7 SELF-GUIDED & ORGANIZED TOURS

FREE BUENOS AIRES CITY TOURISM OFFICE TOURS

The Buenos Aires City Tourism Office offers an excellent array of free city tours. Participants are taken through the city on buses or meet at a designated point and walk through a neighborhood as a guide explains the highlights. Most of the tours are conducted in Spanish; however, a few are in Spanish and English. The possibility of an English-speaking guide being on hand can change at the last minute, but I encourage you to sign up for a tour anyway and see what happens. You can always leave if you do not understand, or someone will more than likely be able to translate.

Ask for information about the tours at the many Buenos Aires **Visitor Information Kiosks** (listed on p. 24). You can also call the hot line for information (*(C* **11/4313-0187**). It's staffed from 7:30am to 6pm Monday to Saturday, and Sunday from 11am to 6pm. Or call the organization directly about the free tours (*(C* **11/4114-5791;** Mon–Fri 10am–4pm; ask to speak with Rubén Forace, who is in charge of them). The tours are on a space-available basis, so you'll have to register for them.

The tours cover the most important neighborhoods—Palermo, San Telmo, La Boca, Recoleta, the Plaza de Mayo, Belgrano, and many others—but are not offered every day. Ask for the brochure *Free Guided Tours,* which tells you when they are scheduled while you are in town, at the Visitor Information Kiosks.

They also offer four specialized free tours that relate to Buenos Aires historic figures. Called *Itinerarios Evocativos,* these include Eva Perón, Carlos Gardel, Jorge Luis Borges, and Federico García Lorca. These will also be listed in the *Free Guided Tours* brochure, but each tour is not held every month. However, each of the Itinerarios Evocativos has its own pamphlet that lists the places, addresses, and a description of each of the sites that would be visited on the tour. You can therefore do these tours on your own on a self-guided basis if they are not offered while you are in town.

Another interesting self-guided, free city tour service offered by the Buenos Aires City Tourism Office is the Cellular Telephone Tours. Ask for the brochure, currently only in Spanish, called *Audio Guía Móvil.* The brochure has instructions for each itinerary, where you call a number and punch codes to hear speeches and other information (in either English or Spanish) when near historical sites. When I tried this system, I didn't think it worked very well, but you might have better luck. While, in theory, this information service is free, don't forget that you will be charged for the airtime itself, making the cost of using this service possibly significant. Still, the system's complete flexibility and ability to allow you to hear recordings from the past certainly makes this different from any other tour option out there.

BIKE TOURS

Bike Rentals Buenos Aires (*(C* **11/4126-2953;** www.bikerentalbsas.com.ar) offers several interesting bike rides, from bicycling through Buenos Aires, combined with a tango lesson, to culinary biking tours, to day trips to Colonia where you ferry across and then bike around. It's run by Raphaella Saar, a young woman who once worked at La Cabaña and loved working with tourists and dreamed one day of having her own company.

Buenos Aires Urban Biking (ⓒ **11/4568-4321** or 11/15-5165-9343 [cell]; www.urbanbiking.com) has four different themes for biking throughout Buenos Aires: northern areas of the city, southern areas including the Ecological Reserve, Buenos Aires at Night, and the Tigre Delta outside of the city. Equipment is provided by the company and prices and trip lengths vary by itinerary, from a half-day to a full 8-hour day. They also operate in La Plata, the capital of the province of Buenos Aires. Guides speak English, Spanish, French, and Portuguese.

La Bicicleta Naranja (ⓒ **11/4362-1104;** www.labicicletanaranja.com.ar) has two offices and two route formats. One begins in San Telmo and looks at the origins of the city in its southern section. The other looks at what it calls Aristocratic Buenos Aires in the northern section of the city.

Lan and Kramer Bike Tours (ⓒ **11/4311-5199;** www.biketours.com.ar) leads groups, which generally meet and start their trips in Plaza San Martín. There are several tour routes, some of which pass through the Ecological Reserve along the Puerto Madero waterfront. Rates vary, depending on the length of the itinerary.

BOAT TOURS

Buenos Aires ignores its riverfront location in many ways and seems to have no real connection to the water other than a view from its tall buildings. The two tours listed below, however, allow you to see the city from the water.

Buenos Aires Boats, La Boca Docks, at the base of Caminito (ⓒ **11/4303-1616;** www.bueboats.com), leaves four times daily from the port in La Boca near where Caminito hits the waterfront. Trips last about 1¹/₂ hours and go from La Boca to the Río de la Plata. Tours cost about $5 (£3.55) for adults, $3.50 (£2.50) for seniors and children, and are free for those younger than 3. Group discounts are available. Only cash is accepted.

Puro Remo Boats and Kayaks (ⓒ **11/15-6397-3545,** -3546 [cell]; www.puroremo.com.ar) leaves from the Puerto Madero Yacht Club and offers various tours where you do all the paddling. Tours vary in length, price, and skill set. Only cash is accepted.

In addition, La Boca also has small **ferry boats** at the base of the now-closed Puente N. Avellaneda (that big metal rusty thing overlooking La Boca that has actually been declared a UNESCO heritage site). These are the boats used by locals to cross the river back and forth to Buenos Aires from the very poor suburbs in Avellaneda. Costing only 50 centavos ($1.75/£1.25), they are fun to ride, but I suggest crossing and coming directly back instead of exploring the other side of the river, because Avellaneda is considered dangerous if you don't know where you're going. Few tourists take these boats, so you will be especially welcomed onboard by locals who rarely meet foreigners. Though it seems farfetched considering the setting, some locals half-jokingly call these boats the La Boca Gondolas, considering the Italian heritage of the area. Whatever you do, do not touch the heavily polluted water full of industrial waste and sewage. Only cash is accepted.

BUS TOURS

Travel Line (ⓒ **11/5555-5373;** www.travelline.com.ar) offers more than 20 tours with various themes within Buenos Aires and into the suburbs. Participants are picked up at their hotels and tours can last anywhere from 4 hours up to a full day; some include meals. Themes include Eva Perón, tango tours, Fiesta Gaucho (which visits an *estancia,* or farm), City by Night, and the Tigre Delta, among many others. Prices vary but range from $10 to $90 (£7.10–£64). American Express, Discover, MasterCard, and Visa are accepted.

CUSTOMIZED & INDIVIDUAL TOURS

BA Local (✆ 11/15-4870-5506 [cell]; www.balocal.com) is run by Christina Wiseman, a young, glamorous American expat from New York. Her tours range from off-the-beaten-path neighborhoods to art galleries, shopping, and other themes, as well as whatever a tourist might want to see. Her tours are particularly good for seeing the city from a young woman's perspective.

CiceroneBA Tours (✆ 11/15-5654-9032 [cell]; www.ciceroneba.com.ar) is run by Buenos Aires native Marcello Mansilla. He offers highly customized and individualized tours on many themes or whatever the client wants. He is a descendant of Lucio Mansilla, an important figure during Argentina's civil war period, who is honored by a street in Barrio Norte.

Diva Tours/Bitch Tours (✆ 11/15-6157-3248 [cell]; www.bitchtours.blogspot.com). As the name suggests, these tours are run by a very sassy woman, Buenos Aires–born Agustina Menendez, who also works as an actress and dancer. She tailors her tours to whatever the client wants and also takes clients on the usual tours but with an attitude, from the Casa Rosada to a slaughterhouse. Her motto is if she's not having fun, you're not having fun.

Marta Pasquali (✆ 11/15-4421-2486 [cell]; marpas@uolsinectis.com.ar). Marta is one of the best private tour guides in Buenos Aires, working with visiting government officials, corporate clients, and individuals. She has an incredible in-depth knowledge of Buenos Aires and imparts not just the facts about a particular building or event, but also how it translates to a deeper understanding of Buenos Aires.

Monica Varela (✆ 11/15-4407-0268 [cell]; monyliv@hotmail.com or varmonica@gmail.com). Monica is an incredibly intelligent, passionate tour guide. Like her friend Martina, she is one of the city's best private tour guides, offering individual and corporate tours. She can run a tour on any theme and has received excellent feedback from *Frommer's* readers who have hired her.

DINING TOURS

Dine at Home Tours (✆ 11/4801-3182, 11/15-6051-9328 or 11/15-5564-9846 [cells]; www.dineathome.com.ar) is an interesting concept for dining at other people's homes, and a good way to get to know English-speaking locals in Buenos Aires. Edward Goedhart started the tours, which clients can select depending on an occupation. So, for instance, if you're an architect and want to know a local architect, this is a way to do it, all depending on schedules. Book through an agent or directly.

GAY TOURS

Mister Papi Tours (✆ 11/4372-4578 or 11/15-5995-8531 [cell]; www.misterpapi.com.ar), run by Fabian Fuentes, offers tours in Spanish and English. He only does them for individuals or very small groups of friends, in a combination of walking, taxi, or rent-a-car, depending on what people want.

JEWISH-THEMED TOURS

Travel Jewish (✆ 877/TANGO-SI [826-4674] in the U.S. or 11/5258-0774 in Buenos Aires; www.traveljewish.com; info@traveljewish.com) is owned by Deborah Miller, an

American who has lived in Buenos Aires, and offers Jewish tours of the city. Trips can be planned from beginning to end, including flights and high-end hotels, adventure kayaking and a day in Tigre, or simply Jewish-themed day tours to enjoy once you are in Buenos Aires. Deborah also offers Spanish language classes. Some facilities they visit may require ID, so you should always have your passport when taking one of these tours.

SHOPPING TOURS

Buenos Aires Boutique Tours (✆ **11/15-3565-1713** [cell]; www.baboutiquetours.com. ar) is run by Australian-born shopping enthusiast Kirsty Noble, who takes a group of shoppers around Recoleta, Palermo, and other neighborhoods. The hunt is for unique Argentina-made items, and even locals have been surprised by the secrets uncovered. The trip begins in a cafe, so all the shoppers, usually women, get to meet each other before hitting the streets. There's a lunch break at a spot where family and friends who don't love shopping can join up and not feel neglected while you max out your credit cards.

SPANISH LANGUAGE TOURS

While **Conocer Buenos Aires** (✆ **11/15-5565-0348** [cell]; www.conocerbue.com.ar) only offers tours in Spanish, its in-depth themes are not found in most English-language tours. They cover major cultural figures in Argentina, immigration, off-the-beaten-path neighborhoods where tourists rarely venture, and other themes, using a combination of walking and minibus, depending on the tour. Check the website for new tours, which are definitely worth taking if you understand Spanish.

SPORTS TOURS

Go Football Tours (✆ **11/4816-2681** or 11/15-4405-9526 [cell]; www.gofootball.com. ar) brings you to the game. Sports lovers will enjoy having all the thinking done for them, from knowing which team is playing when, to getting tickets and getting to the game itself. The company picks you up at the door of your hotel, takes you to the stadium, and then back to the hotel again. Visit their website to find out which games fit into your travel schedule. They also have tours to tennis, polo, and many other sports events. Visa and cash are accepted. Most events run about $40 (£28), including tickets and transportation.

Golf Day (✆ **11/4824-8531** and 11/4826-8531) is perfect for busy executives who don't have the time to plan a day of golf, but want to squeeze in a few holes before leaving Buenos Aires. This company will pick you up, take you to a local golf course, provide lunch, and then bring you back to your hotel. They prefer more than a day's notice, if possible, when making a reservation. Prices range from about $60 (£43) or more.

TANGO TOURS

There are literally hundreds of tours for people interested in tango here in Buenos Aires, the city where it all began. For more information, see "Tango Tours" on p. 230.

VOLUNTEER TOURISM

Voluntario Global (✆ **11/15-6206-9639** [cell]; www.voluntarioglobal.org.ar) is an association that promotes responsible tourism. It offers visitors a chance to see how the other half lives, with trips to *villas miserias,* or slums, surrounding Buenos Aires, where you work alongside nongovernmental agents helping the poor. In some cases, you see where the *cartoneros,* or garbage pickers, live—the ones you've avoided during your trip—and you'd better understand their lives.

See chapter 8 for five walking tours. See "Free Buenos Aires City Tourism Office Tours," above, for a description of walking tours provided by the Buenos Aires Tourist Office.

In addition to the above, **Los Santos Tours** (✆ **11/4325-8100;** turismoxbuenosaires@netafull.com.ar) has several themed walking itineraries through different Buenos Aires neighborhoods. Price and duration will vary by itinerary, but the full-city tour can last up to 7 hours. Prices range from $16 to $24 (£11–£17), and some itineraries include a snack or lunch.

IN VIP Visit BA (✆ **11/15-5063-6602** [cell]; www.invisitba.4t.com) offers highly customized tours, some of which are strictly walking, while others are bus-and-walking combinations. Prices vary by itinerary, but can range from $15 to $25 (£11–£18) or more per person, depending on the group size and itinerary.

8 LANGUAGE COURSES

Argentina I.L.E.E. This school opened in 1986 and uses a cultural immersion program. They can arrange housing with families for students who come to their classes. All teachers have a master's degree in education or literature from the University of Buenos Aires. They also offer tango classes and other local outings.
Callao 339 (3rd floor at Sarmiento). ✆ **11/4782-7173.** www.argentinailee.com. Metro: Congreso.

Borges Spanish School Argentina A project of the International Foundation Jorge Luis Borges, this school has language classes combined with travel tours.
Av. Córdoba 2302 (1st floor, at Uriburu Congreso). ✆ **11/5217-9777.** www.tripnow.com.ar. Metro: Facultad de Medicina.

Español Andando This language school uses a cultural immersion program in a 4-day crash course and fights what it calls "boring" ways to learn Spanish. Rather than a classroom, students travel around Buenos Aires with professors to also use their new language skills in real situations. The school doesn't have an office for drop-by visits, but the first class meetings are at a cafe in San Telmo.
✆ **11/5278-9886.** www.espanol-andando.com.ar.

World Class Language School Whether you know Spanish well or not at all, you'll find several levels of classes with this school. The school is open to tourists and also has many business clients.
Ciudad De La Paz 2476, 1A (at Monroe, in Belgrano). ✆ **11/4116-3535.** www.wclass.com.ar. Metro: Juramento.

9 SPORTS

There's no shortage of sporting events in Buenos Aires, from the highbrow International Polo championships where locals hobnob with European royalty, to soccer events where the crowds are as rowdy as the players. Check the papers for events and times when in town, especially the English-language *Buenos Aires Herald.* If you want to have your experience planned for you (ticket choice, ticket purchase, and being escorted to and from the game), check out the two companies I mention in "Sports Tours" in "Self-Guided & Organized Tours," above.

SPECTATOR SPORTS

HORSE RACING   Over much of the 20th century, Argentina was famous for its thoroughbreds. It continues to send prize horses to competitions around the world, although you can watch some of the best right here in Buenos Aires. In the center of the city, you can see races at **Hipódromo Argentino de Palermo,** Av. del Libertador 4205, at Dorrego (© **11/4778-2839**), in Palermo, a track made in a classical design with several modern additions. The Hipódromo is open all year. Entry is free and race times run from late afternoon until past midnight. In the suburbs, a few miles from Buenos Aires, is also the **Hipódromo de San Isidro,** Av. Márquez 504, at Fleming in San Isidro (© **11/4743-4010**). This modern location is open year-round. Most races begin in the early afternoon and run through early evening, and entry prices range from $1 (70p) to $10 (£7.10), depending on your seating area. Check the *Buenos Aires Herald* for more exact race schedule information for both arenas.

POLO   Argentina has won more international polo tournaments than any other country, and the **Argentine Open Championship,** held late November through early December, is the world's most important polo event. There are two seasons for polo: March through May and September through December, and competitions are held at the **Campo Argentino de Polo,** Avenida del Libertador and Avenida Dorrego (© **11/4576-5600**). Tickets can be purchased at the gate for about $25 (£18) per person. This is one of the most important polo stadiums in the world, and visits by European royalty are not uncommon in season. Contact the **Asociación Argentina de Polo,** Hipólito Yrigoyen 636 (© **11/4331-4646** or 11/4342-8321), for information on polo schools and events. **La Martina Polo Ranch** (© **11/4576-7997**), located 60km (37 miles) from Buenos Aires near the town of Vicente Casares, houses more than 80 polo horses, as well as a guesthouse with a swimming pool and tennis courts.

SOCCER   One cannot discuss soccer (called *fútbol* here) in Argentina without paying homage to Diego Armando Maradona, Argentina's most revered player and one of the sport's great (if fallen) players. Any sense of national unity dissolves when Argentines watch their favorite clubs—River Plate, Boca Juniors, Racing Club, Independiente, and San Lorenzo—battle on Sunday in season, which runs from February until November. There is also a summer season when teams travel, so essentially soccer never really stops in Buenos Aires. Passion for soccer here could not run hotter. Try to catch a game at the **Estadio Boca Juniors,** Brandsen 805 (© **11/4309-4700**), in San Telmo, followed by raucous street parties. Ticket prices start at $3 (£2.15) and can be purchased in advance or at the gate.

OUTDOOR ACTIVITIES

GOLF   Argentina has more than 200 golf courses. Closest to downtown Buenos Aires is **Cancha de Golf de la Ciudad de Buenos Aires,** Av. Torquist 1426, at Olleros (© **11/4772-7261**), 10 minutes from downtown and with great scenery and a par-71 course. Prices are from $7 (£4.95) during the week to $10 (£7.10) on weekends, with additional fees for caddies and other services. **Jockey Club Argentino,** Av. Márquez 1700 (© **11/4743-1001**), is in San Isidro, about 30 minutes from downtown. It has two courses (par-71 and -72). Prices start at $40 to $60 (£28–£43) to enter, but with extra fees for caddies and other services.

City Strolls

Buenos Aires is a great walking city. No matter where you start out, you'll find beautiful architecture and tree-lined streets as you explore various areas. If you get lost, friendly Porteños will help you, as well as offer advice on their favorite sights. I've provided a few itineraries here, but you'll probably figure out a few of your own along the way.

WALKING TOUR 1	HISTORICAL CALLE FLORIDA

GETTING THERE:	Take the metro to San Martin.
START:	Corner of calles Córdoba and Florida.
FINISH:	Calle Florida at Diagonal Norte.
TIME:	2 hours, not including eating or shopping stops.
BEST TIMES:	Daylight hours in the midafternoon, when you can see the buildings most clearly and most are open (some interiors not visible after 8pm).

Pedestrianized Calle Florida mostly has a reputation as a shop-till-you-drop and people-watching destination. However, there is superb architecture and historical interest here as well. I highlight the most beautiful features of the street here, and I recommend that you keep your head up as you walk along (trying, of course, not to bump into anyone or step in Buenos Aires's infamous dog doo-doo.) While many of the buildings on this street have been modernized at storefront level, the facades higher up are often preserved. The last portion of this trip along Calle Florida takes you into Buenos Aires's banking center, nicknamed "La City" after London's financial district. This tour is an easy walk and is also wheelchair-accessible in most cases.

To start the tour, begin at the northeastern corner of Calle Florida, where it hits Calle Córdoba. You will be in front of Córdoba 810, which is the:

❶ Centro Naval

This is one of the city's most exquisite buildings, a masterpiece of cast stone architecture. A nude sea god in a Spanish galleon, announcing triumph through a conch shell, oversees its corner doorway. Naval themes continue along the upper balustrades. The building was opened in 1914 and was designed by Swiss architect Jacques Dunant. It's not generally open to the public, but sometimes they let you into the circular lobby. If you ever get invited to an event here, make sure to go.

Cross Calle Córdoba heading south and stop just after crossing the street, at the:

❷ Galerías Pacífico

The most famous shopping mall in Buenos Aires, Galerías Pacífico was opened in 1891. The building was designed to recall the Galleria Vittorio Emanuele II in Milan, with its long halls, glass cupola, and several tiers of shops. An economic crisis shortly after its opening, however, meant that it was converted into office space for the Pacífico Railroad Company. In 1992, everything old became new again, and the building was converted back into a shopping center. Enter the building and see the central staircase where

(Finds)   More Do-It-Yourself Excursions

The Buenos Aires City Tourism kiosks scattered throughout the city have maps that can be used for self-guided tours. *The Golden Map* (p. 25), available at almost all hotels, also has some self-guided walks for various neighborhoods in the city. One pamphlet that the city provides contains information about a special cell-phone tour, where participants punch in codes at various destinations and hear explanations in English, Spanish, and other languages, including recordings of historical events at the various locations. Ask for this specific brochure, but know that the phone system does not always work well. Other themed tours include "Women of Buenos Aires" or focus on such important historical figures as Evita, Lorca, Borges, or Gardel, with addresses and descriptions of the places you will see. Some of these tours cover large distances not suitable for being covered solely by walking.

all the halls meet. In 1945, while still an office building, paintings about the history of mankind were installed under the main dome, and the shopping center has daily information sessions explaining their history.

TAKE A BREAK
If you're hungry, make a pit stop in the **food court** at the Galerías Pacífico. Try a fast-food *asado* (Argentine grill), and finish your meal with a Patagonian chocolate treat—you won't be sorry!

When you're finished shopping here, head back out the door facing Calle Florida and turn left, walking south on Calle Florida until you get to Lavalle, another pedestrianized street. No need to look out for cars at this busy intersection, which is sometimes full of street performers. (Take a break here and watch if one catches your attention.) After crossing Lavalle, stop midblock and face the building at Calle Florida 460 on your right, or west, side. It's the:

❸ Sociedad Rural Argentina
Surrounded by modern storefronts, this small, ornate French rococo building seems out of place among its ordinary neighbors. The people working inside almost undoubtedly feel the same way, for this is the headquarters of the Sociedad Rural Argentina, an organization created in the mid-1800s by the country's wealthi-

est oligarchs. This society was integral to the creation of Argentina's great agricultural wealth. The door to this important institution is almost always closed, but if you find it open, take a chance and wander in to see the Belle Epoque interior. There are, however, no official visits to the building and you'll likely be quickly sent out the door.

Continue walking south on Calle Florida until you get to Avenida Corrientes. Cross the street and stop in front of Burger King, which was once the site of the:

❹ Ana Díaz Historical Homestead
Women's history buffs take note: While men usually get all the credit for founding cities, Spanish explorer Juan de Garay's 1580 expedition, which permanently founded Buenos Aires, was not without a lady's touch. Ana Díaz, whose house was located on the property where Burger King now sits, came along with him. The first time that the Spanish tried to settle the city of Buenos Aires in 1536, it was an all-male group of explorers and the settlement failed. Who knows how many times it might have taken to settle Buenos Aires if a woman hadn't been around to take care of things the second time around? Still, it's unclear historically what her exact role was in the founding. Was she a Spanish conquistadora, a woman with Indian

Legend:
- (i) Information
- ✉ Post office
- ☕ Take a Break
- Ⓐ Subway
- Ⓓ—Ⓔ Subway transfer

1 Centro Naval
2 Galerías Pacífico
3 Sociedad Rural Argentina
4 Ana Díaz Historical Homestead
5 Galería Mitre/Falabella
6 Banco Francés—Optician Store
7 Gath & Chaves
8 HSBC Building
9 Galería Güemes
10 Bank of Boston
11 Roque Sáenz Peña Monument

0 ——— 1/4 mi
0 ——— 0.25 km

CITY STROLLS

8

HISTORICAL CALLE FLORIDA

blood who served as a guide, or a lover of one of the men? Ana Díaz's original home is long gone, but was located on this corner. A stunning turn-of-the-20th-century home was later built here and was intact until Burger King got its hands on it. Still, enter the hamburger joint and take a walk up the staircase to your left. Try not to gasp in awe as you head upstairs to the colonnaded rotunda, stained-glass ceilings, and various rooms with their ornamental plaster ceilings. Imagine what the ground floor looked like before "ground meat" took over. This is one of the most stunning hidden gems of Calle Florida in terms of both beauty and historical value. On the Corrientes side of the building, you can read plaques that explain more about Ana Díaz and her often-overlooked importance to the founding of Buenos Aires.

Upon leaving Burger King, turn to the right and continue up Calle Florida. Don't stop until you're mid-block between Corrientes and Sarmiento. Then face the east side of the street to see the:

❺ Galería Mitre/Falabella
This is one of the most visually impressive and unusual buildings on Calle Florida. It was designed in a robust Spanish colonial style, imitating the Argentine missions along the Paraguayan border. The most unique feature is the ornamentation around the doorway and the frieze above it, with men in 16th-century Spanish clothing, both executed in a rustic manner. This crude but ornate ornamentation mimics art created by Indian slaves for their Spanish masters in that region of Argentina during the early colonial period in the late 1500s and early 1600s. The building had been closed for many years and is now home to Falabella, the Chilean department store, which opened in Buenos Aires in 2005.

Continue in the same direction on Calle Florida, crossing Sarmiento. Stop midblock before Perón, this time facing the west side of the street, so that you're looking at the:

❻ Banco Francés—Optician Store
At street level, you'll wonder why you've stopped here (no, I don't want you to use the check-cashing store). But look up and you'll see a beautiful 1920s-era building that was once an optician's headquarters. Notice the bronze eyeglasses adorning the windows and beautiful maidens surrounding them. Four-eyed nerds can only dream to have it so good.

Continue up Calle Florida in the same direction, stopping just as you hit Calle Perón, and look to the corner opposite, on the west side, to see:

❼ Gath & Chaves
You'll notice the BANCO MERIDIEN sign under a glass-and-wrought-iron doorway simulating old Parisian subway entrances. Look above and you will still see the old name of this one-time British department store on the corner tower—Gath & Chaves. Like Harrods, it shows the former influence of British culture on Argentina. Inside, only hints of its former beauty remain in the bank lobby.

Continue up Calle Florida to Perón, but don't cross it yet. Instead, face your left, or east, side for a glimpse of the:

❽ HSBC Building
This ornate Spanish Gothic building, one of my favorites, is faced with travertine marble and the corner entrance is covered with heavy bronze doors. It, however, is very often covered with graffiti.

Cross Perón and walk half a block on Calle Florida, stopping on the east side in front of Calle Florida 165, the:

❾ Galería Guemes
The Calle Florida entrance of this turn-of-the-20th-century shopping gallery is nothing special, and the most interesting thing is the sign for Piazzolla Tango, held in the basement theater. However, step through the threshold and you'll find one of the city's most exquisite buildings. It was designed by Francesco Gianotti, an Italian architect, who also designed the now-closed

Confitería del Molino. At night, the gallery is open to those seeing the tango show. However, you can still wander in, as the entranceway is not locked. No matter what time you go, don't miss the ornamental elevator bays with their bronze details while inside.

Continue south on Calle Florida and cross Calle Bartolomé Mitre. Stop immediately, facing the wedge-shaped building on your left, or east, side at Calle Florida 99. This is the:

❿ Bank of Boston

This is another ornate Spanish colonial building, even more impressive than the HSBC bank, full of beautiful details on its facade and within the interior. Much of the limestone and structural steel necessary to make this building came from the United States. The 4-ton bronze doors were made in England. Since the peso crisis, the building has often been a flashpoint for anti-American sentiments and, at times, is covered with "Yankee go home" graffiti. If the building is open, enter its spacious lobby, with slender columns supporting a gilded and coffered ceiling. The building is topped by an enormous and ornate cupola, part of the row of them on Diagonal Norte, marking each

intersection with the connecting streets. (This pattern begins at Plaza de Mayo and continues up Diagonal Norte, where it intersects with Av. 9 de Julio, forming the vista point for the Obelisco.)

When leaving the building, face the plaza and look at the:

⓫ Roque Sáenz Peña Monument

Inaugurated in 1936, this Art Deco monument commemorates Roque Sáenz Peña, president of Argentina from 1910 to 1914, who died while in office. It overlooks Diagonal Norte, which is also sometimes known as Avenida Roque Sáenz Peña. The construction of Diagonal Norte was part of a plan to rebuild Buenos Aires with vista points along the lines of Haussmann's redesign of Paris. Diagonal Norte was completed in the mid-1930s.

This statue marks the end of this walking tour. During the daytime you can head across the street to the Buenos Aires City Tourism kiosk, the modern metal structure with a winged cover, if you need any kind of information or help. Behind it, if you need travel assistance, you'll find the main customer service center for Aerolíneas Argentinas. If you just want to head home after the tour, the D line Catedral subway station is here, or you can walk a little toward Plaza de Mayo for more subway line access (lines A and E).

WALKING TOUR 2   **PLAZA SAN MARTIN & RETIRO**

GETTING THERE:	Take the metro to San Martín.
START:	The east side of Plaza San Martín, facing the Kavanagh Building.
FINISH:	Retiro Station.
TIME:	1½ hours if you're just walking; 3 to 4 hours if you go inside all buildings mentioned.
BEST TIMES:	Monday through Saturday between 11am and 4pm (not at night when things are closed).

At the turn-of-the-20th century, some of Buenos Aires's most fabulous mansions were built overlooking Plaza San Martín, and quite a few remain. The enormous plaza, with its overgrown trees and lazy atmosphere, might call to mind the squares of Savannah, Georgia. The Retiro area spreads down a gentle hill from the plaza and encompasses the train station complex built by the British, once the main entrance to this grand city. This tour has a moderate walking level, but steps and a hill overlooking San Martín, as well as an expanse of Retiro, can be a slight challenge.

Start in the plaza itself, looking toward the east at the:

❶ Kavanagh Building

At the time of its construction in 1936, this was the tallest building in South America, standing at about 120m (394 ft.) with over 30 stories, and designed as a residential structure. However, it took more than 16 years to sell the apartments in this Art Deco building. Since its construction, many buildings have risen higher throughout the city.

Turn to your right and walk a few meters up the park (you'll be making a circle around the plaza) until you see the:

❷ Marriott Plaza Hotel

The grande dame of Buenos Aires's hotels, the Marriott Plaza Hotel (p. 65), opened in 1908, is among the city's most traditional hotels. When it opened, it was considered so far from the main hotel district (along Av. de Mayo) that many assumed it would fail. History, of course, has proven that sentiment wrong, as numerous famous guests and royalty have stayed here. The facade of the hotel was renovated for its 100th anniversary.

> **TAKE A BREAK**
> If you have the time, check out Marriott's **Plaza Grill** (p. 93) to get an idea of the old-style dining once common throughout the city. This spot has been a center of elite dining and socializing in Buenos Aires for nearly a century. Stop in for lunch or dinner, depending on when you are exploring. This is a full-service restaurant, so expect the meal to take longer than if you were running in for just a snack. Or grab a brandy on the rocks at the adjacent Plaza Bar, where local businesspeople often have strategy meetings.

Continue to walk toward your right around the plaza, with Calle Florida to your left shoulder. Stop when you get to where Calle Santa Fe hits the park and look at the:

❸ Círculo Militar & Palacio Paz

Perhaps the most beautiful of the Beaux Arts mansions in Buenos Aires, the Círculo Militar looks plucked from the Loire Valley. It was the home of the Paz family and took almost 12 years to build; the patriarch who commissioned it died before it was finished. The family owned the *La Prensa* newspaper. The Palacio Paz is now home to the Círculo Militar, an elite organization for retired military officers, which bought the building in 1938 when the Depression made keeping such a home a burden. The Museo de las Armas, which sheds light on the Islas Malvinas/Falkland Islands conflict, is also in the building.

Continue walking around the plaza to your right. Stop at the:

❹ General José de San Martín Monument

This fantastic monument celebrates General José de San Martín, who battled against Spain in the wars of independence and is known as the founder of the Argentine nation. Though the statue was originally designed in 1862, it was expanded in 1900 into the over-the-top spectacle here. You'll see San Martín atop his horse in the middle on a raised platform, surrounded by soldiers and their women seeing them off before battle. The statue is a favorite hangout spot for the young, and it's where visiting dignitaries from other countries usually leave a ceremonial wreath. The best time to see this statue is in October and November, when the jacaranda trees are in full bloom. Unfortunately, many of the bronze plaques and wreaths were stolen when the price of copper skyrocketed in recent years. You can see some of their outlines in the granite base.

Turn around so that the statue of San Martín is to your back and cross the very wide Calle Maipú, being careful of traffic in this chaotic intersection. Walk up Calle Arenales, toward the grand marble building slightly to your right, which is known as the:

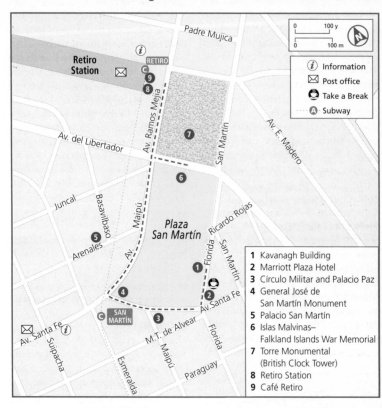

Information
Post office
Take a Break
Subway

Retiro Station

Padre Mujica

Av. del Libertador

Av. Ramos Mejía

San Martín

Av. E. Madero

Juncal

Basavilbaso

Maipú

Plaza San Martín

Ricardo Rojas

San Martín

Florida

Arenales

Av.

Av. Santa Fe

SAN MARTÍN

M.T. de Alvear

Florida

Av. Santa Fe

Suipacha

Maipú

Esmeralda

Paraguay

1 Kavanagh Building
2 Marriott Plaza Hotel
3 Círculo Militar and Palacio Paz
4 General José de San Martín Monument
5 Palacio San Martín
6 Islas Malvinas–Falkland Islands War Memorial
7 Torre Monumental (British Clock Tower)
8 Retiro Station
9 Café Retiro

CITY STROLLS

8

PLAZA SAN MARTIN & RETIRO

5 Palacio San Martín

Another of the grand mansions that line Plaza San Martín, this was the home of the powerful Anchorenas family whose prestige dated to colonial times in Argentina. In 1936, the Ministry of Foreign Affairs took over the building, again largely as a result of Depression-era costs of running such a large home. From the street, you'll mostly be able to see its enormous French gates, although these do have intricate grillwork, which you can look through and see the large circular courtyard. The building is open periodically for free tours.

Retrace your steps from here, and head back to the Plaza San Martín, in front of the San Martín monument. Once you reach the plaza, turn to your left and continue walking forward through the expanse of the plaza, following the balustrade, until you come across a large set of stairs cascading down a hill. This is one of the favorite city tanning spots in warm weather. Try not to gawk too much at the bathing-suit-clad locals—you have other things to do! At the bottom of the stairs, to your right side, you'll come across the:

6 Islas Malvinas/Falkland Islands War Memorial

This monument honors the 700-plus Argentines who died in the war over the Islas Malvinas/Falkland Islands chain in the brief war with Great Britain in early 1982. The war was treated as almost silly by most English-speaking countries that sided with Great Britain, including the United States. Argentina lost the war, but became a democracy once again in the process. The war and sovereignty over the islands still remain sore points among Argentines, and it is best to treat these topics delicately in discussions. The three branches of the military, the Army, Navy, and Air Force, take turns guarding the monument and its eternal flame, and the changing of the guard is worth seeing.

Turn your back to the Islas Malvinas/Falkland Islands War Memorial and head to the crosswalk across Avenida Libertador. Carefully cross this very wide street and head to the middle of the plaza, to the:

❼ Torre Monumental (British Clock Tower)

This 1916 gift from the British community in Buenos Aires, along with all other things British, was renamed in response to the Islas Malvinas/Falkland Islands War and is called the Argentine Big Ben by some. Decorated with British royal imperial symbols, the base was partly destroyed by an angry mob during an Islas Malvinas/Falkland Islands memorial service. Inside the tower, you'll find a small Buenos Aires City Tourism Information Office, as well as an elevator you can ride to the top for an excellent view of the city. The tower was placed here to celebrate the completion of the nearby Retiro Station that was built with British technology.

Walk out of the Torre Monumental and walk to your left in the direction of the:

❽ Retiro Station

The Retiro Station was opened in 1915 and built with British technological assistance. Four British architects designed it, and the steel structure was made in Liverpool, England, and shipped to Argentina to be assembled. For years, the station was the main entry point into Buenos Aires before the advent of the airplane. It's still very busy with trains to the suburbs and the resort area of Tigre. The mint-green circular ticketing area is particularly distinctive, among the many interesting details in this station. The central hallway is enormous, and while some of the interior ornamentation has disappeared, you'll still see some bronze lighting fixtures adorning the walls.

A few other train stations are in this complex—Bartolomé Mitre and Manuel Belgrano among them, as well as the modern Retiro Station Bus Depot.

Enter the station and its main hall. Turn to the left and continue to the end of the hall. Look for signs to the left for the:

❾ Café Retiro

This cafe opened in 1915 along with the station. For years it sat empty until recently being reopened in 2003. Its interior is historically listed and this is one of the *cafés notables* protected by law in the city of Buenos Aires. The ornamentation includes massive bronze chandeliers, stained glass, and columns with gilded capitals. The food here, a branch of the chain Café Café, is simple and Argentine, with coffee and pastries. Now is the time to take a break and celebrate completing this walk.

When you want to leave, the subway Retiro Station is just outside the door.

WALKING TOUR 3	PLAZA LAVALLE & THE TRIBUNALES AREA

GETTING THERE:	Take the metro to Tribunales.
START:	Teatro Cervantes, overlooking Plaza Lavalle.
FINISH:	Obelisco.
TIME:	1½ hours; 3 to 4 hours if you go inside all buildings mentioned.
BEST TIMES:	Monday through Saturday between 11am and 4pm (not at night when things are closed).

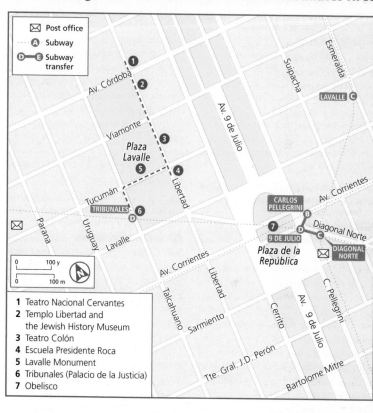

Key:
- ☒ Post office
- Ⓐ Subway
- Ⓓ—Ⓔ Subway transfer

1 Teatro Nacional Cervantes
2 Templo Libertad and the Jewish History Museum
3 Teatro Colón
4 Escuela Presidente Roca
5 Lavalle Monument
6 Tribunales (Palacio de la Justicia)
7 Obelisco

CITY STROLLS

8

PLAZA LAVALLE & THE TRIBUNALES AREA

Plaza Lavalle has been in disrepair for a long time, but the area is receiving a face-lift that should be completed for the 2010 Bicentennial celebrations. As such, some of the buildings in the area might be in scaffolding while you are visiting. The area represents the heart of the country's judicial system, taking its name from the Supreme Court, or Tribunales Building, which is the focus of the plaza. This was also one of the city's main theater districts before the widening of Avenida Corrientes in the 1930s. Teatro Cervantes and the world-famous Teatro Colón testify to this thespian grandeur. This tour is an easy walk and sidewalks are wheelchair-accessible.

Start at the northeast corner of Libertad, where it hits Córdoba, at the:

❶ Teatro Nacional Cervantes

This theater (p. 162), which opened in the 1920s, was the project of Spanish actors working in Buenos Aires. It went bankrupt, was bought by the government, and

has since become a national theater. It is designed in a Spanish Imperial style with the Habsburg double eagles as its main decoration on the outside of the building. The sumptuous interior uses materials from Spain, such as imported carved-wood ornamentation and colorful Seville tiles, on many of the walls and surfaces.

Standing on Córdoba with the Teatro Cervantes behind you, cross Córdoba and walk along Libertad, stopping one building in at Libertad 785, site of the:

❷ Templo Libertad & Jewish History Museum

This Byzantine-style temple was constructed in 1897 by CIRA (Congregación Israelita de la República de Argentina). Next-door, you'll find the Jewish Museum, also known as the Kibrick Museum, which contains religious and historical items related to Buenos Aires's Jewish community. For more information on the temple and museum, see p. 146.

Continue to walk south along Libertad and cross Calle Viamonte. Stop at Libertad 621, between Viamonte and Tucumán, to see the:

❸ Teatro Colón

The Teatro Colón first opened in 1908, and it took more than 18 years to build, largely because of the dramatic tragedies that befell its various architects, especially Víctor Meano, who was murdered in a love triangle. Materials for the theater came from all over Europe, and the building functioned as Buenos Aires's aria to the world, proving that it was a city of culture to be reckoned with. Unfortunately, in a modern tragedy worthy of its own stage production, the much-touted multimillion-dollar renovation of the theater, intended to show it off for its 100th anniversary, went completely wrong. As of this writing, the theater remains in scaffolding, nowhere near finished, and the money for it somehow has mysteriously been spent. While a new completion date is set for mid-2010, its current condition means that date is unrealistic. If and when the renovation is completed, tours and a show are a must while you are in Buenos Aires. But if you're on this walk and the building is open, don't delay going inside, where you'll be able to see marble from all over the world lining the lobby and making up the grand staircase; the wooden and bronze seating area, which soars five levels to an immense chandelier; as well as the underground storage and practice areas where ballerinas practice.

Continue walking along Libertador and cross Calle Tucumán, stopping at the building on the corner, at Calle Libertad 581, site of the:

❹ Escuela Presidente Roca

The employees of this beautiful 1904 Greek revival structure (p. 138) note that people often wander in thinking it's the Teatro Colón. And it's no wonder, with its Doric colonnade and ornamental statues along the central pediment, but this is actually a local school. Technically, it's not open to the public, but polite people will be allowed in the courtyard and maybe even upstairs to see the beautiful ceiling with painted acanthus leaves.

Turn around so that the Escuela Presidente Roca is to your back, and face Plaza Libertad. Head to the column in the center of the plaza, the:

❺ Lavalle Monument

Juan Lavalle fought along with San Martín in the wars for independence as a very young man and continued in the Argentine military, becoming a general. His statue, on a slender column, is the main focus of the center of this plaza. Wander around the plaza, though, and take a look at the various other monuments. Be aware that an underground parking garage was built under the plaza, so you have to watch out for cars, especially at the corner of Libertad and Tucumán, where the entry ramp is located. The plaza, like many in Buenos Aires, is often taken over by protestors who come to make their views known to the people in the next building on this tour. You will sometimes see their camps here.

From the center of the plaza, face west, toward the Supreme Court building, an enormous structure on the southwest corner of the plaza, also known as:

❻ Tribunales (Palacio de la Justicia)

The Tribunales neighborhood takes its name from this building: the Supreme Court, or Tribunales building (also called the Palacio de la Justicia). It is immense and hulking, with strong Greek elements. The facade was cleaned and restored in 2008, though the sides of the building somehow were overlooked in the process. If you are here during the day, try to enter. It used to be fully open to the public, but due to the peso crisis and numerous protests, police barricades often surround it; try to look like you have a reason to enter the building and you'll have a better chance of getting in. Inside, the central courtyard is lined with columns and pilasters. Ornamentation on the walls and between the columns includes symbols imitating the smiling sun from the center of the Argentine flag.

Turn your back to the Supreme Court building and walk along the edge of the plaza in an eastern direction. Look to your right at the edge of the plaza toward the pedestrianized section of Diagonal Norte, also known as Avenida Roque Sáenz Peña, with a vista to Avenida 9 de Julio and the:

❼ Obelisco

The Obelisco (p. 140) was inaugurated in 1936 and built to honor the 400th anniversary of the first (unsuccessful) founding of the city by Pedro de Mendoza. (The second, permanent, founding was in 1580.) This towering 68m (223 ft.) structure marks the intersection of Avenida 9 de Julio and Corrientes. Diagonal Norte stretches behind the Obelisco, which links to the Plaza de Mayo to its south and to the Tribunales, or Supreme Court, to its north. The Obelisco sits in the oval Plaza de República, all of which was once the site of Iglesia de San Nicolás where the Argentine flag was first displayed on August 23, 1812, in Buenos Aires shortly after independence from Spain. This church, of course, was demolished to create the city's most iconic symbol, but an inscription on the north side of the Obelisco honors its noble sacrifice.

This pedestrianized area of Diagonal Norte is lined with cafes and little restaurants, so take a break here if you like. Otherwise, walk up toward the Obelisco itself. If Argentina has won an international event, join the flag-waving crowds here and cheer on the country. Underneath the Obelisco, you have access to three subway lines (B, C, and D), so it is easy to get back to hotels in many parts of the city from here.

WALKING TOUR 4	AVENIDA DE MAYO TO CONGRESO

GETTING THERE:	Take the metro to Bolivar, Perú, Catedral, or Plaza de Mayo.
START:	Casa de Cultura, at Av. de Mayo 575.
FINISH:	Plaza Congreso.
TIME:	2 hours, 5 if buildings and museums are entered.
BEST TIMES:	Monday through Saturday between 11am and 4pm (not at night when things are closed).

Avenida de Mayo opened in 1894 and was meant to be the Gran Via or Champs-Elysées of Buenos Aires, full of lively cafes, theaters, and hotels. The design of the street was just one early part of an even grander plan to rebuild Buenos Aires in preparation for the 1910 Independence Centennial and to declare to the world that Buenos Aires was a city to be reckoned with. Some of the greatest concentrations of Beaux Arts and Art Nouveau buildings in the city are along this route, which connects Plaza de Mayo in the east to Congreso in the west. This is the historical processional route both for grand parades and for when people have something to protest to the president and to Congress. While many buildings along this route are badly in need of repair, others have recently been renovated as the tourism boom brought more attention to this area. It is not hard to imagine how glorious this street must have been in its heyday at the beginning of the 20th century.

This tour is an easy walk, but long distances (about 2.4km/1¹/₂ miles) are covered. Most sidewalks are wheelchair-accessible, but pavement is broken in places. Also, note that you'll be crossing the wide Avenida 9 de Julio, which can take two to three traffic light cycles for pedestrians to cross it; be extra-careful with children.

Start just in from the northeastern corner of Avenida de Mayo and San Martín, at Av. de Mayo 575, site of the:

❶ Casa de Cultura/La Prensa Building

Once the home of the newspaper *La Prensa,* owned by the very wealthy and powerful Paz family, this building is simply sumptuous, with carved granite, bronze ornamentation, and sinuous lanterns among its most striking features. Now home to the Casa de Cultura (the Office of Culture for the City of Buenos Aires; p. 126), it is open for tours on the weekend. The tour is a must-do if you have the time. If you don't, at least enter the building and take a peek at the lobby to get an idea of its splendor.

With the Casa de Cultura to your back, turn right and continue moving up Avenida de Mayo in a western direction. Cross Calle Perú and Calle Maipú and stop at Av. de Mayo 769, location of the:

❷ Palacio Vera

One of the best examples of Art Nouveau along Avenida de Mayo is right here, and the details along its balconies are the most interesting part of the Palacio Vera facade. Now made up of businesses and apartments, it was designed as the home for the Diaz Velez family, who gained prominence at the beginning of the 1800s, just before independence. If the El Ventanal bookstore is open, pop in for its unique collection of antique books and historical front pages for important Argentine events (p. 200).

Continue walking up Avenida de Mayo, cross Calle Esmeralda, and stop when you've reached Av. de Mayo 825, home of the:

❸ Café Tortoni

As the city's most famous cafe (p. 126), this establishment has been graced by numerous political, intellectual, and historic figures from Argentina and around the world. There are tango shows here every night, but the real treat is the ornate interior of the building itself. Above the cafe is the office of the National Tango Academy, which also offers lessons. I have

found recently that with the enormous surge of tourists to Buenos Aires, the door attendant will sometimes limit or refuse entry to foreigners who just want a peek inside the building. If you have a hard time getting in, come back at a less busy time, such as early morning or in the late evening, or better yet, come in for real, sit down, and enjoy a cup of coffee here.

TAKE A BREAK
As long as you're here, you might as well sample the atmosphere and have a bite to eat. Don't expect excellent service, as the waiters seem to ignore the customers. Still, the food is inexpensive, and a tea or coffee with croissants, known here as *medialunas,* makes an excellent snack for more energy along the way.

Continue walking up Avenida de Mayo to the world's widest boulevard:

❹ Avenida 9 de Julio

It will probably take you a few traffic-light cycles to cross this massive street. Construction on this avenida began in the 1930s, with its inauguration in 1937. Expansion, however, continued decades later, up through the 1960s. Unfortunately, during the process of making this boulevard, much of the city's beautiful turn-of-the-20th-century architectural heritage was lost. Spend some time on the avenida in this area, and be sure to see the fountains and the Don Quixote monument inaugurated by Queen Sofía of Spain. During 2006, much of this avenue was renovated with new flowers, plants, sidewalks, brighter lighting and street furniture, making for a nicer experience here than just a few years before that.

Cross Avenida 9 de Julio completely, and continue on to Av. de Mayo 1152, location of the:

❺ Castelar Hotel

One of the jewels of Avenida de Mayo, this hotel opened in 1928. One of its most

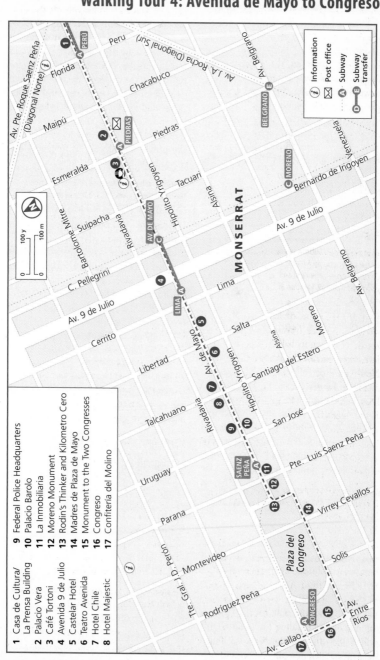

Legend:
- *i* Information
- ⊠ Post office
- Ⓐ Subway
- Ⓓ──Ⓔ Subway transfer

1 Casa de Cultura/
   La Prensa Building
2 Palacio Vera
3 Café Tortoni
4 Avenida 9 de Julio
5 Castelar Hotel
6 Teatro Avenida
7 Hotel Chile
8 Hotel Majestic
9 Federal Police Headquarters
10 Palacio Barolo
11 La Inmobiliaria
12 Moreno Monument
13 Rodin's Thinker and Kilometro Cero
14 Madres de Plaza de Mayo
15 Monument to the Two Congresses
16 Congreso
17 Confitería del Molino

notable features is its extensive Turkish bath on its basement level; it's worth stopping in to get a treatment or just to view the space. The Castelar (p. 70) has a strong association with Spanish literary giant Federico García Lorca, who lived here for many months. His room has been converted into a minimuseum. The eccentric Italian architect Mario Palanti, who also designed the nearby Palacio Barolo (p. 134), designed the Castelar.

Continue walking up Avenida de Mayo and cross Calle Salta to Av. de Mayo 1222, site of the:

❻ Teatro Avenida

This theater, opened in 1908, is largely dedicated to Spanish productions. It presented material by Lorca when he was living in the Castelar down the street in the 1930s. Many other artists from Spain also had work presented here at the time, and the theater was an integral part of making Buenos Aires the center of Spanish-language culture while Spain was engaged in civil war. After a fire in the 1970s, it was partly rebuilt.

Cross the Avenida de Mayo and head to the corner of Santiago del Estero, to the:

❼ Hotel Chile

This is a very unique Art Nouveau hotel with Middle Eastern elements. Take special note of the windows, with their round tops and faience ornamental tiling. The hotel was designed by the French architect Louis Dubois and opened in 1907. Like many other hotels on Avenida de Mayo, Hotel Chile was once luxurious and the utmost in style, but became a rather down-on-its-luck site where the facade is the only clue to its former glory.

Cross Santiago del Estero, staying on Avenida de Mayo, and stop immediately on the corner of the next block to see the:

❽ Hotel Majestic

Opened in 1910 in time for the Centennial celebrations, this is one of the city's most fabled hotels, though it no longer operates as such. Most Porteños point to it

with extreme pride as the place where Infanta Isabel stayed to represent Spain at the celebrations. It was also where the Russian ballet star Vaclav Nijinsky spent his wedding night after getting married in Buenos Aires in 1913. The lobby is sumptuous but extremely dark and badly in need of repair. As one of the most prominent buildings on Avenida de Mayo, it is currently undergoing an extensive renovation. Technically, it is no longer open to the public, but if you ask politely, they might let you peek at the lobby.

Continue walking up Avenida de Mayo and stop at the next building, no. 1333, home of the:

❾ Federal Police Headquarters

Ornate Art Deco buildings are a rarity in Buenos Aires, which did not take to the style in quite the same way as New York, Los Angeles, and Paris. The Federal Police Headquarters, however, is one of the best that you'll find in the city. Take note of the way the windows are treated, with their faceted frames, and the statues adorning the facade. The building was originally opened in 1926 for the *Crítica* newspaper, for which Argentine literary giant Jorge Luis Borges had worked. The building is not generally open to the public, unless you have been the victim of a crime or committed one, but try wandering in and see what happens.

Stay on this block but walk across the street to Av. de Mayo 1370 to reach the:

❿ Palacio Barolo

This, in my opinion, is the most unusual building (p. 134) in all of Buenos Aires. Designed by the eccentric Italian architect Mario Palanti, who also designed the nearby Hotel Castelar, this building is meant to recall Dante's *Inferno.* The lobby symbolizes Hell, with its bronze medallions representing fire and male and female dragons lining the walls. The scale of the building is massive; in fact, it was once the tallest building in South America, though Palanti later designed a similar, taller structure in Montevideo. Originally, a statue of

Dante was in the lobby, but it was stolen in the 1955 revolution deposing Juan Perón and never recovered. The facade was restored in 2007, and the plan is to eventually place a replica of the missing statue in the lobby. Guided tours take you through the building to the lighthouse tower representing God and Salvation, from where you'll get an excellent view up and down Avenida de Mayo and to other parts of the city (p. 50). The 16th floor holds a tango clothing store called Tango Moda (p. 211). With its stunning terrace overlooking the Avenida de Mayo and Plaza de Congreso, it is worth a visit, especially when the store holds its monthly rooftop tango sunset parties.

Continue walking up Avenida de Mayo and cross Calle San José. Stay on this block (btw. San José and Luis Sáenz Peña) and take in:

⓫ La Inmobiliaria

Taking up this entire block, La Inmobiliaria was designed as the office for a real estate and apartment agency. Today, it houses apartments and offices, but the tiled Art Nouveau sign indicating its former use still remains along the top of the facade. The building's most distinctive features are the matching corner towers, which form a kind of endpoint to Avenida de Mayo before it flows into Plaza Congreso.

Continue walking up Avenida de Mayo, crossing into Plaza Congreso, to see the:

⓬ Moreno Monument

This statue, in the first part of Plaza Congreso, quite overgrown by large trees, is of Mariano Moreno, the secretary of the First Government Assembly following independence from Spain. He was also an important journalist who founded both the Argentine National Library and the *Buenos Aires Gazette*. Moreno is memorialized elsewhere in the city, with a street name and subway stop.

Turn around and with Moreno behind you, walk forward to the central walk in the middle of the plaza. Then turn to the left and walk to the next statue:

⓭ Rodin's The Thinker & Kilometro Cero

This is a copy of Rodin's famous statue *The Thinker*, and it's a favorite play area for children. Just next to it is a block marking Kilometro Cero, the point at which all distances from Buenos Aires are marked.

Continue walking through the plaza, but veer toward your left. Cross Calle Yrigoyen and head to Yrigoyen 1584, near the corner of Ceballos, home base of the:

⓮ Madres de Plaza de Mayo

The Madres de Plaza de Mayo (p. 133), who march every Thursday at 3:30pm in the Plaza de Mayo in honor of their missing children, have their main headquarters here. They also run a university, library, bookstore, and a small cafe on the premises. It's worth taking the time to enter and linger here, and maybe have a coffee or a snack. You might also get a chance to talk with one of the by now very old Madres about this heart-wrenching period in Argentina's history, when nearly 30,000 young people were tortured and killed by the military government.

Cross the street and head back into Plaza Congreso, heading toward the enormous no-longer-working fountain in front of Congreso itself, to view the:

⓯ Monument to the Two Congresses

Quite a confection of marble and bronze, this enormous monument celebrates the two congresses that were held in the aftermath of independence from Spain to lay out the foundations for the new nation of Argentina. This multilevel structure has stairs that lead to a fantastic view of Congreso, where you can snap pictures of the building or pose with it behind you. The fountain underwent an extensive renovation in 2007.

Leave the Two Congresses monument and walk toward the Congreso building. Cross the street, being very careful at the crazy intersection, and head to the:

The most imposing building in all of Buenos Aires (p. 132), this structure opened in 1906. It combines influences from some of the world's most famous structures, from the U.S. Capitol to Berlin's Brandenburg Gate. Made of massive blocks of granite, the walls are over 1.8m (6 ft.) thick at their base. Tours will take you through both chambers of the bicameral legislature and are available by asking at the Rivadavia entrance. At night, the porthole windows in the bronze dome are impressively lit.

Walk to your right (north). Cross Calle Rivadavia and stop on the corner to view the:

⑰ **Confitería del Molino**

This fantastic structure (p. 162), in a terrible state of disrepair and closed to the public, was the creation of Francesco Gianotti, an Italian who also designed Galería Guemes and its theater housing the Piazzolla tango show. Once the informal meeting place of politicians from the nearby Congreso, the cafe closed in 1997, though there are plans to renovate and reopen it. Primarily an Art Nouveau structure, stained glass and ornate tile work were once part of the ornamentation here, but these have been covered by tarps to prevent rain damage and further deterioration of the facade. The main visible feature from the street is the windmill top (*molino* means "windmill" in Spanish).

Congratulations, you have finished this walking tour! I recommend you keep walking north along Avenida Callao, which was rebuilt in an almost imperial style after the opening of Congreso. Congreso has a subway stop for the A line, and the C and D lines have nearby stops along Callao.

WALKING TOUR 5	AVENIDA ALVEAR

GETTING THERE:	There are no real public transportation options, so a taxi is best.
START:	The Alvear Palace Hotel.
FINISH:	The Four Seasons Mansion.
TIME:	1 hour, provided you don't get caught up shopping.
BEST TIMES:	Monday through Saturday between 11am and 8pm (not at night when things are closed).

You may have to be wealthy to do your shopping on Avenida Alvear, but you don't need a penny to walk on it. In this tour, I'll touch on the architectural highlights of this exclusive area and only briefly on the shopping. I'll leave that up to you for later. Unlike most walks where the numbers go up, you'll be proceeding down in the numbering system as you follow this tour along Avenida Alvear. This tour is an easy walk and a short distance. However, not all the streets have cutouts for wheelchairs, and there are also some gently sloping hills.

Begin at Av. Alvear 1891, at the intersection of Ayacucho, site of the:

① **Alvear Palace Hotel**

This is the most famous hotel in Buenos Aires (p. 72), and certainly its most elegant. Opened in 1928 and built in a French neoclassical style, the lobby is a gilded marble confection, and the central dining area, known as L'Orangerie, resembles the Palm Court in New York's Plaza Hotel. I highly suggest taking the time for the hotel's brunch buffet. While expensive by Argentine standards ($41–$71/£29–£50 per person), it is a relative bargain compared to a similar setting in Europe or North America. Attached to the hotel is a shopping gallery full of exclusive art and bridal shops.

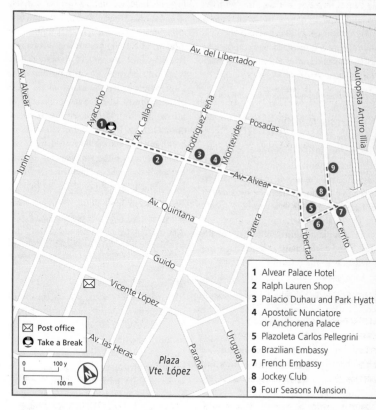

1 Alvear Palace Hotel
2 Ralph Lauren Shop
3 Palacio Duhau and Park Hyatt
4 Apostolic Nunciatore or Anchorena Palace
5 Plazoleta Carlos Pellegrini
6 Brazilian Embassy
7 French Embassy
8 Jockey Club
9 Four Seasons Mansion

⊠ Post office
● Take a Break

CITY STROLLS

8

AVENIDA ALVEAR

Walk out of the Alvear Palace Hotel and with the hotel to your back, cross Avenida Alvear, turn to your left, and then cross Calle Callao before heading to Av. Alvear 1750, home to the:

❷ Polo Ralph Lauren Shop

Shop here if you want, but I recommend taking a look at the building of this Polo Ralph Lauren store, one of the most exquisite of all the shops on this street. It was once a small Art Nouveau mansion. Within the interior, much of the ornate and heavy wood decoration remains, with a stained-glass skylight over the central staircase.

Continue walking down Avenida Alvear, staying on this side of the street. Cross Peña Street to Av. Alvear 1661, location of the:

❸ Palacio Duhau and Park Hyatt

The Palacio Duhau was the spectacular home of the Duhau family, built at the beginning of the 20th century. It is now part of the Park Hyatt Buenos Aires, which maintains an entrance through this building as well as in the new tower built behind on Calle Posadas. The family was involved in the Ministry of Agriculture, and many of the decorations of the building use such agricultural elements as wheat, corn, and cow heads. The Hyatt has worked well in restoring these elements, along with adding modern materials. Make sure to walk inside and take a look at the Piano Nobile or library room off the lobby, with its decorations mimicking Versailles, or the Oak Bar, with its paneling taken from a medieval French castle. The back garden leads to the new building and is a place for tea for the ladies-who-lunch crowd as well as business executives.

Continue walking down Avenida Alvear until you get to no. 1637, the:

❹ Apostolic Nunciatore, or Anchorena Palace

Though originally built for the wealthy Anchorena family, they never lived in this magnificent French-style mansion with its distinctive circular front. The next owner wanted to give the building to the Vatican, but the local representative felt it was too ostentatious and refused to live in it at the time. The Papal insignia, a papal tiara over a pair of keys, is on the building. It remains owned by the Catholic Church.

Continue walking for 2 more blocks until you reach a widening of the street and a small plaza with a statue and fountain, the:

❺ Plazoleta Carlos Pellegrini

I think this is one of the most beautiful of all the small plazas in Buenos Aires, not just for the plaza itself, but also for the buildings that surround it. A large, recently restored statue of Carlos Pellegrini, a famous intellectual and industrialist and a senator representing the province of Buenos Aires, sits in the center of this plaza. The statue was created in France by Félix Coutan and dedicated in 1914. A small fountain and a bench add to the relaxed environment. This plaza is the most Parisian-appearing part of Recoleta, and it gives an idea of all that was lost when Buenos Aires decided to widen Avenida 9 de Julio in the 1960s, destroying other little corners of the city that were similar to this one.

With Carlos Pellegrini to your back, turn to your right and cross the street, heading to Calle Arroyo 1130, site of the:

❻ Brazilian Embassy

First, a note about the name of this street. *Arroyo* means "stream" in Spanish, and one once flowed through this area until it was filled in as the city began to develop. The Brazilian Embassy, one of the city's most beautiful embassies, is one of the two most impressive structures overlooking this plaza. Known as the Palacio Pereda, in honor of its original owner Doctor Celedonio Pereda, it took almost 20 years to build and has details borrowed from the Palais Fontainebleau in France. It was originally designed by the French architect Louis Martin and finished by the Belgian architect Julio Dormal.

With the Brazilian Embassy behind you, turn to your right, cross Calle Cerrito, and stop once you reach the other side. Be aware that this odd intersection has a confusing traffic pattern, so be careful when crossing to see the:

❼ French Embassy

It's hard to believe when you see this beautiful structure, but the plans for the expansion of Avenida 9 de Julio originally included the demolition of this building. Fortunately, the French government refused to give up the building, and it now serves as the vista point for the northern terminus of Avenida 9 de Julio. Created by the French architect Pablo Pater, it became the French Embassy in 1939. The building is a beautiful example of Beaux Arts, and you should be sure to notice the main dome and the grillwork on the surrounding fence. You'll notice *trompe l'oeil* mansard roofs and windows on some of the surfaces of the surrounding modern buildings, an attempt to give an impression of the once surrounding Belle Epoque buildings that were demolished to make way for the expansion of Avenida 9 de Julio.

With the Obelisco on Avenida 9 de Julio to your back, cross Arroyo and Cerritos, stopping at the corner, where you'll find the:

❽ Jockey Club

Carlos Pellegrini, whose statue sits across the street in the plaza out front, started the Jockey Club in 1882 along with other like-minded equestrians. The Jockey Club became a major part of the social networking scene for the wealthy and powerful of Argentina. The Jockey Club's original Calle Florida headquarters were burned to the ground on April 15, 1953, after a Perón-provoked riot against this elite institution. Perón seized the assets of the organization, but it was able to regroup in 1958 a few years after he had been thrown out of power. This current building was once the mansion of the Uzué de Casares family, and the organization moved here in 1966. It is not open to the public, but its interior is full of tapestries, works of art, and a library.

Walk back across Cerritos, walking only for a few feet toward the immense tower a block down, but stop when you get to Calle Cerrito 1455, site of the:

❾ Four Seasons Mansion

The official name of this Louis XIII–style redbrick palace with heavy quoins is Mansión Alzaga Unzue. It was built in 1919 and was given three facades, anticipating the eventual construction of Avenida 9 de Julio to the east of the building. It was designed with an extensive garden complex in front of its northern facade. The mansion is now part of the Four Seasons Hotel, and it is attached to the main tower through a garden courtyard. The tower sits on what were once the mansion's gardens. Some Porteños can still recall the tragic day when the trees here were cut down to make way for the building's foundation. The tower and the mansion were formerly the Park Hyatt until the Four Seasons purchased the property. (A new Park Hyatt has reopened close by.) Renting the entire mansion is the ultimate in luxury, and it's often here where stars party in Buenos Aires. When Madonna filmed the movie *Evita,* she used the mansion's balcony to practice her "Don't Cry for Me, Argentina" scenes as mobs gathered on the street out front trying to catch a glimpse.

Congratulations, you've finished another tour. There are no nearby metro stations, but there are plenty of cabs in the area that can get you wherever you want to go next.

Shopping

Throughout South America, Buenos Aires is famous for its shopping. You'll find it in glitzy malls, along major shopping thoroughfares, and in small boutiques and little out-of-the-way stores. Buenos Aires is most famous for its high-quality leather goods, which, since Argentina is a beef-loving country, should come as no surprise. You won't find as many native crafts here, however, as you will in other South American capitals.

Argentina's peso crisis spawned an interesting trend: With Argentina's inability to import many fashion products, the crisis allowed the creativity of local designers producing for the domestic market to flourish and expand. In particular, you'll find a wealth of young designers catering to the young-women's market, making unique, feminine, and funky fashions found nowhere else in the world. While not the bargain they once were, most items are still reasonably priced, compared to European and North American stores. Antiques, especially in San Telmo, are also a famous part of Buenos Aires's shopping.

Many Buenos Aires stores, particularly those catering to tourists, also allow for tax-free shopping. You'll know them by the blue-and-white logo on the door; ask if you don't see one. Leather-goods stores are exceptionally well versed in the process, and it is often part of the spiel when you enter them. For more details on this process, see the "Just the Facts: Hours, Shipping & Taxes" box below.

Look for the **Mapas de Buenos Aires** shopping map series (www.mapasbsas. com) as well as the **GO Palermo** (www. gopalermo.com.ar) shopping booklet at your hotel and tourism kiosks. The **Florida Street Shopping Association** also puts out a shopping booklet. (www.calle floridastreet.com). **DeDios** has an excellent laminated shopping map, available at Buenos Aires bookstores and online at www.dediosonline.com and www.amazon. com. To help you make sense of it all, tour guides specialize in shopping tours, like Argentine native **Julieta Caracoche** who runs **Al Tuntunno Tours** (© 11/15-4197-238 [cell]; www.altuntunno.com) or the Australian expat **Kirsty Noble** of **Buenos Aires Boutique Tours** (© 11/15-3565-1713 [cell]; www.baboutiquetours.com.ar; (p. 166). Look also for fashion articles in the English-language publications **Buenos Aires Herald** (www.buenosairesherald. com), or **The Argentimes** (www.the argentimes.com), especially anything by Carla Peluffo, a young, beautiful Argentine-American with a keen sense of style.

1 THE SHOPPING SCENE

MAJOR SHOPPING AREAS

Buenos Aires has many shopping areas, but the following places are where you'll find most of the action.

MICROCENTRO Calle Florida, the Microcentro's pedestrian walking street, is home to wall-to-wall shops from Plaza San Martín to all the way past Avenida Corrientes. As you approach Plaza San Martín from Calle Florida, you'll find a number of well-regarded shoe stores, jewelers, and shops selling leather goods. Most of the stores here are decidedly middle class, and some clearly cater to locals and carry things you'd never buy. However, if you're looking for such basic items as electrical converters, extension cords, and other things to help you use electrical goods here, this is where you'll find what you need. Calle Lavalle is also pedestrianized, but most of the stores are of little interest to the tourist. The **Galerías Pacífico** mall is located at Calle Florida 750, at Avenida Córdoba (② **11/4319-5100**), and features a magnificent dome and stunning frescoes (p. 194). Day and night, you'll find street entertainers and tango dancers working the crowds all along Calle Florida. While you'll probably only shop on Calle Florida, other streets do have stores and restaurants, and this neighborhood also has the highest concentration of small travel agencies if you need to change an itinerary or want to add side trips.

AVENIDA CÓRDOBA   Looking for off-season bargains? Then the 3000 block of Córdoba, in the area bordering Barrio Norte and Palermo, is the place to head. Best of all, off-season in Argentina is usually the right season in the Northern Hemisphere, so you won't have to let your purchases sit around for a few months—you can wear them right when you get back home.

AVENIDA SANTA FE   Popular with local shoppers, Avenida Santa Fe has a wide selection of clothing stores with down-to-earth prices typical of stores catering to the local middle class. You will also find bookstores, cafes, ice-cream shops, and cinemas here. The **Alto Palermo Shopping Center,** Av. Santa Fe 3253, at Güemes (② **11/5777-8000**), is another excellent shopping center, with 155 stores open daily from 10am to 10pm.

PALERMO VIEJO   Everything old is new again in Palermo Viejo, divided into Palermo Hollywood and Palermo Soho. Lots of young designers have opened boutiques in this area, or they combine forces on weekends around Plaza Serrano, when restaurants fold up tables and fill with clothes racks. Shopping as a rule is best for women, but men's fashion is definitely catching up.

RECOLETA   Avenida Alvear is an elegant, Parisian-like strip of European boutiques and cafes. Start your walk from Plaza Francia across from Recoleta Cemetery and continue past the Alvear Palace Hotel, along to the French Embassy at Cerrito or Nueve de Julio for one exclusive shop after another, many in French-style mansions. Avenida Quintana provides a similar atmosphere. Nearby **Patio Bullrich,** Av. del Libertador 750 (② **11/4814-7400**), is one of the city's most famous malls. Its 69 shops are open daily from 10am to 9pm. Considered upscale, it has offerings similar to other malls in the city. It has an excellent food court, however, and is a good place to stop for a snack.

SAN TELMO & LA BOCA   These neighborhoods have excellent antiques as well as artists' studios and arts and crafts that celebrate tango. Street performers and artists are omnipresent, especially on weekends. La Boca should be avoided at night, however.

2 OUTDOOR MARKETS

One of the pleasures of Buenos Aires is its open-air markets (called *mercados)* or fairs *(ferias),* many of which combine shopping with entertainment. The bargains you'll find are often accompanied by the wonderful, romantic sounds and sights of tango dancers putting on a show. I've listed below just a few of the many open-air markets you can find all over the city.

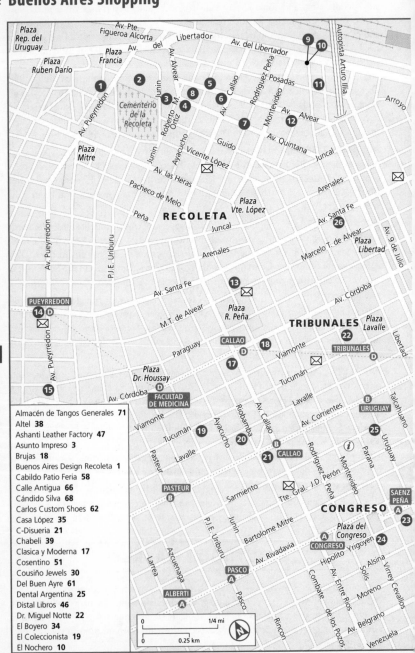

Plaza Rep. del Uruguay

Plaza Ruben Darío

Av. Pte. Figueroa Alcorta

Plaza Francia

Av. del Libertador

Libertador

Av. del Libertador

Autopista Arturo Illia

Arroyo

Cementerio de la Recoleta

Av. Pueyrredon

Roberto M. Ortiz

Av. Alvear

Junín

Callao

Av. Callao

Rodríguez Peña

Posadas

Montevideo

Av. Alvear

Plaza Mitre

Ayacucho

Vicente López

Guido

Av. Quintana

Juncal

Av. las Heras

Pacheco de Melo

Peña

Plaza Vte. López

RECOLETA

Arenales

Junín

P.J.E. Uriburu

Juncal

Arenales

Av. Santa Fe

Marcelo T. de Alvear

Plaza Libertad

Av. 9 de Julio

Av. Santa Fe

M.T. de Alvear

Plaza R. Peña

Av. Córdoba

TRIBUNALES

Plaza Lavalle

PUEYRREDON

Av. Pueyrredon

Paraguay

CALLAO

Viamonte

TRIBUNALES

Libertad

Plaza Dr. Houssay

Av. Córdoba

FACULTAD DE MEDICINA

Tucumán

Lavalle

Av. Corrientes

URUGUAY

Talcahuano

Viamonte

Tucumán

Lavalle

Riobamba

Av. Callao

Rodríguez Peña

Montevideo

Paraná

Uruguay

Pasteur

Ayacucho

CALLAO

Parana

PASTEUR

Sarmiento

Tte. Gral. J.D. Perón

SAENZ PEÑA

CONGRESO

P.J.E. Uriburu

Junín

Bartolome Mitre

Plaza del Congreso

Larrea

Azcuenaga

Av. Rivadavia

CONGRESO

Hipolito Yrigoyen

Alsina

Solís

Virrey Cevallos

PASCO

ALBERTI

0   1/4 mi
0   0.25 km

Combate de los Pozos

Av. Entre Rios

Moreno

Av. Belgrano

Rincón

Venezuela

Almacén de Tangos Generales **71**
Altel **38**
Ashanti Leather Factory **47**
Asunto Impreso **3**
Brujas **18**
Buenos Aires Design Recoleta **1**
Cabildo Patio Feria **58**
Calle Antigua **66**
Cándido Silva **68**
Carlos Custom Shoes **62**
Casa López **35**
C-Disueria **21**
Chabeli **39**
Clasica y Moderna **17**
Cosentino **51**
Cousiño Jewels **30**
Del Buen Ayre **61**
Dental Argentina **25**
Distal Libros **46**
Dr. Miguel Notte **22**
El Boyero **34**
El Coleccionista **19**
El Nochero **10**

Legend / Key:

- ℹ️ Information
- ✉️ Post office
- Ⓐ Subway
- Ⓓ—Ⓔ Subway transfer

Listings:

Ermenegildo Zegna **4**
Escada **12**
Falabella Department Store **52**
Farmacia Suiza **44**
Flabella (Tango Shoes) **50**
Galería El Solar de French **67**
Galería Güemes **53**
Galería Promenade Alvear **5**
Galería Ruth Benzacar **32**
Galerías Pacífico **40**
Gloria Lópes Sauqué **11**
Grand Cru **7**
H.Stern **29, 31**
Jorge Gudiño Antigüedades **68**
Julio Chaile Arte **37**
L'ago **65**
La Cava de la Brigada **70**
Lana's Argentina **36**
Librería de Las Madres—Café Literario Osvaldo Bayer **24**
Librería El Ventanal **57**
Librería Santa Fe **14**
Librerías Turisticas **15**
Libros Cuspide **45**
Louis Vuitton **8**
Lulu of London **13**
MoviCom—BellSouth **41**
Nora Iniesta **60**
Pallarols **69**
Paseo Obelisco **49**
Patio Bullrich **9**
Polo Ralph Lauren **6**
Porto Fem Talles Grandes **26**
Prüne **33**
Raffaello by Cesar Franco **55**
Recoleta Fair (Feria de Plaza Francia) **2**
Rossi & Caruso **16, 43**
San Telmo Market **64**
Saracco **28**
Tango Mina **20**
Tango Moda **23**
Tonel Privado **9, 42**
Vinos Argentinos **48**
Voyager (Luggage) **54**
Walrus Books **63**
Winery **27, 56**
Wussman Gallery **59**

Tips Just the Facts: Hours, Shipping & Taxes

Most stores are open on weekdays from 9am to 8pm and Saturday from 9am until midnight, with some closing for a few hours in the afternoon. You might find some shops open on Sunday along Avenida Santa Fe, but few will be open on Calle Florida. Shopping centers are open daily from 10am to 10pm. Certain art and antiques dealers will crate and ship bulky objects for an additional fee; others will tell you it's no problem to take that new sculpture directly on the plane. If you don't want to take any chances, contact UPS at ℂ **800/222-2877** or Federal Express at ℂ **810/333-3339.** Various stores participate in a tax-refund program for purchases costing more than 70 pesos. Ask for a special receipt, which can entitle you to a refund of the hefty 21% tax (IVA) when you leave the country. Most of these stores have blue-and-white TAX FREE signs, but always ask when making a purchase. The process works by getting a special Global Refund check form that indicates the value of what you will get back when you leave the country. You must have this special form, which participating stores will create for purchases costing more than 70 pesos, to get a refund. Some restrictions do apply, however. The item has to have been made in Argentina and purchased with the intention of taking it out of the country (things such as food do not qualify). The system is used mostly for clothing and leather goods, but you should ask about it whenever making a purchase, even if you do not see the sign. Upon leaving the country, have all of these checks ready and look for the Global Refund desk. At Ezeiza airport, it is located in the immigrations area just before you have your passport stamped to leave the country. For more information, check out the website www.globalrefund.com, and choose Argentina under the selection of countries.

The **San Telmo Antiques Fair** ★★, which takes place every Sunday from 10am to 5pm at Plaza Dorrego, is a vibrant, colorful experience that will delight even the most jaded traveler. As street vendors sell their heirlooms, singers and dancers move amid the crowd to tango music. Among the 270-plus vendor stands, you will find antique silversmith objects, porcelain, crystal, and other antiques. It's especially famous for tango performances that can go on into the late evening, even if most of the vendors themselves close up at 5pm. The star of the show is a dark, handsome dancer known as "El Indio," and you'll see his photos on sale throughout the city at other markets. I highly recommend this fair as a not-to-be-missed sight while in Buenos Aires. Schedule a Sunday in San Telmo when planning your Buenos Aires trip. More information is at www.feriadesantelmo.com.

Head to **Cabildo Patio Feria** when sightseeing in the Plaza de Mayo area. This fair is held on Thursday and Friday from 11am to 6pm in the small garden patio behind the Cabildo, or old city hall. You'll find lots of locally made crafts here, especially pottery, stained glass, and jewelry.

From Friday to Sunday from 11am to 6pm, the Madres (p. 134) hold the **Feria de Madres de Plaza de Mayo** fair in front of their headquarters overlooking Plaza Congreso. Children will also like coming here, as it is next to the park's merry-go-round and other rides. The fair has antiques, crafts, food, and a few interesting book vendors. Sometimes there is also live music. This is among the most casual and least touristy of all of the fairs, so it provides a chance to chat with locals while supporting a good cause.

The **La Boca Fair** is open every day from 10am to 6pm or sundown on the Caminito, the pedestrianized and art-filled thoroughfare in the heart of this neighborhood. It's the most touristy of all the fairs, and most of the items are terribly overpriced. Still, if you need tacky souvenirs in a hurry, you'll quickly get it all done here. Besides, tango singers and other street performers will keep your mind off the inflated prices. Safety has improved somewhat in La Boca, but tourists should still leave the area at night when the police leave and the shops have closed. **Plaza Serrano Fair** ★★ is at the small plaza at the intersection of Calle Serrano and Honduras, which forms the heart of Palermo Hollywood. Bohemian arts and crafts are sold here while dreadlocked locals sing and play guitars. Officially, the fair is held Saturday and Sunday from 10am to 6pm, but impromptu vendors will also set up at night when the restaurants are crowded. Those very same restaurants will fold up their tables in the afternoon and fill the spaces with clothing racks for young designers who cannot afford their own boutiques. It's definitely worth a shopping visit. Plaza Serrano is also sometimes called by its official name, **Plazaleto Jorge Cortazar.**

Recoleta Fair (aka **Feria de Plaza Francia**) ★★, which takes place Saturday and Sunday in front of Recoleta Cemetery from 10am until sunset, offers every imaginable souvenir and type of craft, in addition to food. This has become one of the city's largest fairs, completely taking over all the walkways and then some in the area, and even the Iglesia Pilar, Recoleta Cemetery's church, gets involved by setting up tables of postcards and religious souvenirs in its courtyard. Live bands sometimes play on whatever part of the hill is left vacant by vendors. Officially, the fair is only on weekends, but you will find vendors selling here every day (though they are technically violating the city's vending licenses by doing so). If the police get bored and feel like enforcing the law, you'll sometimes see arguments between them and the vendors. But don't worry; it's just one more part of the entertainment at the fair.

3 MAJOR SHOPPING MALLS & DEPARTMENT STORES

Indoors or out, Buenos Aires has a wealth of shopping areas. Here are some of the best indoor shopping centers in the city. Some, such as Galerías Pacífico, are tourist sites in their own right because of the beauty of their architecture. Even if shopping or shopping malls are not your bag, Galerías Pacífico is not to be missed. The Abasto Shopping Center is a great place to bring the kids, with its special Museo de los Niños in the food court. Until recently, something that made the shopping experience here very different from North America and Europe was a lack of department stores. However, Falabella, the Chilean chain, opened up in 2006 in Buenos Aires with a large store on Calle Florida. Still, most shopping centers are a collection of smaller stores and chains, some uniquely Argentine, others South American—and some that you won't find anywhere else in the world. Most shopping malls are open daily from 10am to 10pm, with exceptions noted below.

Abasto Shopping Center ★★ (Kids) The Abasto Shopping Center is one of the largest in all of Buenos Aires. It was built over a market where the famous tango crooner Carlos Gardel got his start, singing as a child to the fruit and meat vendors who had stalls there. They would give him a few centavos to entertain them, and from this humble beginning, his fame spread. Only a classical stone arch outside of the main shopping center is left from the earlier structure. Now, you'll find an Art Deco–style building with several levels of shopping, mostly aimed at the middle and upper-middle class. This mall is a great place to bring kids, with its extensive food court, enormous arcades with video games, and especially the very fun **Museo de Los Niños,** located in the food court (p. 145). In what used to be one of Buenos Aires's main Jewish neighborhoods, you'll also find the only kosher McDonald's in the world outside of Israel (p. 118). There is also a large cinema complex here. The food court and cinemas here are open later than 10pm. Av. Corrientes 3247 (at Agüero). ✆ 11/4959-3400. www.altopalermo.com.ar (click on "Abasto"). Metro: Gardel.

Alto Palermo   Located on Santa Fe in the Barrio Norte shopping area, Alto Palermo has several floors of shopping, with about 155 stores and services. This mall is significantly less touristy than the Galerías Pacífico. The mall's design is not very straightforward and the connections between levels can be confusing. If shopping with children, this is one in which they can easily become lost. Av. Santa Fe and Coronel Díaz. ✆ 11/5777-8000. www.altopalermo.com.ar. Metro: Agüero.

Buenos Aires Design Recoleta ★★   This is one of my favorite malls in Buenos Aires, and home-design connoisseurs should head here immediately. This small, elegant mall, set behind the Recoleta Cemetery, houses several home-design stores selling high-quality, high-design items, almost all produced in Argentina. Ironically, the peso crisis has created good opportunities for local designers to work, as importing goods from overseas is too expensive. The mall is both indoors and outdoors, with the outdoor section called "La Terrazza," though some people call it "Los Arcos" because of the archways lining this area. It's a pleasant place to relax and have a coffee after seeing the nearby cemetery. There are often changing sculpture exhibits in the gardens. Hours are Monday through Saturday from 10am to 9pm, Sunday and holidays from noon to 9pm. Av. Pueyrredón 2501 (at Libertador). ✆ 11/5777-6000. No metro access.

Falabella   This Chilean department store chain opened its most visible Buenos Aires location in 2006 at Calle Florida 202 at the intersection of Peron. A block up, it has a smaller branch on Calle Florida 343 in the former Galería Mitre, concentrating on housewares. Between both stores, you'll find everything you would find in any department store—cosmetics, jewelry, clothing for men, women and children, housewares, luxury goods, furniture, and even kiosks for buying cellular phones. It's open Monday to Saturday 9am to 9pm, and Sundays noon to 9pm. Calle Florida 202 (at Perón). ✆ 11/5950-5000. www.falabella.com. Metro: Florida.

Galerías Pacífico ★★★   Located on Calle Florida, the pedestrian walking street in the Microcentro, the Galerías Pacífico is probably the most famous mall in Buenos Aires. Architecturally, it is stunning, designed to recall the Galleria Vittorio Emanuele II in Milan, with its long halls, glass cupola, and several tiers of shops. First opened in 1891, in 1945 its main dome was covered with stunning frescoes painted by local artists. There are more than 180 shops here, and they offer a free service whereby all your purchases can be sent to your hotel, so you can shop without the schlep. But Galerías Pacífico is more than shopping: The building also houses the Centro Cultural Borges, where you can see shows, check out art displays, take tango lessons, and see performances by Julio Bocca's Ballet Argentino. Calle Florida 750 (at Av. Córdoba). ✆ 11/5555-5110. Metro: San Martín.

Jumbo Palermo Commercial Center   This mall is near the polo grounds, but is of interest mostly if you plan on staying long-term in Buenos Aires and renting an apartment.

Most of the stores are home-related, with a few clothing stores in the mix. The highlight
of the mall is **Easy,** an Ikea-like store full of inexpensive furniture, construction material, and other things for settling in. Av. Bullrich and Cerviño. © **11/4778-8000.** Metro: Palermo.

Patio Bullrich (Overrated)   This mall is considered one of the most exclusive in Buenos Aires, but most shoppers will find the stores to be middle of the road, catering to the middle and upper-middle classes rather than the truly wealthy. If looking for really exclusive shopping, you'd do better checking out the boutiques on nearby Alvear. There is, however, an excellent food court here, full of the ladies-who-lunch crowd and local businesspeople talking deals. The mall is located in a historic building, and it's worthwhile to take a look at the facade. Hours are Monday through Saturday from 10am to 9pm, Sunday and holidays noon to 9pm. Posadas 1245 (at Libertad, with the historic facade facing Libertador). © **11/4814-7400.** No metro access.

4 OTHER SHOPPING HIGHLIGHTS & CENTERS

You'll find all kinds of interesting indoor shopping areas in Buenos Aires. Check out the ones below for their architecture, interesting atmosphere from decades past, or their extreme exclusivity. Hours will vary for each of these as each store within these centers sets its own hours, but most will be open weekdays from 10am to 5pm.

Galería Güemes ★★ (Finds)   This is a sumptuous building, though its modern entrance on Calle Florida would make you think otherwise. Its back entrance on San Martín, however, still retains all of its original glory from its opening in 1915. This is a shopping gallery with a mix of stores without distinction and several kiosks that obscure the views, but look around at the walls and decorations. The architecture is a mix of Art Nouveau, Gothic, and neoclassical—all heavily ornamented—and was the creation of the architect who designed the now-closed Café del Molino next-door to Congreso. Make sure to look also at the ornate elevator banks that lead to the offices above. The building also houses the Piazzolla tango show (p. 226). The Art Nouveau theater in which it sits was closed for nearly 40 years and was only recently restored. Of all of the tango show palaces in Buenos Aires, this is the most beautiful. Calle Florida 165 (at Perón). Metro: Florida.

Galería Promenade Alvear   Naturally, any place attached to the Alvear Palace Hotel is going to be exclusive. You'll find wedding shops, jewelry stores, antiques, and art boutiques, as well as a few clothing stores. Store hours here vary tremendously, with some shops only open on weekdays and some closing during lunch hours. Others are by appointment only. Each store has a phone number on its window, so if things are closed, write it down and call, or ask the Alvear's concierge for more information. The back of L'Orangerie, the Alvear's lobby restaurant, opens into the central courtyard of the shopping area, making for a pleasant place to grab a coffee. Av. Alvear 1883 (at Ayacucho; attached to the Alvear Hotel). No metro access.

San Telmo Market ★★ (Moments)   Though this is definitely a place to shop, the building is also worth seeing on its own. The San Telmo market opened in 1897 and is a masterpiece not just for its soaring wrought-iron interior, but also for the atmosphere reminiscent of decades before. Half of the market is geared toward locals, with butchers, fresh-fruit-and-vegetable grocers, and little kiosks selling sundries and household items.

This part looks like the kind of place your grandmother probably shopped in when she was a child. I recommend chatting with the staff at these places—they seem to have all the time in the world. The other half is more touristy (but never overly so), with seemingly random antiques (old matchboxes, for example) and vintage-clothing shops. The market is almost a block in size, but squeezed between several other historic buildings, and there are several entrances. It's open daily from 10am to 8pm, but each stand has individual hours. 961 Defensa or Bolívar 998, both at Carlos Calvo. Metro: Independencia.

5 SHOPPING A TO Z

ANTIQUES

Take to the streets of San Telmo, where you'll find the city's best antiques shops. Don't miss the antiques market that takes place all day Sunday at Plaza Dorrego (see "Outdoor Markets," above). There are also a number of fine antiques stores along Avenida Alvear and Suipacha in Recoleta, including a collection of boutique shops at **Galería Alvear,** Av. Alvear 1777. Note that many of the stores listed in the art section in this chapter also sell antiques among their collections. Antiques and art stores along Calle Arroyo and its surroundings in Recoleta near the Israeli Embassy Monument participate in **Gallery Night.** This event is held on the last Friday of every month (though not always in Jan–Feb), and antiques and art stores stay open late and frequently have tea and coffee for patrons. The streets are closed to traffic, creating a comfortable environment for walking and exploring. There is also usually a full moon around this time, so if you're here as a couple, it can be a romantic shopping experience. Keep in mind that most of the museums in Buenos Aires have high-quality art and replica shops, so you might find interesting art and gifts there as well.

Calle Antigua ★★ This store sells religious art, chandeliers, furniture, and other decorative objects. The owner, José Manuel Piñeyro, opened his shop more than 20 years ago. He now has two storefronts, both on the same block of Calle Defensa. The stores accept cash and foreign checks, but no credit cards. Both stores are open daily from 10am to 7pm. Calle Defensa 914 and Calle Defensa 974 (at Estados Unidos). © **11/4300-8782** or 11/15-4472-4158 (cell). Metro: Independencia.

Del Buen Ayre Because this antiques store concentrates on small decorative objects, you're more likely to find an item that can be carried on the plane or packed into your luggage. Most items are turn-of-the-20th-century knickknacks, bronzes, and glass pieces. Cash is preferred here, though checks are accepted. It's open daily from 11:30am to 8pm.

> ⓘ **Tips** **Shopping Tip**
>
> Most antiques stores will come down 10% to 20% from the listed price if you bargain. It is almost impossible to pay for antiques with a credit card in Buenos Aires; virtually no store will accept them, largely because of Customs and tax issues. However, international checks, once verified, are usually accepted by almost all San Telmo stores. Cold cash, of course, is never an issue, whether pesos, dollars, or euros (though British pounds are not generally accepted).

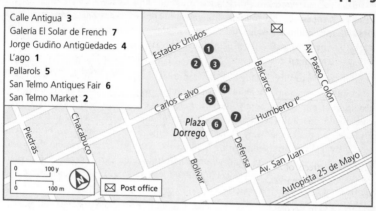

Bolívar 929 (at Estados Unidos). ✆ **11/4361-4534**, 11/4921-8280, or 11/15-4179-7419 (cell). Metro: Independencia.

Galería El Solar de French Built in the early 20th century in a Spanish colonial style, this is where Argentine patriot Domingo French lived. Today, it's a gallery, with antiques shops and photography stores depicting the San Telmo of yesteryear. Most of the shops here are open Monday to Friday from 10am to 7pm. Calle Defensa 1066 (at Humberto I). Metro: Independencia.

Jorge Gudiño Antigüedades Jorge Gudiño, who has more than 20 years of experience selling antiques, opened this store in 1991. The store has beautiful pieces of antique high-end furniture, which are displayed in interesting ways. This makes the store more visually appealing than many others on the street, and it provides ideas for your own use at home. Only cash and overseas checks are accepted. The store is open Sunday through Friday from 10:30am to 7pm. Calle Defensa 1002 (at Carlos Calvo). ✆ **11/4362-0156**. Metro: Independencia.

Pallarols ★ Located in San Telmo, Pallarols sells an exquisite collection of Argentine silver and other antiques. The Pallarols family represents six generations of silversmithing. Their work is featured in various museums in Buenos Aires, and family members will sometimes conduct silversmith workshops at museum stores. The shop is open Monday to Friday from 10am to 7pm, Saturday 10am to noon. Calle Defensa 1015 (at Carlos Calvo). ✆ **11/4362-5438**. www.pallarols.com.ar. Metro: Independencia.

ART STORES & GALLERIES
Atelier Estudio Casa de la Villa This gallery sells very high-end art depicting country life, the Pampas, and many polo scenes. The various artists include Gustavo Rovira, whose work is featured in La Rural and Opera Pampa. Though not in the center of the city, this gallery is worth a trip if you're seeking art that represents Argentina. It's open Monday to Saturday from 6 to 9pm. Gualeguaychú 4104 (at Pareja). ✆ **11/4501-7846** or 11/15-5023-0263 (cell). No metro access.

Buddha BA Asian Art Gallery   In Belgrano's small but delightful Chinatown, this Asian art gallery is attached to a Chinese teahouse and sells high-quality Asian art and antiques. It's open Monday to Friday from noon to 8pm. Arripeña 2288 (at Mendoza). ℰ **11/4706-2382.** www.buddhaba.com.ar/galeria_art.html. Metro: Juramento.

Cándido Silva ★★★   Filled with antiques and religious objects, this store is the standout in the Galería El Solar de French. Objects come in a range of materials—from wood to marble to silver. Many items are centuries-old antiques. Others are tasteful and exquisite reproductions, including a wide selection of canvases painted by indigenous people from throughout South America: Renaissance portraiture comes together with Frida Kahlo's magical realism, in representations of saints, angels, Christ, and numerous renditions on the Virgin Mary. Rural silver and gaucho items are also part of the items on display. Don't worry about fitting it all on the plane—they ship around the world. The store is open Tuesday to Sunday from 10:30am to 7pm. Calle Defensa 1066 (at Humberto I in Galería El Solar de French). ℰ **11/4361-5053;** 11/15-5733-0696 (cell). www.candidosilva.com.ar. Metro: Independencia.

Galería Ruth Benzacar   This avant-garde gallery, in a hidden underground space at the start of Calle Florida next to Plaza San Martín, hosts exhibitions of local and national interest. Among the best-known Argentines who have appeared here are Alfredo Prior, Miguel Angel Ríos, Daniel García, Graciela Hasper, and Pablo Siguier. It's open Monday to Friday from 11:30am to 8pm, Saturday from 10:30am to 1:30pm. Calle Florida 1000, overlooking Plaza San Martín. ℰ **11/4313-8480.** www.ruthbenzacar.com. Metro: San Martín.

Julio Chaile Arte   Julio Chaile has worked as an artist all over the world, and his art has a modern, pop-inspired feel to it. He also creates interesting paint-by-numbers-style works of famous Argentines, which make great conversation pieces for collectors and travelers. Call for an appointment. Paraguay 964, 2L (at Av. 9 de Julio). ℰ **11/4328-2330.** Metro: Lavalle.

Museo Casa—Taller de Celia Chevalier ★★   I don't get excited about much in La Boca, but I highly recommend this place, a boutique and house museum of an artist located just 2 blocks from El Caminito. Celia Chevalier grew up in Buenos Aires and creates whimsical paintings based on her childhood memories. She is charming and open, though she only speaks Spanish. The house is a restored *conventillo*, the type that Italian immigrants moved into when they came to Buenos Aires before the turn of the 20th century. The house dates from 1885 and was made into her studio museum in 1998. Credit cards are not accepted for art purchases. There is a 65¢ (45p) entry fee. It's open weekends and holidays from 2 to 7pm; call for an appointment on other days. Irala 1162 (at Calle Olavarria). ℰ **11/4302-2337.** celia_chevalier@yahoo.com.ar. No metro access.

Nora Iniesta ★   Nora made herself famous within Buenos Aires for her kitschy art, incorporating Argentine symbols such as tango or gauchos. With the combination of the tourist boom and the return of the Peronist political movement to power, Evita-inspired art now dominates much of her work. Beyond that, modern shadow boxes, collages, and montages of detritus, dolls, souvenirs, and buttons are some of the mainstays. Some of her work is sold at Museo Evita, or you can come see the much larger selection here. In general, Nora is in her San Telmo studio during the week from 10am to 5pm, or by appointment. Peru 715, Ste. #2 (btw. Independenica and Chile). ℰ **11/4331-5459** or 11/15-5319-1119 (cell). www.norainiesta.com. Metro: Independencia.

Silvia Freire, Espacio de Arte y Cultura A little bit religious, a little bit New
Age-y, this avant-garde art gallery is housed in a performance space in Palermo Viejo.
While the building is used mostly for theater presentations, you will find a large collection of art for sale hanging along the walls and on tables. Silvia Freire is considered a bit
of a mystic and eccentric and is interesting to meet if she happens to be in the building
when you arrive. It's open Wednesday and Thursday from 10am to 3pm. Cabrera 4849 (at
Acevedo). ✆ **11/4831-1441.** Metro: Plaza Italia.

Wussmann Gallery This is a beautiful gallery with fantastic works of art, concentrating on contemporary work. Among the artists represented is Ral Veroni, a native
Argentine who has lived around the world. It's open Monday to Saturday 10am to 6pm.
Venezuela 574 (btw. Bolivar and Perú). ✆ **11/4343-4707.** www.wussmann.com. Metro: Belgrano.

BEAUTY TREATMENTS
Lulu of London Lulu, whose real name is Jude O'Hara, is a British beauty expert
who has lived in Buenos Aires for several years. A favorite of the local English-speaking
expat community, she offers a variety of beauty treatments, and specializes in waxing and
massage. She is also the force behind the nonprofit Aesthetic Argentina, which advises
foreigners coming to Buenos Aires for plastic surgery and other enhancements. Call for
appointments. Rodriguez Peña 1057 at Santa Fe. ✆ **11/4815-8471;** www.luluoflondon.com.ar.
Metro: Callao.

BOOKSTORES
Asunto Impreso ★★ Its location in the Centro Cultural Recoleta is one indication
that this is a bookstore of distinction, and its tagline, "bookstore for the imagination," is
another. You'll find very high-quality educational and art books here, many of specific
interest for tourists looking to go deeper into the history and culture of Buenos Aires. It's
open Monday to Friday from 10am to 7pm. Junín 1930, in Centro Cultural Recoleta. ✆ **11/
4805-5585.** www.asuntoimpreso.com. No metro access.

Clasica y Moderna ★★ This important bookstore has been saved by extinction in
an interesting way—by putting a restaurant inside to increase traffic. The bookstore
opened in this location in 1938, though the company dates from 1918. Emilio Robert
Diaz was the original owner, and now his grandchildren run it. In 1988, books were
relegated to the back to make way for diners, but it is one of the best bookstores for
English-speaking tourists in the city. You'll find Buenos Aires photo and history books,
as well as Argentine short-story collections, all translated into English. Events of all kinds
are held here too, from literary readings to plays, dance shows, and art exhibitions. It's
open Monday through Saturday 9am to 1am and Sunday from 5pm to 1am. Callao 892
(at Córdoba). ✆ **11/4812-8707** or 11/4811-3670. www.clasicaymoderna.com. Metro: Callao.

Distal Libros Distal is one of Buenos Aires's largest chain bookstores, with branches
throughout the city, including several on the pedestrianized Calle Florida. It has a large
selection of English-language books, including plenty of *Frommer's* books. It's open
Monday through Friday from 8am to 10pm, Saturday from 10am to 10pm, and Sunday
from 10am to 9pm. Calle Florida 436 (Lavalle; there are many other locations on Calle Florida
and other areas). ✆ **11/5218-4372.** www.distalnet.com. Metro: Lavalle.

Librería de Las Madres—Café Literario Osvaldo Bayer ★★ This combination bookstore and cafe offers what few places in Buenos Aires can—the opportunity to

SHOPPING A TO Z

speak with people whose family members disappeared during Argentina's military dictatorship. You'll also find young students who come here to study and continue seeking justice in this cause. The Madres bookstore is just to the side of the cafe, and it's full of books and newspapers on liberal causes from throughout Latin America. It also has one of the largest collections of books on Che Guevara anywhere in the world. An Argentine native, he is a personal hero to many of the Madres, and his image adorns walls throughout the building. In addition to books, there are posters, pamphlets, and other items here, all with a very socialist slant. It's open Monday through Friday from 10am to 10pm, Saturday from 10am to 8pm. Hipólito Yrigoyen 1584 (at Ceballos). ℂ 11/4382-3261. Metro: Congreso.

Libreria El Ventanal ★★   Argentine history buffs should definitely pop into this bookstore with used and antique books, located in the historic Palacio Vera, one of the city's most beautiful Art Nouveau buildings. The sales staff has an old-world professorial air, often wearing suits and bow ties. You'll find wonderful books on Argentine history as well as a trove of old newspapers and other printed collectibles. It's open Monday through Friday from 10am to 6pm. Av. de Mayo 769 (at Piedras). ℂ 11/4345-8800. www.libreriaelventanal.com.ar. Metro: Piedras.

Librería Santa Fe   This store, part of a chain, has a large selection of books on Buenos Aires and Argentina, travel guides, and many books in English, mostly bestsellers. It's open Monday to Saturday from 10am to 8pm. Av. Santa Fe 2376 (at Pueyrredón). ℂ 11/4827-0100. www.lsf.com.ar. Metro: Pueyrredón.

Librería Sigal   Close to the Abasto Shopping Center, this Jewish bookstore and Judaica shop has been in business for more than 70 years, in an area that was once a major Jewish immigration center. Books are mostly in Hebrew and Spanish. They also sell menorahs, yarmulkes, and other items of Jewish interest. Only cash is accepted. It's open Monday through Thursday from 10am to 1pm and 3 to 7:30pm, Friday from 10am to 4:30pm, sometimes later in summer. Av. Corrientes 2854 (at Ecuador). ℂ 11/4861-9501 or 11/4865-7208. www.libreria-sigal.com. Metro: Gardel.

Librerías Turísticas   Every and any kind of tourism book on Argentina and other parts of the world can be found in this store. The company is itself a publisher and seller of books. It's open Monday through Friday from 9am to 7pm, Saturday from 9am to 1pm. Paraguay 2457 (at Pueyrredón). ℂ 11/4963-2866 or 11/4962-5547. www.libreriaturistica.com.ar. Metro: Pueyrredón.

Libros Cuspide   This is one of the biggest chains in Buenos Aires, and you won't have any trouble finding one of its branches in the city's neighborhoods and in other cities of Argentina. I list here the Calle Florida one—it has a large selection of books on Argentina and should be of interest to the tourist seeking to learn more about the country. It's open Monday to Saturday from 9am to 9pm, Sunday noon to 8pm. Calle Florida 628 (at Tucumán). ℂ 11/4328-0575. www.cuspide.com. Metro: San Martín.

Papelera Palermo ★ (Finds)   If you're looking for an unusual only-in-Argentina gift, and beautiful paper to wrap it in, this is the place. You'll find small notebooks, bound in leather or with a handcrafted Evita or Che Guevara cover, to write down your thoughts on Buenos Aires. Artistic photo books and other unique leather office goods are also for sale, along with a large selection of colorful specialty papers and notecards. It's open Monday to Saturday from 10am to 8pm, Sunday 2 to 8pm. Honduras 4945 (at Serrano). ℂ 11/4833-3081. www.papelerapalermo.com.ar. No metro access.

Walrus Books   This unique English-language bookstore was opened by Geoffrey, an American who moved to Buenos Aires after falling in love and marrying Josefina, his Argentine wife. They stock thousands of used English-language books, many translations of historical South American texts and literature, as well as collections of new books and travel guides. It's open Tuesday to Sunday from 10am to 8pm. Estados Unidos 617 at Peru. (C) 11/4300-7135; www.walrus-books.com.ar. Metro: Moreno.

CAMERAS & ACCESSORIES

Cosentino   If you need something for your camera, are looking for a new one, or need high-quality developing services, Cosentino offers it all. If you're having trouble with your camera, they can also refer you to camera-repair service centers. The store is open Monday to Friday from 10am to 6pm, Saturday from 10am to 1pm. Av. Roque Sáenz Peña (Diagonal Norte) 738 (at Perón). (C) 11/4328-9120. Metro: Catedral.

CELLPHONES

Altel   This is a cellphone-rental company aimed at tourists. It offers free delivery and rental; you pay only for calls. Be aware, however, that while a tremendous convenience, cellphone rentals are expensive in Buenos Aires, and you should always read the fine print no matter what company you choose or how good the offer seems to be. Av. Córdoba 417, 1st floor (at Reconquista). (C) 11/4311-5000. www.altelphonerental.com. No metro access.

MoviCom–BellSouth   While this company mostly sells to locals, foreigners can arrange for pay-as-you-go phones and keep the cellular when they leave Buenos Aires. Using a card-value input system, this method can be significantly cheaper than using a standard tourist rental service. Galerías Pacífico (main level), Calle Florida 750 (at Av. Córdoba). (C) 11/5555-5239. Metro: San Martín.

DENTISTS

Dental Argentina ★★   Run by the attractive brother-and-sister team of Gustavo and Marisol Telo, Dental Argentina is a friendly, welcoming place to have your teeth looked at while in Buenos Aires. The two are very savvy with their foreign customers, and they and most of their staff speak perfect English. They are members of the American Dental Association and have excellent rates, much lower than those in North America and Europe. Uruguay 292, 9B at Sarmiento. (C) 11/4828-0821 or 800/481-5427 from U.S. and Canada and 0800/234-1627 from U.K. www.dental-argentina.com. Metro: Uruguay.

Dr. Miguel Notte   Dr. Miguel Notte and the dentists working with him provide excellent and very friendly service, but do not readily speak English. Uruguay 651 Piso 15 J (btw. Tucuman and Viamonte). (C) 11/4372-8881. Metro: Tribunales.

EYEGLASSES & CONTACT LENSES

Saracco   Fast, high-quality vision services are available at Saracco. The eye exam is included in the price of eyeglasses. Eyeglasses and contact lenses cost about a third of what they do in North America, though some designer frames will have similar prices. The company has several branches surrounding Plaza San Martín. Interestingly, because of the large number of descendants of Italian immigrants in Buenos Aires, you'll find the Zyloware Sophia Loren collection is popular and well featured in this and many other eyeglass stores in the city. Juncal 821, near Plaza San Martín. (C) 11/4393-1000. Metro: San Martín.

Palermo is the place for boutiques showcasing young designers who seem to have done well in spite of, or perhaps because of, the peso crisis. The spike in the cost of imported designer clothing helped to fuel local talent. Prices aren't the bargains they once were, but you'll find many unique items your friends will ask you about when you're home. For now, get the Argentina-made goods while you can, as they are some of the country's most interesting products. Women's fashion here is, as a whole, flirty, fun, and, above all, feminine. Though it is mostly made for near-anorexic figures, I list a plus-size shop below as well. You will find the city's top international fashion stores along Avenida Alvear and Calle Quintana in Recoleta. The larger fashion stores in Recoleta tend to take credit cards and have set hours. Many smaller Palermo boutiques may take select credit cards, but many only accept cash. You'll also find most boutiques closed on Sundays, and, in Palermo in particular, hours can sometimes be just a suggestion because of a shop's small staff. If you find a boutique you really like in Palermo, it's often possible to speak directly with the owner about her designs and products and see what new things might be coming up. For women, Palermo shopping can be a very rewarding and unique experience.

Akiabara   This store is a chain, with very pretty, feminine creations, many made in Argentina. It is moderate- to higher-end for Buenos Aires. It's open daily from 10am to 9pm. Honduras 4865 (btw. Serrano and Thames, off Plaza Serrano). ✆ **11/4831-9420.** Metro: Plaza Italia.

Aristocracia   Enter this casually elegant store and the first things you'll notice are the red wall treatments and luxurious, yet casual feel of the place. Lucrecia Gamundi designs most of the items here and has them produced in Argentina. The store also imports clothes from France, Italy, and other countries. The Las Cañitas store is somewhat new, but it was in Recoleta for 10 years before that. The service is excellent in this store that is well known for its interesting window displays. It's open Monday through Saturday from 10am to 9pm. Av. Arguibel 2867 (at Arce). ✆ **11/4772-1144.** Metro: Carranza.

Bakú ★★ (Value)   All the designs in Bakú are the brainchild of Liliana Basili, who opened her own store in 2003 in the Las Cañitas neighborhood of Palermo. She produces unique pocketbooks, leather accessories, belts and belt buckles, and various items of jewelry. All the items are produced in Argentina. Though her shop is in an expensive part of the city, everything here is priced very reasonably. The shop is open Monday from 1 to 10pm and Tuesday through Saturday from 10am to 10pm. Av. Arguibel 2890 (at Arce). ✆ **11/4775-5570.** Metro: Carranza.

Bokura ★ (Value)   The amazing decor of this men's store almost takes away attention from the clothes. Built into a soaring former warehouse, the two-level shop is painted black, with Chinese dragons and other Asian decorations throughout. The store concentrates on jeans, designer T-shirts, and other clothing for young men, all produced in Argentina and perfect if you're looking for something to wear to go clubbing. The shop is open Monday through Saturday from 11am to 8:30pm and Sunday from 2 to 8:30pm. El Salvador 4677 (btw. Armenia and Malabia). ✆ **11/4833-3975.** www.bokura.com.ar. No metro access.

Bolivia ★   One of the city's best casual men's stores, you'll find everything from sportswear and jeans to fashion underwear. The shop is open Monday through Saturday from 11am to 8:30pm. Gurruchaga 1581 (at Honduras). ✆ **11/4832-6284.** www.boliviaonline.com.ar. No metro access.

Ermenegildo Zegna   This famous Italian chain sells outstanding suits and jackets made of light, cool fabrics. If you've landed in Buenos Aires without your suit and find you'll need one, this is among your best options. The shop is open Monday to Friday from 10am to 8pm, Saturday from 10am to 2pm. Av. Alvear 1920 (at Ayacucho). ✆ 11/4804-1908. No metro access.

Escada   This boutique shop sells casual and elegant women's clothing, combining quality and comfort. It's open Monday to Friday from 10am to 8pm, Saturday from 10am to 2pm. Av. Alvear 1516 (at Parera). ✆ 11/4815-0353. No metro access.

Florentina Muraña ★★ (Finds)   This wonderful little store in Palermo Soho takes its name from a character in a Borges story that took place in Palermo. You'll find very pretty, feminine clothing made of interesting materials here. Items include popcorn shag sweaters handmade in Argentina from Italian wool, and crystal jewelry, some designs with ornamental insects such as ladybugs and butterflies. The owner is Gabriela Sivori, and she works in the shop and designs some of the items for sale, all made solely in Argentina. It's open daily from 11:30am to 8pm, though hours fluctuate in the summer. Calle Borges 1760 (at Pasaje Russel). ✆ 11/4833-4137. www.florentinamurania.com.ar. No metro access.

Lupe ★★ (Finds)   Designer Guadalupe Villar opened this white, airy, and always busy store in 2004. Her designs are young and feminine, with an emphasis on casual sportswear at reasonable prices. It's open Monday to Saturday from 11am to 8:30pm and Sunday 3 to 8pm, though hours will vary in summer. El Salvador 4657 (at Armenia). ✆ 11/4833-0730. www.lupeba.com.ar. No metro access.

Mancini ★★ (Finds)   While women can shop till they drop, most clothing stores in Argentina tend to have conservative clothing. Mancini, a chain with both men's and women's clothing, is an exception to the rule. This branch, in Palermo Viejo, sells chic clothing, with an emphasis on black. It's open Monday to Saturday from 10am to 8:30pm, Sunday 11am to 7pm. Honduras 5140 (btw. Thames and Uriarte). ✆ 11/4832-7570. No metro access.

Maria Cher ★   This boutique is a work of art in itself, with its glass-and-steel construction and its own interior bamboo garden. Maria Chernajovky's store has an emphasis on dresses and leather coats and other leather clothing. It's a perfect spot for a woman looking for mature, fashionable clothing with a more sophisticated air. It's open Monday to Saturday from 10am to 8pm, and Sunday 2 to 7:30pm, though hours will vary in summer. El Salvador 4724 (at Armenia). ✆ 11/4833-4736. www.maria-cher.com.ar. No metro access.

Mishka Shoes ★★ (Finds)   If you're a woman with a shoe fetish, head to this small boutique in Palermo Soho. It's not cheap by any means, with prices ranging up to $500 (£355) for Swarovski crystal–beaded sandals, and other unique handmade footwear, but it's definitely a place to splurge. All the shoes are made in Argentina and custom-made sizes and details can also be arranged. If your spouse or partner gets bored, make him wait on the long white settee while you drool over the selection. The shop is open Monday to Saturday from 11am to 8:30pm. El Salvador 4673 (at Armenia). ✆ 11/4833-6566. www.mishkashoes.com. No metro access.

Nana Lou ★ (Finds)   Mariana Lopez Osornio owns this small boutique in the Las Cañitas area of Palermo for which she has designed much of the clothing. Pretty and feminine is the rule here, and many designs also come from Italy. Jewelry is also sold here.

Open late, this shop is a good option if you happen to be dining on Calle Báez, which is much better known for its restaurants than its stores. It's open Sunday through Friday from noon to 1am, Saturday noon to 2am. Calle Báez 283 (at Arevalo). ✆ **11/4772-7826.** www.mlo.com.ar. Metro: Carranza.

Planeta Bs As ★★   More a collection of stores than one store, Planeta Bs As was started by fashion journalist Claudia Jara. Young designers whom she interviewed after the peso crisis kept asking how they could show their designs when they had no money to open a boutique. Claudia answered their questions by opening this space. You'll find maybe 50 vendors selling clothes, primarily for women, with a few men's items thrown in too. Hours and selection, of course, will vary by designer. Nearby, Claudia also opened **Diseno Bs As,** at Jorge Luis Borges 1613, and **Diseno Arg,** at Honduras 5033, all off Plaza Serrano. The shop is open Tuesday through Friday from 3 to 9pm, and Saturday and Sunday from 2 to 9pm. Jorge Luis Borges 1627 (at Plaza Serrano). ✆ **11/4832-2006** or 11/15-5302-7207 (cell). www.mujermilenio.com.ar and www.vol.com.ar. No metro access.

Polo Ralph Lauren   This is the Buenos Aires branch of the famous American luxury retailer. You will find slightly lower prices here than in North America or Europe. The building, an old turn-of-the-20th-century Art Nouveau mansion, is also a reason to come shopping here: The ornate wooden trim and balustrades remain, and a stained-glass skylight oversees the whole shop. It's open Monday to Saturday from 10am to 8pm. Av. Alvear 1780 (at Callao). ✆ **11/4812-3400.** www.ralphlauren.com. No metro access.

Porto Fem Talles Grandes   Who says big girls can't be fashionable? While most of the clothes in Buenos Aires seem aimed at top-heavy stick figures, this store has the same styles in plus sizes, a sure boon for North American shoppers flocking to the city. Be aware that a law passed in 2006 states that all stores are supposed to carry large sizes, but in anorexic Argentina, few stores do. It's open Monday through Friday from 10am to 8pm, Saturday from 10am to 2pm. Av. Santa Fe 1129 (at Libertad). ✆ **11/4813-6219.** www. portofem.com. Metro: San Martín.

Prototype ★   This store features sleek, well-designed men's clothing that can go from office wear to a night on the town. Focusing on solids and simple patterns, the best way to describe the style is a clean, polished, metrosexual look. All the clothes are Argentine-made, and there is also a great selection of shoes and small leather accessories. This store has a furniture section, with an eye to modern male tastes, concentrating on dark leathers, functional lamps, and black-glass knickknacks and other household goods. Part of a chain, the store has locations throughout Buenos Aires. It's open Monday through Saturday from noon to 9pm. Arguibel 2867 (at Arce). ✆ **11/4773-8812.** www.prototypeweb.com. Metro: Carranza.

Raffaello by Cesar Franco ★★   Cesar Franco got his start designing for the theater and tango shows and it comes through in the flare of his clothes. His shop has everything from sportswear to wedding dresses, and truly exquisite leather coats for both men and women, many made by combining leather strips with rich fabrics, in designs that recall Renaissance-era clothing. The shop is open Monday to Friday from 10am to 8pm. Florida 165 (btw. Bartolomo Mitre and Peron), in the Güemes shopping center, 1st floor, shop 127. ✆ **11/4343-1935** or 11/4331-1771. www.raffaellobuenosaires.com. Metro: Catedral.

Rapsodia   There are many branches of this women's clothing store chain that tends to exhibit exotic fabrics and displays, with virtually all of its items made in Argentina. More than six of these stores exist throughout Buenos Aires, but there are two large stores on the same street in Las Cañitas, one selling new clothing and the other mainly vintage

styles. The shop is open daily from 10am to 9pm. Av. Arguibel 2899 and Av. Arguibel 2860,
both at Arce. 📞 **11/4772-2716** or 11/4772-7676. Metro: Carranza.

Rodrigo Reyes   If you're looking for a great selection of well-made, sporty shoes, for
both men and women, this is a great place. It specializes in sneaker shoes, with all the
products made in Argentina, and there's a vast array of funky styles and colors. The shop
is open daily from 11am to 8pm, though hours fluctuate in the summer. Malabia 1682 (at
El Salvador). 📞 **11/4834-6093.** www.rodrigoreyes.com.ar. No metro access.

Tienda de Diseño ★ Finds   Opened at the end of 2008, this small store is a col-
laborative effort by Elianara Lapola, German Iglesias, and other designers. It sells dresses,
sportswear, sunglasses, jewelry, and accessories for women, all with interesting and
unique designs. It's open Monday to Saturday from 10am to 8pm. Malabia 1101 at Niceto
Vega. 📞 **11/4772-6722.** www.tiendadedisenio.com.ar. Metro: Malabia.

HOME DESIGN

Capital Diseño and Objetos   This is one of the most interesting home-design stores
in Palermo Viejo, and you'll find all kinds of well-designed, kitschy, and funky things
here. There's also a large selection of items for children. Among my favorite things are
the decorative key holders and coat hangers designed by Fernando Poggio. There is also
a lot of leather. It's open Monday to Saturday from 10am to 10pm. Honduras 4958 (btw.
Uriarte and Thames). 📞 **11/4834-6555.** www.capitalpalermo.com.ar. Metro: Palermo.

L'ago   Located along the antiques row of San Telmo, this store has creative and modern
designs as well as a few vintage mid-20th-century items. The main focus is lamps, but
there's also an extensive collection of items that can be used for children's rooms or for
those with whimsical, young-at-heart tastes. Virtually all of the new items are made in
Argentina. The store is open daily from 10am to 8pm. Defensa 970 (at Estados Unidos).
📞 **11/4362-4702.** Metro: Independencia.

Tienda Puro Diseño Argentino ★★★ Finds   This is one of my favorite stores in
Buenos Aires, and it features very high quality, high-design items created by more than
120 Argentine designers, with only Argentine materials, in Argentina, all at good value.
The idea came from a design expo of the same name, which in spite of the country's
economic crisis was successful enough to lead to a stand-alone store. The concentration
is on home design, but products also include jewelry, clothing fashions, leather accessories, and children's products. Many of the household items have an updated frontier
feeling. Leather, one of Argentina's most important products, also plays a strong role in
many of the designs. The store has relocated from its former location in the Recoleta
Design Center. It's open from Monday through Saturday from 10am to 8pm. Gorriti 5953
(btw. Arevalo and Ravignani). 📞 **11/4776-8037.** www.purodiseno.com.ar. No metro access.

JEWELRY

The city's finest jewelry stores are located in Recoleta and inside many five-star hotels.
You can find bargains on gold along Calle Libertad, near Avenida Corrientes. Also, make
sure to take a look at the women's fashion section. Many of the small women's boutiques
detailed there also carry handmade jewelry produced locally.

Chabeli   This store has an interesting selection of Argentine jewelry handmade from
crystals and semiprecious stones. It also has women's shoes and pocketbooks, with most
things costing more than $100 (£71). Designs of both leather accessories and jewelry fall
into two main categories: native Argentine to very pretty and feminine, using pink and

pastel materials. They also have another branch in the resort town of Bariloche. The store is open Monday through Saturday from 10am to 8pm, Sunday noon to 7pm. Calle Florida 702 (at Viamonte). ✆ **11/4328-0805.** Metro: San Martín.

Cousiño Jewels   Located in the Sheraton hotel's shopping arcade, this Argentine jeweler features a brilliant collection of art made of the national stone rhodochrosite (also called Inca Rose), a beautiful milky-pink quartz. It's open Monday through Saturday from 9am to 7pm, Sunday from 10am to 6pm. In the Sheraton Buenos Aires Hotel, Av. San Martín 1225 (at Alem). ✆ **11/4312-2336** or **11/4313-8881.** Metro: Retiro.

H.Stern   This upscale Brazilian jeweler, with branches in major cities around the world, sells an entire selection of South American stones, including emeralds and the unique imperial topaz. H.Stern is the top jeweler in Latin America. The Marriott location is open daily from 9am to 7:30pm, but is sometimes closed weekends in winter. The Sheraton location is open Monday to Friday from 9am to 7:30pm, Saturday and Sunday from 9am to 5pm. In the Marriott Plaza, Calle Florida 1005, overlooking Plaza San Martín. ✆ **11/4318-3083.** Metro: San Martín. In the Sheraton Buenos Aires Hotel, Av. San Martín 1225 (at Libertador). ✆ **11/4312-6762.** Metro: Retiro.

KOSHER GROCERS

Autoservicio Ki Tob   This large kosher grocery store also has a kosher meat section. You'll find everything kosher here, from basic staples to junk food. Only cash is accepted. It's open Monday through Thursday from 8am to 8pm, Friday from 8am until 2 hours before sunset, and Sunday from 3 to 8pm. Tucumán 2783 (at Boulogne Sur Mer). ✆ **11/4966-1007.** Metro: Pueyrredón.

Heluini   This small kosher store with friendly service concentrates on Sephardic kosher foods, known locally as Oriental kosher. You'll find spices and other items with a decidedly Middle Eastern flavor here. This is also one of the few places in Buenos Aires that sells peanut butter, a very difficult item to find in Argentina, so if you or the kids have a craving, this is the place to head. The store has been open since 1937. Only cash is accepted. It's open Monday through Thursday from 9am to 9pm, Friday from 9am until 2 hours before sunset. Tucumán 2755 (at Boulogne Sur Mer). ✆ **11/4966-1007.** Metro: Pueyr redón.

LEATHER

With all that beef in its restaurants, Argentina could not be anything but one of the world's best leather centers. If you're looking for high-quality, interestingly designed leather goods, especially women's shoes, accessories, and handbags, few places beat Buenos Aires's selection. Many leather stores will also custom-make jackets and other items for interested customers, so do ask if you see something you like in the wrong size or want to combine items from pieces. While most shops can do this in a day or two, if you are looking to really have something made from Argentina, to avoid disappointment, you should start checking out stores and prices early. If something is complicated to make, it might take more time than usual—and some stores can take as long as a week.

Ashanti Leather Factory ★   This small store on Calle Florida offers a wide selection of leather goods, from men's and women's jackets to funky and interesting women's pocketbooks. The prices on jackets are not the best, but women's accessories are very competitively priced, and you can always bargain. Best of all, the factory is in the basement of the shop, so they can easily custom-make almost anything for you. Ask for a tour so you can meet the craftspeople Roberto, Victor, and Oscar, who sit surrounded by

---

Looking to compare prices and selection in a hurry? Then head to the Murillo Street Leather Warehouse district in the Villa Crespo neighborhood. I've listed several places below in the leather section, including the large Murillo 666, one of the street's main stores. Items are often made above the storefront, or in a factory nearby. Don't be afraid to bargain, or ask if combinations of items can be made if you don't find exactly what you like. The highest density is at Murillo between Malabia and Acevedo, but you'll find about 50 stores total, with everything from leather jackets to purses, luggage, furniture, and more. Many of the smaller stores are owned by Orthodox Jews, and so will be closed on Friday evenings, Saturdays, and certain holidays, so keep that in mind when scheduling your shopping time.

---

sewing machines and colorful bolts of leather. The store is open daily from 10am to 10pm. Calle Florida 585 (at Lavalle). ℂ **11/4394-1310.** Metro: San Martín.

Beith Cuer   You'll find an excellent selection of women's coats and accessories in this store, from hats to purses to items such as fur gloves and hats. For men, you'll find coats, hats, wallets, and belts, too. The staff is very attentive. It's open Monday to Saturday from 9am to 7pm; closed Sunday. Murillo 525 (btw. Malabia and Acevedo in Villa Crespo). ℂ **11/ 4854-8580.** Metro: Malabia.

Casa López ★★   Widely considered among the best *marroquinería* (leather-goods shops) in Buenos Aires, Casa López sells an extensive range of Argentine leather products. There is also a shop in the Patio Bullrich Mall. The store is open daily from 10am to 8pm. Marcelo T. de Alvear 640 (at Maipú, near Plaza San Martín). ℂ **11/4312-8911.** www.casa lopez.com.ar. Metro: San Martín.

Chabeli   In addition to jewelry (see listing above), this store has a wide selection of women's shoes and pocketbooks, with few things costing more than $100 (£71). It's open Monday through Saturday from 10am to 8pm, Sunday noon to 7pm. Calle Florida 702. ℂ **11/4328-0805.** Metro: San Martín.

El Nochero   All the products sold at El Nochero are made with first-rate Argentine leather and manufactured by local workers. Shoes and boots, leather goods and clothes, and decorative silverware (including *mates,* for holding the special herbal tea beloved by Argentines) fill the store. It's open Monday through Saturday from 10am to 9pm; Sunday and holidays noon to 9pm. Posadas 1169, in the Patio Bullrich Mall. ℂ **11/4815-3629.** No metro access.

Gloria Lópes Sauqué ★   Beautiful, exclusive designs await you in this unique leather-design gallery. Gloria Lópes Sauqué is one of Argentina's most creative designers, with her work exhibited in various countries. She is also the only Argentine designer whose work is sold at the Galeries Lafayette in Paris. It's open Monday through Friday from 10am to 8pm, Saturday 10am to 6pm. Posadas 1169 (btw. Libertad and Cerritos). ℂ **11/4815-3007.** www.glorialopezsauque.com. No metro access.

Hard Leather ★   The name might make you wonder if you walked into a Buenos Aires S&M shop, but the selection is anything but. Plus, there's nothing hard about the leather (all of it soft and supple), but the owners missed the double entendre when they looked for a word meaning "durable" to replace *dura*, the Spanish word for "hard." While there are coats for men, women will find a much larger selection. American Express, MasterCard, and Visa are accepted here. The shop is open Monday to Saturday from 9am to 8pm, Sunday 10am to 7pm. Murillo 627 (btw. Malabia and Acevedo, in Villa Crespo). ℂ **11/4856-8920.** Metro: Malabia.

Louis Vuitton   The famous Parisian boutique sells an elite line of luggage, purses, and travel bags here. It's located alongside Recoleta's most exclusive shops. It's open Monday through Friday from 10am to 8pm, Saturday from 11am to 6pm. Av. Alvear 1901 (at Ayacucho). ℂ **11/4802-0809.** No metro access.

Murillo 666 ★★   This store is the main outlet in the Murillo Street Leather District in Villa Crespo neighborhood. There's a large selection of women's coats and accessories, as well as one of the largest assortments of men's jackets. Jackets can also be custom-made. If you're looking for furniture, they have the largest showroom for that as well. Unlike many stores in the district, it is the same price for cash or credit, but sometimes you can still bargain a price down slightly. American Express, Diners Club, MasterCard, and Visa are accepted. The store is open daily from 9:30am to 8pm. Murillo 666 (btw. Malabia and Acevedo, in Villa Crespo). ℂ **11/4856-4501.** www.murillo666.com.ar. Metro: Malabia.

Outlet ★   The name says it all for this store just off Murillo. In addition to large selections of jackets, handbags, gloves, and other items, the store also carries a small selection of shoes. Those couches you're sitting on while your friends try on everything? Those can be bought in various colors as well. In fact, shopping with friends might save you money, as group discounts are offered. This is definitely a place to bargain. There is also a small selection of women's fur coats. American Express, Diners Club, MasterCard, and Visa are accepted. The store is open Monday to Friday from 10am to 7:30pm, Saturday 10am to 6:30pm. Scalabrini Ortiz 5 (at Murillo, in Villa Crespo). ℂ **11/4857-1009.** Metro: Malabia.

Paseo Del Cuero ★   Along with coats and the usual items for men and women, this factory outlet in the Murillo district also has a great selection of men's and women's small luggage carry-ons and gym bags. Feel free to bargain, as the staff often gives you a slightly lower price if you hesitate or offer to pay in cash. Looking for cowhide throw rugs? They're here too! They do take American Express, Diners Club, MasterCard, and Visa. The outlet is open Monday to Saturday from 9:30am to 7:30pm. Murillo 624 (btw. Malabia and Acevedo, in Villa Crespo). ℂ **11/4855-9094.** www.paseodelcuero.com.ar. Metro: Malabia.

Pasión Argentina—Diseños Etnicos ★★   With Palermo Viejo now being over-run by chain stores, it's good to see this store thriving in the heart of it all. Independently owned by Amadeo Bozzi, the store concentrates on leather goods primarily for women, accessories for men and women, and the home. All produced in Argentina, everything is well designed and well made. Some items combine leather with other native materials and are made by members of the Wichi tribe, a native group in the Chaco region. I highly recommend a visit to this store when in Palermo Viejo. It's open Monday through Friday from 10am to 6pm, Saturday 10am to 2pm. Ravignani 1780 (btw. Honduras and El Salvador, in Palermo Viejo). ℂ **11/4773-1157** and 11/4777-7550. www.pasion-argentina.com.ar. Metro: Carranza.

Prüne ★★   This is a chain with additional stores in Alto Palermo, Patio Bullrich, and many other locations in town and throughout Argentina, but the Calle Florida store is among the largest. It's great for women's accessories and small leather goods, and carries some of the best purses in all of Buenos Aires. The store has a light, airy feel and even a back patio. Most of the things here are Argentine products, but a few are Chinese-made. It's open daily from 10am to 11pm. Calle Florida 963 (at Plaza San Martín). ✆ 11/4893-2634. Metro: San Martín.

Rossi & Caruso   This store has some of the best leather products in the city and is the first choice for visiting celebrities—the king and queen of Spain and Prince Philip of England among them. Products include luggage, saddles, and accessories as well as leather and chamois clothes, purses, wallets, and belts. There is another branch in the Galerías Pacífico mall (p. 194). Av. Santa Fe 1377 (at Uruguay). ✆ 11/4811-1965. Metro: Bulnes.

626 Cueros   The blasting disco music here tells you you're in a place a little more edgy than some of the other leather stores in the Murillo district. Here you'll find interestingly designed men's and women's coats, many slightly cheaper than in other stores. You'll also pay less if you pay cash. If you don't have it though, they do accept American Express, Diners Club, MasterCard, and Visa. The store is open Monday to Saturday from 10am to 6pm. Murillo 626 (btw. Malabia and Acevedo, in Villa Crespo). ✆ 11/4857-6972. Metro: Malabia.

LUGGAGE
Voyager   If you've been shopping too much and need a way to get it all home, heading here might be a good idea. The combination of price, selection, service, and location makes it a great place for a new suitcase or any other luggage need. Airport pillows and electric converters are also sold. It's open Monday through Saturday from 10am to 8pm, Sunday from 10am to 7pm. Florida 250 (btw. Sarmiento and Perón). ✆ 11/5032-2578 or 11/5032-2579. Metro: Catedral.

MUSIC
Almacén de Tangos Generales   Tango music and more are available for sale in this small shop overlooking Dorrego Plaza in the heart of San Telmo. CDs of tango music as well as musical scores are sold for those who really want to get to know tango music. In addition, they sell plenty of souvenirs such as mugs, postcards, spoons, and assorted knickknacks to bring back from your trip. The shop is open Monday through Saturday from 11am to 6pm, Sunday from 10am to 8pm. Don Anselmo Aieta 1067 (at Plaza Dorrego). ✆ 11/4362-7190. Metro: Independencia.

C-Disueria   This music store has a variety of CDs and tapes to cover all musical genres. The store has a vast selection of tango music at reasonable prices—you can buy a few CDs to listen to at home and help you remember your trip. Corrientes 1274 (at Talcahuano). ✆ 11/4381-0754. Metro: Tribunales.

ORGANIC & VEGETARIAN FOOD
Bio   This is an organic restaurant with a large selection of organic products one can buy separately. It's a great place for veg-heads to go shopping for snacks to bring back to their hotel. All the ingredients at Bio are organic, and all are strictly grown or produced in Argentina. The small shop has organic chips, teas, cheeses, and even organic wine. They also do takeout. Only cash is accepted. It's open Tuesday through Sunday from noon to

3:30pm and 8pm to 1am, often later on weekends, and Monday from 8pm to 1am. Humboldt 2199 (at Guatemala). ✆ **11/4774-3880.** No metro access.

PET SHOP

Bienfifi   Looking for something special for your pet back home? Head here for unique, Argentine-made collars, leashes, pet carriers, and other items in this store run by Silvana Faldani. Only cash is accepted. It's open Monday through Saturday from 11am to 8pm, and Sunday 2 to 8pm. Cabrera 5050 (btw. Thames and Uriarte). ✆ **11/4899-1924.** No metro access.

PHARMACY

Farmacia Suiza   You won't have a problem finding places to buy medicine in Buenos Aires, but I recommend this place mostly for its atmosphere. It's an old apothecary, tucked into the Microcentro area. The shelves are adorned with wooden carvings and lined with old jars and flasks from the turn of the 20th century. The medicine and services, however, are fully up-to-date. It's open Monday to Friday from 8am to 8pm. Calle Tucumán 701 (at Maipú). ✆ **11/4313-8480.** Metro: San Martín.

POLO & GAUCHO CLOTHING & ACCESSORIES

El Boyero   You'll find high-quality, classic-style polo and other clothing inspired by the gaucho (Argentine cowboy) lifestyle here. There's a large selection of beautiful leather products made in Argentina. Fine silver gaucho jewelry, knives, and other accessories are also available. The store has two branches, one in Galerías Pacífico (p. 194) and the one listed here on Calle Florida. It's open Monday through Saturday from 9am to 8pm (sometimes on Sunday). Calle Florida 953 (at Plaza San Martín). ✆ **11/4312-3564.** Metro: San Martín.

TANGO CLOTHES, SHOES & ACCESSORIES

Abasto Plaza Hotel Tango Shop   Whether you're staying at the Abasto Plaza Hotel or not, it's worth taking a look at this store in the lobby for its tango clothing selection, especially the sexy dresses. Tango music and other items are also sold here. It's open Monday through Friday from 10am to 7pm. Av. Corrientes 3190 (at Anchorena, near the Abasto Shopping Center). ✆ **11/6311-4465.** www.abastoplaza.com. Metro: Carlos Gardel.

Carlos Custom Shoes   This is not a shoe store, but a custom crafter of excellent, high-quality tango shoes. If you call, Carlos will come to your hotel to take measurements and then handcraft your shoes. His work takes longer than most stores with their own factory, up to 10 days or 2 weeks, so make sure to contact him early during your trip. ✆ **11/4687-6026.** No metro access.

Flabella   This is an extremely busy store, selling mostly shoes and other items for tango dancers. The best items are women's shoes, but there's also a variety of men's shoes. Many shoes are in stock for immediate purchase, but many styles have to be custom-made. This can take up to a week, so plan around this during your trip. Shoe prices begin at about $50 (£36) a pair. Eduardo is one of the talented shoe technicians, and he can also offer tips on the tango scene. The store is surrounded by several similar ones, so check out this block for a wider selection. This store is open Monday through Saturday from 10am to 10pm. Suipacha 263 (at Diagonal Norte). ✆ **11/4322-6036.** www.flabella.com. Metro: Carlos Pellegrini.

La Vikinga Tango Fashions ★★ Already famous in Buenos Aires for her Mano a Mano *milonga* (p. 230) Helen Halldórsdóttir, nicknamed La Vikinga because of her Iceland homeland, has started a private tango clothing and shoe boutique. Contact her directly to view her designs, which range from tango dresses and other apparel to tango shoes and even tango sneakers. ✆ **11/4383-6229** or 11/15-5865-8279 (cell); www.lavikinga.eu. Metro: Congreso.

Tango Mina ★ If you've been seduced by Argentine tango, you'll want to spend an afternoon dressing for the part. The designer (a devotee of tango herself) sells cutting-edge women's tango clothing and handmade shoes, inspired by the culture of tango. The styles span classic and traditional to hip and modern. Anne Midón creates inspired clothing designed to move and flow with you in the dance. There is something for everyone among the connoisseurs of tango, and you can find a tango look that fits and functions for every shape and style. After a visit here, you'll be ready for a night on the town. The shop is open Monday through Friday from noon to 7pm, Saturday 11am to 5pm. Riobamba 486, 10th floor (at Lavalle). ✆ **11/4952-3262** and 11/15-5960-8195 (cell). www.tango mina.com.ar. Metro: Callao.

Tango Moda ★★★ There is perhaps no more stunningly situated store in Buenos Aires than this tango clothing store on the roof of the Palacio Barolo. An array of women's and men's tango clothes, accessories, and shoes await you, but it's the view—from the 16th floor of one of the city's most prominent buildings—that will take you away. About once a month, the owner Jorge Arias throws sunset tango parties on the store's gargantuan terrace. Sip wine as you watch couples tango, with the Congreso as the backdrop. You're not dreaming, you're in Buenos Aires. Jorge is also the father of local television-news anchor Luciana Arias, whose early modeling pictures can be seen around the store. The store is open Monday to Friday from 2 to 9pm. Av. de Mayo 1370, 16th floor (at San José in Palacio Barolo). ✆ **11/4381-4049** or 11/15-4033-6746 (cell). Metro: Sáenz Peña.

TOYS & CHILDREN'S ITEMS

Casa Barbie ★★ (Kids) Forget about a little pink plastic house. In Buenos Aires, Barbie gets a three-story mansion, the world's first freestanding store of its kind. Little girls and their mothers can dream away at Barbie wedding displays, or sit and chat at the Barbie tearoom. There is also a beauty salon where you can get a Barbie beauty makeover to impress your own Ken. The shop is open Monday to Saturday from 10am to 8:30pm, Sunday 1 to 8pm. Scalabrini Ortiz 3170 (btw. Cerviño and Cabello). ✆ **0810/4444-BARBIE** (4444-227243); www.barbie-stores.com. Metro: Scalabrini Ortiz.

Ufficio ★★ Most of the products in this store are handmade in Argentina and are solid wood, but they also have a few Chinese imports. Products include lamps, wooden rocking horses, dolls, jigsaw puzzles, guitars, baby bibs, and a few other clothing items. Many of the items are good gifts for kids as an alternative to video games and the usual. The store is open daily from 11am to 8pm. Calle Borges 1733 (at Pasaje Russel). ✆ **11/4831-5008**. No metro access.

VIDEO STORES

Brujas This store sells hard-to-find vintage Argentine videos, DVDs, and music CDs. Keep in mind that Argentine videos differ from the system used in North America. The store is open Monday to Saturday from 10:30am to 9pm. Calle Rodríguez Peña (at Córdoba). ✆ **11/4373-7100**. Metro: Callao.

El Coleccionista   If you're looking for hard-to-find videos, especially of South American and Spanish movies, this is the place to head (however, know that Argentina uses a different VCR system than North America). The store also has DVDs and some used and hard-to-find music. It's in a district with many similar shops, so foreign-film fanatics will do well by poking around here. The shop is open Monday to Saturday from 10am to 8pm. Junín 607 (at Tucumán). ☎ **11/4373-5684.** Metro: Callao.

WINE SHOPS

Argentine wineries, particularly those in Mendoza and Salta, produce some excellent wines. Stores selling Argentina wines abound, and among the best are **Grand Cru,** Av. Alvear 1718; **Tonel Privado,** in the Patio Bullrich Shopping Mall and in Galerias Pacifico; **Winery,** which has branches at L. N. Alem 880 and Av. Del Libertador 500, both downtown; and **Vinos Argentinos** at Tucumán 565 just off Florida Street.

La Cava de la Brigada   Owned by the restaurant of the same name in San Telmo, this store carries more than 350 different wines from more than 40 bodegas winemakers. Prices range from less than $6 (£4.25) a bottle to almost $350 (£249). Locally made and imported whiskeys and other hard liquors are kept in an area on the top floor of the store. It's open daily from 9:30am to 1:30pm and 4 to 9pm. Bolívar 1008 (at Carlos Calvo). ☎ **11/4362-2943.** Metro: Independencia.

WOOL & SWEATERS

Lana's Argentina   The word *lana* is Spanish for "wool." At Lana's Argentina, you'll find a fine selection of Argentine wool sweaters made from the fibers of Patagonian sheep and lambs. The shop also carries many leather goods and accessories to complement your purchase. The store is open Monday to Friday from 9am to 8pm, Saturday 9am to 6pm. Suipacha 984 (at Paraguay). ☎ **11/4328-8798.** Metro: San Martín.

10

Buenos Aires After Dark

When other cities choose to go to sleep, darkness makes Buenos Aires come alive. One thing you'll notice immediately in this city is that people *love* the nightlife. From Avenida Corrientes theaters to tango salons to big techno clubs, Buenos Aires offers an exceptional night out.

The evening usually begins for Porteños with a play or movie around 8pm followed by a late and long dinner. Then, after 11pm or midnight, it'll be time to visit a bar or two, before heading to clubs around 2am. (Disco naps are essential!) On Thursday, Friday, and Saturday, it's time to really stay out late, with Porteños hitting big dance clubs and bars in such places as Recoleta, Palermo, and the Costanera. By the time they start walking home, the sun is coming up. Summertime nightlife is quieter because many flee to the coast, moving their nocturnal activities to places such as Mar del Plata and Punta del Este.

But Buenos Aires's nightlife is not just about clubbing. There's a large number of cultural activities for visitors and residents alike. Nearly 40 professional theaters around town (many located along Av. Corrientes, btw. Av. 9 de Julio and Callao and in the San Telmo and Abasto neighborhoods) show Broadway- and off-Broadway-style hits, Argentine plays, and music revues, although most are in Spanish. Buy tickets for most productions at the box office or through **Ticketmaster** (© 11/4321-9700). The **British Arts Centre,** Suipacha 1333 (© 11/4393-0275), offers theater productions and movies in English.

For current information on after-dark entertainment, consult the English-language **Buenos Aires Herald,** which lists events held in English and Spanish, and often features events by Irish, British, Australian, and North American expats who have moved to Buenos Aires (www.buenos airesherald.com). **The Argentimes,** produced monthly by British expat Kristie Robinson, has similar listings and a user-friendly website (www.theargentimes. com). **Clarín, La Nación,** and many of the major local publications also list events, but only in Spanish. *QuickGuide Buenos Aires,* available in the city's tourism kiosks and in various hotels, has information on shows, theaters, and nightclubs. **Ciudad Abierta** (www.ciudadabiertatv.gov.ar) is a free weekly published by the city government and it lists cultural events all over the city, but in Spanish only. Ciudad Abierta is also an interesting cable-access channel that, like the weekly, highlights cultural and tourist interests around the city; it's usually channel 73 on hotel cable systems. **Llegas a Buenos Aires** lists cultural, arts, tango, and other events. This newspaper is published weekly and distributed free at locations across the city. Visit its website (www.revistallegas.com.ar) to plan ahead for your trip. The websites www.bsasinsomnio.com.ar and www.whatsupbuenosaires.com also list entertainment of all kinds in this city that never sleeps Additionally, you can ask the Buenos Aires City Tourism offices for the "Funny Night Map," which lists bars and clubs throughout Buenos Aires (www.funnymaps.com.ar).

1 THE PERFORMING ARTS

CULTURAL CENTERS

Asociación Argentina de Cultura Inglesa (British Arts Centre) ★★★ This multifunctional facility was established over 77 years ago by a British ambassador who wanted to do more to promote British culture within Argentina. He was highly successful in his efforts, and today the AACI teaches English to over 25,000 students a year, has several film, theater, cultural, and art programs, and generally provides a very welcoming environment for any English speaker who is feeling homesick. Events can range from being completely upper crust (celebrating Shakespeare) to raunchy (*Absolutely Fabulous* TV program showings). Pick up various brochures and event listings at the center itself, or look up listings in the English-language *Buenos Aires Herald.* Take note that during the summer months, December to March, they will have limited programming. Suipacha 1333 (at Arroyo). ✆ 11/4393-2004. www.aaci.org.ar and www.britishartscentre.org.ar. Metro: San Martín.

Centro Cultural de Borges ★★ You can shop all you want in Galerías Pacífico, but if it's culture you're after, you can find it there too. Inside of the shopping mall is this arts center named for Jorge Luis Borges, Argentina's most important literary figure. You'll find art galleries, lecture halls with various events, an art cinema, and an art bookstore. There's also the **Escuela Argentina de Tango,** which offers a schedule of lessons tourists can take with ease (✆ 11/4312-4990; www.eatango.org), and the ballet star **Julio Bocca's Ballet Argentino** performance space and training school—full of young ballet stars and their not-to-be-missed performances (✆ 11/5555-5359; www.juliobocca. com). Hours and fees vary. Enter through Galerías Pacífico or at the corner of Viamonte and San Martín. ✆ 11/5555-5359. www.ccborges.com.ar. Metro: San Martín.

Centro Cultural Recoleta (Recoleta Cultural Center) ★★ This cultural center is just one door over from the famous Recoleta Cemetery. It hosts Argentine and international art exhibits, experimental theater works, occasional music concerts, and an interactive science museum for children, where they are encouraged to touch and play with the displays. The center has recently begun to host controversial and politically oriented artists as well, sometimes with a very anti-Catholic message—defying the center's location in a former church building. Junín 1930 (next-door to the Recoleta Cemetery). ✆ 11/4803-1041. No metro access.

Silvia Freire, Espacio de Arte y Cultura A little bit religious, a little bit New Age-y, this avant-garde art gallery is housed in a performance space in Palermo Viejo. While it's largely meant for theater presentations, you will find a large collection of art for sale here in the building, hanging along the walls and on tables. Silvia Freire is considered a bit of a mystic and eccentric and is interesting to meet if she happens to be in the building when you arrive. Store hours are Wednesday and Thursday from 10am to 3pm. Performance hours vary based on programs; call for information. Cabrera 4849 (at Acevedo). ✆ 11/4831-1441. Metro: Plaza Italia.

DANCE, CLASSICAL MUSIC & OPERA

Julio Bocca and Ballet Argentino ★★★ Julio Bocca is Argentina's greatest ballet and dance star, and many of his performances combine tango movements along with classical dance, creating a style uniquely his own, and uniquely Argentine. He runs a studio in the Centro Cultural de Borges for classical dance and ballet performances, as well as another performance space in Teatro Maipo on Calle Esmeralda, with a range of events from dance to comedy plays. Though Mr. Bocca himself has retired from performance life, his Ballet Argentino troupe is an absolute do-not-miss for lovers of ballet and dance, especially the performances featuring Claudia Figaredo and Hernan Piquin. Ballet Argentino at the Centro Cultural Borges, within Galerías Pacífico at the corner of Viamonte and San Martín. ✆ **11/5555-5359.** www.juliobocca.com. Tickets $5–$19 (£3.55–£13). Metro: San Martín. Teatro Maipo spaces at Teatro Maipo at Esmeralda 449 (at Corrientes). ✆ **11/4394-5521.** Metro: Lavalle.

Luna Park Once the home of international boxing matches, the Luna is the largest indoor stadium in Argentina, hosting some of the biggest shows and concerts in Buenos Aires. Many of these are classical music concerts, and the National Symphonic Orchestra often plays here. Though they had actually met previously, legend has it that a 1944 fundraiser here, for the victims of the San Juan earthquake, was where Juan Perón first met a very young actress named Eva Duarte, changing Argentine history forever. The "Night of a Thousand Stars" song in the musical commemorates this event. Av. Corrientes and Bouchard. ✆ **11/4311-1990.** Metro: L. N. Alem.

Teatro Colón Known across the world for its impeccable acoustics, the Colón has attracted the world's finest opera performers—Luciano Pavarotti, Maria Callas, Plácido Domingo, and Arturo Toscanini among them. Opera season in Buenos Aires runs from April to November. The Colón has its own symphony orchestra, ballet, and choir companies. The main theater seats 3,000. The building is undergoing renovations that have been seriously delayed and are likely not to be completed until 2010. Check the website or call for more information. Calle Libertad 621 (at Tucumán). ✆ **11/4378-7100.** www.teatro colon.org.ar. Tickets $2–$15 (£1.40–£11). Metro: Tribunales.

THEATERS

Grupo de Teatro Catalinas Sur This theater company presents outdoor weekend performances in La Boca. It's in Spanish, but is mostly comedy, and both adults and children are likely to enjoy the productions. Av. Benito Pérez Galdós 93 (at Caboto). ✆ **11/4300-5707.** www.catalinasur.com.ar. Tickets $3–$10 (£2.15–£7.10). No metro access.

Teatro Coliseo This Recoleta theater puts on classical music productions. Marcelo T. de Alvear 1125 (at Cerrito). ✆ **11/4816-5943.** Tickets $2–$8 (£1.40–£5.70). Metro: San Martín.

Teatro Gran Rex Within this large theater, you'll be able to see many national and foreign music concerts. Av. Corrientes 857 (at Suipacha). ✆ **11/4322-8000.** Metro: Carlos Pellegrini.

Teatro Municipal General San Martín This entertainment complex has three theaters staging drama, comedy, ballet, music, and children's plays. The lobby itself, which often hosts exhibitions of photography and art, is worth a special visit during the daytime. The theater has also absorbed many productions that ordinarily would have been at Teatro Colón. Lobby exhibitions are usually free. Corrientes 1530 (at Paraná). ✆ **0800/333-5254.** Metro: Uruguay.

Teatro Nacional Cervantes Some of the city's best theater performances take place here, in this production house originally built by a group of Spanish actors as a thank-you to Buenos Aires. The building is sumptuous, in an ornate Spanish Imperial style, using materials brought from Spain. In 2008 and 2009, a restoration program has helped the detailed facade gleam anew. Calle Libertad 815 (at Córdoba). ✆ **11/4816-4224.** Metro: Tribunales.

The Alamo – Shoeless Joe's **6**
Asia de Cuba **33**
Asociación Argentina de Cultura
  Inglesa (British Arts Centre) **8**
Bar El Federal **43**
Bayres Folk **51**
Bingo Lavalle **26**
Café Tortoni **34**
Casino Buenos Aires **48**
Central Tango **14**
Centro Cultural de Borges **22**
Centro Cultural Recoleta
  (Recoleta Cultural Center) **2**
Chandon Bar **31**
Chueca **35**
Clásica y Moderna **12**
Contramano **3**
El Arranque **18**
El Beso Nightclub **16**
El Niño Bien **20**
El Querandí **37**
El Viejo Almacén **40**
Gran Bar Danzon **7**
Grupo de Teatro Catalinas Sur **49**
Inside Resto-Bar **17**
Julio Bocca's Ballet Argentino **23**
KM Zero/Search **4**
La Coruña **44**
La Divina – The Divine
  Comedy **45**
La Glorietta **1**
La Marshall **50**
La Ventana **38**
Lo de Celia **19**
Luna Park **30**
Madero Tango **47**
Magic Center **28**
Magic Play **27**
Mano a Mano at Plaza
  Bohemia **29**
Medio y Medio **39**
Pappa Deus **42**
Piazzolla Tango **32**
Plaza Bar **21**
Plaza Dorrego Bar **41**
Rey Castro **36**
The Shamrock **5**
Tango Queer **46**
Teatro Coliseo **9**
Teatro Colón **11**
Teatro Gran Rex **24**
Teatro Municipal General
  San Martín **15**
Teatro Nacional Cervantes **10**
Teatro Opera **25**
Teatro Presidente Alvear **13**

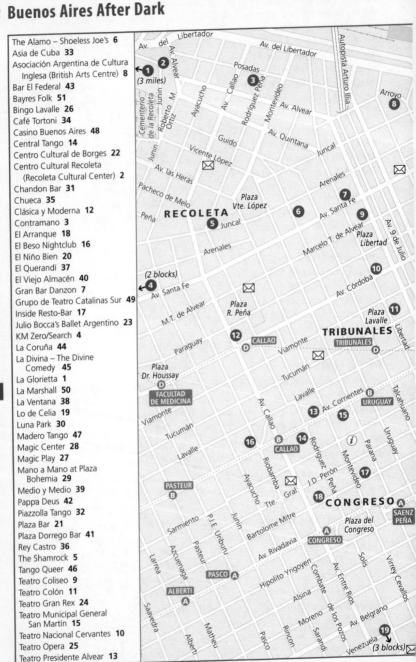

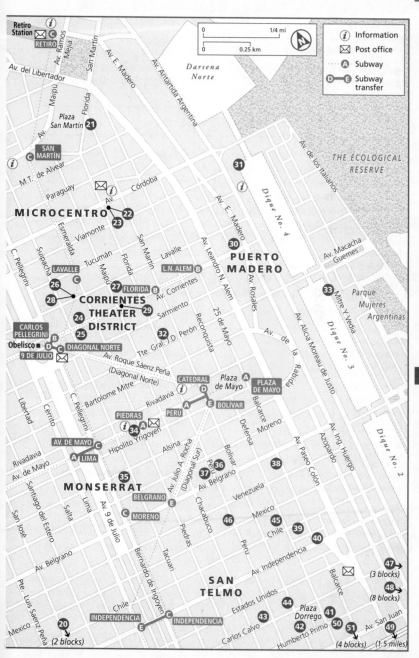

Teatro Opera This futuristic, streamlined Art Deco theater has been adapted for Broadway-style shows. The building itself is a unique and rare example of Art Deco in Buenos Aires. The facade has undergone a partial renovation that has revealed the lightning-bolt glass panels once hidden by advertising signs. Av. Corrientes 860 (at Suipacha). ℂ **11/4326-1335.** Metro: Carlos Pellegrini.

Teatro Presidente Alvear You'll find tango and other music shows at this theater. Av. Corrientes 1659 (at Montevideo). ℂ **11/4374-6076.** Tickets $3–$16 (£2.15–£11). Metro: Callao.

2 DANCE CLUBS

Dancing in Buenos Aires is not just about tango; in fact, the majority of the younger population prefers salsa and European techno. Of course, nothing in life changes quite so fast as the "in" discos, so ask around for the latest hot spots. The biggest nights out in Buenos Aires are Thursday, Friday, and Saturday. Generally, clubs open around midnight, but they don't get busy until 2 or 3am, and they close around 7am. The websites www.adondevamos.com and www.bsasinsomnio.com.ar are great resources for Buenos Aires nightlife. Club entry will generally run $10 to $15 (£7.10–£11). Young women should take note that young Argentine men can be very aggressive in their approach techniques in bars and nightclubs. Most of the advances are harmless, however, even if they may be annoying. Take note that while smoking is officially banned in all indoor spaces in Buenos Aires, most venues take a laissez-faire attitude toward folks lighting up.

Asia de Cuba ★ Come early for a meal at this supper club, and entertain yourself with sophisticated drinking and dancing under the golden Buddha. It's also a place where women are not as likely to be harassed by men on the prowl. P. Dealessi 750 (at Guemes, on Dique 3). ℂ **11/4894-1328** or 11/4894-1329. www.asiadecuba.com.ar. No cover. No metro access.

Kika This club, tucked away in what was once a railroad warehouse, attracts a young, fun Palermo Soho crowd. Most of the music is danceable rock and techno. Honduras 5339 at Juan B. Justo. ℂ **11/4551-6551;** www.kikaclub.com.ar. Cover 40 pesos ($11/£7.80). Metro: Federico Lacroze.

La Diosa A mix of club and resto-bar, La Diosa opens as early as 9:30pm for dinner Thursday through Saturday, but the music is the highlight of the club, which gets a young, glamorous crowd. Rafael Obligado 3731 off Av. Costanera Norte. ℂ **11/4806-9443** or 11/15-4997-2082 (cell); www.ladiosabuenosaires.com.ar. Cover 50 pesos ($14/£9.50). No metro access.

Pachá ★ This club is inside the Costa Salguero riverfront industrial complex, near Palermo, but far enough away to prevent waking up the neighbors. It's modeled in music and style after the iconic Ibiza nightclub. Call ahead for VIP tables. Av Costanera Norte at Pampa. ℂ **11/4788-4280;** www.pachabuenosaires.com. Cover 50 pesos ($14/£9.50). No metro access.

Salsón Some of the city's best salsa dancers stop into this place to boogie the night away. If you want to improve your step, lessons are given on Wednesday and Friday at 9pm. Av. Alvarez Thomas 1166 (at El Cano). ℂ **11/4137-5311.** Cover 30 pesos ($8/£5.70). No metro access.

Tequila Packed every night, this megaclub has a great mix of Latin music and techno. Av. Costanera Norte and La Pampa. ℂ **11/4788-0438** or 11/4781-6555. Cover 40 pesos ($11/£7.60). No metro access.

There is no shortage of popular bars in Buenos Aires, and Porteños need little excuse to party. While dancing isn't the main point at some of them, with DJs spinning into the night, it happens. The following are only a few of the many bars and pubs worthy of recommendation. Strolling along, you're sure to find plenty on your own. You're really in luck when you catch a bachelor or bachelorette party out on the town; they'll be happy to have you come along as friends who embarrass the soon-to-be wedded. Most smoking now takes place outside, though you'll still find plenty of people breaking the ban indoors. Also see section 6 of this chapter for information on gay bars and clubs.

The Alamo-Shoeless Joe's   No matter what time of day it is, you'll find something going on at this American-owned 24/7 bar. The El Alamo-Shoeless Joe's was originally simply called Shoeless Joe's, but when the Texas-born owner Pete found Argentines could not pronounce it, he added an homage to his home state in the name. It's a great gathering place for football games and other American sports events, but even locals come too. Decor is full of wood, with a vaguely "Cheers"-type feel. Breakfast specials are a treat after being out all night clubbing, and there's beer of all kinds by the bottle or on tap in huge pitchers, along with student discounts, free pizza during the happy hour from 8 to 10pm during the week, and other bargains. Food is a simple selection, with most entrees about $3 to $10 (£2.15–£7.10). With the free Internet station, you'll find another reason to come by. Uruguay 1175 and 1177 (btw. Santa Fe and Arenales). © 11/4813-7324. www.elalamobar.com. Metro: Callao.

Chandon Bar   This intimate champagne lounge serves bottles and flutes of Chandon, produced in France and Argentina. In Puerto Madero, adjacent to some of the city's best restaurants, Chandon is perfect for drinks before or after dinner. Light fare is served as well. Av. Alicia Moreau de Justo 152 at Alvear. © 11/4315-3533. Metro: L. N. Alem.

Cronico Bar   The bar has overlooked Plaza Serrano for over 20 years, and its movie posters outside are probably the first thing you'll notice. Inside, you'll find a busy place where people sit at tables painted with nude women in the style of Picasso. There's typical bar food, such as sandwiches and hamburgers, but with a larger menu than most of the surrounding bars. Live rock music sometimes entertains the crowd. Borges 1646 (at Plaza Serrano). © 11/4833-0708. Metro: Plaza Italia.

Gran Bar Danzon   A small, intimate bar, Danzon attracts a fashionable crowd with its small selection of international food and smart, relaxing lounge music. An excellent barman serves exquisite cocktails. Libertad 1161 at Santa Fe. © 11/4811-1108. www.granbardanzon.com.ar. Metro: San Martin.

Jackie O. ★   It might be named for America's favorite First Lady, but this bar seems more English in style than American, with its wood-paneled interior and classic paned windows. Always crowded, even on a Monday, it's an important and very busy fixture on the Las Cañitas bar scene. With three levels, including a covered rooftop patio, it's also one of the largest. A simple menu of Argentine and American food is served, and many patrons come early to eat and then stay to linger over drinks with the rowdy crowd. Báez 334 (at Arguibel). © 11/4774-4844. Metro: Carranza.

La Divina—The Divine Comedy   With a purple-silhouetted naked woman adorning the entry, you might wonder if this is a strip joint or trannie bar. Instead, you'll come across a bit of Miami, a bit of Palermo, and a bit of London thrown together. La Divina,

with a nod to Dante, is a resto-bar upstairs, all in blue for heaven, and in red downstairs for hell, where DJs spin in a tight space for dancing. It's an unusually modern space in retro San Telmo. Defensa 683 (at Chile). ✆ 11/4343-8342. Metro: Moreno.

Macondo Bar ★★ Macondo Bar is one of the stars of Plaza Serrano, with sidewalk seating and lots of levels overlooking the action. Inside, the restaurant twists around several staircases and low ceilings. It's a loud and busy place for sure, but the setup adds a certain sense of intimacy when sharing conversation with friends over drinks and a meal. DJs blast music of all kinds through the bar, from folkloric to techno to electronica. Technically there's no live music, but sometimes people come around and play on the street in front of the bar. Borges 1810 (at Plaza Serrano). ✆ 11/4831-4174. Metro: Plaza Italia.

OMM Bar ★ A small, casual resto-bar by day, it transforms into a crowded, sweaty bar with DJ and dancing on select nights and weekends. At the corner of once-seedy Godoy Cruz, this bar still has an edge to it, something lost in most places in Palermo Viejo as the area gentrifies. Make sure to visit the rooftop terrace. Costa Rica 5198 (at Godoy Cruz). ✆ 11/4773-0954. Metro: Palermo.

Plaza Bar Nearly every Argentine president and his or her cabinet have come here, in addition to visiting celebs such as the queen of Spain, the emperor of Japan, Luciano Pavarotti, and David Copperfield. A vague mix of Art Deco and English country, the bar features mahogany furniture and velvet upholstery, where guests sip martinis and other high-end drinks. Tuxedo-clad waiters recommend a fine selection of whiskeys and brandies. In 2005, *Forbes* magazine declared it among the world's top nine hotel bars, based on several factors—the clientele, the beverage selection, and the way the staff makes everyone feel welcome, even if they come only once in a lifetime. This was at one time the city's most famous cigar bar, but the 2006 anti-smoking law put an end to that decades-long tradition. Nevertheless, add it to your list of things to do. Inside the Marriott Plaza Hotel, Calle Florida 1005 (at Santa Fe, overlooking Plaza San Martín). ✆ 11/4318-3000. Metro: San Martín.

Plaza Dorrego Bar ★ Representative of a typical Porteño bar from the 19th century, Plaza Dorrego displays portraits of Carlos Gardel, antique liquor bottles in cases along the walls, and anonymous writings engraved in the wood. Stop by on Sunday, when the crowd spills onto the street and you can catch the San Telmo antiques market on the plaza in front. Calle Defensa 1098 (at Humberto Primo, overlooking Plaza Dorrego). ✆ 11/4361-0141. Metro: Constitución.

Rey Castro ★ A giant statue of Castro greets you as you enter this club and restaurant. There's an excellent Caribbean menu, and hot salsa and Latin dancing on two levels. From Monday to Thursday, come for the happy hour from 6 to 9:30pm, with an emphasis on *mojitos* and *Cuba Libres*. Calle Peru 342 (at Moreno). ✆ 11/4342-9998; www.reycastro.com. Metro: Moreno.

The Shamrock The city's best-known Irish pub is lacking in authenticity; you're more likely to hear hot Latin rhythms than soft Gaelic music here. That said, it remains hugely popular with both Argentines and foreign visitors, and it's a great spot to begin the night. There is an enormous game room with pool tables and other attractions in the basement. Rodríguez Peña 1220 (at Juncal). ✆ 11/4812-3584. Metro: Callao.

Soul Café and SuperSoul ★★ This retro, funky 1970s-style bar complex is the centerpiece of the Las Cañitas bar scene. Two bars in one, you'll find one side might be more happening than the other, depending on what night you go. Deep inside the space is a small lounge area with live music. There's a velvet rope, but don't get the glamour worries—it's just for show. As long as there's space back there, everyone can have a seat or stand up and watch. Still, most of the action takes place in the front bar, and if you're looking to maybe get lucky Buenos Aires–style, this might be the place to check out on your trip. Báez 352 (at Arguibel). © **11/4776-3905.** Metro: Carranza.

Sugar ★★ Owned by two Brits and an American, this Palermo Soho spot has become trendy with English-speaking expats who have decided to make Buenos Aires their home. When major news or athletic events happen of interest to the English-speaking world, this is where people gather to watch it. There's an inexpensive bar menu, with inexpensive comfort food ranging from $5 to $10 (£3.55–£7.10). On nights and weekends, come for the 5-pesos-a-drink happy hour from 8pm to midnight, and mingling to DJ music. Costa Rica 4619 (at Armenia). © **11/15-6894-2002** (cell). www.sugarbuenosaires.com. No metro access.

Tazz ★ Mexican food for snacking is the highlight of this place, with its blue spaceship-themed interior. The sidewalk space overlooking Plaza Serrano is one of the largest, so this is a great place to come in the summer or in warm weather, even though the crowd here is very young. Serrano 1556 (at Plaza Serrano). © **11/4833-5164.** www.tazzbars.com. Metro: Plaza Italia.

Utopia Bar More cozy and calm than some of the other bars that surround Plaza Serrano, this is an excellent place to grab a drink and a bite to eat in this very trendy area. Yellow walls and soothing rustic wood tables add a sense of calm, though the live music, scheduled on an irregular basis, can be loud at times. Flavored coffees are one of the specialties here. The upstairs, open-air terrace on the roof of the bar is one of the best spots to sit, but its small size, with just a few tables, makes it hard to claim a spot. Because Utopia is open 24 hours, you never have to worry about where you can get a drink at anytime of the night or day. Serrano 1590 (at Plaza Serrano). © **11/4831-8572.** Metro: Plaza Italia.

Van Koning With a model of Van Gogh and its Dutch beers on tap, this is where you go to party Netherlands-style, making sure to toast Princess Maxima, the Argentine beauty who will one day be a Dutch queen. Anyone is welcome to come here, of course, but the first Wednesday of every month around 11pm is when local Dutch expats gather for a communal bash. Báez 325 (at Arguibel). © **11/4772-9909.** Metro: Carranza.

BARS & RESTAURANTS WITH ENTERTAINMENT

You will find that many bars in Buenos Aires offer shows, from flamenco to readings to tango and folkloric dance shows. Here are just a few I recommend, though you'll likely come across many others in your nocturnal wanderings.

Clásica y Moderna ★ This is a combination restaurant and bookstore (p. 199) and a *café notable,* protected in the interest of historical patrimony. Events of all kinds are held here, from literary readings to plays, dance shows, and art exhibitions. Shows are held from Wednesday to Saturday at around 10pm, and there are sometimes two shows, the second one beginning after midnight. Show prices vary from $5 to $8 (£3.55–£5.70) and are not included in the price of dining here. Reservations are recommended for shows. Callao 892 (at Córdoba). © **11/4812-8707** or 11/4811-3670. www.clasicaymoderna.com. Metro: Callao.

Medio y Medio ★★ At night, starting at 10pm, you can stuff yourself and be entertained by Spanish and folkloric singers and guitar players. They charge a 1.50 peso (40¢/28p) service for this pleasure, but don't worry: Beer is cheaper if you buy it with a meal during the show, so that more than makes up for the charge. Chile 316 (at Defensa). ✆ 11/4300-7007. Metro: Independencia.

Pappa Deus ★ An interesting menu, live music shows, folkloric dancing, and jazz on Friday and Saturday nights make this place one of the best alternatives to the tango venues along Dorrego Plaza. Weekdays are much quieter, especially in the upstairs loft, which is a romantic setting for couples who want a break from strolling along the streets of San Telmo. This bar recently relocated from around the corner. Humberto Primo 499 (at Bolívar, near Plaza Dorrego). ✆ 11/4307-1751. Metro: Independencia.

República de Acá ★★ Charcoal drawings of Hollywood actors and other stars decorate the walls of this fun comedy club and karaoke bar overlooking Plaza Serrano. Drinks are the main event here, but food includes pizzas, *picadas* (plates of cut cheese and meat that you "pick at"), salads, and other easy-to-make small items. Drinks come with free use of the Internet, and the menu tells how many minutes of Internet use are included with each drink. About half of this club is taken up by computers. Prices of drinks rise by about 10% after 11pm. At night, the shows begin, and there is entertainment of all kinds. On weekends, live music shows begin at 10pm, followed by comedy routines at 12:30am, karaoke at 3am, and then dancing until way past sunrise. There is a $5 (£3.55) entrance fee after 10pm on weekends, which includes one drink. After 2am, this drops to a little over $3 (£2.15) to enter and still includes one drink. Many mixed drinks are made with ice cream, an adult interpretation of soda floats. TVs wrap around the whole space, so there is always something to watch. Serrano 1549 (at Plaza Serrano). ✆ 11/4581-0278. www.republicadeaca.com.ar. Metro: Plaza Italia.

HISTORICAL BARS & BARES NOTABLES

Buenos Aires is blessed with a large collection of historical bars, cafes, pubs, and restaurants. Most of these are concentrated in San Telmo, Monserrat, the Microcentro, and other older areas of the city. I highly recommend checking them out all over the city, and I have listed some of them in various sections of this book, including the "Where to Dine" chapter. Below are just a few highlights. You should ask for the *Bares y Cafés Notables* map from the Buenos Aires tourism kiosks to see more of these remarkable spaces, which I hope will be preserved.

Bar El Federal ★★ This bar and restaurant, on a quiet corner in San Telmo, represents a beautiful step back in time. It has been in business since 1864, and fortunately, as another *café notable*, it will be preserved forever. The first thing that will strike you here is the massive, carved-wood and stained-glass ornamental stand over the bar area, which originally came from an old pastry shop. Local patrons sit at the old tables whiling away their time looking out onto the streets, chatting, or sitting with a book and drinking tea or espresso. The original tile floor remains, and old signs, portraits, and small antique machines decorate the space. Bar El Federal is among the most Porteño of places in San Telmo, a neighborhood that has more of these establishments than any other. Some of the staff have been here for decades on end, and proudly so. Corner of Perú and Carlos Calvo. ✆ 11/4300-4313. Metro: Independencia.

La Coruña ★ This extremely authentic old cafe and restaurant bar, another of the *cafés notables* protected by law, is the kind of place where you'd expect your grandfather to have eaten when he was a teenager. Young and old alike come to this bar, which is a very neighborhoody spot, with people catching *fútbol* games on television or quietly chatting away as they order beer, small snacks, and sandwiches. The TV seems to be the only modern thing in here. Music plays from a wooden table-top radio that must be from the 1950s, and two wooden refrigerators dating from who knows when are still in use for storing food. The old couple that owns the place, José Moreira and Manuela Lopéz, obviously subscribe to the view that if it ain't broke, there's no reason for a new one. Bolívar 994 (at Carlos Calvo). ✆ **11/4362-7637.** Metro: Independencia.

RESTAURANTS WITH BARS WORTH CHECKING OUT

Bar Uriarte ★ While best known for its excellent cuisine, the name says it all. The mod, very long bar, is an excellent place for drinks, whether you're dining here or elsewhere. Look for drink specials during the 8 to 10:30pm happy hour. Uriarte 1572 (btw. Honduras and Gorritti). ✆ **11/4834-6004.** www.baruriarte.com.ar. Metro: Plaza Italia.

Olsen ★★ Special glass-faced freezers hover over the bar in this Scandinavian restaurant, with a teasing array of vodkas. There are more than 60 choices from around the world, including some specially made for Olsen itself. Enjoy a drink outdoors in the overgrown garden patio, which looks like a living room that has succumbed to nature, or around the central potbellied stove, reminiscent of a 1960s ski-lodge lounge. Olsen is closed on Monday. Gorriti 5870 (at Carranza). ✆ **11/4776-7677.** restaurantolsen@netizon.com.ar. No metro access.

Sullivan's Drink House ★ Many come for the Irish food in this restaurant, but its huge rooftop VIP lounge, which is open to all, serves the best of Irish and English whiskeys. Sullivan's is also a fun choice if you're in town for St. Patrick's Day. El Salvador 4919 (at Borges). ✆ **11/4832-6442.** Metro: Scalabrini Ortiz.

4 TANGO SHOW PALACES

With tango as the main draw, Buenos Aires says, "Let me entertain you." Numerous show palaces, from the simple Café Tortoni (p. 97) to the over-the-top, special-effects-laden Señor Tango, compete for your tourist dollar. All of the shows are excellent, and each is surprisingly unique, proving that tango can mean many things to many people, the performers themselves most of all. Here, I've listed some of the top shows, but new ones seem to open up every other week. Many of the show palaces include dinner, or you can arrive just in time for the show only. Usually the price differential is minimal for seeing only the show, making it worth coming early for dinner. Prices vary tremendously, depending on the venue and how you have booked; the price for show-only is around $50 to $75 (£36–£53), with dinner-and-show about $100 to $120 (£71–£85). Seeing a variety of tango palaces is important, as each show has its own style. Smaller spaces lead to a greater intimacy and more interaction between the dancers and the audience. Sometimes the dancers even grab a few people, so watch out if you're close to the stage! Some of these shows, such as Señor Tango and El Viejo Almacén, have bus services that pick you up at your hotel. Book directly, or ask your hotel concierge for help and bus transfer times, which can be up to an hour before the event. Many local bars also have informal tango shows, where locals come to see decades-old favorites singing. Look for signs in windows, or wander in if you catch one while walking around.

Bocatango This show celebrates tango at one of the neighborhoods associated with its early development. The enormous hall is highlighted by a stage set mimicking the colorful La Boca streets outside. Watch as dancers recount the history and excitement of Buenos Aires's Little Italy from the windows and balconies of their *conventillos,* a form of

(Moments) **Tango: Lessons in the Dance of Seduction & Despair**

It seems impossible to imagine Argentina without thinking of tango, its greatest export to the world. Tango originated with a guitar and violin toward the end of the 19th century and was first danced by working-class men in La Boca, San Telmo, and the port area. Combining African rhythms with the *habanera* and *candombe,* it was not the sophisticated dance you know today—rather, the tango originated in brothels, known locally as *quilombos.* At that time the dance was considered too obscene for women, and as they waited their turn, men would dance it with each other in the brothel lounges.

Increasing waves of immigrants added Italian elements to the tango and helped the dance make its way to Europe, where it was internationalized in Paris. With a sense of European approval, Argentine middle and upper classes began to accept the newly refined dance as part of their cultural identity, and the form blossomed under the extraordinary voice of Carlos Gardel, who brought tango to Broadway and Hollywood, and is nothing short of legendary among Argentines. Astor Piazzolla further internationalized the tango, elevating it to a more complex form incorporating classical elements.

Tango music can range from two musicians to a complete orchestra, but a piano and *bandoneón*—an instrument akin to an accordion—are usually included. If there is a singer, the lyrics might come from one of Argentina's great poets, such as Jorge Luis Borges, Homero Manzi, or Horacio Ferrer. Themes focus on a downtrodden life or a woman's betrayal, making it akin to American jazz and blues, which developed at the same time. The dance itself is improvised rather than standardized, although it consists of a series of long walks and intertwined movements, usually in eight-step. In the tango, the man and woman glide across

slum housing that is characteristic of the area. Your meal is served in an Italian bistro setting, and the food is good enough to make you wonder if Mamma is back there somewhere in the kitchen. Transportation is provided from your hotel. Brandsen 923 (at Practico Poliza). ✆ 11/4302-0808. www.bocatango.com.ar. No metro access.

Café Tortoni ★★   High-quality yet inexpensive tango shows are held in the back room of the Café Tortoni and do not include dinner. There is a show from Wednesday through Monday at 9pm. The tight space here is not for the claustrophobic. What makes some of the Café Tortoni tango shows extremely unique is that women, rather than men, are the main focus. Visit their website for more information and a description of all the upcoming shows including tango, jazz, children's theater, and more. Av. de Mayo 829 (at Piedras). ✆ 11/4342-4328. www.cafetortoni.com.ar. Tickets $10 (£7.10). Metro: Plaza de Mayo.

Central Tango   Among the newest of the shows, Central Tango has eight dancers, two singers, and a six-musician orchestra. Shows are Monday through Saturday; dinner begins at 8:30pm followed by the show at 10:15pm. Rodríguez Peña 361 (at Corrientes). ✆ 11/5236-0055. No metro access.

the floor as an exquisitely orchestrated duo with early flirtatious movements giving way to dramatic leads and heartfelt turns, with the man always leading the way. These movements, such as the kicks that simulate knife movements, or the sliding, shuffled feet that mimic the walk of a gangster silently walking up to murder someone, belie its rough roots when it was the favored dance of La Boca gangsters, in spite of its intense beauty as performed nowadays.

Learning to dance the tango is an excellent way for a visitor to get a sense of what makes the music—and the dance—so alluring. Entering a tango salon—called a *salón de baile* or *milonga*—can be intimidating for the novice. The style of tango danced in salons is more subdued than "show tango." Most respectable dancers would not show up before midnight, giving you the perfect opportunity to sneak in for a group lesson, offered at most of the salons starting around 7 to 9pm. They usually cost between $5 to $8 (£3.55–£5.70) for an hour; you can request private instruction for between $20 and $40 (£14–£28) per hour, depending on the instructor. In summer, the city of Buenos Aires promotes tango by offering free classes in many locations. Visit the nearest tourist information center for updated information. Before you head to Argentina, free tango lessons are also provided by select Argentine consulates in the United States (p. 22 has consulate information).

For additional advice on places to dance and learn tango, get a copy of *B.A. Tango* or *El Tangauta,* the city's dedicated tango magazines. Ongoing evening lessons are also offered at the **Academia Nacional de Tango,** located above Café Tortoni, at Av. de Mayo 833 (ⓒ **11/4345-6968**), which is an institute rather than a tango salon.

Complejo Tango This creative show presents a long range of entertainment for patrons. It begins with an optional tango lesson at 7:30pm, then dinner at 9pm, followed by the show at 10pm. The main hall is in an old converted house with a platform in the middle and a retro interior that looks a bit like a stage set for old New Orleans. The show has three singers, three couples of dancers, and a four-person orchestra providing the music for the show, with international-style dancing, a little bit of folklore, and a humorous presentation. Transportation is provided to and from hotels. Av. Belgrano 2608 (at Saavedra). ⓒ **11/4941-1119** or 11/4308-3242. www.complejotango.com.ar. Metro: Miserere.

El Querandí ★★ El Querandí has the best historically based tango show in the city, showing it from its early bordello roots when only men danced it, to its current leggy, sexy style. You'll also get a great slab of beef and a glass of wine with the show. It's open Monday through Saturday; dinner begins at 8:30pm, followed by the show at 10:15pm. Perú 302 (at Moreno). ⓒ **11/4345-0331.** Metro: Bolívar, Peru.

El Viejo Almacén Shows here involve traditional Argentine-style tango, with little emphasis on the splashy Hollywood style of tango seen in other places such as Señor Tango. Sunday through Thursday shows are at 10pm; Friday and Saturday shows are at 9:30 and 11:45pm. Dinner is served each night before the show starts in the three-story restaurant across the street (guests may opt for dinner-show or show only). Transportation is offered from some hotels. Independencia and Balcarce. ℂ **11/4307-6689.** Metro: Independencia.

Esquina Carlos Gardel ★★ The show here begins with the orchestra playing sad tangos, and then opens up with such a powerful and emotional rendition of Carlos Gardel's signature song, "Mi Buenos Aires Querido" that you'll almost feel like crying. This is perhaps the most elegant of the tango show palaces, built over the location of "Chanta Cuatro"—a restaurant where Carlos Gardel used to dine with his friends and across the street from the Abasto Shopping Center, another location associated with him (p. 193). The luxurious old-time-style dining room here features high-tech acoustics and superb dancers, creating a wonderful tango environment. Doors open at 8pm. Carlos Gardel 3200 (at Anchorena, overlooking Abasto Shopping Center). ℂ **11/4876-6363.** Metro: Carlos Gardel.

La Ventana This show is held in the atmospheric brick-lined cellar of an old building in San Telmo. Performances are a mix of tango, folkloric, and other Argentine styles of dance and music. One of the highlights of the night is a schmaltzy rendition of "Don't Cry for Me, Argentina" complete with a movable balcony and rather glamorous *descamisados* (shirtless ones) holding Argentine flags. Balcarce 431 (at Venezuela). ℂ **11/4331-1314.** www.la-ventana.com.ar. Metro: Belgrano.

Madero Tango Madero Tango prides itself not just on what you see onstage but what you see outside its terraces, too. Located in the Puerto Madero area, this building extends along the waterfront of San Telmo, overlooking the port and boats in the water. It's a more modern, chic, and spacious setting than most of the tango shows in Buenos Aires, and the shows are a bit splashy, too. E. Rawson de Dellepiane 150, Dock 1; alternate address is Moreau de Justo 2100 (at port beginning near where autopista skirts the waterfront). ℂ **11/4314-6688.** www.maderotango.com.ar. No metro access.

Piazzolla Tango This tango show spectacular is held in a stunning theater, an Art Nouveau masterpiece created by the architect who designed the now-closed Confitería del Molino, next-door to Congreso. This theater had been closed for nearly 40 years and was only recently restored. Of all the tango show palaces in Buenos Aires, this is the most beautiful, which adds even more excitement to the well-choreographed show. Calle Florida 165 (at Perón). ℂ **11/4344-8201.** www.piazzollatango.com. Metro: Florida.

Señor Tango This enormous space is more akin to a Broadway production theater than to a traditional tango salon, but the dancers are fantastic and the owner, who clearly loves to perform, is a good singer. The odd shows combine tango, Fosse-esque routines, and even live horses on the rotating stage. The walls are decorated with photos of what appears to be every celebrity who's ever visited Buenos Aires—and all seem to have made it to Señor Tango! Have dinner or come only for the show (dinner is at 8:30pm; shows start at 10pm). Diners choose among steak, chicken, or fish for dinner and, despite the huge crowd, the food quality is commendable. Vieytes 1653 (at Villarino). ℂ **11/4303-0212.** No metro access.

5 MILONGAS (TANGO SALONS & DANCE HALLS)

While the show palaces and their dance shows are wonderful must-sees, there is nothing like the amazing lure of the *milonga* (tango salon) on a trip to Buenos Aires. As with the show palaces, there are more now than ever before. Rather than destroy tango, the peso crisis has created a greater awareness of all things traditionally Argentine. In the same way that the ancestors of today's Porteños turned to tango more than 100 years ago to alleviate their pain, isolation, and worries with a night of dancing away their melancholy, so too have modern Porteños, creating an unprecedented boom in rapidly opening *milongas.* This, coupled with the increase in tourism and expats from Europe and North America who have decided to move here and tango their lives away, means that there are more choices for dancing than ever before. This scene is not without its rules and obstacles, however, especially in terms of how to act with dancers of the opposite sex. Be sure to read "Some Tango Rules" (see below) to get some tips on *milonga* behavior for foreigners before heading out. There's usually an entry fee to a *milonga* of $5 to $8 (£3.55–£5.70).

You should also pick up the *Tango Map,* which has a comprehensive guide to *milongas* in all regions of the city. Find it at the tourism kiosks, the various tango-associated venues listed in this book, and also in select locations in San Telmo. Be aware that the same location may have different events by different names, so keeping track of the address of the venue is important. Also, double-check the listings in **B.A. Tango, El Tangauta,** and **La Milonga,** the city's main tango magazines. Also look for **Punto Tango,** a pocket-size guide with similar information. The numbers that are listed in this section and within the magazines or maps are not necessarily those of the venues, but may be the numbers of the various dance organizations or individual promoters that hold events within the specific dance venue on any given night. See also section 6 of this chapter for gay tango salons that have blossomed on the scene.

El Arranque (Finds) This dance venue looks like a Knights of Columbus hall, but it's one of the most authentic venues for *milongas;* it's also one of the few places that host afternoon dancing. Tango's late-night schedule could drive even a vampire crazy, but here you can dance and still get a real night's sleep afterward. No matter how old and pot-bellied a man is, he can be with any woman in the crowd as long as he dances well. Even older women, however, tend to keep up appearances here, dressing beautifully and stylishly. This place will be very comfortable for older crowds. They strictly enforce traditional tango rules about separating the sexes, however; couples might not even be allowed to sit together. Dancing begins most afternoons at 3pm. Closed Monday. Bartolomé Mitre 1759 (at Callao). © 11/4371-6767. Cover $8 (£5.70). Metro: Congreso.

El Beso Nightclub (Finds) The way to this club may be a little confusing, but follow my directions and you'll be fine. It's unmarked, so the street address is your only indication that you're in the right spot. Walk upstairs, pay your fee, and squeeze past the crowded bar blocking your view. The small space beyond maintains the air of a 1940s nightclub, updated for the modern era with brilliant reds and modern abstractions painted on some walls. Ceiling lamps made from car air filters cast a golden glow on the dancers. Some of the best performers drag their egos with them to the floor, so if you're not so good on your feet, just watch; the last thing you want is to bump into someone. The divisions between the *milongueras* and *milongueros* are not so strong, and the sexes tend to mix informally. Reserve a table ahead of time if you can. Different *milongas* take place on different nights. Check the calendar in advance for details. Snacks, wines, and beers are on sale. Riobamba 416 (at Corrientes). © 11/4953-2794 or 11/15-4938-8108 (cell). Cover $5 (£3.55). Metro: Callao.

El Niño Bien ★★ (Finds) If you want to travel back in time, to an era when tango ruled Buenos Aires, few places will do you better than El Niño Bien. The beautiful main

Tips ## Some Tango Rules

Certainly the seductive sound of the tango is one of the reasons you came to Buenos Aires in the first place. Maybe you just want to see some people perform those fancy kicks and moves onstage. Maybe you'd like to learn some of the steps yourself. Or maybe you're nearly an expert and want your own turn on some of the wooden dance floors where Buenos Aires's best have danced for decades. Whatever your objectives or level of interest, you can do all or any of those options with the choices I have laid out for you in this chapter.

The only places most tourists see tango in Buenos Aires are in the big, and expensive, show palace-restaurants, which feature dancers onstage as tourists eat meals with steak as the centerpiece. While aimed at tourists, the quality of each of these shows is superb, and even the most jaded Porteño cannot help but be impressed by what is onstage. In spite of the quantity of these stage spectaculars, each is also different in its own right. Some concentrate on the dance's history, others the intimacy with the audience; some throw in other dance forms, especially folkloric, or seem to forget tango al together.

However, I think every tourist should also venture out and see more than just those shows if time permits. Head to a *milonga*, a place where the dance is done by those who know it well (usually following a strict protocol of interactions between the sexes). A key concept in these places refers to the *milonga* eyes—perhaps you've heard fairy tales about two sets of eyes meeting across the room and then finding their way to each other on the dance floor. In some *milongas*, men and women sit on different sides of the room, couples only blending together in certain spots. Men and women will try to catch each other's eyes this way, flirting across the smoke-filled distance, adding nods, smiles, and sometimes hand movements for increased effect. The man finally approaches the woman, offering to dance. Often, there is not even a word between the two at this stage until they take the floor.

dance hall is straight from the Belle Epoque; you'll half-expect Carlos Gardel himself to show up behind the mike. Dressed in black, men and women tango, as patrons at side tables respectfully study their techniques. Don't look too closely at anyone, however, unless you know what you're doing: *Milonga* eyes—staring across a room to attract a partner onto the dance floor—are taken seriously. Food is served, but don't bother unless you're famished; it's only so-so. Unfortunately, Niño Bien is becoming a victim of its own success, and many tour groups are starting to unload here. If you're looking to find a tango teacher, one will probably find you first at this venue; many instructors come here seeking students for private lessons. Centro Región Leonesa, Humberto I no. 1462 (at San José). ✆ 11/4483-2588. Cover $5–$6 (£3.55–£4.25). No metro access.

La Glorietta (Finds)   Tangoing in the open air is the highlight of this *milonga*. It also opens in the afternoon, so it is perfect for people who want to experience tango but not be out very late. Snacks and tostados are served. It can be slightly touristy. There's a show at 1am on Friday and Saturday. Once de Septiembre and Echeverria. ✆ 11/4674-1026. Cover $5 (£3.55). No metro access.

This ritual means that tourists need to be aware of a few things. Firstly, never, ever block anyone's view, especially a woman who is sitting by herself. Be aware of divisions between the sexes in seating (which might be enforced by the management anyway for newcomers), and follow the rules. As a foreigner, some very strict places might tell you they simply have no seats; you can overcome this obstacle by saying you are looking for a friend who arrived earlier. Avoid eye contact with members of the opposite sex if you have no idea what you're doing. You might be inviting a dance when all you want to do is watch, confusing some people who are completely absorbed in the rules of the game.

If a woman wants to dance with new men in order to practice the tango, she should not be seen entering the salon with a male friend, because most of the other men will assume she is already taken. If couples want to practice dancing with new people, they should enter the room separately. If you are coming in a group, divide yourselves up by sex for the same reason. Each *milonga*, however, maintains its own grip on these rules—some very strict, others abiding only by some. It's also best not to go to these places in large groups, and rather with a few people at a time or as a couple. The sudden entrance of a large group of noisy curious foreigners who don't know the place can instantly change the overall atmosphere. And importantly, show respect to where you are in terms of how you appear. While you needn't dress to the nines, a baseball cap and sneakers will ruin the atmosphere of the place (if they even let you in).

Find a copy of the *Tango Map*, which lists almost all of the city's *milongas*, as well as specific special events held each night. It is, incidentally, among the best maps, period, of Buenos Aires, and it even includes neighborhoods generally off the beaten tourist path.

La Viruta (Finds) This is one of the most interesting *milongas*. It is authentic, but it attracts a very young crowd of Porteños and expats who have come from all over the world to dance their lives away in Buenos Aires, where the living is good and cheap. Many nights it is just a *milonga*. Other nights host shows and competitions, many involving tango, folkloric, and modern dance. La Viruta is in the cellar of the Armenian Community Center. When decorated with balloons for some events, it looks a little like a high school prom from the 1970s. Armenia 1366 (at Cabrera). ℂ **11/4774-6357.** Cover $8 (£5.70). No metro access.

Lo de Celia (Finds) Don't let the modern setup of this place fool you: This is a very traditional *milonga* where the rules are very strictly applied. Men and women must sit on opposite sides of the dance floor, with couples blending in only at the corners. Music is provided by a DJ. The floors are made of terrazzo, which can make dancing harder on the feet than at other tango venues. The crowd here is generally mature and very experienced in tango. The strict enforcement of sexual separation means women will be treated like absolute ladies in this place. They often hold contests close to the end of the night, which are fun to watch and bring levity to some of the tense late-night tango egoists. Humberto I no. 1783 (at Solis). © **11/4932-8594.** Cover $6 (£4.25). No metro access.

Mano a Mano at Plaza Bohemia Finds   This Thursday night–only *milonga* event is run by Helen Halldórsdóttir, a native of Iceland whom tango lovers all over Buenos Aires simply call La Vikinga. She used to run a *milonga* called Bien Pulenta and uses a similar format here at her new event. It's an excellent choice, with her very welcoming tango classes from 9 to 10:30pm, and a practice *milonga* for students until just after midnight when the real one begins. But don't be intimidated, as Helen mixes up the dancing sets with live performances. There's a bit of flair with live bands, shows, and special guests such as visiting tango champions, so you'll enjoy yourself even if you're a wallflower. Ask Helen also about the line of tango shoes that she designs. Maipu 444 (at Corrientes). © **11/15-5865-8279** (cell). Cover $8 (£5.70). Metro: Florida or Lavalle.

Salón Canning Finds   This is among the most authentic of all of the *milongas*. At the end of a long hallway, spectators crowd around the main dance floor to watch couples make their way around it. Salón Canning is known for its extremely smooth, high-quality wooden parquet floor, considered one of the best for dancing in all of Buenos Aires. This tango hall is among the few things left in Buenos Aires that still bear the name of George Canning—a British diplomat who opened relations between Argentina and Great Britain after independence from Spain. Scalabrini Ortiz 1331 (at Gorriti). © **11/4832-6753.** Cover $8 (£5.70). No metro access.

TANGO TOURS

If you think you might want to try your hand at the authentic *milongas,* it would help to take some lessons beforehand or take a tour with a professional. There are literally hundreds of tours for people interested in tango here in Buenos Aires, the city where it all began. Here are just a few, and all of these people and groups also offer lessons. Also, see below where I list even more instructors (p. 231).

ABC Tango Tours   Gabriel Aspe, who is one of the co-owners of this company, also manages one of the tango shows at the Café Tortoni and is a native of Argentina. The company offers several tango show-palace event tours as well as tours to traditional tango houses. © **11/15-5697-2551** (cell). www.abctango.com.

Amantes del Tango   Eduardo and Nora offer individual tours and private lessons. Both are well-established tango performers and Nora's work has been featured in *National Geographic* magazine. © **11/4703-4104** or 11/15-5753-9131 (cell).

Buenos Aires Tango Off   This company offers several tango-themed tours, including its unusual "Dos Pasiones Argentinas," which takes the "Land of Evita and Tango" phrase to heart by combining tango lessons with a visit to the Museo Evita (though she was known to hate the dance, ironically). © **11/4829-1416** or 11/4829-1417. www.bsastangooff.com.ar.

Tango with Judy   Judy and Jon are an American tango-loving and -dancing couple who live in both Buenos Aires and Arizona. They both know the scene well and offer highly specialized and individual tango tours, some of which can be combined with lessons. They give four weekly classes and also private lessons anytime. Their work has been featured in tango magazines as well as *Caras,* a Buenos Aires celebrity gossip magazine. © **520/907-2050** or 213/536-4649 in U.S., 11/4863-5889 or 11/15-6161-1838 (cell) in Buenos Aires. www.tangowithjudy.com; tangowithjudy@hotmail.com.

Tanguera Tours   The owner, Laura Chummers, is a perky American who really knows the scene and makes it accessible for men and women of any skill level. She and her guides won't let you be a wallflower at any of the places they take you. She began by taking around only women, but now does tours for women and men. You will love her tours and the special places where she takes you. ℂ **408/298-5676** in the U.S. www.tangomina.com.ar/tanguera/index.htm.

TANGO TEACHERS

All of the above tour groups offer tango lessons, either in a group or individually. Alternatively, you can try the professional tango teachers I've listed below as well. More listings for teachers are available in the *B.A. Tango, Tangauta,* and *La Milonga* magazines. Also consider group and individual lessons through the **Escuela Argentina de Tango,** inside of the Galerias Pacifico (ℂ **11/4312-4990;** www.eatango.org).

- **Estudio Zarasa Tango, with Julio Balmaceda and Corina DeLaRosa** (Av. Independencia 2845 at Pichincha; ℂ **11/3527-7840,** or 11/15-4405-6464 and 11/15-5528-9826 [cells]; www.julioycorina.com.ar). Julio and Corina are one of the most accomplished tango couples in Buenos Aires. They have toured the world with their shows, including performing in New York's Carnegie Hall, and now impart their incredible talent to their students.

- **Julieta Lotti** (ℂ **11/4774-5654;** julietalotti@hotmail.com) has taught and danced tango for years. She is a member of the Las Fulanas troupe of dance professionals. She does not speak much English, however.

- **Maite Lujan** (ℂ **11/15-5992-5041** [cell]; maritelujan@yahoo.com) has taught tango for years and speaks English and Portuguese. She has also advised various tango clubs catering to tourists.

- **Marie Soler** (ℂ **11/15-5411-7208** [cell]; tangomariemar@hotmail.com) is a young woman who knows the tango scene well. She speaks English and often enters various competitions and shows in the La Viruta *milonga.*

- **Pedro Sánchez** (ℂ **11/4923-2774;** pedromilonguero@yahoo.com.ar) has been dancing tango for more than 50 years, and many women I know swear by his instruction methods. He speaks little English, but always makes himself understood. He will give private lessons, and also has Monday evening sessions for small groups, which might be a good way to get to know him and see his techniques.

- **Patricia Herrera (Yuyu;** ℂ **11/4805-1457;** yuyuherrer_tango@yahoo.com.ar). An excellent and patient teacher, Patricia, who goes by the nickname Yuyu, teaches from her home in Recoleta or will visit people at their home or hotel.

6 GAY & LESBIAN DANCE CLUBS, RESTO-BARS & TANGO SALONS

Buenos Aires has a thriving gay and lesbian scene. It's one of the most impressive on the South American continent, rivaled only by Brazil's Rio de Janeiro. Most of the action is centered in Barrio Norte, which has always been the traditional gay neighborhood of Buenos Aires. With the rapid gentrification of San Telmo, however, this historic neighborhood has seen many gay men move in, as well as being the site of the city's two gay hotels. Gay nightlife begins late, with few people hitting a club before 2am. Nightclubs

Buenos Aires: Latin America's Gay Tourism Capital

For the past few years, Buenos Aires has reigned as Latin America's preeminent gay travel capital. Gays and lesbians are estimated as being as high as 15% to 20% among international tourists, and many mainstream places stress their gay-friendliness. One reason for the boom is simply economics, but there has also been an effort by the city to make sure that gay tourism is officially recognized. Legal advances have also helped, with CHA (Comunidad Homosexual de Argentina) pressing for legal recognition of same-sex couples in 2003. CHA President Cesar Cigliutti and CHA Treasurer Marcelo Sondheim, long-term partners, were the first couple joined under the law. With its enormous collection of bars, dance clubs, restaurants, and tango halls catering to the community, no other city in Latin America rivals what Buenos Aires has to offer for visiting gays and lesbians. Despite all these positive advances, most gays and lesbians remain somewhat closeted, and there are few openly gay stars in the media. Violence against the transgendered is also a serious problem.

open around midnight, are busiest at 2 to 3am, and then close at around 7am. Bars might open as early as 8pm, around dinner time.

DANCE CLUBS & BARS

Amerika This is the city's most popular gay club, and even straight people come for the great music. In general, straights hang out on the uppermost level of the club near the glassed-in area that resembles a spaceship pod, while gays, lesbians, and others mix throughout the rest of the many levels in this enormous venue. Open Thursday through Sunday only. Gascón 1040 (at Córdoba). © 11/4865-4416. Cover $10 (£7.10). Metro: Angel Gallardo.

Bulnes Class ★★ A popular lounge-y venue with class, from white leather couches to crystal chandeliers, this place has some of the most handsome men in Buenos Aires socializing with friends. Bulnes 1250 (at Cabrera). © 11/4861-7492. No cover. Metro: Guemes.

Contramano Popular with a mature crowd, this was the first gay bar or dance club opened in Buenos Aires, just after the fall of the last military government in the early 1980s. The dance floor area is now closed, though may eventually reopen. Rodríguez Peña 1082 (at Alvear). No phone. Cover $4 (£2.85). No metro access.

KM Zero/Search Those who have been to Buenos Aires will remember this was formerly the Titanic Bar. It's the same space, with different themed parties and open each night of the week, including for dancing. It's popular at times with a rougher crowd than you'll find in some of the more glamorous bars. Av. Santa Fe 2516 (at Puerreydon). © 11/4822-7530. Cover $6 (£4.25) Fri–Sat and special nights. Metro: Puerreydon.

Sitges One of the city's largest and most popular gay bars. It has a stage that sometimes features very silly acts. Av. Cordoba 4119 (btw. Palestina and Pringles). © 11/4861-3763. No cover. Metro: Angel Gallardo.

RESTO-BARS

A resto-bar is an Argentine concept of a restaurant-bar combination. People either come for a meal or stop by for drinks only. In general, the bar portions of resto-bars do not get busy until after 11pm or midnight. These are more relaxed than traditional bars and it is easier to chat with locals.

Chueca   Named after the gay district in Madrid, this is one of the most popular of the city's gay resto-bars. It gets very crowded here after midnight. Alsina 975 (btw. Suipacha and Yrigoyen/9 de Julio). © 11/4334-9869. Metro: Avenida de Mayo.

Inside Resto-Bar   The waitstaff and the owners provide great, attitude-free service in this resto-bar. It's a good place to go just for drinks at their small bar, where many locals gather for conversation. On weekends, they have special tango shows and male strippers, too. Ask about their return coupons, offering great discounts for people who come back during their slow early weeknights. Bartolomé Mitre 1571 (at Montevideo). © 11/4372-5439. Metro: Congreso.

TANGO SALONS & LESSONS

Tango was originally only danced by men together, because it was at first considered too obscene a dance for women to do with men. In the modern era, gay Porteños take this a step further, with three gay tango salons bringing back old-fashioned, same-sex tango.

Bayres Folk   The new kid on the block, these events combine both same-sex tango dancing as well as folkloric and other traditional dances, including the gaucho-esque Zamba, on Monday nights, with lessons beginning at 8pm and *milonga* a few hours later. Cochabamba 360 (at Defensa). © 11/15-5654-1658 (cell). Metro: Constitution.

La Marshall   The originator of the gay tango spots in Buenos Aires, La Marshall has moved around over the years. It begins with a group lesson, then on to a show and *milonga* at Plaza Bohemia. The event is held on Wednesday only, but the La Marshall group also runs gay tango lessons on Sunday evenings at the gay hotel El Lugar Gay in San Telmo (p. 71). Maipu 444 (at Corrientes). © 11/15-5458-3423 (cell). www.lamarshall.com.ar. Metro: Florida, Lavalle.

Tango Queer   Run by women, but aimed toward both sexes, Tango Queer is an event and an organization. There's no real schedule for the *milonga* events, which may happen once a month or less often. In addition, there are shows, classes, and individual lessons for gays, lesbians, and others on Tuesday at the Buenos Aires Club. Double-check their website for events and locations. Perú 571 (at Mexico). © 11/15-3252-6894 (cell). www.tangoqueer.com. Metro: Belgrano.

7 FILM

Buenos Aires has over 250 movie theaters showing Argentine and international films. One of the best is the 16-screen **Village Recoleta,** V. López and Junín (© 11/4805-2220). There are also cinemas at two shopping malls: **Alto Palermo,** Av. Santa Fe 3251, at Agüero (© 11/4827-8000), and **Galerías Pacífico,** at Calle Florida 753 and Córdoba (© 11/4319-5357). Other convenient Microcentro locations include the six-screen **Atlas Lavalle,** Lavalle 869, at Esmeralda (© 11/5032-8527; www.atlascines.com.ar), and the four-screen **Monumental Lavalle,** Lavalle 739, at Maipú (© 11/4322-1515).

Most films are American and shown in English with Spanish subtitles; however, some are Argentine films, which are not subtitled. The average cost of a movie ticket is 15 pesos ($4/£2.85). Check the *Buenos Aires Herald* for current film listings. Every April, Buenos Aires hosts an international independent film festival (www.bafilmfest.com).

8 CASINOS, ARCADES & BINGO HALLS

There are several places in Buenos Aires for both adults and kids to test their luck. Calle Lavalle, with its bright lights and big-city tackiness, is the perfect place for adults and teenagers to drop a coin into a slot or place a bet on the table. This can often be done together with a movie viewing, since many of the cinemas are here as well.

Bingo Lavalle   If you think bingo is just for seniors living out their retirement days, think again. Porteños of all ages love bingo, and here is where you'll find some of the most competitive on a night out. This is a huge, smoke-filled space—the smokiest of any environment I've ever experienced in all of Buenos Aires. I recommend spending some time here to check out this interesting scene with its cross-section of locals. Alcoholic drinks and bar snacks are served. Bingo Lavalle is surrounded by arcades and movie theaters, but you must be at least 18 to enter. It's open Monday to Thursday from 9am to 3am, Friday 9am to 6am, Saturday noon to 6am, and Sunday noon to 3am. Lavalle 842 (at Esmeralda). ℂ 11/4322-1114. Metro: Lavalle.

Casino Buenos Aires   Feel like trying to win some money to upgrade your hotel accommodations? This 24-hour casino is the place. The casino is housed in a Mississippi riverboat parked on the Buenos Aires docks. There are over 117 gaming tables, hundreds of slot machines, and other ways to win (or lose). Parking is nearby and there are restaurants onboard. It's open 24 hours daily. Elvira Rawson de Dellepina, Darsena Sur Puerto de Buenos Aires (Southern Port beyond Puerto Madero). ℂ 11/4363-3100. No metro access.

Magic Center (Kids)   Built into an old theater, you'll find more nonelectronic games (net games and Skee-Ball) here than at most entertainment centers. It's open daily from 9am to 1am. Lavalle 845 (at Esmeralda). ℂ 11/4394-9200. Metro: Lavalle.

Magic Play (Kids)   This is a great place for the kids during the day, and teenagers later at night. Slots, racing cars, pool, and video games keep them entertained. It's open daily from 9am to 1am. Lavalle 672 (at Maipú). ℂ 11/4322-5702. Metro: Lavalle.

Side Trips from Buenos Aires

If you're spending more than 4 or 5 days in Buenos Aires, you might want to consider taking a side trip—especially if you're visiting in summer, when many Porteños have already fled town.

During the summer months, Porteños hit the beach resorts. **Mar del Plata** is the country's most popular resort area. During the summer season, so many people head here from Buenos Aires that the capital can feel like a ghost town in certain neighborhoods. Calling Mar del Plata crowded is an understatement, as more than eight million people visit this city during the summer months.

Just outside of Buenos Aires's suburbs is the **Tigre Delta,** a beautiful complex of islands and marshland full of small bed-and-breakfasts, resorts, and adventure trails. You can take a day trip here on mass transit from Buenos Aires or make it an overnight stay.

Gualeguaychú, little known outside of Argentina, is home to the national Carnaval, a 2-month-long spectacle held in January and February. While it doesn't rival Rio's big party, it makes for a very fun excursion nevertheless. The small size of the town means it's also an easy place to meet people involved in the event on the streets or in the local bars.

Just over the river in Uruguay is the day-tripper's paradise of **Colonia,** a UNESCO Heritage City, less than an hour away by boat.

The Pampas surround Buenos Aires, and here's where to go to find gaucho culture. The main town at the center of it all is **San Antonio de Areco,** about 1 1/2 hours north of the capital. Few people stay in the town, preferring to stay at the surrounding *estancias* (ranches), several of which are detailed here.

The Office of Tourism of the Nation, at Suipacha 1111, will have brochures on various side trips from Buenos Aires, including some listed here.

1 MAR DEL PLATA

400km (248 miles) S of Buenos Aires

Argentina's most popular beach resort is a sleepy coastal city of about 700,000 long-term residents—until mid-December, when Porteños flock here through March for their summer vacation. Nearly eight million vacationers will pass through in the summer season, the vast majority of them Argentines. Although it's not as luxurious as Uruguay's Punta del Este—the beach favorite of many jet-setting Argentines—Mar del Plata is closer to Buenos Aires and far cheaper. Its long, windy coastline is known for its beaches crowded with tan bodies, and quieter seaside coves, with beautiful landscapes farther inland, leading to the edge of the grassy Pampas. The resort was at one time very exclusive, but during the Perón era, many hotels and high-rises were built for labor unions and the middle class, changing both the social and physical makeup of the city forever. Some of the magnificent French and Tudor-style mansions, which housed Argentina's summer elite residents in the early 20th century, have been meticulously preserved as museums.

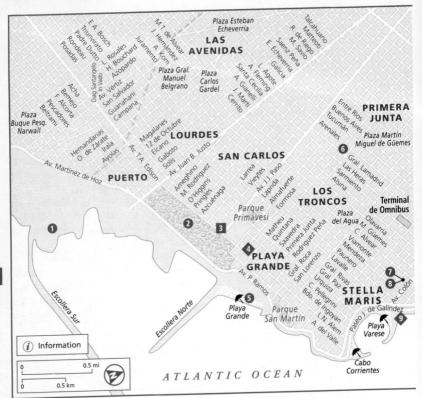

Mar del Plata offers excellent nightlife in summer, when independent theater companies from Buenos Aires come to town, and nightclubs open their doors to passionate Latin partygoers. The months of December, January, and February are the most crowded, wild, and expensive for visiting. In March, families with children and retired couples on vacation make up the bulk of visitors, who take advantage of a more relaxed atmosphere and the slight reduction in prices. Many hotels and restaurants remain open year-round; though the weather is chillier, people do vacation here on weekends in winter too. While Argentines will tell you stories about family vacations here over the generations, the city only hit the international radar during the November 2005 Summit of the Americas, when massive protests took place against the presence of then U.S. President George W. Bush. Much of the city was blocked off during that time period, disrupting locals from their daily lives, and many people still have much to say about the visit.

ESSENTIALS

GETTING THERE   You can reach Mar del Plata by plane, car, bus, train, or boat. The airport lies 10 minutes from downtown and is served by **Aerolíneas Argentinas** (𝄐 **800/333-0276** in the U.S. or 0810/222-86527 in Argentina; www.aerolineas.com.

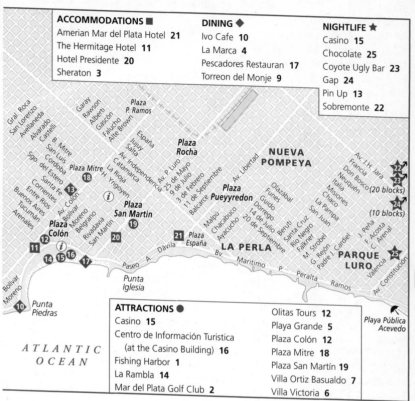

ACCOMMODATIONS ■
Amerian Mar del Plata Hotel **21**
The Hermitage Hotel **11**
Hotel Presidente **20**
Sheraton **3**

DINING ◆
Ivo Cafe **10**
La Marca **4**
Pescadores Restauran **17**
Torreon del Monje **9**

NIGHTLIFE ★
Casino **15**
Chocolate **25**
Coyote Ugly Bar **23**
Gap **24**
Pin Up **13**
Sobremonte **22**

ATTRACTIONS ●
Casino **15**
Centro de Información Turistica
(at the Casino Building) **16**
Fishing Harbor **1**
La Rambla **14**
Mar del Plata Golf Club **2**
Olitas Tours **12**
Playa Grande **5**
Plaza Colón **12**
Plaza Mitre **18**
Plaza San Martín **19**
Villa Ortiz Basualdo **7**
Villa Victoria **6**

ar). Flights last just under an hour, and there are about three flights a day. Cabs will cost about $12 to $17 (£8.50–£12) into the center of town. The RN2 is the main highway from Buenos Aires to Mar del Plata; it takes about 4 to 5 hours to drive between these cities. More than 50 bus companies link Mar del Plata with the rest of the country. Buses to Buenos Aires, which leave from the central bus terminal at Alberti 1602 (© 223/451-5406), are comfortable and cost less than $30 (£21) each way. They arrive in Buenos Aires at the Retiro Bus Station. A train run by the company Ferrobaires also connects Mar del Plata with Buenos Aires, and it's only slightly more expensive than the buses. It leaves Buenos Aires from **Constitución,** in the southern part of the capital, and runs three times a day. In Mar del Plata, purchase tickets at the train station at avenidas Luro and Italia (© 223/475-6076 in Mar del Plata, or 11/4304-0028 in Buenos Aires). Bus and train trips take about 4 to 5 hours.

VISITOR INFORMATION The **Centro de Información Turística,** Bulevar Marítimo PP Ramos 2270, at the Casino building (© 223/495-1777; www.mardelplata.gov.ar), has a knowledgeable, helpful staff that provides maps and suggested itineraries. It is open daily from 8am to 9pm. There is also a branch at the airport. An additional website for tourism information is www.mdp.com.ar.

La Rambla marks the heart of the city, the seaside walk in front of the casino and main city beach. You can walk around this area, with restaurants and other businesses clustered here and between the nearby bus station and **Plaza San Martín.** Farther south, the Los Tronces neighborhood houses the city's most prominent residences, as well as **Playa Grande** (the main beach), the Sheraton hotel, and the **Mar del Plata Golf Club.** Mar del Plata has 47km (29 miles) of Atlantic coastline, so if you plan to go to that part of the city, you'll need to take a taxi or rent a car. **Avis** (© **223/470-2100;** www.avis.com.ar) rents cars at the airport.

WHAT TO SEE & DO

The main reason to visit Mar del Plata is the beaches, all of which spread out from the city's heart at **Plaza Colón.** Here, you'll find the **Mar del Plata Casino** (© **223/495-7011;** www.loteria.gba.gov.ar). The red brick and granite structure guarded by sea lion sculptures is the social center of the city. Walkways and steps lead from here to the beach, with many people posing in front of the giant granite sea lions for their only Mar del Plata photos. In the early evening, as the crowds head home from the beach, you'll often see street performers and musicians here. (Watch your pockets if you stand and admire.) With long, slow breaks, **Waikiki** is the best spot for surfing. The coastline is nice, but you should not come expecting to find the Caribbean—the Atlantic remains fairly cold, even during summer. Once you've brushed off the sand, visit the **fishing harbor,** where hundreds of red and yellow boats unload their daily catches. The harbor houses a colony of 800 male sea lions that come to bathe on the rocky shores. (Be warned that between the sea lions and the fishing boats, it's an olfactory disaster.) Next to the colony, there's an ugly but intriguing boat graveyard where rusty boats have been left to rot away.

In the Los Tronces neighborhood, **Villa Victoria,** at Matheu 1851, at Arenales (© **223/492-0569**), showcases the early-20th-century summer house of wealthy Argentine writer Victoria Ocampo, who published the early-20th-century Argentine literary magazine *Sud* and was the first female member of the Argentine Academy of Letters. Some of Argentina's greatest authors have stayed here visiting her writing salons, including Jorge Luis Borges. It is open year-round, Thursday to Tuesday from 1 to 8pm, with an admission charge of about $3 (£2.15). In summer, musical and theatrical performances are held in the gardens, with various entry prices depending on the event. **Villa Ortiz Basualdo,** Av. Colón 1189 (© **223/486-1636**), is an English-style Victorian mansion decorated with exquisite Art Nouveau furniture from Belgium. The building is open daily from 10am to 10pm with an entry charge of just over $1 (70p). In the same neighborhood, the **Museo del Mar,** Av. Colón 1114, at Viamonte (© **223/451-9779;** www.museodelmar.com), houses a collection of 30,000 seashells. Stop in for a bite at the cafe surrounded by tanks of sharks staring at you and your meal. This is an ideal spot for visiting if you're with kids, and the rooftop terrace has an amazing view to the ocean, a few blocks away. In summer, it is open from Sunday to Friday 9am to 7pm, and Saturday 9am to 10pm. During the winter, it's open daily from 9am to 1pm. Admission is about $2 (£1.40) for the museum, with various prices for lectures and other events at the adjacent auditorium.

Twenty minutes from the city center, **De Los Padres Lake and Hills** is a picturesque forest with wide parks surrounding the lake, perfect for an afternoon picnic. Nearby in the Barrio Sierra de los Padres, the **Zoo El Paraíso,** Ruta 266, Km 16.5 (© **223/463-0347;** www.zooelparaisoonline.com.ar). The park is open daily from 10am to 7pm, with admission of $8 (£5.70) for adults and $3 (£2.15) for children. It features a wonderful collection of flora and fauna, including plants and trees from all over Argentina as well as lions, pumas, monkeys, llamas, and other animals. For information on surfing, deep-sea fishing, mountain biking, horseback riding, trekking, and other adventure sports, contact the tourism office.

The tour company **Olitas Tours** also does half-day city tours, as well as a special tour for children on a bus filled with clowns. Visit its kiosk at Plaza Colón, or call ✆ **223/472-6810** (www.olitas-tours.com.ar).

WHERE TO STAY

Amerian Mar del Plata Hotel   The Amerian is an Argentine chain hotel, and this branch in Mar del Plata overlooks Plaza España and La Perla Beach. The hotel is surrounded by several nightclubs, so it can be noisy at night. Prices can differ depending on sea or city views. Rooms are spacious, however, especially for the price category. Junior suites, positioned at angles, all have some form of sea view, even if it's not direct. Suites come with Jacuzzi tubs and all the bathrooms are large, no matter the category. The lobby has a small computer station. There is no gym or pool, though staff will help guests arrange to visit one nearby.

Av. Libertad 2936 (at La Rioja and Yrigoyen), 7600 Mar del Plata. ✆ **223/491-2000.** Fax 223/491-2300. www.amerian.com. 58 units. From $75 (£53) double; from $150 (£107) suite. Rates include breakfast buffet. AE, DC, MC, V. Free parking. **Amenities:** Restaurant; bar; concierge; access to nearby health club; Internet in business center; room service. *In room:* A/C, TV, hair dryer, Wi-Fi, minibar.

The Hermitage Hotel   This is Mar del Plata's grande dame hotel, opened in 1943, and where celebrities often make an appearance. The gilded Louis XV lobby has an often star-studded bar and sets the tone for the decor. The hotel acquired the Torre Colón in 2002 and renovated all the rooms in the old building at the same time. The rooms in the new building are nicer and pricier, with either sea or city views, though units are spacious throughout the hotel. Rooms in the old wing have classic touches, such as painted wooden moldings and wood-framed furniture. You'll find a more modern decor in the new towers, a contrast of dark woods and neutral tones. An underground passageway connects the hotel with a private casino and stretch of sand. The beach has its own bar and towel service. The heated rooftop pool has a spectacular view to the sea. The formal restaurant Luis Alberto serves three meals daily. The hotel has three rooms for travelers with disabilities.

Bulevar PP Ramos 2657 and Av. Colón 1643 (overlooking the Casino), 7600 Mar del Plata. ✆ **223/451-9081.** Fax 223/451-7235. www.hermitagehotel.com.ar. 300 units. Doubles from $159 (£113) in old building, from $181 (£129) new; suites $256–$288 (£182–£204). Rates include breakfast buffet. AE, DC, MC, V. Parking $10 (£7.10). **Amenities:** Restaurant; bar; babysitting; concierge; small health club and spa; Internet in business center; heated outdoor pool; room service. *In room:* A/C, TV, hair dryer, minibar, Wi-Fi.

Hotel Presidente   This small four-star hotel, owned by the Spanish chain Hoteles Alvarez, is about a block from the beach. An older property, it's full of dark woods, and some of the rooms are on the small side. The pleasant staff more than makes up for any faults in the decor. Some amenities—such as the restaurant Tartufu, where breakfast is served, and the small gym—are shared with the neighboring Hotel Iruña, owned by the same company. Some of the side rooms have sea views and rooms facing the sea cost a little more, but overall this hotel is a good choice for those who want good service on a reasonable budget. Each room comes with a small desk and vanity and, while there is no air-conditioning, the ceiling fan keeps the room comfortable. A small convention center

SIDE TRIPS FROM BUENOS AIRES

MAR DEL PLATA

on the eighth floor hosts meetings, and the lobby bar can be very busy. Here, you'll also find two computer terminals with free Internet access.

Corrientes 1516 (at Diagonal J. B. Alberdi), 7600 Mar del Plata. ⒞ 223/491-1060. Fax 223/491-1183. www.hotelpresidente.com. 53 units. Doubles from $110 (£78) with city view, from $124 (£88) sea view; suites from $105 (£75). Rates include breakfast buffet. AE, DC, MC, V. Parking $8 (£5.70). **Amenities:** Restaurant; bar; babysitting; concierge; small health club and spa; room service. *In room:* TV, hair dryer, Wi-Fi.

Sheraton ★★ ⓀⒾⒹⓈ   The Sheraton overlooks the golf course and the military port, near Playa Grande. Rooms were renovated in 2005, including the trademark Sheraton Suite Sleeper beds. The airy rooms, including the standard ones, seem oversize, and suites have Jacuzzi tubs. The hotel's children's area and video arcade make this a great choice for families. Two restaurants are in the hotel: the informal **La Pampa,** open for all meals, with an international menu; and the formal **Las Barcas,** open for dinner from Wednesday to Sunday. A $15 (£11) charge applies to use of the indoor pool, connected to the health club and spa. The gym received all-new equipment in 2007 and it has stunning views of the sea. A garden surrounds the outdoor pool, which is free of charge, but only open in the summer. Former U.S. President George W. Bush stayed here for the 2005 Summit of the Americas. The Sheraton also has two rooms for travelers with disabilities.

Alem 4221 (overlooking the golf course), 7600 Mar del Plata. ⒞ 0800/777-7002 or 223/414-0000. Fax 223/499-0009. www.sheratonmardelplata.com.ar. 191 units. Doubles from $259 (£184) with city views; from $286 (£203) ocean views; suites from $416 (£295). Rates include breakfast buffet. AE, DC, MC, V. Parking $15 (£11). Small pets accepted. **Amenities:** 2 restaurants; bar; babysitting; children's center; concierge; nearby golf course; large health club and spa; Internet in business center; indoor pool and heated outdoor pool; room service. *In room:* A/C, TV, hair dryer, minibar, Wi-Fi.

WHERE TO DINE

Ivo Cafe ★★ GREEK/ARGENTINE   I can't say enough about this fantastic Greek restaurant at the bottom of a high-rise condo overlooking the ocean. It's a two-level restaurant, with sidewalk seating. The Greek owners serve Greek food along with an Argentine *parrilla* (grill). They have oversize Greek salads, excellent souvlaki, and many other Greek choices. The chic black table is also set with olives and eggplant pastes for dipping bread. Also, while they have an English-language menu, ask for the Spanish one if you can read it; it has more and better choices. From the plate-glass windows, diners have a view of the sweeping arc of lights on the Mar del Plata shoreline. Come for dinner shows each Thursday, beginning at 9pm, with Greek dancing for a charge of about $15 (£11), which includes a meal, but not drinks. Still, come in the wee hours on any day, and you'll find the staff breaks into piano-playing, singing, and traditional dancing.

Bulevar Marítimo 3027 (at Güemes). ⒞ 223/486-3160. www.ivocafe.com. Main courses $6–$12 (£4.25–£8.50). AE, MC, V. Daily 24 hr. in summer; winter Sun–Thurs 8am–3am, 24 hr. Fri–Sat.

La Marca ★★ ARGENTINE   This restaurant became famous for serving a whole cow upon special request, for large groups of 50 or more people. It's not often that it does that anymore, but La Marca remains the town's best *parrilla*, serving thick rump steaks, tenderloins, barbecued ribs of beef, flanks, and other cuts of beef. The tender filet mignon with mushroom sauce is delicious. The menu includes pork chops, sausages, sweetbreads, black pudding, and other delights as well. The salad bar is extensive. Service is polite and unhurried. Make sure to try the *dulce de leche* (caramelized milk) before you leave.

Almafuerte 253. ⒞ 223/451-8072. www.lamarcarestaurant.com.ar. Main courses $3–$10 (£2.15–£7.10). AE, DC, MC, V. Daily noon–3pm and 8:30pm–1am.

Pescadores Restaurant ★★ SEAFOOD   You see this restaurant the moment you
pull into Mar del Plata, only because it's under the enormous Quilmes neon billboard
sign on the pier. This three-level seafood restaurant juts into the ocean and is one of the
best in town. Built into the Fisherman's Club, it's the next best thing to catching the fish
yourself. Fish of all kinds—sole, salmon, calamari, lobster, oysters, and everything else
local or shipped in—is here. Landlubbers will find pasta, salads, and *parrilla* offerings
too, and some of the fish sauces double as pasta sauces. Naturally, there are a lot of white
wines on the menu. We list a high top price here, but most main courses run about $10
(£7.10).

Bulevar Marítimo and Av. Luro (in the Club de Pesca, on the city pier). ✆ **223/493-1713.** Main courses
$3–$22 (£2.15–£16). AE, DC, MC, V. Daily noon–3pm and 8pm–midnight.

Torreon del Monje ★★ ARGENTINE   It's hard not to notice this restaurant in Mar
del Plata, inside a castlelike structure dating from 1904 and overlooking the Atlantic
Ocean. Day or night, the plate-glass windows that open onto the street also afford a fantastic view of the sea. Food runs from simple sandwiches to a *parrilla*, with steak, chicken,
and, of course, locally caught seafood. Almost each night, dinner shows take place while
you dine, beginning at 10pm. Some are tango, others flamenco and folkloric. There is no
additional charge for the shows; they're part of the experience of dining here. If you've dined
elsewhere, stop in for drinks at the beautiful oak bar. During the day, many people come
for the flavored and alcoholic coffee specials in the Esmeralda lounge.

Paseo Jesús de Galíndez (at the Puente del Monje, on the seafront). ✆ **223/451-9467.** www.torreondel
monje.com. Main courses $4–$10 (£2.85–£7.10). AE, DC, MC, V. Daily 8am–2am; until 4am Fri–Sat.

MAR DEL PLATA AFTER DARK

Nightlife follows closely behind beaches as Mar del Plata's biggest draw. In summer,
theater companies leave Buenos Aires to perform in this coastal resort; ask the tourism
office for a schedule of performance times and places. The city's most popular bars are
south of Plaza Mitre, off Calle San Luis. The best dance clubs are along Avenida Constitución, 3km (2 miles) from downtown, including **Chocolate,** Av. Constitución 4445
(✆ **223/479-4848;** www.chocolatemdq.com.ar); **Gap,** Av. Constitución 5780 (✆ **223/
479-6666**), which features live rock music; and **Sobremonte,** Av. Constitución 6690
(✆ **223/479-7930**). **Pin Up,** Santiago del Estero 2265 (no phone; www.pinupweb.
com), is one of the most popular gay discos. **Coyote Ugly Bar,** Av. Constitución 6690
(✆ **223/479-2600**), is a favorite Mexican restaurant and bar that breaks into salsa and
merengue dancing as the night goes on.

2 TIGRE & THE DELTA

36km (22 miles) NE of Buenos Aires

The Tigre River Delta is, in essence, a wild natural suburb of Buenos Aires, but it seems
a world apart from the city. The delta is formed by the confluence of five rivers, where
they flow from the Pampas into the Río de la Plata. This marshy complex is full of silt
and hundreds of tiny islands. Over time, it's continuing to grow down the Río de la Plata.
The delta area has grown considerably since the Spanish Conquest. In theory, within
several hundred years, the Río Tigre Delta will actually reach the capital. The islands here
are a mix of grassland, swamp, and true forest, with a variety of animal and plant life.

The development of the Tigre Delta into a resort area is a result of two concurrent historical circumstances in Buenos Aires in the 1870s. One was the construction of railroads from Buenos Aires into the rest of the country. The other was the 1877 outbreak of yellow fever, which caused wealthy Porteños to seek out new parts of the city for new year-round homes, as well as summer vacation spots. The British were in charge of much of the construction here, so many of the older neo-Gothic and mock-Tudor mansions and bed-and-breakfasts that line the banks of the river passages look like Victorian London buildings transplanted into the wild marshes of the Pampas.

Today, many Porteños come here on weekends to relax, ride horseback, hike, fish, swim, or do nothing at all. It's also a convenient destination for tourists, since it's easy to come here just for the day, tour the islands by boat, and return to Buenos Aires in time for dinner. There is a year-round population of residents on these car-free inner islands, and they go to school, work, and shop for groceries using a system of boats and docks.

ESSENTIALS

GETTING THERE   The Tigre Delta is best reached by train from Buenos Aires and then a boat or launch from the train station. Trains from Buenos Aires leave from **Estación Retiro** for Estación Tigre, at Avenida Naciones Unidas, every 10 to 20 minutes along the Mitre Line. Tickets run about $3 (£2.15) round-trip. Call © **11/4317-4445** for schedules and information, or visit www.tbanet.com.ar. Within Tigre, the **Estación Fluvial Tigre,** where the boats depart to head through the various rivers and islands, is on the next block over from **Estación Tigre,** at Mitre 305. Many companies run launches and services on both banks of the river here; you have to know where you want to go, or simply choose one and go wherever it takes you. Among the many companies are **Catamaranes Interisleña** (© **11/4731-0261**); **Líneas Delta** (© **11/4749-0537**); and **Catamaranes Río Tur** (© **11/4731-0280**). To reach **Martín García Island,** one of the most remote parts of the delta, you have to travel with **Cacciola** (© **11/4749-0329**). Most of these companies service the various islands, but allow you to ride on the boat until the end of the trip and then simply return. Ticket prices vary, but range from less than $1 (70p) and up. I highly recommend that you find out when the last few boats leave from your destination; toward the end of the day, boats can fill up quickly, leaving some passengers to wait for the next boat. Extra boats are dispatched at peak times, but you still may have to wait a few extra hours at the end of the day, especially on Sunday. Build this time into your plans or you may literally get stuck in the mud. Many tour companies in Buenos Aires also provide excursions to the Tigre Delta, and I have included that information below.

VISITOR INFORMATION   In theory, there are two **Centros de Información Turística** in Tigre. There is one in Estación Tigre, but it never seems to be open. Within Estación Fluvial Tigre, at Mitre 305 (© **0800/888-TIGRE** [888-84473] or 11/4512-4497; www.tigre.gov.ar), another office is open daily from 8am to 8pm. It is a very busy office, providing information on the islands, hotels and rentable bungalows, and other activities. You may have to wait a little while for help, but most of the staff speaks English. Another useful tourism website is **www.puntodelta.com.ar**.

GETTING AROUND   Within the town of Tigre itself, where both the train station and the docks are, one can easily walk along both banks. There are restaurants, playgrounds for children, and a few tourist-oriented shops along the waterfront and on the streets heading to the Puerto de Frutos (see below). To get around and see the delta, however, you will need a boat. I have listed the companies that provide these services above. Of course, if you have the skills and stamina, swimming is another option.

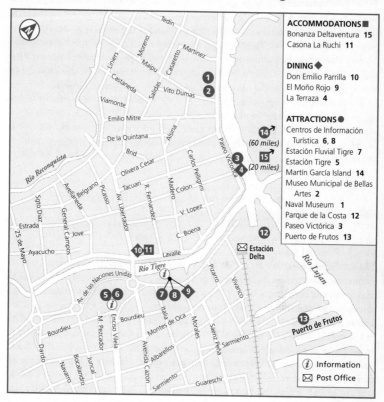

WHAT TO SEE & DO

The main thing to see in Tigre is the delta itself and the various islands and resorts that dot the area. Within the town of Tigre, where the train station and boat docks are, there are a few services and various other places of interest. Many people simply stay in this area and dine in the restaurants, sunbathe along the shoreline, or wander the town. Ponies march up and down the eastern shoreline in the city center, near the intersection of calles Lavalle and Fernández (no address or phone); children love riding them. From this area, head along what is called **Paseo Victórica,** a collection of Victorian mansions along the waterfront of Río Lujan, until it intersects with Río Conquista. This is one of the prettiest parts of Tigre, and you will find many people sunbathing along the shore here also. In the midst of all this Victorian splendor is the **Naval Museum,** Paseo Victorica 602, at Martínez (© 11/4749-0608). On the other bank, across from here, is the **Parque de la Costa,** Vivanco, at Montes de Oca (© 11/4732-6000), full of rides for kids and grownups. Just outside of the center of Tigre is the famous **Puerto de Frutos** (© 11/4512-4493), at Calle Sarmiento 160, along Río Lujan. Fruit farming was integral to the early development of the Tigre Delta, and this market is a leftover from those days. Most people rave about seeing this site, but in general, I have always found it disappointing, with almost no fruit. Besides the traditional basket weavers who create their wares using the reeds growing in the delta, the market is now mostly full of odds and ends and less interesting crafts that can be found in many other places. Still, it is worth a quick visit. Definitely worth a visit however is the **Museo Municipal de Bellas Artes,** Paseo Victorica 972 (© **11/4512-4528**), built into what had been the Tigre Casino. The building is among the most impressive Argentine Beaux Arts buildings outside of Buenos Aires and took years to restore. The redesign of the casino as a museum was done by Gabriel Miremont, the curator of the Museo Evita and numerous museums throughout Argentina. The museum has free admission and is open Wednesday to Friday from 9am to 7pm, Saturday and Sunday from noon to 7pm.

A 3-hour boat ride each way from the center of Tigre will take you to **Martín García Island.** It is famous for its upscale political prison where various Argentine presidents, including Juan Perón, have been incarcerated, but exploring here will take a full day once you account for the round-trip boat ride.

If you are doing any trekking on the islands, even in hot weather, you will need hiking boots, long pants, and long-sleeved shirts. Sawgrass and other very sharp forms of plants inhabit the area and will rip into unprotected skin. You should also bring mosquito repellent, though malaria is not a problem in the delta, only painful itching. It's also a good idea to pack binoculars, to view birds and other wildlife.

Travel Companies Providing Tigre Delta Excursions

Various travel companies in Buenos Aires provide day-trip excursions to the Río Tigre delta or will arrange longer stays in the numerous bed-and-breakfasts, bungalows, and adventure lodges in the area. **Say Hueque Tourism,** Viamonte 749, Office 601, 1053 Buenos Aires (© **11/5199-2517**) or Guatemala 4845 Office 4, 1425 Buenos Aires (© **11/4775-7862;** www.sayhueque.com), is one that I highly recommend, especially for longer trips and adventure excursions to see the natural beauty of the area. **Travel Line** (© **11/4393-9000;** www.travelline.com.ar) offers Tigre Delta day tours, among many other excursions. The full-day Tigre tours are Sundays only (ask for an English-speaking guide) and include lunch, a ride to and from Tigre by train, and a boat ride along the rivers of the Tigre Delta for about $65 (£46) per person.

WHERE TO STAY

Bonanza Deltaventura ★★ If you want to get away from it all, head to this hotel on one of the islands in the Río Tigre delta. It has miles of walkways through the grasslands for bird-watching and horses for riding along the shoreline. Or you can just swim off the dock out front. Guests can rent four small but comfortable rooms as either singles or doubles, for a total of eight people in the lodge. The living style is communal, with shared bathrooms and kitchen. The price is for 2 days and 1 night and includes meals and trekking excursions, but alcoholic drinks cost extra. The staff also speaks English. You will need to call ahead of time to stay here, to ensure that space is available and that you take the right boat company. The hotel is on the Carapachay River islands section of the delta, about a 1-hour boat ride from the center of the town of Tigre.

Carapachay River Islands, 1648 Tigre. © **11/4728-1674** or 11/15-5603-7176 (cell). www.deltaventura. com. 4 units. From $106 (£75) per person. Rates include breakfast and trekking excursions. No credit cards.

Casona La Ruchi ★★ This charming bed-and-breakfast overlooks the waterfront across the bank from the Estación Fluvial. Owners Dora and Jorge Escuariza and their children run the place, and guests who stay in the six-room, 1893 mansion are treated like family. Guests have use of the kitchen and they can gather and barbecue at the backyard grill near the outdoor pool. Rooms are furnished with quaint Victorian antiques, and some have windows looking out onto the waterfront. The place is open year-round, but it's busiest during summer weekends. Guests have 24-hour access to the hotel, though the family does not have an actual overnight staff person. Call if you're arriving late in the day to verify that someone can let you in. You will enjoy the warmth and hospitality at this place.

Lavalle 557 (at Av. Libertador), 1648 Tigre. ℂ **11/4749-2499.** www.casonalaruchi.com.ar. 6 units, some with shared bathroom. $55 (£39) double. Rates include continental breakfast. No credit cards. **Amenities:** Outdoor pool; Wi-Fi.

WHERE TO DINE

Don Emilio Parrilla ARGENTINE/PARRILLA   A rustic interior and a casual atmosphere with tables in bright Provençal yellow await you in this *parrilla* overlooking the waterfront. The food here is great, and a complete meal will run you about $10 (£7.10) a person. Unfortunately, it's only open on weekends.

Lavalle 573 (at Av. Libertador). ℂ **11/4631-8804.** Main courses $3–$6 (£2.15–£4.25). No credit cards. Fri 8pm–1am; Sat–Sun 11:30am–5pm and 8pm–2am.

El Moño Rojo ★ ARGENTINE/INTERNATIONAL   An enormous restaurant complex overlooking the waterfront near the Estación Fluvial, this is one of the best places to come for a meal with entertainment. The atmosphere is brilliantly red, festive, and very kitschy, full of posters of tango stars, pictures of Argentine actors and actresses, and old Peronist memorabilia. On Friday, they stage a tango show. The food is a mixture of pizzas, snacks, sandwiches, and traditional *parrilla* grilled meat, so there should be something to please everyone here.

Av. Mitre 345 (at Estación Fluvial Tigre). ℂ **11/15-5644-8058** (cell). Main courses $4–$7 (£2.85–£4.95). No credit cards. Daily 8am–2am.

La Terraza ★ ARGENTINE/INTERNATIONAL   This two-level restaurant looks as if it were dropped in from a tropical island, with its wraparound verandas and overhanging palm trees. A full *parrilla* offers some of the best steak dining in Tigre. You'll also find chicken, salads, and Italian cuisine. There is a beautiful view to the Río Lujan while dining here.

Paseo Victoria 134 (at Colon Tigre). ℂ **11/4731-2916.** www.laterrazatigre.com.ar. Main courses $4–$7 (£2.85–£4.95). No credit cards. Tues–Sun noon–5pm; Fri–Sat 8pm–1am, sometimes later.

3 GUALEGUAYCHU & ARGENTINA'S NATIONAL CARNAVAL

250km (155 miles) N of Buenos Aires

Carnaval might be more associated with neighboring Brazil, but that doesn't mean you won't find entertainment of a similar nature in Argentina. The Argentine Mesopotamia region, which encompasses the provinces of Missiones, Entre Ríos, and Corrientes, is where many of these festive events are held. The most popular of all these, made so by a huge amount of marketing and proximity to Buenos Aires, is that of Gualeguaychú, in the southern part of Entre Ríos province. Unlike in Rio, however, where Carnaval is concentrated in a few days, Gualeguaychú's event is held every Saturday in January, it's a great destination for a side trip.

The town of 100,000 people gears up for this all year. Each weekend during the event, nearly 30,000 visitors descend on the town to see the *comparsas,* or schools, which are groups of people who band together to produce the Carnaval spectacle. They perform in all their feathered finery and compete with other *comparsas.* At the end of the 2 months, one *comparsa* is chosen as the winner. The stadium where the Carnaval is held is called the **Corsodromo** and is built over an old train station. Beauty and bodies reign during this period, with both men and women nearly naked in the arena. Though the Indians are long gone, the name of the town comes from the native Guarani and means "The River of the Big Tiger"; that theme is often celebrated in Carnaval.

Gualeguaychú is more than worth the trip, as it's both an interesting diversion from Buenos Aires and a chance to see how Argentina does its Carnaval. The city is not well set up, however, for international travelers, as most visitors come from Buenos Aires and other parts of Argentina (though a few do come from Brazil and Uruguay). In other words, it's difficult to find anyone who speaks English at the hotels, the Corsodromo, or the Tourism Information Centers, though the city will soon engage in a project to promote the learning of English. Still, this makes it all the more fun and authentic and very different from English-ubiquitous Buenos Aires. In addition to Carnaval, the area is surrounded by beaches along the Río Gualeguaychú and the Río Uruguay. Many Porteños choose to vacation here for the beaches, camping, and fishing.

The fun has recently been overshadowed by the controversy surrounding the construction of a paper mill in Fray Bentos, Uruguay, across the Río Uruguay directly opposite Ñandubaysel beach, the city's favorite beach, about 19km (12 miles) outside of town. Protests against the mill created a diplomatic mess for Uruguay and Argentina and massive protests shut down transportation between the two countries, which still periodically happens. Argentines feared pollution, and though this did not happen once the mill was opened in October 2007, it clearly has impacted the vista. Ironically, international tourism has increased with the controversy. You might recall the photos of a certain bikini-clad beauty, Angelina Carrozzo, the Gualeguaychú Carnaval Queen of 2006, who disrupted the Latin American and Caribbean Business Summit, held in Vienna in May 2006, bringing world attention to the tiny resort.

For such a small town, Gualeguaychú also has intense nightlife, with several bars and clubs hugging the Costanera (the walkway along the Río Gualeguaychú) and near the Corsodromo. Gualeguaychú was also an area of mass German and Eastern European immigration after World War II, so it has a disproportionate number of blondes in relation to other areas of Argentina, adding to the mystique of women from the region. The German influence is present in some of the food, architecture, hotels, and even language throughout the city. Be aware that this is a town that still adheres to the practice of siestas, so you should expect that nearly everything, other than some restaurants and a few small convenience stores, closes between about 1 and 4pm.

ESSENTIALS
GETTING THERE   You can reach Gualeguaychú by bus or car. There is no nearby airport with commercial services, and rail transport ended long ago. (In fact, the train station was converted into the Carnaval stadium, so it is unlikely that train service will ever return to the town.) If traveling by car from Buenos Aires, take Ruta 12 north from Buenos Aires to where it intersects with Ruta 14, which you then take north. Buses for

Gualeguaychú from Buenos Aires leave from the **Retiro Bus Station** and go to the
Gualeguaychú Terminal de Omnibus at Boulevard Jurardo and Boulevard Artigas
(© **3446/440-688**). The journey takes about 3 hours. Various companies will make the
trip, which runs about $10 (£7.10), including **FlechaBus.** Call © **3446/440-776** in
Gualeguaychú or © **11/4315-2781** in Buenos Aires for tickets, schedules, and information or visit www.flechabus.com.ar. Many travel agencies in Buenos Aires also have special
bus day trips to the Carnaval. These trips leave Buenos Aires in the late afternoon, stay in
Gualeguaychú for the Carnaval event, and then return to Buenos Aires after 3 or 4am.

VISITOR INFORMATION   There are two **Centros de Información Turística** in Gualeguaychú. One is at the bus station (© **3446/440-706**). The main center is at the Plazoleta de los Artesanos, at Paseo del Puerto along the waterfront (© **3446/423-668** or
3446/422-900). Both are generally open daily from 8am to 8pm. In the summer, however, the main branch on the port is open 8am to midnight Friday through Sunday. It
provides a selection of maps, hotel information, and help with finding accommodations,
which can be very difficult in high season. Their website, though only in Spanish, is the
best tourism website I've ever used in Argentina, based on its logical format, ease of use,
and wealth of information. Access it at www.gualeguaychuturismo.com. Within Buenos
Aires, the province of Entre Ríos has a tourism information center at Suipacha 846
(© **11/4326-2573**), which also provides information on Gualeguaychú as well as other
carnivals in the region.

GETTING AROUND   Within Gualeguaychú, most of what you need is accessible
within a small walking distance of the center of the city along the Costanera, the walkway
along the Río Gualeguaychú. Within this area, you will find beaches and camping sites,
all within sight of downtown. Even the Corsodromo, once the old railroad station, can
be reached on foot from downtown in about 20 minutes. The best close beach is the
Solar del Este, just northeast of town. Other excellent camping sites and beaches exist
within a few miles of downtown Gualeguaychú. A car makes things much easier when
you're here, but there are no car-rental services in Gualeguaychú or in the surrounding
cities. The solution is to rent a car in Buenos Aires and drive to Gualeguaychú. You can
also take taxis wherever you need to go or make arrangements to have a driver take you
to the beach in the morning and pick you up at a specified time in the afternoon. One
24-hour cab company is **Remiss Boulevard** (© **0800/888-4010** or 3446/434-010).
Another is **Remiss Plaza** (© **0800/444-0644** or 3446/431-136). Cabs do not use
meters, and instead set the price when you enter. You can also ask your hotel concierge
to make arrangements for you. Cabs can be flagged down on the street, but can be hard
to find at peak times. Hitching rides is not uncommon, but not to be recommended for
women traveling solo.

WHAT TO SEE & DO

The main reason for coming to Gualeguaychú is for the Carnaval. It is held every Saturday in January and February and the first week of March, usually at about 10pm, and
runs for about 5 hours. It is a massive party, held within the **Corsodromo,** which was
built over the site of the old railroad station at the intersection of avenidas Rocamora and
Piccini. Beauty pageants are part of the season, with Miss Gualeguaychú Tourism usually
selected at the end of January and the new Carnaval Queen at the end of February. Ask
the tourism office for exact dates and plan long ahead for these special weekends. Tickets
can be reserved by calling the Corsodromo's ticket office (© **3446/430-901**). Once
reserved, tickets need to be paid for and picked up by either Friday before the event or

Saturday noon on the day of event. Tickets are about $12 (£8.50) for adults and $4 (£2.85) for children. The sooner you reserve your ticket, the better your seating assignment will be, as a limited amount of seating exists within the bleachers of the stadium. Late ticket purchasers simply stand along the route of the event in a fenced-in area of the Corsodromo. If you forget to buy tickets, there are always scalpers. Visit the main tourism website www.gualeguaychuturismo.com for more information or see www.carnaval delpais.com.ar.

While the Corsodromo ticket office has the best selection of tickets, individual Corsos and organizations also buy up sets of tickets in blocks and resell them to the public so that an entire group can sit in one area of the stands and cheer on the performers together. One of the largest sellers of individual tickets is the **Club Sirio Libanés,** which runs the **Kamar Corso** group (© 3446/425-673), one of the city's most popular. New for 2009 is a special VIP seating area. You must already have a ticket and pay about an additional $25 (£18) per person for this area, but you get free beer, comfortable seating, and a better view from the restricted judging area (© 3446/420-807).

Within the town, there are a few interesting sites, most of them centered on the **Plaza San Martín.** The town is relatively young, only established by the Spanish in 1783, and this was the original Plaza Mayor. A statue of San Martín on horseback sits in the center of the plaza. Nearby are busts of various local heroes and heroines, though vandals unfortunately have destroyed the noses of most of them. A merry-go-round, swing sets, and kiosks selling ice cream and candy make the park an ideal place to bring children. Overlooking the park, on Calle San José, is **Catedral San José.** Its facade is ornamented by Corinthian columns, and the interior has a gilded altar and frescoed ceilings with scenes of the lives of various saints. The **Police Headquarters** overlooks the plaza on Sáenz Peña, but it is not open to the public, unless you need to report a crime or plan to get caught committing one in the drunken stupor that is Carnaval. It is a churchlike Italianate structure with a columned facade and central tower. Most of the remainder of the buildings on the plaza are nondescript, save for a turn-of-the-20th-century school building.

There are two historic house museums in Gualeguaychú. One is the **Museo de la Ciudad Casa Haedo,** at the intersection of Rivadavia and San José (no phone). Built around 1801, it is a Spanish colonial structure with original floors and other remaining details. It is full of Victorian furniture, an old gun collection, and portraits of the Haedo family. Legend has it that one of the young female members of the Lapalma family died of a broken heart and haunts the **Museo de la Ciudad Azotea de Lapalma,** at calles San Luis and Rioja (© 3446/437-028). This beautiful 1835 former hacienda, built on what was once the edge of town, contains material related to the founding of the city. Both museums are open from Wednesday to Sunday from 9am to noon and Friday and Saturday from 5 to 8pm. Along the waterfront is the long **Costanera.** People stroll here day and night, and the beaches under this promenade are full of people fishing, sunbathing, and picnicking. It's normal for people here to begin to chat with strangers and invite them to sit down and share *mate,* the Argentine herbal tea, with them, so don't be surprised if that happens to you. During Carnaval weekends, the area is packed with revelers from the nearby clubs, and thousands of young people dancing on the beach.

Farther down the Costanera, just to the south of the center of town, is the **Paseo del Puerto,** a continuation of the Costanera, but with small grassy plazas along the route. This is where the tourism office is located. The **Plazoleta de los Artesanos,** full of local craftspeople, is also in this area. Most stalls are open in January and February on the weekends from about 8am to 1am. Some are also open daily during those hours in those months. Various boat companies are also located here and offer rides along the river and around the **Isla Libertad,** an island in the center of the river. One company with these services is **Paseos Náuticos** (✆ **3446/423-248**), which runs the trips six times a day for $5 (£3.55) per person in high season. About 19km (12 miles) from town is **Ñandubaysel** beach, which is famed for its sunsets. Because so many people camp here overnight, you'll pass many tents between the parking lot and the beach. From here, the Río Uruguay is relatively narrow and the country of Uruguay seems almost reachable by swimming. Outside of town, there are also thermal spa resorts, *estancias* (ranches), and luxury cabin camping grounds. Ask the tourism office for more information.

WHERE TO STAY

While many hotels accept credit cards, reservations often must be done via cash deposits into the Buenos Aires bank accounts of their owners, making it difficult to reserve if you are unaware of the process. Ask at a travel agent unless you want to experience this for yourself. During Carnaval, a 3- or 4-night stay is often required by the hotels, which often fill up months before the season.

Aguay Hotel ★★   The Aguay Hotel is one of the city's newest and best-situated hotels, opened in 2001. It directly overlooks the Costanera, and the top-floor rooms as well as the rooftop pool have incredible views over the river and surrounding land. All rooms have balconies, and suites have Jacuzzis in the bathrooms. The hotel is also close to the casino and the bars on the Costanera, so it can be noisy in the evening, but you'll be right in the middle of all the action. A front garden and walkway by a waterfall add to the ambience. The hotel has two restaurants, the fancy Italian Di Tulia in the lobby and a rooftop drink-and-snack bar where breakfast is served. I recommend coming here for drinks even if you are not staying in the hotel, as the view is unmatched anywhere in the city.

Av. Costanera 130 (at Bolívar), 2820 Gualeguaychú. ✆ **3446/422-099.** www.hotelaguay.com.ar. 18 units. From $90 (£64) double; from $110 (£78) suite. Rates include continental breakfast. AE, MC, V. Free parking. **Amenities:** 2 restaurants; exercise room; Internet in lobby; small rooftop pool; room service. *In room:* A/C, TV, hair dryer, minibar, Wi-Fi.

Hotel Alemán   This charming little hotel is owned by a family of German descent, and the architecture is mildly Bavarian on the outside to give a hint of their former homeland. The hotel is about 50 years old, but as of this writing, it is about halfway through an expansion and renovation process. Renovated or new rooms have wood paneling, floral-pattern bedspreads and drapes, and modernized bathrooms. Rooms overlook a brilliantly sunny courtyard, and upper-level rooms have small patios.

Bolívar 535 (at 3 de Febrero), 2820 Gualeguaychú. ✆ **3446/426-153.** 26 units. From $48 (£34) double. Rates include continental breakfast. No credit cards. Free parking. *In room:* A/C, TV, hair dryer, Wi-Fi.

Hotel Berlin   This small hotel offers friendly service along with a convenient location between downtown and the Corsodromo. Wood-paneled rooms are small, but the bathrooms with shower stalls were renovated in 2007. The staff is welcoming and loves to chat with visitors about their impressions of Carnaval.

Bolívar 733 (at Peron), 2820 Gualeguaychú. ✆ **3446/425-111.** www.hotelberlin.com.ar. 19 units (shower only). From $60 (£43) double. Rates include continental breakfast. AE, MC, V. Free parking. **Amenities:** Babysitting; bikes. *In room:* A/C, TV, hair dryer, Wi-Fi.

Viedma Hotel   Don't be put off by the very modern architecture on the outside of this building. With its friendly service and country Victorian–style decor full of honey pine furniture, the Viedma is a pleasant place to stay in Gualeguaychú. Rooms are very large, with wood paneling and wainscoting in some, adding even more of a country touch. The hotel, though a few blocks away from the coveted Costanera area, has no views to the waterfront because the buildings near it are all the same size. However, it is quiet at night, an important consideration. Rooms can accommodate one to four people in varying combinations, and suites come with an extra room. All bathrooms come with shower stalls only.

Bolívar 530 (at 3 de Febrero), 2820 Gualeguaychú. ② **3446/424-262.** viedmahotel@ciudad.com.ar. 28 units (shower only). From $45 (£32) double. Rates include continental breakfast. DC, MC, V. Parking $4 Sat–Sun in high season; free at other times. *In room:* A/C, TV, Wi-Fi.

WHERE TO DINE

Bahillo ICE CREAM   Head to this ice-cream parlor for ice cream, sorbets, and other sweet treats, and eat them on the sidewalk benches like all the Argentine tourists. This is a great place to bring the kids or to take a break yourself when walking around in the summer heat.

Costanera (at San Lorenzo). ② **3446/426-240.** Ice cream $2–$4 (£1.40–£2.85). No credit cards. Daily 10am–3am or later.

Di Tulia ★★ ARGENTINE/ITALIAN   Located in the lobby of the Aguay Hotel, this is the best restaurant in Gualeguaychú. It concentrates on northern Italian cuisine, as well as some seafood, and it also has an excellent selection of wine.

Av. Costanera 130 (at Bolívar). ② **3446/429-940.** Main courses $4–$10 (£2.85–£7.10). AE, MC, V. Daily noon–4pm and 8pm–1am.

Lo De Carlitos ★ ARGENTINE/ITALIAN/PARRILLA   Carlos has run this family establishment on the waterfront for years. The interior is simple, with an emphasis on the service, and a small sidewalk outdoor-dining area is also provided. The restaurant serves mostly basic Argentine food from the *parrilla,* as well as a large selection of seafood and basic Italian dishes, all in large servings.

San Martín 206 (at Costanera). ② **3446/432-582.** Main courses $3–$8 (£2.15–£5.70). No credit cards. Daily noon–3pm and 8pm–2am.

GUALEGUAYCHU AFTER DARK

For such a small town, Gualeguaychú has a good nightlife scene, based around the Costanera and a few surrounding streets. The newest highlight of nightlife here is not a bar but the **Gualeguaychú Casino,** Costanera and San Martín (② **3446/424-603**), which opened in February 2005. The owners call it the world's only Carnaval-themed casino, and it has been beautifully decorated by local artists. About 100 slot machines, several card and roulette tables, and other forms of gambling entertainment await you. In addition, there are bars and restaurants, along with a live theater and a babysitting service.

The most popular nightclub in town is the enormous **Bikini,** Costanera at 25 de Mayo (no phone). It holds a few thousand people with a main dance floor and an outdoor patio and Tiki bar. It is only open Friday and Saturday from 2am to 9am. The crowds spread from here onto the street and the beach. **El Angel,** San Lorenzo 79 (② **3446/432-927**), offers drag shows and other entertainment from Thursday to Sunday beginning at 11pm and has a gay following. The sleek, Miami-style **Macuba Disco,** at the corner of Maipu and Piccini across from the Corsodromo (no phone), is especially packed after Carnaval, with many *comparsa* members coming in their costumes. The bar and dance club **Ciudad de Samba,** Bolivar 834 at Italia (② **3446/15-501-571** [cell]), is

4 COLONIA DEL SACRAMENTO, URUGUAY

140km (87 miles) W of Buenos Aires

The tiny gem of Colonia del Sacramento, declared a World Heritage Site by UNESCO, appears untouched by time. Dating from 1680, when it was established by Manuel Lobo as a buffer colony by the Portuguese against the Spanish, the old city boasts beautifully preserved colonial artistry down its quiet, bougainvillea-draped, cobblestone streets. A leisurely stroll into the **Barrio Histórico (Historic Neighborhood)** leads you under flower-laden windowsills to churches dating from the 1680s, past simple single-story homes from Colonia's time as a colonial settlement, and on to local museums detailing the riches of the town's past. The Barrio Histórico contains brilliant examples of colonial architecture and many of Uruguay's oldest structures. A mix of lovely shops, tiny posadas, and cafes with and restaurants with delicious food make the town more than a history lesson.

The majority of visitors take day trips to Colonia from Buenos Aires. However, staying overnight or exploring the region has certain advantages. Colonia is surrounded by wineries and *estancias* and some of Uruguay's most beautiful landscapes, as well as spa resorts, but very few visitors get to see this. Only recently experiencing a tourism boom, many of these sites have a more authentic atmosphere than their counterparts in Argentina. As small as it is, staying overnight in Colonia allows you to have the town to yourself after the day-trippers have left, to wander the cobblestone streets unencumbered. Photography buffs in particular will find this delightful. For those who come as a couple, the small town is serenely romantic for watching a sunset together and then heading to candlelit restaurants serving steaks, locally caught fish, and wines from the surrounding vineyards.

ESSENTIALS
Getting There
The easiest way to reach Colonia from Buenos Aires is by **ferry. FerryLíneas** (© 02/900-6617) runs a fast boat that arrives in 45 minutes. **Buquebús** (© 02/916-1910) also offers two classes of service. Prices range from $35 to $58 (£25–£41) each way. A new ferryboat-and-bus combination service opened in 2006 to compete with what had been a monopoly for Buquebús. **Colonia Express** (© 54/11-4313-5100 in Buenos Aires, or 02/901-9597 in Montevideo; www.coloniaexpress.com) offers similar prices, but has a less frequent schedule.

Colonia is a good stopping-off point if you're traveling between Buenos Aires and Montevideo. **COT** (© 02/409-4949 in Montevideo) offers **bus service** from Montevideo and from Punta del Este.

Citizens of the United States, the United Kingdom, Canada, and New Zealand need only a passport to enter Uruguay (for tourist stays of up to 90 days). Australian citizens must get a tourist visa before arrival.

Visitor Information
The main **Oficina de Turismo,** General Flores and Rivera (© 052/23700 or 052/26141), is open daily from 8am to 8pm. Just outside the gates to the Barrio

Histórico and with the same hours is a smaller **Oficina de Turismo** at Calle Manuel Lobo, 224 between Ituzaingo and Paseo San Miguel (© **052/28506**). Speak with someone at the tourism office to arrange a guided tour of the town, or contact the Asociacion de Guias Profesionales de Turismo del Departamento de Colonia (© **052/22309** or 052/ 25068; asociacionguiascolonia@gmail.com). Visit www.colonia.gub.uy or www.uruguay natural.com for information about Colonia and the surrounding region. The website www.guiacolonia.com.uy has useful information, and keep an eye out for the bi-monthly booklet **Güear** (www.guear.com), which has shopping, restaurant, hotel and nightlife listings, as well as profiles of local chefs and other information. A PDF of the booklet can be downloaded before your visit.

Money

The official currency is the **Uruguayan peso** (designated NP$, $U, or simply $); each peso is comprised of 100 **centavos.** Uruguayan pesos are available in $10, $20, $50, $100, $200, $500, $1,000, and $5,000 notes; coins come in 10, 20, and 50 centavos, and 1 and 2 pesos. The Uruguayan currency devalued by half in July 2002, due to its close kinship with the Argentine peso. The current exchange rate is approximately 23 pesos to $1. Because the value of the peso fluctuates greatly with inflation, all prices in this guide are quoted in U.S. dollars. Most locations listed here take Argentine pesos, Uruguayan pesos, euros, and U.S. dollars.

WHAT TO SEE & DO
A Walk Through Colonia's Barrio Historico

Your visit to Colonia will be concentrated in the **Barrio Histórico (Old Neighborhood),** located on the coast at the far southwestern corner of town. The sites, which are all within a few blocks of each other, can easily be visited on foot within a few hours. Museums and tourist sites are open Thursday through Monday from 11:15am to 4:45pm. For about $2 (£1.40), you can buy a pass at the Portuguese or municipal museums, which will get you into all the sites. Many locations in Colonia don't have real addresses, but often an intersection of two streets is used for direction. Individual museums don't have phone numbers either, so make sure to get a map at the tourist office. While the town is small and convenient for walking, almost nothing in the center of Colonia is handicapped accessible. It is a difficult visit for anyone in a wheelchair, except to see the exteriors of important structures.

Start your tour at **Plaza Mayor,** the principal square that served as the center of the colonial establishment. To explore Colonia's Portuguese history, cross the Calle Manuel Lobo on the southeastern side of the plaza and enter the **Museo Portugués (Portuguese Museum),** with exhibits portraying European customs and traditions that influenced the town's beginnings. Its most important holding is the final Portuguese royal medallion to grace the city walls before the city finally fell into Spanish hands. Leading behind the Museo Municipal is the **Street of Sighs,** or the **Calle de Los Suspiros,** so called because it was where the prostitutes worked their trade in olden days when the military barracks were just off the Plaza Mayor. It remains the most intact colonial street in the city, with its angled cobblestone drain leading to the waterfront. You also see side by side the difference between Portuguese and Spanish colonial construction. If the roof is flat, it is Spanish. If the roof is angled with tiles, it is Portuguese. Nearby are the **Ruinas Convento San Francisco (San Francisco convent ruins).** Dating from 1696, the San Francisco convent was once inhabited by Jesuit and Franciscan monks, two brotherhoods dedicated to preaching the gospel to indigenous people. You can crawl over the ruins, or climb the adjacent 100-foot-high **Faro** or **Lighthouse** after paying the $1 (70p) fee. The wind is strong up there and you can see Buenos Aires on a clear day. The lighthouse is open daily from 10am to 8pm and is overseen by the Uruguayan navy, which has a small base just off Plaza Mayor.

Around the corner is the **Casa de Brown (Brown House)**, which houses the **Museo Municipal (Municipal Museum).** Here, you will find an impressive collection of colonial documents and artifacts, a must-see for history buffs. For those with a more artistic bent, make sure to check out the **Museo del Azulejo (Tile Museum),** close to the waterfront on Calle Misiones de los Tapes at Paseo de San Gabriel, a unique museum of 19th-century European and Uruguayan tiles housed in a gorgeous 300-year-old country house. Upon exiting the museum, turn right for a walk along the water and then make a right onto Calle de la Playa, enjoying the shops and cafes along the way, heading up to the **Iglesia Matriz,** originally dating from 1680. Various conflicts and fighting meant the church was reconstructed several times, and today's building is a mix of colonial and neoclassical styles. To the side of the church is **Plaza de Lobo,** with its excavated **Ruinas Casa del Gobernador (House of the Viceroy ruins),** built by the Portuguese and destroyed in 1777 by the Spanish. The House of the Viceroy captures something of the city's 17th- and 18th-century magistracy, when the port was used for imports, exports, and smuggling. Complete your walk by heading back toward the Plaza Mayor. To the left, you'll see the **City Gate** or **Portón de Campo** and what remains of the ramparts that once served to protect the city. Climbing them and contemplating the view out to the Río de La Plata and the world beyond will help you understand that, in spite of its tiny size, Colonia played a pivotal role in the global struggle between two European empires to dominate a continent an ocean away.

WHERE TO STAY

Staying overnight in Colonia allows you to explore the town at a slower pace or couples to have a romantic evening.

Hotel La Misión   This hotel overlooking the Plaza Mayor was partly renovated in 2008, with rooms that mix modern and traditional styles, and new bathrooms. The original building dates from 1762. A lobby filled with antiques leads to a small courtyard dripping with bougainvillea.

Misiones de los Tapes 171, CP 70000, Colonia. ✆ **052/26767.** www.lamisionhotel.com. 11 units. From $100 (£71) double. Rates include breakfast buffet. AE, MC, V. **Amenities:** Restaurant; concierge; Internet in business center; room service. *In room:* A/C, TV, minibar, Wi-Fi.

Posada Plaza Mayor   Among the most charming hotels in the center, this hotel has several rooms around a tranquil central courtyard with a fountain. Rooms are a mix of modern and rustic, and the breakfast room has a spectacular view over the Río de la Plata.

Calle de Comercio 111, CP 70000, Colonia. ✆ **052/23193.** www.posadaplazamayor.com. 15 units. From $110 (£78) double. Rates include breakfast buffet. AE, MC, V. **Amenities:** Restaurant; concierge; Internet in business center; room service. *In room:* A/C, TV, hair dryer, minibar, Wi-Fi.

Outside Colonia

Four Seasons Carmelo ★★ (Kids)   One of the most luxurious, award-winning resorts in South America, the Four Seasons Carmelo is about 90km (56 miles), or a 1-hour car ride, from the center of Colonia, set on the Río de la Plata. The enormous rooms and suites, about 1,000 to 1,300 square feet and with fireplaces and cathedral ceilings, are set in individual bungalows in a landscaped garden surrounding the pool, making for a romantic getaway or honeymoon spot. The spa offers extensive treatments in a calming, Asian-inspired setting. There is also a golf course, polo grounds, and other amenities, as well as special children's programs. The hotel runs a shuttle service from Colonia's port, for $88 (£62) one way and $132 (£94) round-trip, per person.

Ruta 21, Km 262, CP 70000, Carmelo. © **0542/9000.** Fax 0542/9999. www.fourseasons.com. 44 units. From $410 (£291) double; $435 (£309) suite. Rates include breakfast buffet. AE, DC, MC, V. **Amenities:** Restaurant; bar; babysitting; children's center; concierge; deluxe health club and spa; Internet in business center; 2 indoor/outdoor pools; room service. *In room:* A/C, TV, hair dryer, Internet, minibar.

Sheraton Colonia ★★ (Kids)   Opened in 2005, the Sheraton Colonia is a 10-minute cab ride from the center of town. Built over a golf course, with a view to the Río de la Plata, it's a family-friendly resort-style option if you want to spend more time in the area. Rooms are in neutral tones and have large windows overlooking the surrounding waters. Large desks and other surfaces make the rooms a great work environment, even if you're here to relax. The pool cascades with several levels in a landscaped garden and is spectacular at sunset. A lobby restaurant serves three meals, and dinner is also available at the golf clubhouse, set in the gardens. The health club area is large, with new equipment and enormous glass windows overlooking the river. The large spa has 18 treatment rooms and offers a romantic champagne whirlpool treatment for couples, among many other options. Some suites come with kitchens.

Continuación de la Rambla de Las Américas s/n, CP 70000, Carmelo. © **052/29000.** Fax 052/29001. www.sheraton.com. 92 units. From $265 (£188) double; from $380 (£270) suite. Rates include breakfast buffet. AE, DC, MC, V. **Amenities:** Restaurant; bar; babysitting; children's center; concierge; golf course; deluxe health club and spa; Internet in business center; 2 indoor/outdoor pools; room service. *In room:* A/C, TV, hair dryer, Internet, minibar.

WHERE TO DINE

El Drugstore ★ URUGUAYAN/JAPANESE/SEAFOOD   This restaurant across from Iglesia Matriz has a colorful, kitschy interior with posters and bric-a-brac. It's owned by Argentine Guillermo Azulay, who says, "I want to do something that makes people happy." Its most unusual feature is an antique car parked outside, converted into a dining area. Traditional *chivitos*, fish, steak, pastas, and Japanese food are on the menu. Live music, an executive menu for $15 (£11), and an open kitchen make this an interesting place to dine.

Vasconcellos 179 (at Portugal, across from Iglesia Matriz). © **052/25241.** Main courses $3–$12 (£2.15–£8.50). No credit cards. Daily noon–midnight.

Lobo ★ URUGUAYAN/FRENCH/INTERNATIONAL   Lobo's food has a formal presentation with a casual touch. Head chef Nicolas Diaz Ibarguren had previously worked at the Alvear Palace in Buenos Aires and cooks some of the most creative dishes in Colonia, such as carpaccio, leak and bacon raviolis, and gourmet *chivitos* at surprisingly reasonable prices. The decor mixes old and new, with brick walls, wooden framed doors, and modern lighting accents. There's live music on weekends.

Calle de Comercio (at La Playa). © **052/29245.** www.loborestaurante.com. Main courses $6–$8 (£4.25–£5.70). AE, MC, V. Tues–Sun 12:15pm–midnight.

Mesón de la Plaza ★ URUGUAYAN   Among the most traditional and elegant spots in Colonia, this restaurant serves fine steaks and other Uruguayan cuisine. It's in a large colonial building with high ceilings, across from Iglesia Matriz.

Pulpería de los Faroles ★ URUGUAYAN   Waiters with vests add a formality to this old institution, with ancient brick walls offset by pastel tablecloths. Traditional food includes locally caught fish, steaks, and pastas.

Calle Misiones de los Tapes 101 (at Comercio, on the Plaza Mayor). 𝕮 **052/25399.** Main courses $8–$15 (£5.70–£11). AE, MC, V. Daily noon–midnight.

COLONIA AFTER DARK

Believe it or not, there is nightlife in Colonia, whether it's locals partying after work, or tourists staying in the local *posadas* and the surrounding spa-hotels. Bar life begins at 10 or 11pm, but for serious dancing, expect things to get started after 1am. With its white leather lounges and blue-neon back-lit bar, **Mar Dulce Resto Pub** at Virrey Cevallo 232 and General Flores (𝕮 **098/500898** [cell]) looks like it was plucked from Miami Beach and has live music, DJs, and dancing. **Patrimonio** at Calle de San Jose 111 at España (𝕮 **099/187911** [cell]; www.patrimonioloungebar.com), offers live rock and jazz and a spectacular back patio that cascades over the Río de La Plata. **Trescuarto** at Av. Méndez 295 (𝕮 **052/29664** or 099/523043 [cell]; www.trescuarto.com), is the town's mega-disco, a four-level venue with three different kinds of music, hence the name. It's open only on Friday and Saturday.

5 SAN ANTONIO DE ARECO & PAMPAS ESTANCIAS

111km (69 miles) NW of Buenos Aires

San Antonio de Areco is a quiet little town about 90 minutes north of Buenos Aires, deep in the heart of Argentina's famous Pampas. The city is best known as the center for gaucho culture, Argentina's version of American cowboy tradition. Few people stay in San Antonio, choosing to visit it as a day trip from Buenos Aires, or as a base for exploring the nearby *estancias* that surround the town.

The city is compact, built in 1730 around an old colonial church dedicated to San Antonio de Padua, from which the town takes its name. Colonial and turn-of-the-20th-century buildings abound, all reached on walkable cobblestone streets that radiate from the church and Plaza Ruiz de Arellano, the town's main square. The Río Areco divides the town in two parts. Here along the river is a monument-lined green space called Parque San Martín, crossed by an old pedestrian bridge to Parque Criollo, where the city's most famous site, the Museo Gauchesco Ricardo Güiraldes, sits.

The city's main shopping streets are Alsina and Arellano, heading south from Plaza Arellano. It's a year-round tourism destination, but it lives for the annual **Día de la Tradición,** generally held around November 10. Gauchos—real and wannabe—fill the town, playing gaucho games of skill such as the *sortija,* in which they catch rings from poles while riding horses, giving them as gifts to beautiful women in the audience. San Antonio doesn't have many hotels, and those it has fill up fast at this time of year. (Of course, there is always the gaucho's pad, if he hands you his *sortija* ring.) See also the section on *estancias,* below; all are within a short drive of the center of San Antonio.

GETTING THERE   San Antonio de Areco can be reached by car from Buenos Aires by driving north along Ruta 8. The drive takes about an hour and a half. Most people come by bus, however. **Chevallier** offers hourly bus service from Buenos Aires's Retiro Bus depot (© **2326/453-904** in San Antonio, 11/4000-5255 in Buenos Aires, or 0800/222-6565 toll-free).

VISITOR INFORMATION   The **Dirección de Turismo de San Antonio de Areco** tourism information center (© **2326/453-165;** www.pagosdeareco.com.ar) is in Parque San Martín along the Río Areco waterfront, near the intersection of Avenida Zerboni with Calle Zapiola and Calle Arellano. It is open 7 days a week from 8am to 7pm. The website, www.sanantoniodeareco.com, also provides more tourism information.

GETTING AROUND   Within San Antonio itself, your feet can take you most of the places you need to go. Even the most distant actual attraction, the Museo of the Gaucho, is only a 15-minute walk from the center of town. Because many people use the town as a base for exploring other parts of the Pampas, such as the numerous *estancias, remises* are a must. Contact the 24-hour **Remis Zerboni,** Zerboni 313, near Alsina (© **2326/453-288**). The town is also great for bike riding; most hotels provide free bicycles.

WHAT TO SEE & DO

The center of San Antonio de Areco is the leafy **Plaza Arellano,** surrounded by cobblestone streets and overseen by a statue of Juan Hipólito Vieytes, a local involved in the Argentine war for independence from Spain. His memorial sits in an acoustic circle, so you'll have fun talking here, especially if you bring kids. The statue faces south to Mitre Street, staring at the church from which the town draws its name, **San Antonio de Padua,** rebuilt in the late 1800s over the original 1730 colonial version. Colonial on the outside, the interior mixes Gothic and neoclassical styles with frescoes of angels and saints in niches on the walls, all overseen by a coffered ceiling. On the plaza's north side is the Belle Epoque **Municipal Hall,** a long pink building at Lavalle 363 with an attractive central courtyard. Nearby is the **Draghi Museum and Shop,** Lavalle 387 between Alsina and Arellano (© **2326/454-219;** daily approximately 10am–5pm, though technically by appointment only). Opened by the late Juan Jose Draghi, a master silversmith who began his career more than 45 years ago, making ornamental items for gauchos, it is now run by his son Mariano. The museum is in itself a work of art, with its exquisite stained-glass ceiling. The museum also has its own hotel (p. 257). A few blocks away, you can watch other silversmiths at work in the small **Artesano Platero,** Alsina at Zerboni, facing the Parque San Martín (© **2326/454-843,** or 2325/15-656-995 [cell]; www.arecoplateria.com.ar; daily 9:30am–12:30pm and 3–9pm).

From here, head to **Parque San Martín,** on the south side of the Río Areco. It's lined with trees and monuments, full of vine-covered walkways called *glorietas.* Families picnic, and kids play soccer or climb over the small dam constructed in the river. Two bridges cross the park here, but the most picturesque is the **Puente Viejo,** originally constructed in the 1850s as a toll crossing. The other end of the river has Parque Criollo, and here sits the city's most famous site, the **Museum of the Gaucho** (aka **Museo Ricardo Güiraldes,** in honor of the author of *Don Segundo Sombra*), Camino Ricardo Güiraldes at Sosa (© **2326/455-839;** Wed–Mon 10am–4:30pm). Written in 1926, the novel immortalized the noble gaucho, making him an honored part of Argentine history. The museum combines an authentic 1830 *pulpería,* or country general store, where gauchos gathered with a museum designed in a colonial style by Argentine architect José María

Bustillo in 1936. Here, you will find the author's personal effects, photos, books, and other gaucho memorabilia. It's a bit kitschy (think rooms filled with gaucho manne-quins), but if you speak Spanish, a conversation with the museum's guide and historian, Omar Tapia, will help you put the gauchos in their proper historical context.

Travel Companies Providing San Antonio & Estancia Visits

Various travel companies in Buenos Aires arrange day trips to San Antonio de Areco, with or without overnight stays on nearby *estancias*. **Borello Travel & Tours,** 7 Park Ave., Ste. 21, New York, NY 10016 (© **800/405-3072** or 212/686-4911), or Perú 359, Ste. 407, Buenos Aires 1067 (© **11/5031-1988;** www.borellotravel.com), a firm specializing in upscale travel, can arrange a visit to San Antonio with stays in the local *estancias*. Buenos Aires–based **Say Hueque Tourism,** Viamonte 749, Office 601, 1053 Buenos Aires (© **11/5199-2517**), or Guatemala 4845, Office 4, 1425 Buenos Aires (© **11/4775-7862;** www.sayhueque.com), also provides trips to this area.

WHERE TO STAY

Draghi Paradores ★ The Draghi Paradores is a small apartment hotel opened in 2006 behind the Draghi museum and store. It is the newest and one of the nicest of San Antonio's hotels, with a slightly romantic feel. Built in a Spanish colonial style, the entrance is graced by a small pool and fountain in an enclosed courtyard. The five rooms are clean with a country feel to them, with a rich use of woods, frilly white bedding, and terra-cotta tiles on the floor. Two of the rooms also come with small kitchens, making them ideal for families or long-term stays in San Antonio.

Lavalle 387 (btw. Alsina and Arellano), 2760 San Antonio de Areco. © **2326/455-583** or 02326/454-515. www.sanantoniodeareco.com/paradores. 5 units, 2 with kitchens. From $74 (£53) double. Rates include breakfast. AE, DC, MC, V. Free parking. **Amenities:** Bikes; concierge; heated outdoor pool; room service. *In room:* A/C, TV, hair dryer, minibar, Wi-Fi.

Hostal de Areco This small family-style hotel is in a historical, turn-of-the-20th-century red house, set back from the street and surrounded by a small garden. There are seven small, spartan rooms with tiled floors, and each has a full-size bed and a bathroom. Dark-green curtains and bedspreads give the rooms an even smaller appearance. The accommodations are very basic, with no air-conditioning and only a ceiling fan.

Zapioli 25 (near the intersection of Zerboni), 2760 San Antonio de Areco. © **2326/456-118.** 7 units. From $41 (£29) double. Rates include breakfast. No credit cards. Free parking. **Amenities:** Bikes; concierge. *In room:* TV.

Hotel San Carlos ★ Though it seems like a motel, overlooking the Parque San Martín, this is the most businesslike hotel in town. You'll find a sun deck equipped with an *asado* grill, a Jacuzzi, two outdoor heated pools in the courtyard, and a fountain decorated with a mosaic of San Antonio de Padua. (It's one of the few places in all of Argentina where you'll see bikini-clad women frolicking in front of religious icons.) Some rooms are on the small side, but they're larger in the hotel's new wing. Many come with hydro-massage tubs or Jacuzzis in the bathrooms, and a few two-bedroom apart-ments have kitchens. The hotel added a spa in late 2008.

Av. Zerboni (on the west corner at the intersection of Zapiola), 2760 San Antonio de Areco. © **2326/456-119.** www.hotel-sancarlos.com.ar. 30 units. From $41 (£29) double; from $74 (£53) apt. Rates include breakfast. Spa packages available. AE, MC, V. Free parking. **Amenities:** Bikes; concierge; health club and spa; Internet in lobby; Jacuzzi; 2 heated outdoor pools; room service. *In room:* A/C, TV, hair dryer, minibar (in some), Wi-Fi.

Los Abuelos   Alberto Cesar Reyes is your grandfather at this motel-style property overlooking Parque San Martín and the Río Areco—the hotel's name literally means "the grandparents." The hotel is basic, with white metal and Formica furnishings, and tiled floors in the rooms. The beds are covered with green chenille bedspreads. Some bathrooms have tubs and showers, while others have only showers. Every room has a new air-conditioner and a ceiling fan. An aboveground pool is surrounded by a small deck in the back of the property, near the parking lot. A nice warm touch is a gas fireplace in the front lobby, surrounded by simple pine chairs and tables.

Av. Zerboni (on the corner at the intersection of Zapiola). 2760 San Antonio de Areco. ℂ 02326/456-390. www.sanantoniodeareco.com/losabuelos. 9 units. From $42 (£30) double. Rates include breakfast. No credit cards. Free parking. **Amenities:** Bikes; concierge; outdoor pool; room service. *In room:* A/C, TV, hair dryer, Wi-Fi.

WHERE TO DINE

Almacén de Ramos Gerelos ARGENTINE/SPANISH   This is one of the best-known restaurants in San Antonio de Areco, with a *parrilla* and international items on the menu. It also serves a broad selection of paellas. The restaurant is in a turn-of-the-20th-century building. Its interior, with rich wooden details, will take you back in time.

Zapiola 143 (at Segundo Sombra). No phone. Main courses $4–$8 (£2.85–£5.70). AE. Daily noon–3pm and 8–11pm.

Corner Pizza ARGENTINE/INTERNATIONAL   This simple place overlooks the Parque San Martín and the Río Areco. You'll find a selection of fast-food items on the menu, from hot dogs and hamburgers to pizza. Many people just come here to down a beer and look at the park. It's ideal if you're on a low budget.

Av. Zerboni (at Alsina, overlooking Parque San Martín). No phone. Main courses $1–$4 (70p–£2.85). No credit cards. Daily 10am–11pm.

La Esquina de Merti ★ ARGENTINE   This restaurant has an old turn-of-the-20th-century feel to it, with exposed brick walls, an ancient copper coffeemaker on the bar, wooden tables, and shelves full of apothecary jars. But it's all a trick: La Esquina de Merti opened in late 2005, in the location of an old *almacén*, or Argentine general store. In any case, the food, concentrating on the beef for which the region is famous, is great. You'll find a beef and chicken *parrilla*, and a selection of pastas and empanadas. The house specialty is *mollejas* with cream, lemon, and champagne (*mollejas* are the softly grilled, melt-in-your-mouth pancreas or thymus of a cow, which might be worth trying for an only-in-Argentina experience). A large wine selection complements everything on the menu.

Arellano 147 at Segundo Sombra (overlooking Plaza Arellano). ℂ 2326/456-705. Main courses $4–$10 (£2.85–£7.10). AE, V. Daily 9am–2am; Fri–Sat 9am–3am.

PAMPAS ESTANCIAS

San Antonio is a popular base for exploring Argentina's famous *estancias,* which doubled historically as both farms and fortresses, built throughout the country along trails from Buenos Aires as a means of conquering and stabilizing territory originally controlled by the Indians. The majority of Argentina's *estancias* date from the middle to late 1800s. After General Roca's Campaign of the Desert in the 1870s, in which he murdered most of the Indian population within 150 miles of Buenos Aires, *estancia* culture, and the cattle and grain tended on them, flourished. Despite the bloody history that gave birth to them, today they're seen as a retreat from the chaos and stress of Buenos Aires. They are popular among Porteños on weekends or for day trips. With the increase of tourism to Argentina, many foreigners are beginning to delight in them as well.

Most of the *estancias* listed here are a half-hour from San Antonio, and no more than 2 hours from Buenos Aires. You can drive to all of them on your own, or use a bus service from Buenos Aires to San Antonio and then catch a taxi from there. For a fee in the range of $80 (£57) to $100 (£71), almost all the *estancias* will also provide transportation from your hotel or the airport in Buenos Aires. Because many *estancias* are accessed by dirt roads, it is advisable to rent a 4WD vehicle if you decide to drive yourself, especially if rain is predicted during the time of your visit. The websites of the *estancias* listed here post detailed driving maps.

Services and features vary, but the atmosphere at most *estancias* is a cross between a rustic resort and a bed-and-breakfast. Nothing relieves stress like a day or a few in the country, and horseback riding, trekking, lounging by the pool, and eating and drinking aplenty are all part of a day in the Pampas. In general, the rates for *estancias* include a full board of four meals—breakfast, lunch, afternoon tea, and dinner—and sometimes all drinks including alcohol. Lunch, the highlight of a dining experience on an *estancia,* is usually an *asado* or barbecue where everyone, including the workers, gathers to socialize. Day rates generally include only lunch and limited activities. Most *estancias* are real working farms, with hundreds of acres and cows, horses, and other animals attended by real gauchos (not all of whom dress in the traditional way). If you're in the mood to milk a cow or watch the birth of a colt, you just might have the chance.

El Cencerro   Smaller, cozier, and more rustic than some other places listed here, this working *estancia* makes you feel like you're part of the farm's daily goings-on. Rooms and public areas are filled with antiques and odd objects. Activities include horseback riding, helping with the animals, carriage rides, bicycle rides, and trekking. Only 3km (2 miles) away is the historical Capilla del Señor, a charming town established in the early 1700s. You can walk or bike there on your own, or ask for optional guided tours. Similar to San Antonio de Areco in feel, it's virtually unknown to non-Argentines, and thus more authentic, with real gauchos wandering the downtown. The area is also the center of Argentine ballooning, an added option for $150 (£107) per person. The main house, renovated in 2008, contains five bedrooms, three of which are suites with private bathrooms and large enough for a family of four. An additional house has been opened in the adjacent ranch, with two units, also large enough for families. A gourmet chef cooks dinner, and there's a game room and small home theater. One of the charms of this 21-hectares (52-acre) property is the wooded creek flowing through it. You can access the *estancia* by bus from Buenos Aires to Capilla del Señor and then a $6 (£4.25) taxi ride. By *remise* from Buenos Aires, 80km (50 miles) away, it's about $80 (£57).

Buenos Aires Provincial Ruta 39; 2812 Capilla del Señor. © **11/4743-2319** or 11/15-6093-2319 (cell) in Buenos Aires. www.estanciaelcencerro.com.ar. 7 units. From $150 (£107) double, $200 (£142) suite. Rates include all meals and some drinks; $75 (£53) day rate includes lunch. No credit cards. Free parking. **Amenities:** Bikes; outdoor pool; room service. *In room:* Wi-Fi.

El Ombú de Areco   El Ombú takes its name from the tree that dominates the Pampas. It's among the most historic *estancias* near Buenos Aires, and the general atmosphere and overgrown row of trees out front are reminiscent of a plantation in the southern U.S. The rooms in the old house are best, with their high ceilings. But you really can't go wrong here; all the rooms have romantic appeal, decorated with brass beds, floral linens, and a strong country atmosphere. Several game rooms are on the grounds, and it's easy to mingle with the friendly staff. This is a working ranch, with 300 hectares (741 acres) of land and more than 400 cows and other animals. Enjoy horseback riding, cattle round-ups, carriage rides, bicycling, and other activities. Some rooms have hydro-massage tubs or a tub/shower combination. Rooms are not air-conditioned, but have ceiling fans. The *estancia* is about 10km (6¼ miles) from San Antonio and 120km (75 miles) from Buenos Aires. Their *remise* service costs $85 (£60) from Buenos Aires and about $105 (£75) from Ezeiza airport. A taxi from San Antonio de Areco is about $11 (£7.80).

Buenos Aires Provincial Ruta 31, Cuartel 6, 2760 San Antonio de Areco. ℂ **2326/492-080,** or 11/4737-0436 in Buenos Aires. www.estanciaelombu.com. 9 units. From $200 (£142) single, $320 (£227) double. Rates include 4 meals and drinks (10% discount if paid in cash); $70 (£50) day rate includes lunch. AE, MC, V. Free parking. Pets accepted. **Amenities:** Babysitting; bikes; concierge; 2 outdoor pools; room service. *In room:* Hair dryer.

El Rosario de Areco   This *estancia* is among the most pleasant to visit, with its barn-red buildings and bougainvilleas scattered among the grounds. The *estancia* dates from 1892, but the rooms, many of which are former horse stalls, have surprisingly modern interiors. The waitstaff is a little different here too, dressed in chic black uniforms instead of gaucho outfits. One of the owners cooks the lunch *asado.* The public rooms and even some of the gardens have Wi-Fi, which is rare for an *estancia.* There are 16 double rooms, all with large private bathrooms. Rooms are not air-conditioned, but they come with ceiling fans, and some rooms also have fireplaces. The owners are building a small hotel with 30 rooms on the 80-hectare (198-acre) grounds; it's set to open in mid-2009. Presently, guests enjoy a small polo field, horseback riding, and carriage rides, as well as TV, pool, and video games. The hotel is 7km (4⅓ miles) from San Antonio de Areco and 100km (62 miles) from Buenos Aires. From San Antonio, a taxi will run about $8 (£5.70), and their *remise* service is $110 (£78) from Buenos Aires.

Buenos Aires Provincial Ruta 41 (mailing address is Castilla de Correo 85), 2760 San Antonio de Areco. ℂ **2326/451-000,** or 11/15-3562-8500 (cell) in Buenos Aires. www.rosariodeareco.com.ar. 16 units. $224–$284 (£159–£202) double. Rates include all meals and drinks; $75 (£53) day rate includes lunch (call for availability). No credit cards (except at new hotel when open). Free parking. **Amenities:** Babysitting; bikes; concierges; 2 outdoor pools; room service. *In room:* Hair dryer, Wi-Fi.

Estancia Villa Maria   While you can definitely stay overnight in this *estancia,* its location within a half-hour drive from Ezeiza Airport makes it ideal as a day trip before taking a night flight home. The main house is a beautiful mock Tudor mansion set in a rolling garden landscape, originally built in the late 1800s and expanded in 1919. You'll enjoy horseback riding, polo grounds, carriage riding, and other activities in the game rooms, or you can just lounge by the pool. Some rooms have fireplaces, heavy wooden molding, and gorgeous views through windows with Gothic stained-glass accents. The 11 units are in the main house and a nearby Victorian mansion, and include one suite and one apartment. The *estancia* is now part of a new housing development, but it's designed so as not to be visible from the main house. Villa Maria is 48km (30 miles) from Buenos Aires and about 15km (9 miles) from Ezeiza Airport. A taxi from Buenos Aires is about $60 (£43), and about $17 (£12) from the airport.

Buenos Aires Provincial Ruta 205, Km 47.5. 1814 Partido de Ezeiza. ℂ **11/6091-2064.** www.estanciavilla maria.com. 11 units. $300–$450 (£213–£320) double. Rates include all meals and drinks; $100 (£71) day rate includes lunch. No credit cards. Free parking. **Amenities:** Babysitting; bikes; concierge; outdoor pool; room service; tennis courts. *In room:* A/C, TV, hair dryer, Wi-Fi.

La Bamba   This is one of the most gorgeous and romantic *estancias* near Buenos Aires. The original building opened in 1830 as a stagecoach stop along the old Camino Real, linking Buenos Aires with other colonial cities. The buildings are Pompeiian-red with white trim, contrasting with the rich green landscape. The Argentine movie *Camila,* about a forbidden romance in the 1840s, was filmed here and nominated for Best Foreign Film in the 1984 Academy Awards. This place is ideal for honeymooners—especially the isolated Torre Room in the main house, on the third floor. Guests enjoy swimming, horseback riding, carriage rides, trekking, and other activities. The 150-hectare (371-acre) property has cows and soy and wheat fields. The *estancia* is 13km (8 miles) from San Antonio and 123km (76 miles) from Buenos Aires. A taxi from San Antonio is about $8 (£5.70), and a *remise* service from Buenos Aires is $55 (£39). The *estancia* is closed for a renovation that should be completed by October 2009. New electrical wiring, air-conditioning, and improvements to the pool and polo ground will enhance the historical nature of this *estancia*. In the meantime, La Bamba is partnering with the nearby Estancia Bamba Chica for guests. (Buenos Aires Provincial Ruta Nacional 8, 2760 San Antonio de Areco; ✆ **11/4732-1269;** www.bambachica.com.ar).

Buenos Aires Provincial Ruta 31, 2760 San Antonio de Areco. ✆ **2326/456-293.** www.la-bamba.com.ar. 12 units. $300–$350 (£213–£249) double. Rates include all meals and drinks; $100 (£71) day rate includes lunch. AE, DC, MC. Free parking. **Amenities:** Babysitting; concierge; Internet; outdoor pool; room service; sauna. *In room:* A/C, hair dryer, Wi-Fi.

Santa Susana & Fiesta Gaucha   Close to Buenos Aires, this oft-visited *estancia* hosts day-trippers who come for the Fiesta Gaucha, a touristy but fun event. The tour bus leaves from Buenos Aires and gauchos give you glasses of Argentine wine and empanadas on arrival. Watch as they tend to the *asado,* preparing a meal for hundreds, or take a horse or carriage ride to build up your hunger. The *estancia* has a small chapel and a museum inside of the main house built in the 1830s, displaying gaucho boots and saddles, turn-of-the-century clothing, and the *boleadore,* a three-balled rope used to catch animals. In a riding arena, you can watch gauchos play *sortija* and other games of skill. Cyrillo, one of the gauchos, will show off his *rasta,* a coin-adorned belt. Within the main dining hall that holds 600 guests, you'll be served from the *asado* as you watch a show combining tango with traditional folkloric dances. At the end, the band plays a waltz, and guests join the dance. If you don't have time for a working *estancia* and want a taste of gaucho culture geared to an international audience, this is ideal. Even the most jaded will come away with a smile. A gift shop sells souvenirs, with copies of museum items. In general, these trips are booked through an agent, though actually you could show up on your own. The *estancia* is about 75km (47 miles) from Buenos Aires on Ruta 6, and package tours run about $85 (£60) with lunch, drinks, and transportation.

Buenos Aires Provincial Ruta 6, 2814 Los Cardales. ✆ **2322/525-016.** www.esantasusana.com.ar.

Appendix A: Fast Facts & Websites

1 FAST FACTS: BUENOS AIRES

AMERICAN EXPRESS The American Express building is next to Plaza San Martín, at Arenales 707 (© **11/4310-3000**). The travel agency is open Monday through Friday from 9am to 6pm; the bank is open Monday to Friday from 9am to 5pm. In addition to card-member services, the bank provides currency exchange, money orders, check cashing, and refunds.

AREA CODES The city area code, known locally as a *caracteristica*, is **011.** Drop the 0 when calling from overseas with Argentina's country code, **54.** Also see "Telephones," below.

ATM NETWORKS/CASHPOINTS See "Money & Costs," p. 34.

BUSINESS HOURS Banks are open weekdays from 10am to 3pm. Shopping hours are weekdays from 9am to 8 or 10pm and Saturday from 10am to 1 or 5pm. Many stores will have similar Sunday hours, or be closed. Shopping centers are open daily from 10am to 8 or 10pm, though individual stores in some complexes will set other hours. Some small family-owned stores close for lunch.

CAR RENTALS See "Getting There & Getting Around," p. 29, and "Toll-free Numbers & Websites," p. 265.

DENTISTS See section 5 in chapter 9.

DRINKING LAWS The drinking age in Argentina is 18. However, ID is rarely requested, so it's easy for underage drinking to occur.

DRIVING RULES See "Getting There & Getting Around," p. 29.

DRUGSTORES Ask at your hotel where the nearest pharmacy *(farmacia)* is. In Buenos Aires, the chain **Farmacity** is open 24 hours, with locations at Lavalle 919 (© **11/4821-3000**) and Av. Santa Fe 2830 (© **11/4821-0235**). Farmacity will also deliver to your hotel.

ELECTRICITY Bring a **connection kit** of the right power and phone adapters, a spare phone cord, and a spare Ethernet network cable—or find out whether your hotel supplies them to guests. Electricity in Argentina runs on 220 volts. Most Argentine plugs are slanted double prongs, like that of Australia, though some use double round prongs, as in continental Europe. Note that most laptops operate on both 110 and 220 volts. Luxury hotels usually have transformers and adapters available.

EMBASSIES All embassies are located in Buenos Aires: **U.S. Embassy,** Av. Colombia 4300 (© 11/5777-4533); **Australian Embassy,** Villanueva 1400 (© 11/4777-6580); **Canadian Embassy,** Tagle 2828 (© 11/4805-3032); **New Zealand Embassy,** Carlos Pellegrini 1427, 5th floor (© 11/4328-0747); **United Kingdom Embassy,** Luis Agote 2412 (© 11/4803-6021).

EMERGENCIES The following numbers are valid in Buenos Aires and throughout Argentina. For an **ambulance,** call ℂ **107;** in case of **fire,** call ℂ **100;** for **police** assistance, call ℂ **101.** The tourist police have a special line: ℂ **0800/999-5000.**

GASOLINE (PETROL) The cost of gasoline (petrol) is around 4 pesos per liter ($1.10/80p), or about $4 per gallon.

HOLIDAYS See "Holidays," p.27 and "Calendar of Events," p. 28.

HOSPITALS For an English-speaking hospital, call **Clínica Suisso Argentino** (ℂ **11/4304-1081**), or **Hospital Britanico** (ℂ **11/4309-6600**). Also, see "Health," p. 36.

INSURANCE For travel overseas, most U.S. health plans (including Medicare and Medicaid) do not provide coverage, and the ones that do often require you to pay for services up front and reimburse you only after you return home.

If you require additional medical insurance, try **MEDEX Assistance** (ℂ **410/453-6300;** www.medexassist.com) or **Travel Assistance International** (ℂ **800/821-2828;** www.travelassistance.com; for general information on services, call the company's **Worldwide Assistance Services, Inc.,** at ℂ **800/777-8710**).

Canadians should check with their provincial health plan offices or call **Health Canada** (ℂ **866/225-0709;** www.hc-sc. gc.ca) to find out the extent of their coverage and what documentation and receipts they must take home in case they are treated overseas.

Travelers from the U.K. should carry their European Health Insurance Card (EHIC), which replaced the E111 form as proof of entitlement to free/reduced cost medical treatment abroad (ℂ **0845-606-2030;** www.ehic.org.uk). Note, however, that the EHIC only covers "necessary medical treatment," and for repatriation costs, lost money, baggage, or cancellation, travel insurance from a reputable company should always be sought (www.travelinsuranceweb. com).

Travel Insurance The cost of travel insurance varies widely, depending on the destination, the cost and length of your trip, your age and health, and the type of trip you're taking, but expect to pay between 5% and 8% of the vacation itself. You can get estimates from various providers through **InsureMyTrip.com**. Enter your trip cost and dates, your age, and other information, for prices from more than a dozen companies.

U.K. citizens and their families who make more than one trip abroad per year may find an annual travel insurance policy works out cheaper. Check **www.money supermarket.com**, which compares prices across a wide range of providers for single- and multitrip policies.

Most big travel agencies offer their own insurance and will probably try to sell you their package when you book a holiday. Think before you sign. **Britain's Consumers' Association** recommends that you insist on seeing the policy and reading the fine print before buying travel insurance. **The Association of British Insurers** (ℂ **020/7600-3333;** www.abi.org.uk) gives advice by phone and publishes Holiday Insurance, a free guide to policy provisions and prices. You might also shop around for better deals: Try **Columbus Direct** (ℂ **0870/033-9988;** www.columbusdirect.net).

Trip Cancellation Insurance Trip-cancellation insurance will help retrieve your money if you have to back out of a trip or depart early, or if your travel supplier goes bankrupt. Trip cancellation traditionally covers such events as sickness, natural disasters, and Department of State advisories. The latest news in trip-cancellation insurance is the availability of **expanded hurricane coverage** and the **"any-reason"** cancellation coverage—which costs more but covers cancellations made for any reason. You won't get back 100% of your prepaid trip cost, but you'll be refunded a substantial portion. **TravelSafe** (© **888/885-7233;** www.travelsafe.com) offers both types of coverage. Expedia also offers any-reason cancellation coverage for its air-hotel packages. For details, contact one of the following recommended insurers: **Access America** (© 866/807-3982; www.accessamerica.com); **Travel Guard International** (© 800/826-4919; www.travelguard.com); **Travel Insured International** (© 800/243-3174; www.travelinsured.com); and **Travelex Insurance Services** (© 888/457-4602; www.travelex-insurance.com).

INTERNET ACCESS Cybercafes called *"locuturios"* are found on every corner in Buenos Aires, so it won't be hard to stay connected. Access is reasonably priced (usually averaging just under $1 per hour) and connections are reliably good. Wi-Fi has become ubiquitous, even in budget hotels, but call to ask. See "Staying Connected," p. 47.

LANGUAGE Argentines speak Spanish, which locally is not *español* as in other countries, but is instead referred to as *castellano*. Within most shops, hotels, and restaurants catering to tourists, you'll almost always find English-speaking staff. However, this is not always the rule in nontouristy places or in budget hotels and restaurants. For daily Spanish phrases, see the glossary in appendix B.

LAUNDROMATS Nearly all hotels have both laundry and dry-cleaning services, which can be very expensive in luxury hotels. Laundromats exist all over Buenos Aires, but they are wash-and-fold places called *lavanderías,* and there are virtually no self-service laundromats. Service runs about $2 (£1.40) to wash, dry, and fold a pound of clothes, usually available by the afternoon if dropped off in the morning. Dry cleaners are called *tintorerias.*

LEGAL AID Contact your embassy if you require legal aid. Also, see section 8,

"Women Travelers," in chapter 3 if you're a woman who has been the victim of an assault.

LOST & FOUND Be sure to tell all of your credit card companies the minute you discover your wallet has been lost or stolen and file a report at the nearest police precinct. Your credit card company or insurer may require a police report number or record of the loss. Most credit card companies have an emergency toll-free number to call if your card is lost or stolen; they may be able to wire you a cash advance immediately or deliver an emergency credit card in a day or two.

MAIL Airmail postage for a standard letter or postcard from Argentina to North America is 4.50 pesos ($1.22/86p) and to Europe is 5 pesos ($1.35/95p). Mail takes, on average, between 7 and 10 days to get to the U.S. and Europe.

MAPS Reliable maps can be purchased at the offices of the **Automóvil Club Argentino,** Av. del Libertador 1850, in Buenos Aires (© 11/4802-6061 or 11/4802-7071). You can also purchase maps from DeDios ahead of time at www.dediosonline.com or Amazon. See "Getting There & Getting Around," p. 29.

MEASUREMENTS See the chart on the inside back cover of this book for details on converting metric measurements to nonmetric equivalents.

PASSPORTS See "Entry Requirements," p. 25.

POLICE For **police** assistance, call © **101.** The tourist police have a special line: © **0800/999-5000.**

SMOKING People who hate smoke can rejoice. Anti-smoking laws have finally been passed in Buenos Aires, as well as a few other Argentine cities. It's among the few laws actually obeyed in Argentina. However, clubs and bars tend to have a few smokers and no one minds.

TAXES Argentina's value-added tax (VAT) is 21%. You can recover this 21% at the airport if you have purchased certain local products totaling more than 70 pesos ($19/£13) (per invoice) from stores participating in tax-free shopping. Forms are available at the airport and participating stores, but be aware that you may be asked to display your purchases when leaving.

TELEPHONES See "Staying Connected," p. 47.

TIME In 2007, Argentina introduced daylight saving time in the east of the country, with Buenos Aires and the coast moving forward 1 hour from December 30 to March 16. Buenos Aires will be 3 hours ahead of Eastern Standard Time in northern winter.

TIPPING A 10% tip is expected at cafes and restaurants. Give at least $1 (70p) to bellboys and porters, and 5% to hairdressers. There is no need to tip taxi drivers, but you can round to the nearest peso.

TOILETS Public toilets are rare, though some exist in the train stations, sometimes for a small fee or a tip of 50 centavos. Bathrooms are available in shopping centers and, if you ask politely, most restaurants will allow you to use their toilet, even if you're not a customer.

USEFUL PHONE NUMBERS
U.S. Dept. of State Travel Advisory ✆ **202/647-5225** (manned 24 hr.)
U.S. Passport Agency ✆ **202/647-0518**
U.S. Centers for Disease Control International Traveler's Hotline ✆ **404/332-4559**. Also, see "Online Traveler's Toolbox," p. 48.

WATER In Buenos Aires, the water is perfectly safe to drink. But if you are traveling to more remote regions of Argentina, it's best to stick with bottled water for drinking.

2 WEBSITES

MAJOR U.S. AIRLINES

American Airlines
www.aa.com

Continental Airlines
www.continental.com

Delta Air Lines
www.delta.com

Northwest Airlines
www.nwa.com

United Airlines
www.united.com

MAJOR INTERNATIONAL AIRLINES

Aerolineas Argentinas
www.aerolineas.com.ar

Air Canada
www.aircanada.com

Air France
www.airfrance.com

British Airways
www.british-airways.com

Iberia
www.iberia.com

KLM
www.klm.com

LAN Airlines
www.lan.com

Lufthansa
www.lufthansa.com

Qantas Airways
www.qantas.com

Swiss Air
www.swiss.com

TAM
www.tam.com.br

CAR RENTAL AGENCIES

Avis
www.avis.com

Dollar
www.dollar.com

Hertz
www.hertz.com

Thrifty
www.thrifty.com

MAJOR HOTEL & MOTEL CHAINS

Crowne Plaza Hotels
www.ichotelsgroup.com/crowneplaza

Four Seasons
www.fourseasons.com

Hilton Hotels
www.hilton.com

Holiday Inn
www.holidayinn.com

Hyatt
www.hyatt.com

InterContinental Hotels & Resorts
www.ichotelsgroup.com

Marriott
www.marriott.com

Sheraton Hotels & Resorts
www.starwoodhotels.com/sheraton

Appendix B:
Survival Spanish

Argentine Spanish has a rich, almost Italian sound, with the double "ll" and "y" pronounced with a "j"-like sound. So *llave* (key) sounds like "*zha*-ve" and *desayuno* (breakfast) sounds like "de-sa-*zhu*-no." *Usted* (the formal "you") is used extensively, and *vos* is a form of "you" that's even more familiar than *tú* (informal "you"). Peculiar terms you may come across only in Argentine include: *bárbaro* (very cool); Porteño (a resident of Buenos Aires); *pasos* (steps in a tango); *bandoneón* (a cousin of the accordion, used in tango music); and *subte* (the Buenos Aires subway). **Uruguayan Spanish** closely resembles the Spanish spoken in Buenos Aires.

BASIC WORDS & PHRASES

English	Spanish	Pronunciation
Good day	**Buenos días**	*bweh*-nohss *dee*-ahss
How are you?	**¿Cómo está?**	*koh*-moh ehss-*tah*
Very well	**Muy bien**	mwee byehn
Thank you	**Gracias**	*grah*-syahss
You're welcome	**De nada**	deh *nah*-dah
Goodbye	**Adiós**	ah-*dyohss*
Please	**Por favor**	pohr fah-*bohr*
Yes	**Sí**	see
No	**No**	noh
Excuse me (to get by someone)	**Perdóneme**	pehr-*doh*-neh-meh
Excuse me (to begin a question)	**Disculpe**	dees-*kool*-peh
Give me	**Déme**	*deh*-meh
Where is . . . ?	**¿Dónde está . . . ?**	*dohn*-deh ehss-*tah*
the station	**la estación**	lah ehss-tah-*syohn*
a hotel	**un hotel**	oon oh-*tel*
a gas station	**una estación de servicio**	sehr-*bee*-syoh
a restaurant	**un restaurante**	oon res-tow-*rahn*-teh
the toilet	**el baño**	el *bah*-nyoh
a good doctor	**un buen médico**	oon bwehn *meh*-dee-coh
the road to . . .	**el camino a/hacia . . .**	el cah-*mee*-noh ah/*ah*-syah
To the right	**A la derecha**	ah lah deh-*reh*-chah
To the left	**A la izquierda**	ah lah ees-*kyehr*-dah
Straight ahead	**Derecho**	deh-*reh*-choh

English	Spanish	Pronunciation
I would like . . .	Quisiera . . .	kee-*syeh*-rah
I want . . .	Quiero . . .	*kyeh*-roh
to eat	comer	koh-*mehr*
a room	una habitación	*oon*-nah ah-bee-tah-*syohn*
Do you have . . . ?	¿Tiene usted . . .?	*tyeh*-neh oo-*sted*
a book	un libro	oon *lee*-broh
a dictionary	un diccionario	oon deek-syoh-*nah*-ryoh
How much is it?	¿Cuánto cuesta?	*kwahn*-toh *kweh*-stah?
When?	¿Cuándo?	*kwahn*-doh?
What?	¿Qué?	kay?
There is (Is there . . . ?)	(¿)Hay (. . . ?)	eye
What is there?	¿Qué hay?	keh eye
Yesterday	Ayer	ah-*yer*
Today	Hoy	oy
Tomorrow	Mañana	mah-*nyah*-nah
Good	Bueno	*bweh*-noh
Bad	Malo	*mah*-loh
Better (best)	(Lo) Mejor	(loh) meh-*hor*
More	Más	mahs
Less	Menos	*meh*-nohss
No smoking	Se prohibe fumar	seh pro-*hee*-beh foo-*mahr*
Postcard	Tarjeta postal	tar-*heh*-tah poh-*stahl*
Insect repellent	Repelente contra insectos	reh-peh-*lehn*-teh *cohn*-trah een-*sehk*-tohss

MORE USEFUL PHRASES

English	Spanish	Pronunciation
Do you speak English?	¿Habla usted inglés?	*ah*-blah oo-*sted* een-*glehss*
Is there anyone here who speaks English?	¿Hay alguien aquí que hable inglés?	eye *ahl*-gyehn ah-*kee* keh *ah*-bleh een-*glehss*
I speak a little Spanish.	Hablo un poco de español.	*ah*-bloh oon *poh*-koh deh eh-spah-*nyol*
I don't understand Spanish very well.	No (lo) entiendo muy bien el español.	noh (loh) ehn-*tyehn*-doh mwee byehn el eh-spah-*nyol*
The meal is good.	Me gusta la comida.	meh *goo*-stah lah koh-*mee*-dah
What time is it?	¿Qué hora es?	keh *oh*-rah ehss
May I see your menu?	¿Puedo ver el menú (la carta)?	*pweh*-doh vehr el meh-*noo* (lah *car*-tah)
The check, please.	La cuenta, por favor.	lah *kwehn*-tah, pohr fah-*bohr*

English	Spanish	Pronunciation
What do I owe you?	¿Cuánto le debo?	*kwahn*-toh leh *deh*-boh
What did you say?	¿Cómo? (colloquial expression for American "Eh?")	*koh*-moh?
I want (to see) . . .	Quiero (ver) . . .	*kyehr*-oh (vehr)
a room	un cuarto or	oon *kwar*-toh, *oon*-nah
	una habitación	ah-bee-tah-*syohn*
for two persons	para dos personas	*pah*-rah dohss pehr-*soh*-nahs
with (without) bathroom	con (sin) baño	kohn (seen) *bah*-nyoh
We are staying	Nos quedamos aquí	nohs keh-*dah*-mohss
here only . . .	solamente . . .	ah-*kee* soh-lah-*mehn*-teh
one night	una noche	*oo*-nah *noh*-cheh
one week	una semana	*oo*-nah seh-*mah*-nah
We are leaving . . .	Partimos (Salimos) . . .	pahr-*tee*-mohss (sah-*lee*-mohss)
tomorrow	mañana	mah-*nya*-nah

TRANSPORTATION TERMS

English	Spanish	Pronunciation
Airport	Aeropuerto	ah-eh-ro-*pwer*-toh
Flight	Vuelo	*bweh*-loh
Rental car	Arrendadora de autos	ah-rehn-dah-*doh*-rah deh *ow*-tohss
Bus	Autobús	ow-toh-*boos*
Bus or truck	Camión	kah-*myohn*
Local bus	Micro	*mee*-kroh
Lane	Carril	kah-*reel*
Baggage (claim area)	Equipajes	eh-kee-*pah*-hehss
Luggage storage area	Custodia	koo-*stoh*-dyah
Arrivals gates	Llegadas	yeh-*gah*-dahss
Originates at this station	Local	loh-*kahl*
Originates elsewhere	De Paso	deh *pah*-soh
Stops if seats available	Para si hay lugares	*pah*-rah see eye loo-*gah*-rehss
First class	Primera	pree-*meh*-rah
Second class	Segunda	seh-*goon*-dah
Nonstop	Sin escala	seen eh-*skah*-lah
Baggage claim area	Recibo de equipajes	reh-*see*-boh deh eh-kee-*pah*-hehss
Waiting room	Sala de espera	*sah*-lah deh eh-*speh*-rah
Toilets	Baños	*bah*-nyoss
Ticket window	Boletería	boh-leh-teh-*ree*-ah

SURVIVAL SPANISH

B

SURVIVAL SPANISH

INDEX

See also Accommodations and Restaurant indexes, below.